Taiwan's Imagined Geography

Chinese Colonial Travel Writing and Pictures, 1683–1895

Harvard East Asian Monographs 230

Taiwan's Imagined Geography

Chinese Colonial Travel Writing and Pictures, 1683–1895

Emma Jinhua Teng

Published by the Harvard University Asia Center
Distributed by Harvard University Press
Cambridge (Massachusetts) and London, 2004

Printed in the United States of America

The Harvard University Asia Center publishes a monograph series and, in coordination with the Fairbank Center for East Asian Research, the Korea Institute, the Reischauer Institute of Japanese Studies, and other faculties and institutes, administers research projects designed to further scholarly understanding of China, Japan, Vietnam, Korea, and other Asian countries. The Center also sponsors projects addressing multidisciplinary and regional issues in Asia.

Library of Congress Cataloging-in-Publication Data

Teng, Emma.
    Taiwan's imagined geography : Chinese colonial travel writing and pictures, 1683–1895 / Emma Jinhua Teng.
        p. cm. – (Harvard East Asian monographs ; 230)
    Includes bibliographical references and index.
    ISBN 0-674-01451-0 (hardcover : alk. paper); ISBN 0-674-02119-3 (pbk.: alk. paper)
    1. Taiwan--Description and travel. 2. Travelers' writings, Chinese--History and criticism. I. Title: Chinese colonial travel writing and pictures, 1683–1895. II. Title. III. Series.
    DS799.15.T46 2004
    915.124'9043--dc22

                                                                    2004001500

Index by Mary Mortensen

☺ Printed on acid-free paper

First paperback edition 2005

Last figure below indicates year of this printing
14 13 12 11 10 09 08 07 06 05

For Stephen

Acknowledgments

In writing this book I have benefited greatly from the support and advice of numerous people, and I thank them all. Patrick Hanan, Stephen Owen, and Peter Perdue directed this project in its first incarnation as a doctoral dissertation on Qing travel writing. Judith Zeitlin has offered continual inspiration and guidance since the beginning of my graduate study. Isabelle de Courtivron has been an equally inspiring mentor since I joined the faculty at MIT, and this book was born from her challenge to move beyond the dissertation. The senior faculty of the Foreign Languages and Literatures Section at MIT—Isabelle de Courtivron, Elizabeth Garrels, Shigeru Miyagawa, Margery Resnick, Edward Baron Turk, William Uricchio, and Jing Wang—and Peter Perdue in History read the first draft of the manuscript and provided invaluable feedback and encouragement. Numerous others gave generously of their time to read versions or sections of the manuscript: Leo Ching, Rey Chow, Thomas Christensen, Robert Eskildsen, Joshua Fogel, Patterson Giersch, Joanna Handlin Smith, Jonathan Hay, Dorothy Ko, Joanna Levin, Lydia Liu, Victor Mair, Susan Mann, James Millward, Stephen Owen, David Palumbo-Liu, Michael Puett, Harriet Ritvo, Murray Rubinstein, John Shepherd, Richard Smith, Stephen Teiser, David Der-wei Wang, Eugene Wang, Stephen West, Ellen Widmer, and Judith Zeitlin. Thanks also to the anonymous reviewers of the manuscript and related articles.

At Academia Sinica, Taiwan, Tu Cheng-sheng, Liu Tsui-jung, Pan Ying-hai, Ka Chih-ming, Chang Lung-chih, and Chan Su-chuan generously shared their expertise in Taiwan studies with me, as have John Shepherd and Murray Rubinstein, stateside. Thanks to Robert Eskildsen for sharing his research on Japanese imperialism and Charles Le-Gendre, to Evan Dawley for sharing his research on the Taiwan cession crisis, and to Antonio Tavares for sharing his research on camphor in Taiwan. Li Hsien-li provided essential assistance on research on the Taiwan gazetteers.

I also thank the countless people who offered advice on research methodology, sources, and analysis over the past several years, including Allan Barr, Peter Bol, Chu Ping-tzu, Nichola di Cosmo, John Dower, Stevan Harrell, Robert Hymes, Laura Hostetler, William Kirby, Leo Lee, Sebastian Liao, Susan Naquin, Elizabeth Perry, Haun Saussy, Hue-tam Ho Tai, Tang Wen-hui, Thongchai Winnichakul, and Wu Hung. I have benefited greatly from conversations on travel with Ali Behdad, Marion Eggert, Tobie Meyer-Fong, Mary Fuller, Shirley Geok-lin Lim, and Hu Ying. Pat Giersch and Chang Lung-chih were essential partners over the past several years in discussions about imperialism, colonialism, internal colonialism, and the Chinese frontiers. Julian Wheatley, Chen Tong, Zhang Jin, and Kurt Fendt enthusiastically helped with various translation issues.

Material for "Taiwan as a Living Museum: Savagery and Tropes of Anachronism" and "Fashioning Chinese Origins: Nineteenth-Century Ethnohistoriography" first appeared in the article "Taiwan as a Living Museum: Tropes of Anachronism in Late-Imperial Chinese Travel Writing," *Harvard Journal of Asiatic Studies* 59, no. 2 (Dec. 1999): 445–84, and is reprinted here with permission of the editors. Material for Chapter 6 first appeared in the essay "Texts on the Right and Pictures on the Left: Reading the Qing Record of Frontier Taiwan," in *Writing and Materiality in China*, ed. Judith T. Zeitlin and Lydia H. Liu (Harvard University Asia Center, 2003), pp. 451–87, and is reprinted here with permission of the Asia Center. An earlier version of Chapter 7 first appeared as the article "An Island of Women: The Discourse of Gender in Qing Travel Accounts of Taiwan," *International History Review* 20, no. 2 (June 1998): 353–70, and is reprinted here with permission of the editors. Selections of my translation from Yu Yonghe's travelogue appeared in "Exploring China's Last Frontier: Excerpts from Yu Yonghe's *Small Sea Travelogue*," *Asian Pacific American Journal* 4, no. 1 (Spring/Summer 1995): 89–107, and in "*Pihai jiyou*: An Early Exploration Account of Taiwan," in *Hawaii Reader of Traditional Chinese Culture*, ed. Victor Mair (University of Hawaii Press, 2003). An earlier version of my translation from Ding Shaoyi's travelogue first appeared as *"A Brief Record of the Eastern Ocean* by Ding Shaoyi," in *Under Confucian Eyes: Texts on Gender in Chinese History*, ed. Susan Mann and Yu-Yin Cheng (University of California Press, 2001), pp. 350–62, 457–61. The cartographic design in this book, unless otherwise noted, was provided by Patrick Florance and Martin Gamache/AMG.

Vital support and encouragement for this project were provided by Dean Philip Khoury at MIT, the American Association of University Women, the Foreign Languages and Area Studies Program, and the Whiting Foundation. The final research and writing were generously supported by a Postdoctoral Fellowship in the History of the Arts and Humanities from the J. Paul Getty Foundation. Thanks to the MIT Class of 1956 for the granting of a Career Development Professorship, which provided support for the writing and production of this book.

The research for this project was facilitated by the wonderful librarians of the Harvard-Yenching Library, Widener Library, Rubel Library, Fu Ssu-nien Library of Academia Sinica, Taiwan Central Library, Taiwan Provincial Library, The British Library, Bodleian Library, Oxford, Cambridge University Library, Institut des Hautes Etudes Chinoises, College de France, Herzog August Bibliothek, Wolfenbuttel, National Library of China, and MIT Humanities Library. Thanks also to the staffs of the National Taiwan Museum, the National Palace Museum, Taipei, the National Palace Museum, Beijing, and the National Museum of Chinese History.

My heartfelt gratitude to the tremendously helpful staff at Foreign Languages and Literatures, MIT, and at East Asian Languages and Civilizations, Harvard. Nancy Lowe provided crucial logistical and moral support throughout this project. Charles Broderick, Pamela Grimes, and Marcus Henzer supplied vital support through numerous computer crises. Thanks also to my research assistants, Rebecca Deng and Jeremiah Yu.

Among the numerous friends who offered support and help with this project I must mention Rania Huntington, Min-Min Liang, Daisy Ng, David Schaberg, Min Song, Sophie Volpp, and Nicholas Wey Gomez.

My parents have provided continual moral and financial support since the beginning of my graduate work. My mother offered crucial editorial assistance that enabled me to meet the deadline for this manuscript. My mother-in-law kept us going with endless supplies of food and humor. Thanks to Panamai and Perry, whose good cheer and generosity of spirit sustained me through the solitude of writing, and to Laura and Elfine who offered much-needed respites. Most of all, to my husband, Stephen Chung, whose support and boundless faith in me made this book possible. Finally, to my son, Jonathan, whose patience as an infant allowed me to finish the final editing of the manuscript.

E.J.T.

Contents

Appendixes

Reference Matter

Figures and Color Plates

Figures

Color Plates (following p. 186)

Note on Romanization

The *pinyin* system of romanization is used throughout the text, with the exception of place-names like Taipei, Keelung, and Amoy that are familiar to English readers in these forms. I have also chosen to render proper names of Taiwanese and American authors in the system of romanization preferred by the individual author, especially when the author has published under that spelling (e.g., Chang Yao-ch'i and not Zhang Yaoqi). If the author's preference is not known, the pinyin system is employed.

Dates of Selected Eras

Xia	ca. 22nd c.–ca. 17th c. B.C.
Shang	ca. 17th c.–ca. 11th c. B.C.
Zhou	ca. 11th c.–221 B.C.
Qin	221–206 B.C.
Han	206 B.C.–221 A.D.
Three Kingdoms	220–80
Six Dynasties	222–589
Western Jin	265–317
Southern and Northern Dynasties	317–589
Sui	581–618
Tang	618–907
Five Dynasties	907–60
Song	960–1279
Yuan	1280–1368
Ming	1368–1644
Qing	1644–1911
Dutch rule of Taiwan	1624–61
Zheng rule of Taiwan	1661–83
Qing rule of Taiwan	1683–1895
Japanese rule of Taiwan	1895–1945

Taiwan's Imagined Geography

Chinese Colonial Travel Writing and Pictures, 1683–1895

Introduction

Winter 1697

After four days and nights aboard a junk crossing the treacherous waters of the Taiwan Strait, Chinese traveler Yu Yonghe excitedly spotted the peaks of Taiwan's mountains on the horizon.[1] In sight at last was the frontier island that he had longed to see since the Chinese conquest of Taiwan fourteen years earlier. As Yu wrote in his travel diary:

Taiwan lies far beyond the Eastern Ocean and has never, since the dawn of Creation, sent tribute to China. Now we have made . . . Taiwan the ninth prefecture of Fujian. By nature I am addicted to distant travel and I am fearless of obstacles and danger. Ever since Taiwan was put on the map, I have said that I would not be satisfied until I could see the place for myself.[2]

Yu Yonghe's wish came true at last in 1697, when he volunteered for an expedition to Taiwan to obtain sulfur, a vital strategic item used to manufacture gunpowder. Friends and associates warned him against the voyage: the Taiwan Strait was perilous, filled with obstacles such as the notorious "Black Water Ditch," which had capsized countless junks; Taiwan itself was a dangerous place, a mountainous jungle inhabited by "savages" and rife with deadly tropical diseases. Travelers told stories of shipwrecked sailors cannibalized by the islanders and of headhunting raids across the Taiwan Strait. Taiwan had also gained infamy as a "pirates' lair." Above all, the island was known as a stronghold for the Ming loyalist forces of Koxinga,[3] who had waged a war of resistance against the new Manchu Qing dynasty

(1644–1911), and whose defeat by Qing forces in 1683 resulted in Taiwan's becoming an imperial possession for the first time in Chinese history. It was this feat that sparked Yu Yonghe's desire to travel to the island.

Despite the risks the journey presented, Yu was intrigued by the notion of seeing the empire's newest frontier. Before the Qing conquest, few Chinese literati had traveled to this "savage island." This voyage was Yu's chance for adventure, his opportunity to go beyond the old boundaries of China and explore uncharted terrain.

Yu's enthusiasm for the Taiwan frontier stands in sharp contrast to the disdain expressed by many of his contemporaries, who regarded the acquisition of this new territory as a waste of imperial resources. As one critic declared, "Taiwan is merely a ball of mud beyond the seas, unworthy of development by China. It is full of naked and tattooed savages, who are not worth defending. It is a daily waste of imperial money for no benefit."[4] Such objections reflected the prevailing Chinese perception of Taiwan as a barren wilderness, an insignificant parcel of land beyond the pale of civilization. So deeply ingrained was this notion that the court had proposed in 1683 to abandon the newly conquered island after repatriating Ming loyalist troops to the mainland. Admiral Shi Lang, who had led the capture of Taiwan, vigorously protested this decision. In a memorial submitted to the emperor in February 1684, Shi argued for the importance of annexing Taiwan on both strategic and economic grounds.

I have personally traveled through Taiwan and seen firsthand the fertility of its wild lands and the abundance of its natural resources. Both mulberry and field crops can be cultivated; fish and salt spout forth from the sea; the mountains are filled with dense forests of tall trees and thick bamboo; there are sulfur, rattan, sugarcane, deerskins, and all that is needed for daily living. Nothing is lacking. . . . This is truly a bountifully fertile piece of land and a strategic territory.[5]

Shi Lang could speak with authority because he, unlike the emperor's other advisers, had traveled to Taiwan and observed local conditions with his own eyes. Opponents of annexation knew little about Taiwan beyond the cliché of the island as a "miasmal wilderness," for there was a dearth of information about the island in the Chinese histories and geographical records. With his personal knowledge of the island, Shi was uniquely empowered to speak as an expert on this subject. The emperor was sufficiently persuaded by Shi's eyewitness account of the island and its riches to convene a meeting to debate the issue of annexing this territory. Shi's faction eventually carried the day, and in the spring of 1684, Taiwan was officially incorporated into the Qing empire. Over two hundred years later, in 1887, the court would grant the island full status as a province of China.

This book deals with the place of travel writing, pictures, and maps in Taiwan's transformation from a "savage island" located "beyond the seas" (*haiwai*) into a "Chinese province," an integral part of the Chinese empire. Qing travelers like Shi Lang and Yu Yonghe played a crucial role in the production of geographic knowledge about this newest addition to the Qing domain. Their writings helped to demonstrate that far from being a "ball of mud" inhabited by "naked and tattooed savages," Taiwan was endowed with land worth cultivating and populated by natives deserving of inclusion as subjects of the empire.

The Qing incorporation of this island involved not only a reconsideration of Taiwan's place in imperial geography but also a reconceptualization of the Chinese domain itself. The Ming conviction that Taiwan was not part of this domain was rooted in the traditional conception of China as a territory bounded by natural geographic features, such as mountains, rivers, the desert, and the sea.[6] Since Taiwan was separated from the Chinese mainland by the Taiwan Strait, it was, ergo, outside China. The Qing expansion into territory "beyond the seas" entailed a shift from the established conception of China to a new spatial image of an empire that transgressed the traditional boundaries.

The annexation of Taiwan was only one incident in the much larger phenomenon of Qing expansionism, a phenomenon that scholars have recently begun to treat as an example of imperialism, comparable to European imperialisms.[7] Following the conquest of China proper, the Manchu rulers of the Qing dynasty pursued numerous military campaigns on China's frontiers. These campaigns were driven largely by the Qing need to consolidate the empire and eliminate potential military rivals, including the Ming loyalist regime in Taiwan and the Mongols and Russians on the Central Asian frontiers.[8] A gradual process that spanned approximately a century, Qing expansionism was also motivated in part by economic interests and by population

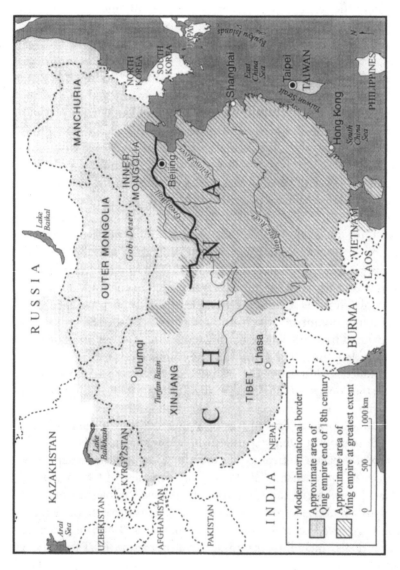

Fig. 1 Expansion of the Qing empire
(cartographic design by Patrick Florance and Martin Gamache/AMG)

pressures in China proper, which generated a demand for new arable lands. Having annexed Taiwan in 1684, the Qing turned its attention to Central Asia, "pacifying" the Mongols and bringing eastern Turkestan and Lhasa, the capital of Tibet, under Qing rule. The Qing further expanded its control in south and southwest China, subjecting various non-Chinese peoples of this region to Qing domination. At its height, in the eighteenth century, Qing influence extended into Korea, Vietnam, Laos, Thailand, Burma, and Nepal, all of which came under the suzerainty of the empire.

By 1760, the Qing had achieved the incredible feat of doubling the size of the empire's territory (see Fig. 1), bringing various non-Chinese frontier peoples under its rule. The impact of Qing expansionism was thus tremendous, as the Qing not only redefined the territorial boundaries of China but also refashioned China as a multiethnic realm—shifting the traditional border between Chinese (*Hua*) and barbarian (*yi*). In doing so, the Qing created an image of "China" that differed vastly from that of the Ming.

In order to promote this new conception of the Chinese empire, the court commissioned a number of major projects to depict the expanded imperial domain. Among them were the Kangxi-Jesuit atlas (1717), a comprehensive survey of the empire; *The Comprehensive Gazetteer of the Great Qing Realm (Da Qing yitong zhi*; ca. 1746), a compendium of geographic information about the empire; *The Qing Imperial Tribute Illustrations (Huang Qing zhigong tu*; ca. 1769), an illustrated catalogue of the peoples of the empire and other "tributaries"; and the *Imperial Glossary of the Five Dynastic Scripts (Wuti Qingwen jian*), an encyclopedic, multilingual glossary of the five major languages of the empire. These texts at once served to define the extent of the empire and to articulate the vision of a geographically diverse and multiethnic imperial realm.

In this book, I argue that travelers' representations of frontier regions such as Taiwan played an important role in the creation of the new imagined geography of the expanded Qing empire. Frontier travel writing emerged as a vital genre during the Qing, as Chinese literati, military men, and merchants traveled to the frontiers in unprecedented numbers. Not only did frontier travelers compose written accounts of their journeys, but a good number of them produced various kinds of *tu* (maps, pictures, illustrations) as visual records of their observations. These *tu* included pictorial maps, ethnographic images, drawings of flora and fauna, architectural renderings, and pictures commemorating battles and other events on the frontier. (Henceforth, I will refer to these various *tu* as "topographical pictures.") As the empire expanded, travelers' accounts and topographical pictures became an important source of geographic knowledge about the newly acquired lands, knowledge that was crucial for strategic and administrative purposes. Travel writing and pictures also served an important ideological function. In representing the distant lands and the ethnically diverse peoples of the frontiers to audiences in China proper, these works transformed places once considered non-Chinese into familiar parts of the imperial realm and thereby helped to naturalize Qing expansionism through the production of a re-imagined imperial geography.

The legacy of Qing imperialism for modern China has been profound: because the People's Republic of China (PRC) now claims sovereignty over virtually all the territory acquired by the last dynasty, the impact of Qing expansionism continues to be felt by the people of Tibet, Xinjiang, Taiwan, and other former frontier regions. Separatist ("splittist" in PRC jargon) movements in all these areas have met with staunch opposition from the Chinese state, which considers such lands inseparable parts of China's sacred territory. Hence, the PRC claims Taiwan—which was a Japanese colony between 1895 and 1945 and which has been ruled by a separate (and recently democratic) government as the Republic of China (ROC) since 1949—as "sovereign territory" that must be returned to the Chinese motherland with due speed. Ironically, the "territorial integrity" that Chinese nationalists seek to defend is based on a territorial image of "China" created by an invading Manchu dynasty, and not the older Ming image.

Of the former Qing frontiers, Taiwan is of particular interest because the question of the island's sovereignty in the postwar era remains unresolved and hotly contested: Is Taiwan de facto a "sovereign state," or is it, in the words of the U.S. media, a "renegade province" of China?[9] Taiwan's relationship to the PRC and the question whether Taiwan might officially declare independence were leading issues in the 2000 presidential race in Taiwan. In an attempt to influence the outcome, the PRC issued a thinly veiled threat of force: "To safeguard China's sovereignty and territorial integrity and realize the reunification of the two sides of the straits, the Chinese government has the right to resort to any necessary means."[10] The "Taiwan issue" (and U.S.

arms sales to Taiwan) is the prickliest thorn in U.S.-China relations and has the potential to bring the two powers into armed conflict.[11] The geopolitical importance of Taiwan combined with Taiwan's emergence since 1987 as a "Chinese democracy" have contributed to the growth of Taiwan Studies as an important new field in Asia and the United States.

In examining the process by which Taiwan was incorporated into the imagined geography of the Qing empire, this book helps to explain how an island that was *terra incognita* for the better part of Chinese history came to be regarded as an integral part of China's "sovereign territory." This study views Taiwan-China relations as a product of a particular history—that of Qing expansionism—rather than as a matter of vague "ancestral ties."[12] By elucidating the nature of this historical relationship, I seek to add to our understanding of current political events in the region.

Expanding Colonial Discourse Studies

Although the primary focus of this book is the Qing construction of Taiwan's imagined geography, in writing this book I also hope to challenge prevailing preconceptions of "the colonizer" and "the colonized" by examining a non-Western imperial power. The presumption that colonizers were European and the colonized non-European is deeply entrenched both inside and outside the academy. The very notion of studying "Chinese colonialism" thus seems alien to many. On more than one occasion, I have been asked: "What do you mean by 'Chinese colonial travel writing'? Do you mean European colonial travel writing about China?" The idea that "imperialism" is essentially a Western phenomenon has also been reinforced by scholars of modern China's "postcoloniality," who have tended to focus on China's historical experiences with Western imperialism while ignoring China's own history as an imperialist power.[13] This is due in no small part to the PRC's ardent denials that the Chinese were ever anything but victims of imperialism; hence official PRC discourse refers to Qing expansionism as "national unification," and talk of "Chinese imperialism" is heresy.[14] I seek to remedy this situation by asserting that China's postcoloniality must also be understood in terms of the legacy of Qing expansionism.

Expanding colonial discourse studies to include imperial China is no easy task, for one immediately runs into terminological difficulties. Scholars (both Western and Chinese) frequently argue that terms such as "imperialism" or "colonialism" cannot be applied to China on the grounds that Qing expansionism does not fit the model of European imperialism. Of course, the Chinese had an empire, just as Rome had an empire, it is often argued, but an empire is not the same as "imperialism." Yet the notion of "European imperialism" is itself problematic. The scholarship of the past several decades has shown that there is no single model of European imperialism: British imperialism differed from French and German imperialisms; nineteenth-century imperialism differed from the earlier conquests of the New World and the mercantile colonialism of the seventeenth and eighteenth centuries. And then there is the matter of American "neo-imperialism" or "neo-colonialism." Theorists have debated whether imperialism is best understood primarily as a political system (as in late nineteenth-century England) or as an economic system (as by early twentieth-century critics). Definitions of "imperialism" range from Lenin's (1916) restrictive "monopoly stage of capitalism" to Michael Doyle's broadly inclusive "imperialism is simply the process or policy of establishing or maintaining an empire."[15] Thus, there is no universal agreement, even among Europeanists, on the precise definition of "imperialism."

Theorists have also been concerned with distinguishing "colonialism" from "imperialism," although the two terms are often used interchangeably. Again, there is no consensus on this score, with some theorists taking "colonialism" as a subset of "imperialism" (e.g., Benita Parry) and others taking "colonialism" as the more general term and "imperialism" as the particular, late nineteenth-century European phenomenon (Nicholas Thomas).[16] Because of this ambiguity, there will necessarily be some slippage in discussing theoretical approaches to "imperialism" and "colonialism" here. Like "imperialism," "colonialism" is a complex and multivalent term that refers to a variety of historical and regional experiences, ranging from the "settler colonialism" of Australia to the "internal colonialism" of the American ghetto.[17] Since "colonialism" derives from the Latin *colere* (to cultivate), the distinction that I find most useful is Edward Said's: "'Colonialism,' which is almost always a consequence of imperialism, is the implanting of settlements on distant territory."[18] This distinction notwithstanding, following convention I employ the term "colonial discourse," rather than "imperial discourse," to describe the complex of signs and practices within which the Qing empire was known. As David Spurr writes: "In speaking of the discourse of colonialism, the distinction [between colonialism and imperialism] tends to collapse, since the basic principles of this discourse . . . also constitute the discourse of imperialism."[19]

My use of the term "Qing imperialism" therefore rests on the premise that, to quote Raymond Williams, "imperialism, like any word which refers to fundamental social and political conflicts, *cannot be reduced, semantically, to a single proper meaning.* Its important historical and contemporary variations of meaning point to real processes which have to be studied in their own terms" (italics added).[20] To this end, I use the word "imperialism" in this study to refer to the Qing conquest of vast tracts of non-Chinese lands through military force, their rule of these distant lands from an imperial center, and their incorporation of significant numbers of ethnically distinct, non-Chinese peoples as subjects of the empire. Since an important aspect of Qing imperialism was the implanting of Han Chinese settlements on distant frontier territories, I consider Qing expansionism at once an imperial and colonial phenomenon.

More fundamentally, I use the term "imperialism" to denote the set of practices, policies, and ideologies through which the Qing empire was fashioned and maintained. In this I follow Edward Said's definition: "'Imperialism' means the practice, the theory, and the attitudes of a dominating metropolitan center ruling a distant territory."[21] I find Said's definition useful, since it is neither so restrictive that it inhibits cross-cultural comparison nor so general that it loses theoretical rigor. Moreover, it cuts to the heart of the matter studied here, for this book is primarily concerned not with imperialism as an economic or political system but with imperialism as a set of attitudes and power relations: precisely those aspects of imperialism that seem to be the most intransigent and that some argue have outlasted formal colonial rule. These power dynamics are vividly visualized in a painting depicting a Qing colonial official's tour of inspection of Taiwan (see Color Plate 1), embodied in the hierarchal relation between the official, seated high above and flanked by banners symbolizing imperial authority, and the natives who kneel in submission on the ground beneath him offering tribute from their land. In shifting the focus to the cultural and ideological dimensions of imperialism/colonialism, I draw on Nicholas Thomas's argument.

Colonialism is not best understood primarily as a political or economic relationship that is legitimized or justified through ideologies of racism or progress. Rather, colonialism has always, equally importantly and deeply, been a cultural process; its discoveries and trespasses are imagined and energized through signs, metaphors and narratives; even what would seem its purest moments of profit and violence have been mediated and enframed by structures of meaning.[22]

I would argue that it is in imperialism/colonialism as a cultural process that we can begin to find the common ground on which "European imperialism(s)" and "Qing imperialism" can be discussed. This is not to deny the historical specificity of late nineteenth-century European imperialism or of Qing imperialism. Nor is it a plea for a return to general, universal theories of imperialism. Rather, it is an attempt to extend the ground on which particular, historical, and localized accounts of imperialisms and colonialisms can be delineated. It is an attempt to initiate a dialogue where there has been none.

My intent in reclaiming the use of the word "imperialism" for China studies is not to suggest the equivalence of Qing and European imperialisms; although recent scholarship in the China field has shown that, despite the manifest differences, Qing and early modern European imperialisms bear enough similarities in terms of institutions and processes to merit comparison.[23] What I want to do instead is to suggest a problematic: Why is it that Qing expansionism, which involved territorial conquest, political control, economic exploitation, and cultural hegemony, cannot be considered "imperialism"? What does it mean to call the Qing an empire without "imperialism"? What difference would it make if we were to see Qing expansionism as imperialism and not simply as an imperium? I address this problematic further in the Epilogue and suggest that it informs our understanding of China-Taiwan relations today.

Setting Qing expansionism within the broader framework of colonial studies rather than confining it within the perimeter of "area studies" allows us to see China in the context of global historical processes, rather than as a unique and timeless civilization unto itself.[24] An intriguing statement made by a nineteenth-century travel writer demonstrates that there were Chinese literati who perceived the Qing imperial project in global terms. This traveler, Ding Shaoyi, compared his own observations of Qing Taiwan to Guileo Aleni's description of the European colonization of North America:

The savagery of the native barbarians of the newly opened frontiers of North America is no different from that of the savages of Taiwan. In the past, they were extremely ferocious, yet Europeans have managed to guide them with their senseless, confused religion and have finally changed the native customs. So it is a real injustice to say that the raw savages of Taiwan have absolutely no human morals despite their human appearance and that they cannot be civilized with our Kingly Governance (*wangzheng*)![25]

Ding addressed his comments to contemporaries skeptical about the possibility of civilizing the "savages" of Taiwan. Since the Europeans had succeeded in North America, he concluded, surely the Chinese, with their superior civilization, would prevail in Taiwan. Although recognizing differences in specific beliefs and institutions, Ding perceived fundamental parallels between European and Chinese expansionism and their civilizing enterprises. Historian Laura Hostetler has also demonstrated that the Qing emperors were keenly aware of imperialism as a global phenomenon and perceived themselves as players in an international game of territorial expansionism.[26]

The notion of "Chinese imperialism" is rendered particularly complex by the fact that the Qing was itself a conquest dynasty. The majority, Han Chinese population of China proper was subjugated to the Manchu ruling class. Yet the Qing adopted many of the fundamental political, economic, and cultural institutions of the Chinese imperial system, becoming somewhat "sinicized" in the process. At the same time, ethnic Han Chinese participated actively in the military and political life of the Qing, becoming part of the ruling class and perhaps somewhat "Manchuized" in the process.[27] This ethnic complexity only intensified with Qing expansionism. Whereas the Qing army, with its multiethnic troops, conquered the frontier territories, the colonists who settled these frontiers were nearly exclusively Han Chinese.[28]

What we find in frontier regions such as Taiwan, then, is no simple dichotomy of colonizer/colonized, but a multilevel hierarchy of colonial officials (both Manchu and Han), Han Chinese settlers, and indigenous peoples. Each group had its own interests—sometimes these interests competed with those of other groups; sometimes they intersected. Qing administrators did not necessarily view Han Chinese settlers as natural allies on the frontiers. Indeed, given the island's history as a base for Ming loyalists, Qing officials regarded the settlers in Taiwan with suspicion. During the initial years of Qing expansionism, in particular, the court often adopted policies that favored indigenous peoples over Han Chinese colonists, in large measure to prevent costly ethnic unrest.[29] The study of Qing imperialism therefore seems particularly apt at a time when scholars of colonial studies are arguing for the need to rethink older models of a strict colonizer/colonized dichotomy and to consider the complexity of ethnic interactions in colonial contexts.[30]

The analysis of frontier travel writing and topographical pictures promises to enhance our understanding of the Qing frontier experience greatly. Historians have produced excellent studies of the political, economic, and military administration of the Qing frontiers, but relatively little has been written on cultural representations of the frontiers.[31] Like European imperialisms, Qing imperialism was a complex and dynamic convergence of strategic, economic, political, cultural, and ideological interests. Studies of Western imperialism have emphasized the vital role of colonial discourse in sustaining empires and producing colonial subjects.[32] I would argue that if we wish to understand the Qing formation of a geographically and ethnically diverse empire, scholars of China must similarly attend to the role of colonial discourse in this process and the cultural dimensions of the frontier experience. Travel literature and topographical pictures, both of which constitute forms of colonial discourse, are valuable resources for such a project: these texts express and articulate ideologies of imperialism even as they engender ideas about the frontiers.

The study of colonial discourse has largely been inspired by Edward Said's *Orientalism* (1978). Although widely critiqued as reductionist or one-sided in the decades since its publication, this provocative work nonetheless remains a foundational text in the field. Said described "Orientalism" as a complex set of ideas and images through which European culture defined the East as "other" to Western civilization. Chinese representations of the frontiers as exotic, uncivilized, and barbarous bear fundamental similarities to European Orientalism. If European culture, as Said argued, derived its sense of identity and strength by setting itself off against the Orient, Chinese civilization gained its sense of identity as "the Middle Kingdom" (*Zhongguo*) in opposition to the "barbarians of the four directions" (*siyi*). Both traditions attempted to establish their own civilization as the normative ideal and to project "over there" qualities and traits (lasciviousness and indolence, for example) that they sought to repress in their own societies. Painted in the broadest strokes, European Orientalism and Chinese discourse on barbarians can be regarded as comparable. Indeed, the similarities are striking and point to the existence of shared, cross-cultural modes of constructing foreign "others."

My study of Qing travel literature and topographical pictures considers Chinese representations of the frontiers as a form of discourse roughly equivalent to Orientalism yet shaped by the particular conditions of the Qing imperial enterprise.[33] Much as European Orientalism has outlasted European colonialism, its Chinese counterpart has outlasted the particular institutions and circumstances of Qing imperialism and lives on in contemporary representations of ethnic "minorities" in the modern Chinese nation-state. This phenomenon has been described by anthropologist Dru Gladney as "oriental orientalism" and by anthropologist Louisa Schein as "internal orientalism."[34] Expanding the scope of colonial studies allows us to view China not simply as the object of Orientalist discourse or as a mimic of Western Orientalism but also as the producer of its own brand of exoticist discourse.

One aspect of my project is to ask what the concepts of "race" and "ethnicity" meant in the Qing context.[35] Were Qing representations of frontier peoples culturalist or racialist? Or a combination thereof? Like "imperialism" and "colonialism," "race" and "ethnicity" are two terms that bear comparative treatment across cultural contexts. These two terms are perhaps the more difficult pair, for they are inadequately defined (even in contemporary American usage) and, moreover, have long and complicated histories tied to the histories of imperialism and conquest. Anyone trying to define these terms quickly enters a swamp in which concepts of race, ethnicity, culture, nation, and tribe are inextricably tangled. "Race" and "ethnicity" are, furthermore, loaded terms in English; "race," in particular, immediately brings to mind racism and eugenics. Using the word "race," even in reference to a historical idea or construct, is often mistaken as a signal that one believes in race as an objective fact—which I certainly do not.[36]

Without entering too deeply into this terminological morass, it is safe to assert that both race and ethnicity essentially refer to the categorization of peoples based on some notion of difference; how this difference has been defined has varied historically and culturally (witness the latest U.S. Census Bureau attempts to redefine its categories of race and ethnicity).[37] As such, my analysis focuses on the ways in which Qing writers conceptualized human difference and categorized groups of people within the empire.[38]

In frontier travel writing, Chinese literati were concerned with a range of human differences—physical, cultural, linguistic, intellectual, and moral, as well as in human nature (*xing*). For Qing authors, the relative significance of these types of differences was a matter of debate. In my analysis of Chinese sources on Taiwan, I identify two discourses concerning human difference: what I call a "racialist discourse" and an "ethnical discourse." I roughly define the first as a discourse that focuses on physical differences and innate differences in human nature. The racialist discourse further constructs difference as categorical and absolute, along the lines of the distinction between humans and animals. In contrast, ethnical discourse focuses on cultural differences and constructs difference as a matter of degree within certain human universals.

In labeling these discourses "racialist" and "ethnical," I imply certain parallels with Western discourses that place "race" on the side of nature and "ethnicity" on the side of nurture, in the "nature" versus "nurture" debate on human difference. However, in drawing these parallels, I by no means suggest that Qing concepts of race and ethnicity are precisely equivalent to their Western counterparts (of any place or period).[39] Why, then, use a loaded word like "race" at all? Why not stay with a seemingly more neutral term like "ethnicity"? Like Pamela Kyle Crossley, I argue that "unless one has resort to the term 'race,'. . . 'race' and 'ethnicity' would remain mingled with each other, the process of differentiation forever muddled by the notion that 'ethnic group' is just a better word for what was once called 'race.'"[40] I therefore use the word "race" primarily to distinguish what I call "racialist discourse" from "ethnical discourse," rather than to highlight the similarities between Western and Chinese thinking on race, as does Frank Dikötter in his *Discourse of Race in Modern China*.

As a form of colonial discourse, travel texts provide crucial data for the analysis of Qing constructions of race and ethnicity, for they allow us to see in greater detail Qing views on frontier peoples beyond official pronouncements on ethnic policy. In my analysis of Qing accounts of Taiwan, I demonstrate how the Qing ideology of empire, which sought to accommodate different ethnic groups and to suppress the distinction between Chinese (*Hua*) and barbarian (*yi*), came into conflict with older attitudes of Han Chinese chauvinism, often expressed in racialist terms.

The Qing vision of the imperial domain—articulated most clearly by the Qianlong emperor (r. 1736–95)—was of a conglomerate of five major peoples—Manchus, Han Chinese, Mongols, Tibetans, and East Turkestanis—joined into one polity under a universal emperor. But where did the Taiwan indigenes (not to mention other indigenous peoples of southern China) fit into this scheme? After we examine a range of Qing representations of the Taiwan indigenes and the Taiwan frontier, we will return to this question in the Conclusion.

Imagined Geography

The "imagined geography" of my title is intended to distinguish between the geography that exists on the ground and geography as a cultural construct. Thus, although Taiwan never moved from its position at 23.5 degrees north / 120 degrees east, 96 miles from the Chinese coast, in terms of the Chinese geographic imagination, between the seventeenth and nineteenth centuries the island shifted from "far, far beyond the seas" to a location firmly situated within the Chinese empire. Then, between 1895 and 1945, the island that had only recently "become Chinese" "became Japanese," as Leo Ching demonstrates.[41] In focusing on the role of discourse in these processes, I concur with Edward Said that the "struggle over geography . . . is complex and interesting because it is not only about soldiers and cannons but also about ideas, about forms, about images and imaginings."[42] My use of the term "imagined geography" draws on Said's notion of "imaginative geography," as well as the concept of "imagined communities" introduced by Benedict Anderson.

In *Orientalism*, Said proposed the notion of "imaginative geography" to denote the complex set of ideas and images by which geographic entities such as the "Orient" and the "Occident" were historically produced. Said argued that it is through "imaginative geography" that meaning is assigned to the space "out there," beyond one's own territory. As Said wrote: "All kinds of suppositions, associations, and fictions appear to crowd the unfamiliar space outside one's own."[43] Said thus highlighted what he saw as the arbitrary and imaginative dimensions of geographic knowledge. Following Said, the term "imaginative geography" has been used to refer to the culturally constructed nature of geography and to the role of discourse in producing geographic knowledge. Whereas Said's work in *Orientalism* primarily focused on European texts about the Orient, recent scholars such as Joan M. Schwartz, Anne Godlewska, and Derek Gregory have considered imaginative geography as the product of a variety of representations—literary, cartographic, pictorial, photographic, and so forth—working in concert.[44]

The concept of "imagined communities" derives from Anderson's pioneering work on nationalism, in which he described the nation as an imagined political community—"imagined" because "the members of even the smallest nation will never know most of their fellow-members, meet them, or even hear of them, yet in the minds of each lives the image of their communion."[45] Borrowing from Anderson, I suggest the Qing empire not as a community but as an "imagined geography," a defined and limited spatial image that existed in the minds of Qing elites despite the fact that most would never travel to the distant reaches of the empire. This imagined geography delineated the territory that belonged to the "our land" of the Qing empire, in distinction to the "barbarian lands" that lay beyond its boundaries. As such, imagined geography describes the process by which the "geo-body" of an empire is produced.

The term "geo-body" was first used by Thongchai Winichakul in 1994 to describe the territoriality of the Thai nation:

Geographically speaking, the geo-body of the nation occupies a certain portion of the earth's surface which is objectively identifiable. It appears to be concrete to the eyes as if its existence does not depend on any act of imagining. That, of course, is not the case. The geo-body of the nation is merely an effect of modern geographical discourse whose prime technology is a map.[46]

Although there are essential differences between empires and nation-states, since Thongchai concedes that the definition of the term is neither strict nor conclusive, I will also use the term "geo-body" in reference to the Qing empire, which I regard as an effect of multiple geographic discourses—textual, pictorial, and cartographic.[47]

My use of the term "imagined geography" thus distinguishes this particular form from other forms of imaginative geography more generally. "Imaginative geography," as Said described it, tends to dramatize the distance and difference of what is "out there." Following *Orientalism*, studies of imaginative geography have generally focused on the "barbarian land" side of the "our land–barbarian land" distinction that Said posited as fundamental to imaginative geography.[48] In my formulation, "imagined geography" is concerned primarily with defining "our land" and thus focuses on the other side of the equation. More specifically, the imagined geography of empire describes the process by which "their land" is converted into "our land." Rather than simply dramatizing distance and difference, imagined geography at once exoticizes the other and attempts to convert otherness into familiarity and we-ness. I use the variant form "imagined geography" to connote this slight shift of focus.

Yet because attempts to construct identity out of difference can never be wholly successful, Qing imagined geography was characterized by an inner dissonance. The tension between dramatizing difference and domesticating it marked Qing representations of Taiwan and other frontier regions of the empire. It is this tension between difference and sameness, distance and union, the exotic and the familiar, that I explore in tracing Taiwan's transformation from "savage island" into "Chinese province."

Frontier Travel Writing and Pictures

Frontier travel writing and pictures had an intimate connection with the Qing imperialist project. These works served as vital sources of information about the new regions of the empire, especially during the early years of expansionism, when other sources of empirical geographic information were not readily available. Frontier officials relied on travel accounts, maps, and other topographical pictures to familiarize themselves with local conditions—the terrain, natural resources, local customs, relations between various local tribes, and so forth. Compilers of local gazetteers likewise employed such texts as sources for the production of these compendia of geographic and historical information and crucial administrative aids. Travel accounts also served as important source materials for general geographic and historical works, encyclopedias, guidebooks, and even the *zhiguai* (records of anomalies) collections that Chinese literati read for entertainment.

Frontier officials themselves seriously engaged in the collection of geographic information about the frontiers. An excerpt from an eighteenth-century travel account gives us a picture of how officials went about this activity:

In the course of my duties, I toured around and inquired after customs and strange products. I saw all kinds of unusual and weird things that have never been seen in China proper. . . . In my spare time from official duty, I ordered a painter to make illustrations of those concrete things that I had seen and heard. . . . I will keep [this pictorial album] in my travel trunk, so that when I return I may present it to the learned and accomplished gentlemen at the capital and thereby expand their knowledge.[49]

Officials produced such textual and pictorial accounts both as personal mementos and as aids for colonial administration. In addition, they sometimes submitted travel accounts, maps, or illustrations to the emperor as records of conditions on the frontiers or of their own achievements in frontier service. The court itself occasionally ordered frontier officials to submit geographic information and illustrations for use in the compilation of grand, empirewide projects such as the *Comprehensive Gazetteer of the Great Qing Realm* or *The Qing Imperial Tribute Illustrations.*[50]

The subjects taken up by travel writers were shaped to a large degree by the conventional categories of geographical recording—topography, climate, buildings and institutions, transportation routes, local ethnic groups and their customs and languages, flora and fauna, local products, geographic marvels, and so forth. Although the subjects of travel writing were fairly uniform, travelers chose to compose their accounts in a variety of formats—the travel diary, the essay, the notation book, or the geographical record (a genre consisting of short entries under various categorical headings)[51]—each with its own generic conventions.[52]

Topographical illustrations, which were produced either by the travel writers themselves or by professional painters in their employ, generally focused on similar subjects. For the most part, frontier pictures can be divided into three main categories—maps or landscape pictures (*ditu* or *shanchuantu*), ethnographic illustrations (*fengsutu*), and illustrations of flora and fauna (*fengwutu*)—but a wide range of *tu* exist outside these categories. There are architectural drawings of civil, military, and religious structures, pictures of local industries, and illustrations commemorating events such as the annual review of troops or an official's tour of inspection. As with travel writing, a variety of generic conventions shaped these pictorial representations.[53]

The development of frontier travel literature in the Qing was encouraged not only by the demands of expansionism but also by the new status accorded geography as a discipline. According to Benjamin Elman, the *kaozheng* (evidential scholarship) movement—one of the major intellectual trends of the late imperial era—elevated geography to a key discipline through important methodological innovations in the seventeenth century.[54] The new geography emphasized empirical observation, the systematic gathering of data, and philological research. It often focused on topics related to issues of frontier or maritime defense. Evidential scholarship also generated interest in historical geography, including the historical geography of China's frontiers and borders. Thus, in frontier geography colonial imperatives coincided with the scholarly interests of Qing literati, and these interests reinforced one another.

Other cultural trends of the late imperial era also stimulated interest in the frontiers. This era has been described by many literary scholars as an age of surfeit, an age when everything seems to have been done, everything seems to have been said.[55] This was particularly true in the case of travel literature, for all the famous mountains, all the scenic spots in China, had been overinscribed with the writings of earlier travelers.[56] In conventional travel writing, the traveler was expected not so much to describe the scene before him but to meditate on his relationship to those who had come before him. Paintings of the famous scenic spots similarly were bound by convention and the precedents of famous masterworks. Frontier travel gave the literatus the opportunity to do something new and fresh, to cover new ground, as it were. Liberated from the need to dwell on historical models, the traveler as explorer and eyewitness observer took center stage. Travelers to Taiwan had perhaps the greatest leeway for originality, for unlike travelers to the Central Asian frontiers, for example, there were virtually no literary precedents for their journeys.

Qing travel literature evinced a new attitude toward the frontiers. Canonical Tang dynasty (618–907) literary treatments of the frontiers were filled with images of hardship and suffering—whether the bitter winds of the Central Asian frontier or the miasmas of southern border lands. The theme of exile permeates this literature, with unfamiliar terrain causing tears of homesickness and alienation to well up in the eyes of the poet. As Han Yu wrote from exile in Chaozhou in the south:

> Typhoons for winds, crocodiles for fish—
> Afflictions and misfortunes not to be plumbed!
> South of the county, as you approach its boundary.
> There are swollen seas linked to the sky;
> Poison fogs and malarial miasmas
> Day and evening flare and form![57]

In contrast, we find Qing travelers, like Yu Yonghe, proclaiming a passion for "distant travels" (*yuanyou*) and even relishing the danger and strangeness of the frontiers. As Yu Yonghe declared: "In searching for the exotic and visiting scenic spots, one must not fear terrible inclinations: if the voyage is not dangerous, it will not be exotic; if the inclination is not terrible, it will not be exhilarating."[58] In similar terms, another traveler vowed: "If the journey is not distant, then it will not be lusty; if the journey is not dangerous, it will not be exotic."[59] These sentiments were echoed by numerous other frontier travelers who insisted on the unconventional and adventurous journey as the only authentic form of travel.

In the classic *Chinese World Order* (1968), John King Fairbank argued that traditional Chinese relations with non-Chinese peoples were colored by the concept of sinocentrism and the assumption of Chinese superiority. One would expect Chinese accounts of frontier peoples to be marked by this attitude of Han Chinese superiority. As I shall demonstrate, in frontier travel literature this was not, however, uniformly the case. Rather, Chinese views of the other were complex and often contradictory. As in Western travel literature, encounters with the other provided Chinese travelers with an opportunity to look back at the self, and literati representations of Taiwan and its indigenous people frequently expressed, and were colored by, their author's political, social, or philosophical concerns.

Encounters with difference on the frontiers also prompted travelers to engage in cultural reflection, leading them to new understandings of Chinese culture and often to cultural relativism. Questioning the universality of Chinese culture, travel writers suggested that it was fitting for each place to have its own customs and tastes: as many a writer proposed, "Perhaps our culture seems just as strange to them." Traditional Western historiography has presented China as culturally static and self-satisfied until the encounter with the West in the nineteenth century. However, an examination of frontier travel writing demonstrates that long before the "response to the West," Chinese intellectuals were interested in exploring the ways in which other cultures challenged their own societal norms.

Qing literati expressed a penchant for reading about exotic geographies and for collecting ethnographic illustrations of exotic peoples such as the Miao of southwestern China or the "savages" of Taiwan. Their enthusiasm for the subject is reflected in the number of anthologies devoted to travel writing produced during the Qing. Travel accounts and pictures originally circulated in manuscript form among the author's friends and colleagues, as well as among frontier officials. Many such manuscripts were subsequently published, either as part of an author's collected works or in collectanea. Wang Xiqi's mammoth *Geographic Collectanea of the Little Fanghu Studio* (*Xiaofanghuzhai yudi congchao*, published 1877), for example, reproduced over a thousand travel accounts representing exotic locales from Taiwan to Turfan.[60] Travel literature and topographical pictures thus appealed to a dual audience: frontier officials and others who needed practical geographic information and armchair travelers who sought to experience the thrills of the frontier vicariously.

Unfortunately, although a significant corpus of late imperial travel writing was preserved through reprinting in collectanea, due to the difficulties of reproduction, pictures were generally not included in such reprintings.[61] Subsequently, many pictures have been lost or exist only in rare manuscript editions in museums or private collections. Sometimes our only clue that pictures once accompanied a particular travel account is a colophon writer's lament that "it is a pity that the pictures have long been lost."[62] Thus, although travel literature and topographical pictures originally circulated within the same milieu, the modern reader of Qing travel anthologies generally reads as though texts existed in isolation from pictures—a practice reinforced by the academic distinction between literary studies and art history. I argue, however, that travel writing is best understood within a system of geographic representation that includes visual materials.

Travel and Visuality

Indeed, visuality plays a central role in the practices of travel and travel writing. As Mary Louise Pratt has shown in *Imperial Eyes: Travel Writing and Transculturation*, it is primarily through the sense of sight that the traveler constructs the other.[63] The claim to have "seen for oneself" is a recurring motif in late imperial Chinese travel literature, with travelers insisting that "I have been there myself and seen with my own eyes," or "I am only recording that which I have seen with my own eyes."[64] Another frequent move is for the traveler to refute common beliefs about a place based on what he has seen firsthand. As Ming literatus Zhang Hong explained after a journey to eastern Zhejiang in 1639, "About half [of the things I saw there] did not agree with what I had heard. So when I returned I got out some silk and used it to depict what I had seen, because relying on your ears is not as good as relying on your eyes."[65] The privileging of the eye as the most reliable sense is related to the privileging of experiential knowledge in travel writing.[66] The ears, in contrast, are associated with hearsay, a type of knowledge regarded as particularly suspect in travel literature.[67] It is the traveler's claim to have been an eyewitness to all he records that confers authority on the travel account.[68]

The role of the eyewitness acquired a special importance in Chinese accounts of the frontiers, as it did in European accounts of the New World. In the absence of a canon of texts concerning these "uncharted terrains," only firsthand experience could lend credibility to the explorer's report.[69] As one Qing literatus asserted:

> Of all the books written about Taiwan, works such as Ji Qiguang's *Brief Account of Taiwan* [sic] and Xu Huaizu's *Random Jottings on Taiwan* are based on unsubstantiated rumor. . . . Only Lan Dingyuan's *Record of the Pacification of Taiwan* and Huang Shujing's *Record of a Tour of Duty in the Taiwan Strait* are written by men who really went there themselves and traversed the territory. Therefore, what they have to say about the mountains and streams, the environment, customs, and products can be trusted.[70]

Thus, among the various forms of geographic records available to Qing readers, travel writing, as a document of personal experience, had privileged status. Travel writers themselves frequently claimed that only those with firsthand experience could produce reliable geographic knowledge—thereby bolstering their own authority. Qing literati also considered it crucial for topographical pictures, especially maps, to be based on empirical observation. This does not mean that artists necessarily drew pictures from life. Rather, pictures might be produced (either by the traveler or by a professional painter) based on the traveler's memory of what he had seen or perhaps samples of plants and other products that he had collected. Nonetheless, the basis in firsthand experience is what theoretically separated the topographical picture from an imaginative painting, just as it separated the travel account from fiction.[71]

Given the importance of "seeing for oneself," it is not surprising that travelers like Zhang Hong chose to record their experiences in visual as well as textual forms. Indeed, art historians have written much on the association between domestic Chinese tourist travel and landscape painting (*shanshui hua*). But comparatively little has been written on the traveler's involvement with the class of visual materials known as *tu*, a broad term that includes pictures, illustrations, maps, charts, and diagrams.[72] This neglect is largely due to the low status of vernacular visual forms within the discipline of art history. As art historian James Cahill writes of Chinese pictorial maps: "Many such picture-maps were painted in China from early to recent times, but they have received little attention from either Chinese or foreign scholars, because they have been considered (usually with good reason) to have practical rather than aesthetic value."[73] At the same time, historians and scholars of cartography have traditionally discounted pictorial maps on the grounds that such maps have more aesthetic than practical value.[74] Pictorial maps and other kinds of topographical pictures have therefore largely fallen between the cracks of disciplinary divisions.

Craig Clunas has recently argued for the importance of pictures (*tu*) and visuality in early modern China and demonstrated that pictures permeated virtually every aspect of life in this period.[75] Certainly, visual materials, especially maps and astronomical charts, had long been considered vital to geographic knowledge in China.[76] By the Ming, illustrated books of all kinds, including geographic works, were widely available. Thus, readers were accustomed to looking at pictures in conjunction with texts. Robert Hegel's study of Ming and Qing illustrated fiction has also greatly added to our understanding of the theory and practice of reading texts with pictures. Following the approach suggested by scholars like Clunas and Hegel, I seek to reinsert the reading of pictures into the reading of travel literature.[77]

The idea that topographical pictures represent an important complement to written texts in the production of geographic knowledge was succinctly expressed by Xia Xianlun, the compiler of a nineteenth-century collection of Taiwan maps:

The ancients had histories on their right and maps (*tu*) on their left, granting equal importance to visualizing and perusing (*guanlan*). When [Han dynasty general] Xiao He entered the passes, the first thing he did was to collect maps and written records. Without maps, one cannot have comprehensive knowledge of all the roads and their obstacles, of the terrain and its strategic passes.[78]

Xia emphasized the importance of looking in addition to reading, implying that images allow for a different way of comprehending space and place than words alone. Thus text and pictures are essential to one another: visual knowledge was an important counterpart to textual knowledge.

Word and image enjoyed a kind of complementary division of labor in late imperial geographic representation. Cordell Yee and others have demonstrated that gazetteer maps, for example, were primarily intended as illustrative accompaniments to the gazetteer text, which contained verbal descriptions of the geography. Maps provided a general idea of the topography and aided in understanding the spatial relations between these landmarks. The text supplied such detailed information as distances between locations and the names of villages, mountains, and other topographical features. Map and text thus assumed complementary functions, with maps allowing for qualitative understandings of the terrain and texts providing quantitative geographical information. This complementary relation was expressed in the idea that the "narration of events without maps is not clear, and maps without explanation are not intelligible."[79] A similar dynamic can be seen in a genre known as "pictures with explanations" (*tushuo*), which combined pictures and explanatory text. Thus, word and image worked together in the production of geographic knowledge.

The Qing court clearly recognized the political importance of visual in addition to textual knowledge of the frontiers. For the Qing, the visual representation of the frontiers, especially mapping, was bound up with the assertion of imperial power on both the practical and the symbolic levels.[80] And so the Qing sponsored works such as the Kangxi-Jesuit atlas and the *Qing Imperial Tribute Illustrations*. The

Qianlong emperor also commissioned a series of French copperplate engravings to commemorate Qing conquests on the frontiers. Such pictures helped not only to visualize the extent of Qing imperial possessions but also to define, order, and celebrate these possessions. Pictures therefore played an important role in the fashioning of empire.

Although the surviving visual record of the Qing frontiers is far smaller than the textual record, it is no less significant. Like travel writing, pictures are a highly mediated form of representation: thus, these images reveal a great deal about how Qing travelers "saw" the frontier. In reinserting pictures into the reading of travel literature, I demonstrate that an examination of pictures may bring to the fore issues or perspectives that do not emerge from an examination of literary texts alone. Therefore, a more complete understanding of the cultural meanings that the frontier had for the Qing can be gained by examining pictures in conjunction with texts such as travel accounts and gazetteers.

As a study of Qing colonial discourse, this work necessarily privileges both texts and the perspective of the Qing elite.[81] This is largely a function of my sources, the Qing travel accounts, gazetteers, maps, pictures, and other documents produced by Qing literati on which the research for this project is based. Neither the perspective of the Taiwan indigenes nor that of the Han Chinese settlers is represented here. This project makes no claim to uncover the voice of the subaltern. The rich oral traditions of the Taiwan indigenes and early Chinese settlers of Taiwan are beyond the scope of this book. Following the predilections of Qing travel writers, I have for the most part left aside the story of the Han Chinese settlers of Taiwan, a story that has long been at the center of Taiwan Studies.[82] Moreover, my sources present an entirely male perspective; unlike Mary Louise Pratt and Susan Morgan, I have found no evidence of female-authored travel accounts. Therefore, I make no apology for using the pronoun "he" to refer to Qing travelers in this book.

Since my concern is with discourse, this work does not include in-depth discussion of the cultures and histories of the Taiwan indigenes and the Han Chinese settlers of Taiwan (the "real world" stuff of anthropology and history), both of which have been extensively documented elsewhere. I make no presumption that Qing texts or pictures are "accurate" representations of Qing Taiwan and its inhabitants; rather, I treat them as forms of Qing "imagined geography."[83]

This work does not aim to be explicitly comparative in a methodological sense, for my intent is not to prove that Qing imperialism
fits the model of, say, British or Spanish imperialism but to explore
what happens when we treat Qing texts from the vantage point of
colonial discourse theory: How does colonial discourse theory help
us identify and elucidate relations of power and cultural dominance
that pervade Qing constructions of Taiwan?[84] Nonetheless, readers
familiar with European colonialism will no doubt find much that is
familiar here: the construct of the "savage," primitivism, the feminization of the other, and so on. They will also no doubt find much
that is unfamiliar. Those interested in more explicit comparisons between Qing and European imperialisms should refer to the work of
Peter Perdue, John Shepherd, Michael Adas, and Laura Hostetler.[85] It
is also beyond the scope of this book to compare Qing colonial policy and Japanese colonial policy on Taiwan, the subject of Chang
Lung-chih's research.[86]

The Qing Transformation of Taiwan

After the Qing conquest of the island, Qing Taiwan policy went
through a number of phases over the course of the next two centuries.
John Shepherd's *Statecraft and Political Economy on the Taiwan Frontier, 1600–1800* gives a detailed and thorough account of these policy
shifts during the first century of Qing rule on Taiwan. According to
Shepherd, the Qing court alternated between a pro-quarantine approach and a pro-colonization approach to Taiwan policy throughout
this period.[87] Pro-quarantine policies sought to preserve the status quo
on the island by restricting Chinese immigration to Taiwan and protecting the indigenes' land rights. Pro-colonization policies promoted
Chinese immigration and the aggressive appropriation of indigenous
lands for Chinese settlers. Policymakers alternated between these two
orientations, as they sought to balance the interests of the indigenous
people and the Chinese settlers and thereby avoid costly conflict on
the frontier.

Despite the efforts of pro-quarantine officials, the Qing could not
stem the tide of Han Chinese immigration to this frontier, and by the
nineteenth century, the court had decided to proceed with the final
colonization of the island as a whole. In 1875, the Qing adopted the
"Open the Mountains and Pacify the Savages" (*kaishan fufan*) policy.

This policy legalized the entry of Han Chinese settlers into the last of the remaining indigenous territory on the island. In order to accomplish this appropriation of lands, the Qing employed the military to "pacify the savages." With the adoption of this policy, the tenuous balance between Han Chinese interests and indigenous interests definitively tipped in favor of the Chinese settlers. When Taiwan was promoted to provincehood in 1887, it seemed that the island was to be once and for all Chinese terrain.

When the Qing first conquered Taiwan, there were only a handful of firsthand accounts of the island. Thus, the Ming image of the island as a "ball of mud" predominated. Over the course of two centuries of Qing colonial rule, Chinese literati produced a significant corpus of travel accounts, maps, and pictures of Taiwan, providing a wealth of knowledge about the once-unknown island and concomitantly transforming its image. The pioneering Qing writers strove to make the island known and struggled with the question whether the island was worth colonizing. In the eighteenth century, when the issue of annexation had been settled, colonial officials recognized the need for accurate geographic information about the island. Eighteenth-century authors rejected the works of the earlier period as unreliable and attempted to replace these writings with their own empirical observations. It was during this second phase that the dominant tropes of Qing colonial discourse about Taiwan emerged. The bulk of this book is, therefore, devoted to eighteenth-century works. By the nineteenth century, Chinese attitudes toward Taiwan and the material conditions of the colony had changed so dramatically that "the ball of mud" was now considered a "land of Green Gold."[88]

In this book, I trace changes in Chinese representations of Taiwan and its indigenous people as the Qing gradually converted the island from an "inhospitable wilderness" into an agricultural colony producing lucrative cash crops such as sugar, rice, and tea. Focusing on the related images of the landscape, the indigenous people, and natural resources, I examine discursive shifts in these representations and show how these shifts were related to changes in Qing colonial policy—for example, the decision to "Open the Mountains and Pacify the Savages" in the late nineteenth century.

I begin, in Chapter 1, by considering the annexation debate of 1683 and examining the conflict between older Ming notions of Taiwan's geography and emerging Qing representations of the island. Resis-

tance to the annexation of Taiwan stemmed from traditional presumptions about what lay "beyond the seas," in the domain known as
the "Wilderness." As we will see, maps and travel writing helped to
reconceptualize an island long considered "beyond the seas" as a part
of the Qing domain.

Chapter 2 examines how seventeenth- and eighteenth-century
travel writers constructed Taiwan as a living museum of Chinese antiquity. Representations of the Taiwan indigenes as anachronous people were used both to denigrate and to idealize these people.

Chapter 3 situates eighteenth-century representations of Taiwan
within the context of the early Qing debate over whether to quarantine
or colonize the island with Chinese settlers. Travel writers viewed
Taiwan's landscape through the lens of its agricultural potential. Over
the course of the eighteenth century, the early Qing image of Taiwan as
a horrid wilderness was gradually replaced by an image of Taiwan as a
fertile, land of bounty, an "abundant paradise," in the words of one
writer.

Chapter 4 examines how Qing writers dealt with the question of
whether the Taiwan indigenes were a "separate breed" or whether they
were essentially no different from the Chinese. Qing writings exhibit a
tension between the traditional assumption that there was a fundamental division between Chinese and barbarians (the "racialist discourse")
and Qing imperial ideology, which denied this categorical division.

In Chapter 5, I analyze the Qing division of Taiwan's land and natives into the categories of "raw" and "cooked." Qing concepts of the
raw and the cooked captured the complex intersection of ideas about
acculturation, political submission, and environment, and Qing writers used the metaphor of "cooking" to demonstrate that the Taiwan
indigenes were "worth incorporating into the empire." These classifications have, in turn, informed the modern construction of Taiwan
"mountain aborigines" and "plains aborigines" as two distinct ethnic
groups.

Chapter 6 examines how graphic illustrations of Taiwan indigenes
served to visualize "racial difference." In these pictorial representations, native dress, adornment, and bodies were seen as overt manifestations of cultural difference. Visual representations of the Taiwan indigenes help us to see how ideas about physical difference, cultural
difference, and moral difference intersected in Qing constructions of
race and ethnicity.

Chapter 7 explores how gender and ethnicity are closely inter-twined in Qing ethnographic discourse on the Taiwan indigenes. Qing colonial discourse used the trope of gender in multiple ways to signify relations of power. In particular, "gender inversion," like the tropes of anachronism discussed in Chapter 2, was central to the Qing construction of savagery.

Chapter 8 demonstrates how nineteenth-century scholars used the methodology of evidential scholarship to "prove" that the Taiwan in-digenes were the living ancestors of the Chinese. This argument was used to link the Taiwan indigenes more closely with the Chinese and also to critique those who looked down upon the "savages" as rude and uncivilized. Through evidential scholarship, Qing literati linked the study of "primitive" customs in Taiwan to the project of "recover-ing antiquity" then in vogue among Chinese intellectuals.

In Chapter 9 I examine the dramatic changes in the representations of Taiwan's landscape and indigenous people in the wake of the 1875 decision to "Open the Mountains and Pacify the Savages." The adop-tion of this aggressive colonization policy represented a radical break with the passive policy pursued by the Qing since annexation. "Open-ing and Pacifying" signified a new Qing determination to make Tai-wan's land and indigenous people "Chinese." The end goal of the new colonization policy was to assert Chinese sovereignty over the entire island of Taiwan, paving the way for Taiwan's promotion to provincehood.

Finally, in the Conclusion I turn to nostalgic accounts of Taiwan, composed after the island was ceded to the Japanese in 1895. Nostalgic writers figure the cession of the island as the severance of a limb from the national body. This image vividly demonstrates that Taiwan had come to be conceptualized as an integral part of the Chinese geo-body, rather than as a lone entity "beyond the seas."[89] The "loss" of the is-land to the Japanese served only to convert Chinese nationalists even more ardently to this idea. The history of frontier travel literature thus traces the emergence of Chinese nationalist sentiment toward Taiwan.

The Conclusion also draws together some of the themes of earlier chapters to consider the shifting space occupied by Taiwan and its in-digenous people in the imagined geography of the far-reaching and multiethnic Qing empire. In particular, I ask how the Taiwan "sav-ages" fit into the Qing vision of the empire as a "great unity" of five major ethnic groups: the Manchus, Han Chinese, Mongols, Tibetans, and East Turkestanis. This book thus seeks both to elucidate the historical relation between China and Taiwan—a subject that is particularly germane in light of current tensions in the region—and to address issues of wider concern to scholars of Qing imperialism and comparative colonial studies.

The Epilogue offers some thoughts on the impossibility of theorizing Taiwan's postcoloniality and asks: What are the consequences when we label certain conquests "colonial" and refuse to apply the label to others? I further suggest the possibility of "meeting points" between Chinese and Western colonial discourses and ask how this concept might help us to move beyond the "West versus the Rest" dynamic that underlies contemporary postcolonial discourse.

Interlude 1

Taiwan is a small, mountainous island approximately the size of Switzerland, located nearly 100 miles from China's southeastern coast, across the Taiwan Strait (see Fig. 2). Despite this proximity, the island's indigenous population, whom modern anthropologists consider "Austronesian," had little contact with the Chinese before the sixteenth century. Taiwan straddles the Tropic of Cancer, and its subtropical climate—characterized by intense heat, high humidity, and frequent precipitation, especially during the monsoon season—creates ideal conditions for the vigorous growth of jungle vegetation. Even today, despite massive industrialization and urbanization, more than half the island remains covered by forest. The island is divided down the middle by the Central Mountain Range, which separates the alluvial plains of the western coast from the narrow lowland area of the eastern coast. Notoriously difficult to cross, these mountains effectively cut off the eastern half of Taiwan from the western half for much of Taiwan's history.

Taiwan's isolation was broken with the expansion of naval commerce in the East Asian region in the sixteenth and seventeenth centuries. The island's location along the trade routes linking China, Japan, and the Philippines drew attention to the once-obscure island, and Taiwan soon became, as John Shepherd describes it, "a political pawn contested by the Chinese state, assorted naval warlords and pirates, and European maritime empires."[1] Sixteenth-century Portuguese explorers were the first Westerners to encounter Taiwan, to which they gave the name "Ilha Formosa," or "Beautiful Island." In 1624, the Dutch—seeking to compete with the Portuguese (who had Macao) and the Spanish (who had the Philippines) in the China trade—established an entrepôt in southern Taiwan and began to

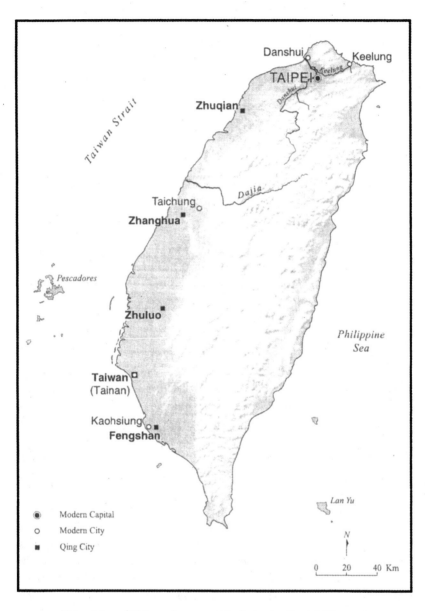

Fig. 2 Map of Taiwan (cartographic design by Patrick Florance
and Martin Gamache/AMG)

colonize the island. The Spanish arrived in 1626 and attempted to establish a colony in the north of the island but were soon ousted by the Dutch. In turn, the Dutch were driven out by the Chinese Ming loyalist Koxinga, who established his own regime on the island in 1661 and used Taiwan as a base to fight the Qing. Taiwan thus had a complex colonial history before the Qing conquered the island. Throughout this time, however, much of the island remained under indigenous control, and indigenes played a major role in the flourishing trade in deerskins, deer horns, and venison with China and Japan.

The Dutch had established a colony in the southwestern coastal region of the island, centered on what is now the city of Tainan. They organized the deer trade, which had previously been dominated by Chinese and Japanese traders and pirates, by selling village monopoly rights to Chinese traders. These monopoly merchants traded salt, iron, cloth, porcelain, and other goods with the indigenous people for deer products, which fetched a handsome price in Japan and China. Although they were primarily interested in trade, the Dutch made some attempts to turn Taiwan into an agricultural colony. They established sugarcane and rice plantations in southwestern Taiwan and recruited Chinese farmers from southern Fujian to work the fields. By the time Koxinga expelled the Dutch from Taiwan in 1661, these plantations had become quite profitable.

When Koxinga and his Ming loyalist troops retreated to Taiwan, the new "Zheng" regime essentially followed the Dutch practices of recruiting Chinese settlers to reclaim farmland and selling monopoly rights to Chinese traders.[2] Although it continued to be concentrated in southwestern Taiwan, Chinese settlement expanded beyond the old Dutch core, with smaller colonies of Chinese farmers scattered along the western coast up to what is now the northern port of Keelung. Therefore, when Shi Lang landed on Taiwan in 1683, he found a sizable Chinese population, significant agricultural output, and a thriving deer trade. Estimates put the Chinese population of the time at slightly less than 100,000, and the indigenous population at slightly more.[3] Traces of the Dutch presence were still noticeable on the island since some of the indigenes had converted to Christianity and local scribes had learned the Dutch (Roman) alphabet.

By the end of the seventeenth century, then, Taiwan had been transformed from a small and isolated island into a coveted entrepôt strategically located at a nexus of expanding East Asian maritime trade.

CHAPTER I

An Island Beyond the Seas
Enters the Map

"Taiwan is no bigger than a ball of mud. We gain nothing by possessing it, and it would be no loss if we did not acquire it."

—*Veritable Records of the Kangxi Emperor*, November 27, 1683

Such was the emperor's response when officials came to congratulate him on the capture of Taiwan from Ming loyalist forces in the autumn of 1683. A Manchu ruler oriented toward Inner Asia, the Kangxi emperor (r. 1662–1722) had little appreciation for maritime affairs and saw no benefit in acquiring a small island a hundred miles away from China. As he explained to his well-wishers, "Taiwan is a place beyond the seas; it is of no consequence to us."[1] Portuguese sailors may have dubbed the island "Ilha Formosa" (the beautiful island), but to the emperor Taiwan was nothing more than a ball of mud.

The Kangxi emperor's attitude set the tenor for discussions of the disposition of the newly conquered territory. The court proposed to abandon the island once the rebel troops and the Chinese civilian population had been evacuated. This plan was presented by the court's emissary, Su Bai, at a meeting of high officials convened at the end of 1683 to discuss Taiwan's fate. The majority in attendance supported this proposal: after all, the aim of the expedition against Taiwan had been to force the surrender of the rebel forces based on the island and not to acquire new territory. Only Shi Lang, the admiral who had led the conquest of Taiwan, voiced an objection. He had fought fiercely to take the island and was loath to relinquish it.

The ensuing debate whether to abandon or to annex Taiwan
hinged on a central issue: Would the benefits of acquiring the new territory outweigh the costs of maintaining the island frontier? Those
who opposed annexation argued that since Taiwan was "beyond the
seas," it would be difficult and costly to control. The expense was un-
warranted now that the threat to the empire's security had been
eliminated. Echoing the emperor's sentiments, these officials asserted
that China had nothing to gain from this island: in the words of one,
"If we were to take the land, it would not even be worth plowing; if
we were to take the people, we could not even make officials out of
them."[2] This cost-benefit assessment reflected the prevailing Chinese
view of Taiwan as a barren wilderness inhabited by ignorant savages.

Shi Lang countered that there were both strategic and economic
reasons for annexing the island, which he laid out in a detailed memorial that he submitted to the emperor along with a map of Taiwan.
Warning that foreign powers were already "drooling" over Taiwan, he
demonstrated the threat to China's coastal security were a hostile nation to claim the island.[3] Shi also cautioned that an "abandoned" Taiwan was likely once again to become a lair for pirates, a scourge on
the south China coast. Shi further contended that the new territory
need not become a drain on the imperial treasury. Far from being a
wasteland, he asserted, Taiwan was amply endowed with natural resources and arable lands. Shi's eyewitness description bears repeating:

I have personally traveled through Taiwan and seen firsthand the fertility
of its wild lands and the abundance of its natural resources. Both mulberry and field crops can be cultivated; fish and salt spout forth from the
sea; the mountains are filled with dense forests of tall trees and thick
bamboo; there are sulfur, rattan, sugarcane, deerskins, and all that is
needed for daily living. Nothing is lacking. . . . This is truly a bountifully
fertile piece of land and a strategic territory.[4]

The picture of Taiwan presented in Shi Lang's memorial was dramatically at odds with the dominant conception of the island as a barren wilderness. Shi's rhetorical tactic in this testimony was to assert
the authority of his version of Taiwan based on his extensive maritime experience and his firsthand knowledge of the island. In order to
discredit his opponents, he pointed out that they had never set foot on
the island and implied that their knowledge of Taiwan was based on
mere hearsay. The annexation debate thus became not only a matter

of cost-benefit analysis but also a contest between two opposing understandings of Taiwan's geography.

Indeed, as Shi Lang implied, the conception of Taiwan inherited from the Ming was based less on solid geographic knowledge than on traditional presumptions about the geographic configuration of the world and generic images (both literary and historiographic) of oceanic islands. Two ideas dominated the discourse about Taiwan: it was "beyond the seas" (*haiwai*), and it belonged to a realm known as "Wilderness" (*huangfu*). In terms of the established ideological conception of the Chinese empire, both these ideas worked against the annexation of Taiwan. The Qing incorporation of Taiwan would necessitate a reconfiguration of these geographic constructs.

This chapter examines how geographic representation helped the Qing reconceptualize a territory "beyond the seas" as a part (albeit a peripheral part) of the Chinese domain. The annexation of Taiwan in the late seventeenth century coincided with the emergence of geography as a precise discipline in China. The new geography emphasized empiricism and evidential methods. One of its aims was to correct the "mistakes" and omissions of the existing geographic record. Shi Lang and other advocates of annexation relied on this notion of "correcting" the Ming understanding of Taiwan to argue in favor of incorporating the island. As I hope to show, this reconceptualization of Taiwan involved not simply the replacement of old "myths" about Taiwan with accurate "facts" but also the development of new discursive constructs and geographic paradigms. Chief among these was the metaphor of Taiwan as a "hedgerow" for the Chinese empire.

Beyond the Seas:
China as a Naturally Bounded Territory

What did it mean to be "beyond the seas"? The constant reference in the annexation debate to Taiwan's location "beyond the seas" was more than a physical description of the island's geography: it was a statement about Taiwan's relationship to the Chinese domain. Certainly, the Taiwan Strait was not an enormous physical barrier between China and the island, for fishermen, traders, and pirates had been frequenting Taiwan on a regular basis since at least the sixteenth century, despite the dangers of the crossing. Symbolically, however, the strait represented a major boundary between China and the world beyond the pale (*huawai*).

Since antiquity, many Chinese thinkers had held that the Chinese domain was defined by Heaven-endowed geographic features such as rivers, mountains, deserts, and seas. This conception of China as a naturally bounded territory had its roots in canonical texts such as the "Tribute of Yu" ("Yugong") chapter of the *Classic of History* (*Shujing*, composed ca. fifth century B.C.), which was required reading for educated gentlemen in imperial China.[5] Extending this idea, the Tang dynasty astronomer and geographer Yixing (682–727) proposed a theory that China's mountains and rivers formed natural boundaries that defended the terrain against foreign invaders.[6] By the late imperial period, this conception of the Chinese domain was deeply ingrained in Chinese literati culture. During the Ming, as Andrew Waldron and James Millward have shown, debates over wall building reinforced the importance of a territorial definition of China.[7]

Ming maps conventionally depict the spatial image of a Chinese domain centered on the Central Plains and bordered by natural geographic features. *The Comprehensive Gazetteer of the Great Ming Realm* (*Da Ming yitong zhi*, 1461), for example (see Fig. 3), represents the Chinese empire bordered by the sea to the east and the south, mountains to the north and the west, and the desert to the northwest. A slightly later map, the *Comprehensive Map of the Great Ming Realm* (*Huang Ming dayitong ditu*, 1636), depicts the Chinese domain sandwiched diagonally between ocean to the southeast and desert to the northwest.[8] Such cartographic representations served to naturalize the spatial image of a territorially bounded China.

The importance of the seas as a symbolic boundary is highlighted by the fact that Chinese cartographers sometimes graphically represented China's terrestrial borders as aquatic borders. On the Ming *Map of Imperial Territories* (*Yu ditu*, 1526), for example, the border between southwestern China and neighboring states in southeast Asia, and the area where the Liaodong peninsula merges into the landmass of northeast Asia are represented as stylized ocean waters.[9] Luo Hongxian also represented the Ming domain as bounded by seas to the south in his *Enlarged Terrestrial Atlas* (*Guangyu tu*, compiled ca. 1540), which served as a basic model for many Ming and early Qing

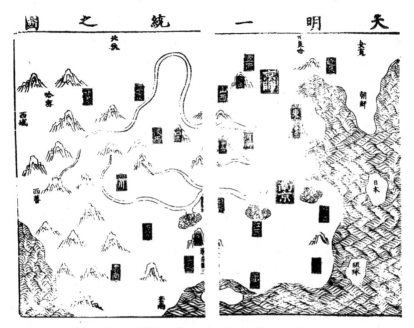

Fig. 3 Map of China from the *Comprehensive Gazetteer
of the Great Ming Realm* (1461)

maps including the *Unified Map of Chinese and Barbarians* (*Huayi yitong tu;* see Fig. 4) in Wang Qi's famous encyclopedia *Pictorial Compendium of the Three Powers* (*Sancai tuhui,* 1607).[10]

Taiwan's location "beyond the seas," therefore, placed it definitively outside the natural territorial boundaries of China proper. Late
Ming and early Qing descriptions of the island reinforced the notion
of Taiwan's separation from China. Taiwan was commonly described
as "faraway overseas," "hanging alone beyond the seas," "an isolated
island surrounded by ocean," or "far off on the edge of the oceans."[11]
This, despite the fact that Taiwan is located less than 100 miles from
China's shore.

The deeply ingrained notion that the seas defined the natural limits
of the Chinese realm underlay the reluctance to annex Taiwan. As the
Kangxi emperor's advisers argued, "Since antiquity, no oceanic islands
have ever entered the imperial domain."[12]

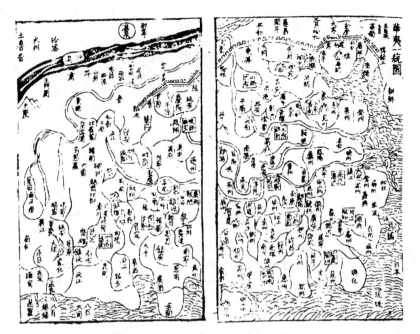

Fig. 4 "Unified Map of Chinese and Barbarians" from Wang Qi's
Pictorial Compendium of the Three Powers (1607)

A SAVAGE ISLAND

Islands occupied a special place in Chinese geographic lore: as seemingly isolated realms unto themselves, removed from the world, islands elicited a certain fascination and were thus made the staging grounds for the fantastic. As one Qing literatus put it, "I often read the accounts recorded in the *Classic of Mountains and Seas* (*Shanhai jing* [sixth c. B.C.–first c. A.D.]), and I noted that all the extraordinary things mostly came from far off on the distant seas."[13] Conceptually, strangeness correlates with distance from the normative center or to location outside a boundary.[14] In this case, the boundary is the sea.

In the absence of a reliable body of geographic knowledge about Taiwan, Ming assumptions about the inhabitants of Taiwan were shaped by stock images of islands in the Chinese histories and fiction. The Chinese histories and geographies were filled with accounts of islands inhabited by cannibals—monstrous-looking beings who wore nothing but skins and feathers on their hideously tattooed bodies. Stories told of shipwrecked sailors falling prey to these ferocious savages and of periodic raids on the south China coast by marauding headhunters. Islands in the China seas also gained the reputation of harboring pirates, including the notorious "dwarf pirates" of Japan.

In addition to these historical accounts, works of geographic marvels like the *Classic of Mountains and Seas* told of fantastic lands like the Country of Dogs, the Country of Hairy People, the Country of Women, and the Country of Two-Bodied People—all said to be located somewhere "overseas." Other legends told of islands inhabited by the monstrous Rakshas, minions of hell. By the late imperial period, many of the fantastic lands from the *Classic of Mountains and Seas* had come to be associated with the geographic area near Taiwan. It is not uncommon to find maps that depict these fantastic lands alongside other islands such as Japan, the Ryukyus, and the Philippines. [15] A late Ming map, Cao Junyi's *Complete Map of Allotted Fields, Human Traces, and Travel Routes Within and Without the Nine Frontiers Under Heaven* (*Tianxia jiubian fenye renji lucheng quantu*, 1644), which served as a principal model for Qing cartographers, portrays a number of these fantastic lands as islands in the sea off China's southeastern coast. [16] A Chinese world map of 1743, held by the British Library, similarly depicts Taiwan in proximity to places such as the Country of Women and the Country of Hairy People (see Color Plate 2).

Counterbalancing the tales of cannibals and monsters, the histories and geographies told of islands that were marvelously fecund and full of hidden treasure. Blessed with summer-like weather year round, these islands were filled with fragrant flowers and delicious tropical fruits, and gold, sulfur, and other riches could be found deep within their mountains. Chinese legends also told of magical islands located somewhere on the seas. The most famous of these were the three fairy isles of Penglai, Fangzhang, and Yingzhou, which were inhabited by immortals who dined on magical gems and herbs and imbibed the springs of eternal life. [17] Such tales inspired adventurers and pirates to risk the rumored perils of cannibals and miasmas and travel beyond the seas in search of treasure.

Just as the opposition's depiction of Taiwan drew on cliched images of cannibal islands, Shi Lang's representation of Taiwan as a place where "fish and salt spout forth from the sea" alluded to such stock images of islands as realms of boundless fertility and treasure. Shi Lang's report exemplifies how even "eyewitness" accounts of Taiwan were always informed by pre-existing figments of the geographic imaginary.

TAIWAN IN THE DOMAIN OF WILDERNESS

If natural boundaries shaped Ming conceptions of the Chinese domain, so did cultural and political boundaries. An alternative to the territorial definition of the Chinese realm was articulated in cosmographic conceptions of the world laid out by ancient texts such as the "Tribute of Yu."[18] This classic work represented the world as a series of concentric zones centered on the imperial capital; the lands within 500 *li* of the capital were the "Royal Domain"; the next zone was the domain of the feudal princes and lords; the next, the "Zone of Pacification"; the next, the territories of "Allied Barbarians"; and the last, "Wilderness" (*huangfu*). Although the original work contained only a verbal description, later texts commonly rendered these zones graphically as a series of nested rectangles (see Fig. 5).[19] The zones of the "Tribute of Yu" represented spatially the notion of diminishing political and cultural ties to the imperial center.[20] In this cosmography, cultural and political distance replaced physical, geographic distance as a measure of foreignness.

In a similar fashion, the *Ritual of Zhou* (*Zhouli*, second c. B.C.) laid out a series of nine domains (*jiufu*), which again were rendered in later texts as a series of concentric rectangles.[21] As with the scheme of five zones in the "Tribute of Yu," the nine zones rendered cultural and political relations in spatial terms. Once again, these domains are centered on the royal capital, with areas of increasing political and cultural distance radiating outward. The outermost zones of the nine domains consisted of various grades of barbarians: Man, Yi, Zhen, and Fan, each more barbarous than the last.[22] Located in the domain farthest from the center, the Fan were the most removed from civilization and hence the most barbarous.

The assumption that Taiwan belonged to the domain of Wilderness derived in no small part from the island's lack of a historical relationship with China. Pre-Qing histories and geographies contained scant

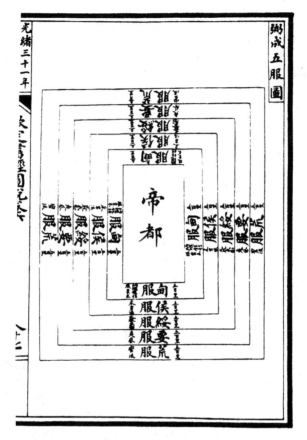

Fig. 5 Chart of the Five Zones from the *Yugong*
as depicted in the *Shujing tushuo*

information about Taiwan: the name "Taiwan" did not even appear in Chinese sources until the late Ming. "Taiwan," as such, was thus an unknown entity for the greater part of Chinese history. Moreover, according to Chinese records, Taiwan had never sent tribute to China, even after Chinese traders had established a flourishing trade with the island in the sixteenth century. Taiwan was, therefore, outside the tributary system that played a significant role in maintaining the idea of a cosmographic world order—and hence, even farther removed than the "Allied Barbarians," who sent annual tribute to China. Qing writers constantly reiterated the fact that Taiwan had never sent tribute to China.

Those on both sides of the annexation debate made constant reference to Taiwan's location in Wilderness. As the zone farthest from the imperial center, *huangfu* was a domain of uncultivated land and cultureless savagery, utterly beyond the influence of Chinese civilization. The term *huangfu* evokes images of barrenness, starkness, untamed growth, and waste, for the word *huang* (meaning "wild" or "uncultivated"), when used in various combinations, refers to fallow fields, desert, jungle, or wild forest. These images shaped the traditional disdain for the borderlands of China—the steppe to the north beyond the Great Wall, the desert to the northwest, and the jungle to the south—as untamed expanses.

Moreover, the indigenous people of Taiwan were known to the Chinese as *fan* (savages), a label that associated them with the outermost zone of Fan.[23] Although the homophones *fan* and Fan are written in slightly different forms in Chinese, they are etymologically related and sometimes interchangeable words. Fan, as in the "domain of Fan," has the meaning of a hedge—or, when used figuratively, a boundary or frontier—and is, therefore, located at the edge of the world.[24] The term *fan* refers to savages or foreigners, those conceptually located at the edges of the earth, and who, therefore, lack any knowledge of culture. Qing sources sometimes alluded to the close relationship between *fan* (savages) and the domain of Fan. Taiwan's association with that domain paralleled its location in the realm of Wilderness, both spaces far removed from the imperial center.[25]

Thus, despite Taiwan's relative physical proximity to China, in terms of cosmographic space it lay on the outermost periphery of the world. A "remote wilderness" beyond the seas, Taiwan was culturally and politically distanced from the center of Chinese civilization. For opponents of annexation, the images of barrenness and miasmas associated with Wilderness supported their contention that Taiwan was an undesirable acquisition. The assumption that the inhabitants of the island were strange and uncivilized savages buttressed the claim that the natives were not worth incorporating into the Chinese empire.

In the course of the annexation debate, Shi Lang not only struggled to replace the older image of Taiwan as a barren wilderness with a new image of the island as a bountiful land but also implicitly proposed a new paradigm of Taiwan's geography, one that linked the island to China. Shi emphasized Taiwan's geographic proximity to China, describing the island as "linked" to Jiangsu at its northern tip and "connected" to Guangdong at its southern tip. Although Taiwan was "originally beyond the pale," he argued, if Taiwan were annexed, this strip was perfectly situated to be a hedgerow or fence (*fanli*) for China's southeastern provinces. He thus reconfigured Fan/Wilderness as *fanli*/hedgerow. In Shi's conception, the island no longer lay outside the boundary of the Chinese domain but served as a kind of palisade protecting China from outside invaders. Shi's metaphor of Taiwan as a hedgerow furthermore implicitly suggested a new paradigm of the Chinese empire—one that extended beyond the seas.

Putting a Wilderness Island on the Map

This extended definition of the Chinese domain was set into place after Shi Lang's side won the annexation debate (largely on the strength of his strategic arguments). Taiwan officially "entered the map" in the spring of 1684. Qing texts frequently employ the terms "entering the map" (*ru bantu*) or "entering the map and records" (*ru tuji*) to denote Taiwan's incorporation into the Qing empire. As the editor of one of Taiwan's early gazetteers declared: "Since antiquity Taiwan had been a remote wilderness, a place beyond the reaches of civilization. Now the emperor has been on the throne for twenty-one years, the vast seas are calm and clear, and there is peace throughout the land; even this wilderness has entered the map."[26] In a sharp reversal of the court's original anti-annexation stance, officially sanctioned rhetoric now celebrated the incorporation of a wilderness island into the empire. The fact that Taiwan lay beyond the seas was held up as evidence that Qing power and influence extended far beyond that of the Ming. In the coming decades, Qing writers would similarly celebrate the additions of other frontiers (the Xinjiang area in 1759, for example) to the imperial map.[27] With Taiwan's entry onto the map, the Qing reconfiguration of the island's geography would begin.

The act of adding Taiwan to the map of the imperial domain carried great symbolic significance and indicated Qing dominion over the terrain. Since antiquity (at least since the third century B.C.), the possession of maps had been regarded as symbolically equivalent to the possession of territory. Hence, the offering of maps to the ruler was conventionally known as the "presentation of rivers and mountains" (*xian jiangshan*). This trope expresses both the strategic importance of maps in war and conquest and the role of the map as a simulacrum of the terrain it represents. In keeping with this practice, Shi Lang, too, submitted a map of Taiwan to the emperor after his conquest of the island.

With annexation, Taiwan "entered the map and records" not only in a symbolic sense but also in a literal sense. Before the Qing conquest of the island, Taiwan was essentially terra incognita to Chinese cartographers. The Song dynasty (907–1276) *Easy-to-Use Maps of Geography Through the Dynasties* (*Lidai dili zhizhang tu*, 1098–1100, supplemented 1162), a collection of 44 historical maps of dynastic territories from antiquity to the Song, shows no evidence of Taiwan on its "General Map of the Ancient and Present Territories of China and Barbarians" ("Gujin huayi quyu zongyao tu"). Important Ming maps, such as Luo Hongxian's *Enlarged Terrestrial Atlas*, the *Map of Advantageous Terrain, Past and Present* (*Gujin xingsheng zhi tu*, 1555), and Cao Junyi's *Complete Map of Allotted Fields, Human Traces, and Travel Routes Within and Without the Nine Frontiers Under Heaven* continued to omit Taiwan. Perhaps most important, the imperially sponsored *Comprehensive Gazetteer of the Great Ming Realm* (see Fig. 3) fails to show Taiwan. The island was literally "off the map" as far as Chinese cartographers were concerned.

The same held true to a degree for the textual record. As Yu Yonghe noted: "In past dynasties there were no links to China; the Chinese did not know that this piece of land existed. Even geographic maps, the Imperial Comprehensive Geographies, and other such books that contain records of all the barbarians, do not include the name Taiwan."[28] Now that Taiwan had "entered the map and records," Qing officials faced the daunting task of mapping the island and recording its geography—for reliable geographic information would be vital to the successful administration of the new territory. As Matthew Edney so succinctly puts it in his work on the geographic construction of British India: "to govern territories, one must know them."[29] This was no less true for the Qing empire than for the British or Roman empires that Edney discusses. Emphasizing empirical methods, comprehensiveness, the systematic gathering of data, and precision, the emerging Qing discipline of geography readily lent itself to the needs of imperial administration.

The Kangxi emperor, himself an avid enthusiast of geography, early recognized the need for comprehensive geographic knowledge of his empire. To meet this need, the emperor established a bureau for the collection of geographic data in 1685. As he stated:

Our territory is complicated, broad and vast, extending 10,000 *li*. . . . climatic conditions vary, and the people's customs differ. These have not been compiled. How is one to know them completely? We observe that writers on geography have been fairly numerous since the Han dynasty. But their accounts vary in their amount of detail, and reports produced then and now differ. We therefore order that a bureau be set up to collect all kinds of documents, verify the gazetteers, and compile a book.[30]

In addition to this work, which would be titled the *Comprehensive Gazetteer of the Great Qing Realm*, the emperor further commissioned Jesuits to complete a comprehensive cartographic survey of the empire, as mentioned above. These projects were the most massive undertakings of their kind in Chinese history. The *Map of a Complete View of Imperial Territory* (*Huangyu quanlan tu*, AKA the Kangxi-Jesuit Atlas), completed in 1717, and the *Comprehensive Gazetteer of the Great Qing Realm*, completed in 1746, went far beyond their Ming equivalents in terms of both scope and precision, and they did much to expand Chinese knowledge of the frontiers.

Local geographic knowledge was essential to these large-scale projects, and local officials were enlisted in the effort to produce material for the imperial compilers. In 1685, only one year after the annexation of Taiwan, Qing officials on Taiwan set about compiling a local gazetteer in response to the emperor's call for the production of the *Comprehensive Gazetteer*. Editors were instructed to collect information on such subjects as strategic passes, mountains, streams, customs, and local products and personages, as well as to draw maps.[31] Following the conventional procedures for compiling a gazetteer, the editors conducted field investigations and consulted the textual record. The dearth of historical materials on Taiwan meant that the compilers had few written sources. Travel writing was one of their few resources.

Indeed, travel writing was a key element in the bottom-up system of producing geographic knowledge for the compilation of the *Comprehensive Gazetteer*. Not only did the compilation bureau collect such accounts, but they were also key sources for local gazetteers, which in turn were used in compiling the provincial gazetteers and then the empirewide *Comprehensive Gazetteer*. Travel writing played an important role in this system because it was presumed to be based on firsthand experience: it therefore had the authority of empirical knowledge. (I say more about this presumption of empiricism below.) Thus, travel writers became implicated, indirectly in most cases, in the larger project of producing imperial knowledge of Taiwan.

The earliest Chinese literati to travel to Taiwan recorded the island's geography with enthusiasm, and numerous accounts were produced in the first years after annexation. Among Taiwan's pioneering travel writers were: Ji Qiguang, one of Taiwan's first county magistrates; Lin Qianguang (fl. 1672), Taiwan's first instructor of Confucian schools; Xu Huaizu, a literatus who traveled in Taiwan for a year; Yu Yonghe, a literatus who went to Taiwan from Fujian on a sulfur-prospecting expedition; and Wu Chenchen, a literatus in the retinue of an official assigned to Taiwan. The earliest gazetteer compilers were Jiang Yuying, in charge of Taiwan's first draft gazetteer (1688), and Gao Gongqian, in charge of the first published gazetteer (1696). These writers did much to expand Chinese knowledge of the Taiwan frontier and to fill in historical lacunae. As on other frontiers, the expansion of geographic knowledge went hand in hand with the extension of government control, which enabled more and more terrain to be explored and mapped. Therefore, the documentation of the island's geography proceeded in a piecemeal fashion at first, for numerous logistical difficulties attended attempts to survey the terrain beyond centers of direct Qing control.

Following Dutch and Ming patterns of settlement, the Qing established three counties on the island: Taiwan county, in the southwestern coastal region that had been the core of Dutch settlement in the seventeenth century; Fengshan county, encompassing the western coastal plains to the south of Taiwan county; and Zhuluo county, encompassing the western plains to the north as far as the Dajia River. The center of the island's administration, Taiwan prefecture, was located within the bounds of Taiwan county. The rest of the island, including the northern third of the western plain, above the Dajia River, was indigenous territory—beyond the direct control of the Qing. There were two major roads on the island: the Northern Route, extending north from Taiwan prefecture, and the Southern Route, extending south.

In the first years following annexation, local officials and their staffs rarely dared to travel beyond Taiwan's prefectural capital or the three county seats for fear of remnants of rebel troops, hostile natives, and contagion. As a result, many of the earliest travel writers confined their descriptions of Taiwan to the centers of Chinese settlement. Much of what was known about the rest of the island was hearsay, garnered from traders and old hands who had been on the island since Ming times. Yu Yonghe was one of the first Chinese literati to travel extensively in Taiwan's hinterland, despite warnings from local officials about the dangers. His *Small Sea Travelogue* (*Pihai jiyou*) was the most detailed account of the Taiwan frontier during these early years, and it became an important source for later travelers and colonial officials.

EMPIRICISM AS PROMISE AND PROBLEM

Although my research on Taiwan travel writing and gazetteers confirms that empiricism was highly *privileged* within the emerging discipline of geography, this does not translate into the general assertion that Qing geography was characterized by empiricism. There is a subtle but important distinction between the two statements. Qing geographic texts derived authority from their claim that they were based on firsthand experience and direct observation (although this is by no means unique to the Qing era).[32] Over and over commentators declared that the only reliable texts were those written by people who had traversed the territory themselves. The eyewitness as author was thus raised above others.

Qing writers on Taiwan frequently foregrounded their concern over distinguishing reliable from unreliable knowledge, empirical data from hearsay and invention. A particular source of anxiety was the impossibility of producing knowledge of terrain that was difficult to explore. Taiwan's first county gazetteer, the *Gazetteer of Zhuluo County* (1717), for example, contained a lengthy disquisition on the problems of mapping wilderness:

Creation has recklessly set down transformations in a miasmic barbarian corner of the earth, jumbled together among layered mountains and lofty peaks, twisting streams and winding bays, hidden away in a distant place. If one desires to capture it all on a map drawn on a foot of silk, can one possibly capture the reality (*zhen*)? If one insists on capturing that which cannot be captured, one will only succeed in confusing the reality. From what I have seen, there are at least ten maps of Taiwan, and yet not one of them has captured the reality.[33]

Since accurate mapping depended on empirical observations, the gazetteer argued, it was nearly impossible to provide reliable maps of Taiwan when so much of the island had not yet been fully explored. Therefore, the editor cautioned, maps should be taken only as a general picture of the island's topography and not as perfect copies of "reality."

Yet this concern with the authority and limitations of direct observation does not translate into empiricism in practice. To put it simply, the *claim* to empiricism should not be mistaken for *actual* empiricism. Writers lie—and travel writers are notorious in this respect. A writer's claim to have seen something with his own eyes does not preclude it from being pure invention. On this point I strongly disagree with Laura Hostetler's contention that Qing ethnography "was increasingly characterized by the rigor of direct observation and empirical method."[34] There is no doubt that direct observation and empiricism were *valued* in Qing ethnography. But just as Qing literati did, we must grapple with the dilemma of distinguishing a "real" eyewitness account from hearsay that borrows its authority. I argue that it is impossible to distinguish "real" from "false" eyewitnessing with any certainty. For the purposes of this book, which focuses on discourse, the difference is unimportant, since it is the *claim* to empiricism and to the authority of "eyewitnessing" that interests me. The liar's claim to eyewitnessing only underscores the value of empiricism and its function in authorizing the text. But it also alerts us to the need for caution in taking the trope of "I'm only recording what I've seen with my own eyes" at face value. (By the same token, hearsay is not necessarily false; it simply has a different epistemological status.) Moreover, as this book demonstrates for Qing Taiwan, eyewitness accounts are always already constructed by the imaginary.

In addition, my research reveals that although early eighteenth-century accounts of Taiwan aimed to be rigorously empirical, as geographic knowledge of the island became codified, later authors tended more and more to rely on prior texts, often copying or summarizing large passages from earlier writers (with or without attribution). This practice underscores the fact that empiricism was not the only authority structure of Qing geography. This is not surprising, of course, since textual research and collation were key aspects of evidential research.

In the case of Taiwan, geographic representation relied on a dual structure of authority: eyewitnessing and the textual record. This is clearly demonstrated in Huang Shujing's *Record of a Tour of Duty in* the Taiwan Strait (*Taihai shicha lu*, 1736), a work that is still considered by many to be the most authoritative Qing geographic account of Taiwan. An evidential scholar in his methodology, Huang assembled all available written records concerning Taiwan past and present while simultaneously leading a team of investigators to systematically gather geographic information from local sites. He then collated the textual record against the empirical data. Qing commentators considered this work authoritative because of Huang's thorough knowledge of previous texts and his rigorous efforts to collect information through direct observation.[35]

Huang's insistence on collating the textual record against empirical data reveals the evidential scholar's distrust of either text or personal observation alone. The textual record may be flawed with inaccuracies, omissions, or even hearsay. Personal observation cannot be trusted because personal experience is limited. Collation ensures greater reliability, with text confirming direct observation and direct observation verifying the written record. Text and experience thus guarantee each other's reliability.

The limitations of empiricism led Qing literati to ponder another epistemological conundrum: that is, if eyewitnessing is privileged as an instrument of "truth" or reliable knowledge, how can we avoid the mistake of dismissing out of hand that which we have not seen for ourselves? Taiwan travel writers frequently ruminated on this quandary. As Lan Dingyuan wrote after seeing a volcano for the first time:

As for strange tales about foreign lands, is there anything we have not heard? I take what I have personally seen and heard to be reliable, and yet there is much that is beyond my experience. A mountain producing fire: this story is almost ludicrous. Fire emerging from water: this is even more ridiculous. Perhaps so, but such things do exist.[36]

The epistemological challenge of wonders was a favorite theme for Taiwan travel writers, who like Lan performed the double move of claiming the authority of the eyewitness even as they questioned an epistemology that made empiricism the sole foundation of knowledge.[37] Warning against the fallacy of the "summer insect who knows not of ice," these writers posed the tension between skepticism and open-mindedness as an epistemological problematic of an age in which the privileging of empiricism was matched by the greater flow of information about the outside world (including the frontiers and the West) and all its strange wonders.[38]

These ruminations are meant as a caution against a flattened characterization of Qing geography as "increasingly empirical." Clearly empiricism was important to Qing geographers, but it wasn't the only game in town. "Strange tales about foreign lands" remained popular throughout the Qing and continued to play a role in Chinese representations of Taiwan, as we shall see below.[39]

ADDING TAIWAN TO THE MAP

Qing efforts to expand the textual record of Taiwan were matched by attempts to augment the cartographic record. Immediately following the annexation of Taiwan as the ninth prefecture of Fujian province, the compilers of the 1684 edition of the *Gazetteer of Fujian Province* (*Fujian tongzhi*) scrambled to add a map of this new territory to the already completed draft of the gazetteer. Although Taiwan is still missing from the gazetteer's overall map of the Fujian coast, the gazetteer contains a separate map of the island entitled "A Map of Taiwan Prefecture and Its Three Counties." This map shows a greatly abbreviated image of the island, focused on important Chinese landmarks such as the prefectural and county seats, the old Dutch forts, and Lu'ermen Bay, the central port of entry to Taiwan since Dutch times. The island is depicted face-on from the perspective of the Fujian coast, with the Pescadores in the foreground. The relative size of Taiwan's western coastal plain—where Chinese settlements and Qing administrative seats were located—is greatly exaggerated. The map projects an image of Taiwan dominated by the southwestern region that had been the core of Chinese settlement since Dutch times.

This map derives its basic shape and features from the *Sketch Map of Taiwan* (*Taiwan lüetu*) held by the National Palace Museum, Taiwan, or one like it. The *Sketch Map*, which exists in both Manchu and Chinese versions, is very possibly the only extant pre-conquest Chinese map of Taiwan.[40] It was certainly drawn for strategic purposes, specifically for use in the attack against the "Rebel Zheng," whose presence on the island is noted several times on the map. As indicated by the title, the map gives a schematic outline of the island. Although Taiwan is a long, narrow island, this map depicts the island as roundish, almost doughnut like, with the southern bay of Lu'ermen occupying a prominent position at the center of the map. The map provides important navigational information about the bays and approaches to the island, with notations such as "one can land here," reflecting the map's strategic purpose. The *Sketch Map of Taiwan* clearly represents the perspective of an external naval force approaching the island from the Chinese coast. In following the essential shape and features of this map, the Fujian gazetteer continued to project a pre-conquest image of Taiwan as a small, roundish island isolated beyond the seas.

By the time the next edition of the Fujian gazetteer was published (1737), Taiwan had made it onto the general map of the Fujian coast.[41] The island appears as a small half-circle just barely peeking up from the bottom edge of the map. Along with other maps, such as the National Palace Museum's *Map of Fujian Province* (*Fujian sheng ditu*, ca. 1684), this map served to create a new spatial image of Fujian. Showing the province from a bird's-eye perspective, these maps represent Fujian not as the "Eight Min" (as it had been known for centuries) but as eight-plus-one, with the new appendage of Taiwan situated just off the coast. On the *Map of Fujian Province*, in particular, the sea no longer serves as a barrier between the imperial domain and the outside world. Rather, Fujian province extends beyond the sea to include an island hovering close by.

Mapping also altered the spatial image of the Chinese empire as a whole. Taiwan began to appear on maps of the empire soon after annexation. Whereas Taiwan was absent from Luo Hongxian's *Enlarged Terrestrial Atlas*, it appeared on a Qing reinterpretation of this map: Cai Fangbing's general map of the Qing empire (see Fig. 6) from his *Enlarged and Revised Complete Atlas of the Record of the Expanded Territory* (*Zengding Guangyu ji quantu*, late seventeenth c.). Similarly, Taiwan was absent from the *Comprehensive Gazetteer of the Great Ming Realm*, but it appeared in the first edition of the *Comprehensive Gazetteer of the Great Qing Realm* (*Da Qing yitong zhi*, 1746). When the Kangxi emperor commissioned French Jesuits to survey and map the empire beginning in 1708, Taiwan was included in this project.[42] The Kangxi-Jesuit Atlas, presented to the emperor in 1718, showed Taiwan as an integral part of the Chinese empire. In representing Taiwan as a component of the imperial domain, maps such as these marked a departure from Ming cartographic models.

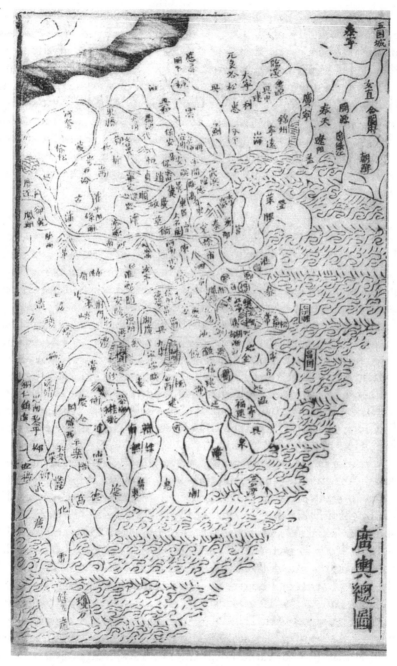

Fig. 6 "General Map of the Expanded Territory" (right-hand panel) from Cai Fangbing's *Enlarged and Revised Complete Atlas of the Record of the Expanded Territory* (17th century) (reproduced by permission of the Herzog August Bibliothek Wolfenbüttel [Cod. Guelf. 148 Blankenb.])

Qing maps also demonstrated a changing attitude toward the sea as a natural boundary of the Chinese domain. The treatment of the seas in Cai Fangbing's general map of the Qing empire differs greatly from that in his Ming model. Where Luo Hongxian represented the empire's southern boundary as sea, Cai presented southwestern China as landlocked.[43] Moreover, whereas Luo's map shows a great expanse of sea to the east of the Chinese domain, Cai's map has the ocean abruptly ending in empty space just beyond Taiwan. Thus, the role of the seas as a boundary appears to be diminished in this map. Rather, it is the line where the ocean stops and empty space begins that defines the realm beyond the pale.

ON THE MAP, BUT STILL BEYOND THE SEAS

Despite these cartographic innovations, the idea of the seas as a natural boundary of the Chinese domain would prove stubborn. As a newly incorporated frontier, Taiwan continued to be distinguished from "China proper" (*neidi*) or the realm "within the seas" (*hainei*). Early Qing writings still referred to Taiwan as "beyond the seas" even as they spoke of the island serving as the outer barrier for Fujian province. As the first published gazetteer of Taiwan noted: "Taiwan is separated by the seas and rimmed by mountains. It is located beyond the zones of the Allied Barbarians and Wilderness."[44] The tendency to distance Taiwan rhetorically indicates that seventeenth-century literati had not yet fully accepted the reconfiguration of the Chinese domain beyond its Ming boundaries.

Pictorial maps of the island also represented Taiwan as "alone overseas." Seventeenth- and eighteenth-century scroll maps of Taiwan conventionally depicted the island face-on from the perspective of the China coast rather than from a bird's-eye perspective. Taiwan is thus shown in isolation and not as a part of the larger Qing empire. The Taiwan Strait is pictured in the foreground, standing between the viewer and the island. Some maps continued to emphasize the role of the Taiwan Strait as a boundary. The woodblock print map from the *Gazetteer of Taiwan County* of 1720, for example, shows pages and pages of ocean between Taiwan and the Pescadores and beyond, highlighting the sense of distance. Even into the Qianlong period, we find a scroll map (1787 or earlier) depicting the Taiwan Strait as a body of

Fig. 7 Chen Lunjiong, "General Map of the Four Seas" from
Record of Things Seen and Heard at Sea (ca. 1723–30)

enormous waves with dramatic surf, highlighting the separation engendered by these waters. Small ships tossed on these giant waves
visually convey the risky nature of the crossing and underscore the
impression of Taiwan's isolation.[45]

Qing world maps also continued to distance Taiwan from China
proper. Chen Lunjiong's "General Map of the Four Seas" ("Sihai zongtu," drawn 1723–30), for example (see Fig. 7), which shows the Eastern
Hemisphere from a bird's-eye perspective,[46] depicts Taiwan at the
very edge of the world, beyond both Japan and the Ryukyus. In terms
of the scale of the map, the Taiwan Strait forms an enormous gulf between China and the island. Taiwan's separation is further conveyed
by the fact that China is labeled the "Great Qing Empire," whereas

Taiwan is simply "Taiwan," making it ambiguous whether Taiwan is part of the Qing empire. Similarly, an anonymous world map of 1743 (see Color Plate 2) shows Taiwan separated from mainland China by enormous, fierce waves.[47] China's southeastern coast is bordered by a thick, black line, which marks Fujian off from Taiwan prefecture. This map, therefore, continues to project an image of the Chinese domain bounded by the seas (and other natural features). Such cartographic representations produced the impression that Taiwan was not fully incorporated into the empire. Indeed, the creation of a new spatial image of a Chinese realm that extended beyond the seas would be a gradual process.

SYMBOLIC GEOGRAPHY: LINKING
TAIWAN TO THE CHINESE DOMAIN

Despite the new geography's emphasis on empiricism and evidential inquiry, traditional symbolic geography continued to figure in the geographic representation of Taiwan. Symbolic geography, which dominated Song-Ming scholarship, was grounded in metaphysical thought and cosmographical models. It posited a system of moral correspondences between heaven and earth, within which geographic features were interpreted. Although symbolic geography played a diminished role in Qing representations of Taiwan, it is in this arena that we see some of the most striking attempts to reconfigure the island's geography to reflect its entry onto the map.

The opening sections of Taiwan gazetteers conventionally included an entry on astrology devoted to the question of Taiwan's location within the field-allocation system (*fenye*), the ancient astrological system that correlated sectors of the heavens with territories on earth. Firmly established by the Han dynasty, this system assigned celestial fields to each of the nine geographic regions of China. Through such pairings, astrological signs could be used to predict political events in the corresponding terrestrial region. In ideal terms, the division of the celestial fields matched the political boundaries of territories on earth. But by the Ming, Chinese literati were seriously questioning this cosmological paradigm, since the heavenly fields established in antiquity no longer corresponded perfectly to the political reality of China's vastly expanded territory. Nonetheless, Qing gazetteers continued to employ the field-allocation system as a crucial means of establishing the astrological influences of a locale.

Since Taiwan was terra incognita in the Chinese histories, Qing literati had no references for ascertaining Taiwan's location within the field-allocation system. They thus determined Taiwan's celestial field according to the island's relation to the Chinese domain. "Before Taiwan entered the map," stated the *Gazetteer of Taiwan Prefecture* of 1696, Taiwan's field-allocation "belonged to the realm beyond the pale."[48] Now that Taiwan had entered the map, its celestial field would have to follow suit: "Since Taiwan is now attached to Fujian province, its field-allocation should follow that of Fujian."[49] Assigning Taiwan the astrological correspondence of Fujian province served to tie the island closer to China proper.

Another cosmographic tradition reflected in Qing representations of Taiwan is that of *fengshui*, geomancy or siting. For example, descriptions of Taiwan as situated with "its back to the mountains and its face to the sea" ascribed auspicious siting to the island. The characterization of the island as "facing" the west, with its "back" toward the mountains in the east became conventional among Qing literati, who thus imagined Taiwan as facing the Chinese mainland.[50]

Similarly, in describing Taiwan's geographic location, early Qing writers attempted to link the island more closely to the mainland by matching points on the island with corresponding points on the Chinese coast. Such descriptions served to downplay Taiwan's distance "beyond the seas" and highlight its relation to the mainland. Writers on Taiwan's geography further offered the hypothesis that Taiwan's Central Mountain Range was an extension of various mountains in Fujian, again strengthening the ties between the overseas prefecture and its mother province.

The gazetteers even went so as far as to claim that the Qing annexation of Taiwan had initiated a metamorphosis of the island's geographic conditions. Several eighteenth-century gazetteers asserted that Taiwan's climate had begun to change with annexation to the Chinese domain, as a result of the beneficial cosmic influence of the emperor, which influenced heavenly conditions and, thereby, the weather. These changes included modifications in rainfall, temperature, miasmas, and so on. As the *Gazetteer of Taiwan Prefecture* of 1742 put it, "Recently Taiwan's climate is gradually coming to resemble that of

China proper."[51] Again, this assertion rested on the assumption of moral correspondences between heaven and earth, which influenced the flows of *qi* and the transformations of the cosmological elements of yin and yang. Climatological changes were the manifestations of these transformations.

These shifts in the representation of Taiwan, which served to minimize the distance between Taiwan and China proper, took place almost immediately after annexation. Although travel accounts and gazetteers almost invariably opened with the conventional litany "Taiwan was originally a remote wilderness beyond the seas, which had no contact with China," Qing literati began to reconfigure Taiwan's cosmographic location—no longer in Wilderness—through the use of symbolic geography. Thus, despite the harsh critiques leveled by evidential scholars against symbolic geography, these systems of thought continued to operate in the gazetteers and other forms of geographic representation and provided theoretical frameworks for linking the island symbolically to the Chinese imperial domain. As such, while empirical geography served the practical needs of imperial administration, symbolic geography served an important discursive function.

METAPHORICAL GEOGRAPHY: TAIWAN AS HEDGEROW

Early Qing representations of Taiwan's geography also lent support to the metaphorical conception of Taiwan as a "hedgerow" for China, or a "Great Wall for the ocean frontier," as supporters of annexation had hoped it would be.[52] The *Record of the Naval Defenses of Fujian Province* (*Fujian haifang zhi*), for example, noted: "[Taiwan] extends from the northeast to the southwest like a standing screen; it is the outer boundary for China's four [coastal] provinces."[53] Cartographic and textual representations of Taiwan's mountains as a screen or barricade further supported this notion. As the *Gazetteer of Taiwan Prefecture* of 1696 wrote: "Taiwan is the outer barricade for Fujian province. All its mountains face China proper."[54] Constructed as facing China, Taiwan's mountains seemed to provide a natural barrier protecting the Chinese coast from outside forces. This image was reinforced by descriptions of Taiwan's Central Mountain Range as an unbroken chain of lofty peaks, standing tall like a screen wrapped around Fujian.[55]

Kangxi maps also depicted the Central Mountain Range as such a barrier (see Color Plate 3). As mentioned above, early Qing maps of Taiwan showed the island from the perspective of the China coast. As a result, these maps showed only the western side of the island, with the Central Mountain Range on the horizon line. The tall mountains on the horizon thus served visually as a barrier, marking the back edge of Taiwan. Such textual and cartographic representations of Taiwan as "leaning against," backed, or rimmed by mountains reified the metaphor of Taiwan as a fence.

Thus, where the sea had once served as the boundary between the Chinese domain and the realm beyond the pale, the island of Taiwan itself now served as this boundary. The notion of Taiwan as a hedgerow reflects the partial nature of Taiwan's incorporation into the Qing empire during the initial stage of Qing colonization. As a hedgerow, Taiwan occupied a somewhat liminal position: it was neither fully outside the Chinese domain nor fully within it; rather, it was itself the boundary between inner and outer.

CHAPTER 2

Taiwan as a Living Museum

Savagery and Tropes

of Anachronism

Strange indeed, these Eastern Savages! The island is so close that if one sets out sailing with a northerly wind from a harbor such as Lieyu, one can reach the Pescadores in one day and night, and then in another day and night one can reach [Mu]Jialaowan. Yet, here there are still people who do not have a calendar, who do not have officials and superiors, who go about naked, and who use a knotted string for calculations. Is that not strange?

— Chen Di, *Record of the Eastern Savages*

Late Ming traveler Chen Di (1540–1617), author of the earliest extant eyewitness account of Taiwan, expressed surprise that only a short distance from China's shores was an island so culturally and technologically remote from Chinese civilization. He figured this cultural difference in terms of temporal distance, as though the "Eastern Savages" (*dongfan*), as he dubbed Taiwan's indigenous inhabitants, remained stuck in the past, in a time before the invention of calendars, clothing, writing, and other accoutrements of civilization. Following Chen Di, Qing travel writers commonly constructed the Taiwan indigenes as anachronous beings. They represented what might be termed "primitive" customs—for example, tattooing and the wearing of animal skins—as analogues of practices recorded in such ancient texts as the *Records of the Grand Historian* (*Shiji*) and the *Book of Rites* (*Liji*). For Qing writers, Taiwan was a living museum where they could observe customs long ago abandoned in China.

The use of historical analogy to explain seemingly strange and alien cultural practices was a common feature of late imperial ethnographic descriptions of non-Han peoples on the Chinese frontiers.[1] The idea that the barbarians preserved customs or practices once found in China dates to early texts such as the *Chronicle of Zuo* (*Zuozhuan*), the *Records of the Grand Historian*, and the *History of the Later Han* (*Hou Hanshu*). By the late imperial era, this notion had become an established historiographic convention.[2] For Chinese writers like Chen Di, the comparison of frontier peoples to the ancients was an effective way of representing their crudeness or primitiveness. This projection of cultural "others" into the past bears a striking similarity to the use of temporal displacement in Western anthropological discourse. As Johannes Fabian demonstrates in *Time and the Other: How Anthropology Makes Its Object*, in traditional Western ethnography the "denial of coevalness," or a distancing in time, is a central mode of constituting people as primitives:[3] using a scale of evolutionary development, ethnographers represent their subjects as "backward" relative to modern Western civilization and thereby relegate them to the past. The denial of coevalness, according to Fabian, serves primarily to distance the observed from the observer.

In an analysis of premodern Chinese, Western, and Chinese Communist representations of non-Han peoples on the Chinese frontiers, anthropologist Stevan Harrell identifies the denial of coevalness (which he calls the "historical metaphor") as a shared feature of all three discourses.[4] He argues that the construction of "peripheral peoples" as ancient serves to demonstrate their cultural inferiority and to legitimate the civilizing project of the hegemonic "center."[5] The historical metaphor legitimates the civilizing project by establishing that peripheral peoples can indeed be civilized: if peripheral peoples represent an earlier stage of development, one that the civilizers themselves once went through, then the project of civilization is simply a matter of bringing these peoples forward in time. Harrell asserts that it is by means of such discursive strategies that the center "assumes the task of civilizing, and with it the superior political and moral position from which the civilizing project can be carried out."[6] In short, the historical metaphor is essentially a tool of denigration.

This chapter examines the ways in which Taiwan functioned as a living museum in Chinese travel accounts from the late seventeenth and early eighteenth centuries. As we shall see, travel writers used the historical metaphor not only to denigrate the "savages" but also to idealize them. The historical metaphor served two contradictory rhetorical modes—which I call the "rhetoric of privation" and the "rhetoric of primitivism."[7] With the "rhetoric of privation," the savage is constructed as backward and culturally inferior. With the "rhetoric of primitivism," the savage is romanticized as the preserver of an ancient righteousness lost among the moderns—a "Noble Savage" of sorts.

Although both forms of rhetoric rely on the denial of coevalness, they represent conflicting conceptions of history. The rhetoric of privation derives from the view of history as progress, a movement away from the brutish original condition of humanity, and a cumulative development of civilization. This view was particularly prevalent in expansionist eras such as the Tang and the Qing, which sought to surpass the achievements of past dynasties. The rhetoric of primitivism, in contrast, derives from the notion of history as a process of degeneration from an idealized past, a notion that can be found in both Confucian and Daoist schools of thought. As early as the Warring States period, Confucians constructed the early Zhou as a Golden Age of perfect virtue. Daoist classics, such as the *Laozi* and the *Zhuangzi*, advocated a return to a primordial era of natural simplicity. The rhetorical effect of displacing the other into the past thus varies depending on which past—a brutish one or an exemplary one—is the point of reference.[8] As a result, a bifurcated image of the Taiwan indigene as savage brute and noble savage emerged in late imperial travel writing. Thus, the historical metaphor was not used solely as an ideological justification of Qing colonial dominance in Taiwan but also as a means of critiquing Han Chinese exploitation of the indigenes.

Chen Di and the Rhetoric of Primitivism

The basic model for the rhetoric of primitivism in Taiwan travel writing was established by Chen Di's *Record of the Eastern Savages* (*Dong-fan ji*), one of the most celebrated premodern accounts of the island. One of the few Chinese literati to travel to Taiwan before the Qing conquest, Chen Di made his voyage to the island in 1603 as a companion of Admiral Shen Yourong, who was leading a punitive expedition against Japanese pirates based on the island. Although Chen Di had been involved in frontier defense before his retirement, he did not participate in this campaign but simply went along as an observer because he had a "taste to see the sea."[9] During his twenty-two-day stay on the island, Chen Di covered the terrain from Tainan along the southwest coast to Kaohsiung.[10] After returning to China, Chen composed the *Record*, a report of his observations of indigenous culture on the island. Although Taiwan was inhabited at this time by several different groups, Chen Di was not fully cognizant of this diversity and thus spoke of the indigenes generically as the "Eastern Savages."

Chen Di's account exemplifies how the rhetoric of privation and primitivism expressed Chinese ambivalence toward the Taiwan indigenes. Chen began with images of indigenous privation: the people wear no clothing; they lack the ritual etiquette of bowing and kneeling; they have no calendar, no writing. In Chen's view, the indigenes thus lacked the very basic elements of civilization: *wen* (writing and texts), *shi* (history—without a calendar to mark time, there can be no history), and *li* (ritual or propriety). Through these images of privation, Chen underscored the indigenes' cultural inferiority in relation to the Chinese.

Chen complicated these images in a comment that serves as a final evaluation of indigenous culture. In this longish passage, Chen mused on what he saw as the "strangeness" (*yi*) of the indigenes. He constructed this strangeness in large part by denying the coevalness of the indigenes. Styling himself the "unofficial historian" (*yeshi shi*), Chen wrote:

The Unofficial Historian says: Strange indeed, these Eastern Savages! . . . Here there are still people who do not have a calendar, who do not have officials and superiors, who go about naked, and who use a knotted string for calculations. Is that not strange? . . . Also, they live on an ocean [island], yet they do not fish. They live unsegregated and yet are not promiscuous. They bury the dead in the same place where the living dwell. They hunt deer the entire year, and yet the deer have not been exterminated. If you counted all their islands together, the terrain would be equivalent to about one county. They reproduce among themselves. To this day they have no calendrical system, nor any writing system, and they do not feel the lack. Is that not strange? The Southern Dwarves and Northern Barbarians all have writing systems, similar to the "bird tracks" of the ancient *zhuan* script; must there not have been a clever person at the beginning who established [this system]? And this place alone lacks writing; why is that? But they eat their fill and amuse themselves, happy and contented; what use would they have for clever people? They are the people of Lord No-Cares (Wuhuai shi) and Getian.[11]

The ambiguity of history, as both progress and degeneration, allows Chen Di to move smoothly from privation to primitivism in this passage. His ambivalence toward the past emerges most sharply in his discussion of writing and its relationship to civilization. Chen Di took the absence of writing among the indigenes as an index of both their technological backwardness and their primitive virtue. On the one hand, Chen marveled that the indigenes still used knotted strings for calculations, a practice regarded by the Chinese as a form of proto-writing.[12] He was astonished that the Taiwan indigenes alone among the barbarians had no writing system. They thus appeared to him even more backward than the Southern Dwarves and Northern Barbarians, who at least possess the archaic writing system known as *zhuan*. On the other hand, the practice of knotting strings and the lack of writing prompted Chen to figure the indigenes as the people of Lord No-Cares and Getian, legendary rulers of a primordial era of peace and natural simplicity, since he associated their "preliterate" state with a contented and carefree existence. In a typically primitivist move, Chen Di turned privation on its head and refigured a lack of technological development as a positive sign of the indigenes' moral condition.

Chen was able to achieve this reversal because writing functions as both a sign of progress and a sign of loss. The centrality of writing to Chinese civilization dates to the earliest times of the Shang and the Zhou. Early myths held that the sage-kings Fu Xi and Huang Di invented writing and gave it to the Chinese people in order that they might be civilized. The possession of writing distinguished those who were civilized from the barbarians, who were not privy to the teachings of the sage-kings. By at least the Warring States period, as Mark Edward Lewis demonstrates in *Writing and Authority in Early China*, writing and texts had become fundamental to cultural and state authority.[13] Therefore, the lack of writing could readily be made to stand for the antithesis of civilization and centrist state authority. According to Daoist critiques of the complexities of civilization, the invention of writing spelled the end of a simpler, natural age. Both the *Laozi* and the *Zhuangzi* called for a return to a way of life that antedated the invention of writing, when people used knotted strings for calculations and record keeping. It is this association of "knotted strings" with Daoist images of a primitive utopia that enabled Chen Di to read the practice as a sign of the indigenes' simple virtues, rather than as mere index of technological backwardness. The simple life is described thus in the *Laozi*:

> Make the state small and its people few.
> Let the people give up use of their tools.
> Let them take death seriously and desist from
>   distant campaigns.
> Then even if they have boats and wagons, they
>   will not travel in them.
> Even though they have weapons and armor, they
>   will not form ranks with them.
> Let people revert to the practice of rope-tying
>   [instead of writing].
> Then they will find their food sweet,
> Their clothes beautiful,
> Their houses comfortable,
> Their customs enjoyable.

People from neighboring states so close that they can see each other and hear the sounds of each other's dogs and chickens will then grow old without ever visiting each other.[14]

This description of a Golden Age represents a vital Daoist critique of the competition, striving, and greed associated with civilization and progress.[15] An alternative to this life is presented in the form of the idealized small state. Chen Di repeatedly alluded to this passage from the *Laozi* in his account: he described Taiwan as small and the villages as isolated; the people do not use boats to travel on the ocean, and they still knot strings. The main body of his text concludes: "Therefore, until old age and death they have no contact with other barbarians."[16] Chen, it seems, fancied that on Taiwan he had found a primitive community matching the Daoist ideal. Sadly, he saw the modern world intruding on this utopia: "Since communication has been established with China, they have begun to have desires, and unscrupulous people cheat them with inferior goods. They are also gradually becoming aware [of the ways of the world], and I am afraid that their days of pure simplicity are ending."[17] For Chen Di the establishment of communications with China represents a rupture with the indigenes' original state of isolation and innocence.

Chen Di's construction of the indigenes as a people free from both worldly desires and knowledge again draws on the *Laozi*, this time a passage on ideal governance:

Do not honor the worthy,
And the people will not compete.
Do not value rare treasures,
And the people will not steal.
Do not display what others want,
And the people will not have their hearts confused.
A sage governs this way;
He empties people's minds and fills their bellies.
He weakens their wills and strengthens their bones.
Keep the people always without knowledge and without desires,
For then the clever will not dare to act.
Engage in no action and order will prevail.[18]

This passage from the *Laozi*, like the one on "knotted strings," serves as an important source for primitivist tropes. Chen Di not only constructed the Taiwan indigenes as a people with neither knowledge nor desires but also represented them as a people with "full bellies" who have no need for "clever people." He further claimed that the people of Taiwan do not steal, a claim repeated by numerous other Chinese travelers to Taiwan. His *Record* is so replete with allustion to the *Laozi* that one might almost read it as a gloss on this classic text.

The *Laozi* was not Chen Di's only source for images of primitivism. Tao Qian's "Account of Peach Blossom Spring" ("Taohuayuan ji"), a text that is itself a rearticulation of the Daoist discourse on primitivism, also influenced Chen. Tao Qian's famous account tells of a mythical hidden refuge at Wuling, where people who had fled the oppressive Qin rule lived in a timeless utopian world. Oblivious to the passage of time and the changing of dynasties, the residents of this refuge preserved ancient customs intact. Tao described this idyllic primitive realm as a world that had no calendars, where planting instead followed the natural rhythm of the seasons. Dogs and chickens could be heard calling to one another, but roads were so overgrown that neighbors never visited one another. The villagers enjoyed a carefree existence and felt no need to exert their intellect. There is some speculation that Tao's account may have been based on non-Han tribal peoples of southern China.[19] Late imperial readers of *Record* certainly would have sensed echoes of Tao Qian's Peach Blossom Spring in Chen Di's representation of primitive Taiwan.

A reading of Chen Di's *Record* against the *Laozi* and "Peach Blossom Spring" demonstrates that the rhetoric of primitivism was grounded in Daoist critiques of Chinese civilization and the centrist state. As is evident in Chen Di's comment, primitivism served as a ready vehicle for self-reflexive critiques of Chinese society. Chen explicitly contrasted the virtuous and innocent primitives with unscrupulous Chinese traders, who cheat the naïve indigenes with inferior goods. With the introduction of these goods also comes the introduction of desire and knowledge; China therefore becomes a source of corruption, a threat to the primitives' idyllic way of life. Chen's *Record*, like much travel literature in general, serves as a vehicle for the author's reflections on his own society. Representations of the Taiwan indigenes, then, might have more to do with a traveler's dissatisfaction with Chinese society than with his actual perceptions of indigenous society. Chen's romanticization of the primitives expresses an anxiety that material advancement might paradoxically bring moral decline.

Between Chen Di's time and the Qing conquest, there seem to have been no firsthand Chinese accounts of the Taiwan indigenes, a lack that even Qing authors found mysterious. Early Qing travelers to Taiwan, who recognized Chen Di as the "first" Chinese literatus to write an account of the island, took him as an important model. Chen Di was, of course, positioned differently from these Qing literati, since he traveled to Taiwan before the Qing colonized the island. He therefore had no need to deal with the issues of colonial relations that would confront Qing authors. Nonetheless, as a central early text, the *Record* set out some of the basic terms in which Qing literati would understand the Taiwan indigenes, as well as the relation between indigenous culture and Chinese civilization.[20] According to Jia Ning, Chen Di was the first to label Taiwan's tribal villages "she," which would become the standard Qing term. He was also the first to name the Taiwan indigenes the "Eastern Savages" (*dongfan*) or "Barbarians of Eastern Savagery" (*dongfan zhi yi*).[21]

In doing so, Chen associated the Taiwan indigenes with the Eastern Barbarians (*dongyi*), a category that included the Koreans and the Japanese. This is significant because historically, for geographic reasons, Chinese expansion to the east had been limited in comparison, for example, to the historical expansion southward.[22] Although numerous non-Han Chinese peoples of the south had been conquered and gradually absorbed into the Chinese empire over the centuries, the Eastern Barbarians had for the most part maintained the more autonomous relationship of "tributaries" to China. Certain other pre-

suppositions also followed from the categorization of the Taiwan indigenes as Eastern Barbarians: the classic characterization of this group
in the *Book of Rites* was that "they had their hair unbound and tattooed their bodies. Some of them ate their food without its being
cooked with fire."[23] These images greatly informed early Qing expectations of Taiwan's natives.

Lin Qianguang and the Rhetoric of Privation

Whereas Chen Di's *Record* established a model for the rhetoric of
primitivism, Lin Qianguang's *Brief Notes on Taiwan* (*Taiwan jilüe*),
one of the earliest accounts written after the Qing conquest, was central in the development of the rhetoric of privation. Between 1687 and
1691, Lin Qianguang, a native of Fujian, served as the first instructor
of Confucian schools in the prefectural government of Taiwan. *Brief
Notes*, following the format of the genre of geographic records (*dili
zhi*), is divided into various categories, with one section devoted to indigenous customs (*fengsu*).

Lin Qianguang's representation of the Taiwan indigenes forms a
sharp contrast to Chen Di's primitivism. Lin began his description of
savage customs with a declaration of their cultural inferiority:

The native savages (*tufan*) . . . are a stupid people. They have no family
names, no ancestral worship, and apart from their own father and
mother, they do not recognize [kin such as] paternal or maternal uncles.
They are unfamiliar with the calendar. Moreover, they do not know their
own ages. By nature they like to kill people.[24]

In some details, Lin's description matches Chen Di's, but his language
is much more explicitly contemptuous of the indigenes. As had Chen
Di, Lin projected the indigenes back into the past, but with radically
different results. This becomes apparent when Lin turned to the indigenes of Taiwan's Central Mountain Range, an area that the Chinese
regarded as inhospitable wilderness during the early stage of Qing
colonization.

As one goes deeper into the mountains, the people have the appearance of
apes, being shorter than three feet. When they see people, they climb into
the treetops. If people want to capture them, then they draw their bows
and confront them. There are also those who burrow out caves to live in,
just like the folk of high antiquity.[25]

In comparing the indigenes to the "folk of high antiquity" (*taigu zhi min*), Lin drew on a vision of antiquity at odds with Chen Di's primitive utopia. "High antiquity," in Lin's usage, is a rude and brutish past when people lived like beasts. For Lin, history is unambiguous: history means progress and the indigenes' backwardness is an unequivocal sign of their inferiority. By using the tropes of cave-dwelling and tree-climbing to describe the indigenes of the mountains, Lin Qianguang constructed the Taiwan indigenes as atavistic beings surviving from the dawn of history. The image of archaic peoples as cave-dwellers and tree-climbers derives from a standard Chinese narrative of the evolution of civilization, one version of which was recorded in the "Liyun" chapter of the *Book of Rites*:

Formerly the ancient kings had no houses. In winter they lived in caves which they had excavated, and in summer in nests which they had framed. They knew not yet the transforming power of fire, but ate the fruits of plants and trees, and the flesh of birds and beasts, drinking their blood, and swallowing (also) the hair and feathers. They knew not the use of flax and silk, but clothed themselves with feathers and skins.[26]

According to the *Book of Rites*, this crude state of human existence was left behind as the sages arose and taught people to build houses, cook with fire, fashion tools, and weave. The sages who introduced the arts of civilization to the Chinese people, bringing them step by step out of the brutish state of high antiquity, were important cultural heroes. First, there was Fu Xi, the Ox-Tamer, who taught people the arts of hunting, fishing, and cooking meat, and who invented the family. Then, there was Shen Nong, the Divine Farmer, who invented the plow and hoe and taught people the art of husbandry. Next, there was Huang Di, the Yellow Emperor, who invented boats and carts, the bow and arrow, ceramics, silk, writing, and a calendar. The notion that the sages introduced the arts of agriculture and civilization is an important one in early Chinese historiography, for the knowledge the Chinese gained from the sages distinguished them from the barbarians, who lacked such civilizing heroes and therefore remained stuck in a lower state of development.

The *Book of Rites'* picture of high antiquity served as one of the most important *locus classici* for the rhetoric of privation: it is a picture of the lowest stage of development, when human beings were little more than the beasts. The image of "high antiquity" as a brutish age was commonplace in Chinese texts. The *Book of Changes* (*Yijing*), for example, also described the ancients as "dwelling in caves and living in the wilderness" (*xueju yechu*). Later texts, such as the Song dynasty *Lushi*, similarly stated that "the people of high antiquity dwelt in caves and lived in the wilderness," and "the people of early antiquity (*shanggu*) ate fur and smeared blood on their mouths."[27] These images of a brutish past significantly informed Qing conceptualizations of savagery.[28] From such classical sources derived the stock phrases of the rhetoric of privation: "eating fur and drinking blood," "dwelling in caves and nesting in trees," "wearing skins and feathers," and "loose hair and tattooed body." Just as the *Laozi* and the *Zhuangzi* became important sources for the rhetoric of primitivism, the *Book of Rites* and the *Book of Changes* established the rhetoric of privation.

Thus, references to the "folk of high antiquity" stood for the brutish age of development and were standard in the rhetoric of privation. In contrast, the figures of Fu Xi, Shen Nong, and Huang Di stood for an idealized stage of development, a time when the Chinese people had left behind the brutish existence of animals but had yet to be beset by the complexities, conflicts, and corruption of advanced civilization. Allusions to this time and to the civilizing heroes were commonplace in the rhetoric of primitivism.[29] The idea of a brutish stage followed by an idealized primitive stage would become fundamental to the construction of the "raw" savages and the "cooked" savages, a subject to which I turn in Chapter 5.

Overall, the rhetoric of privation dominated early Qing representations of the Taiwan indigenes. Early Kangxi texts often depicted the indigenes in terms of the stock phrases of privation, which were less empirical descriptions of their customs than figural representations of their backwardness. A popular metonym for the indigenes, for example, was "tattooed and black-toothed [people]." Lin Qianguang's work played a large role in promoting the rhetoric of privation in Qing accounts. His *Brief Notes* became quite well known because it served as the source for the "Native Savage Customs" ("Tufan fengsu") section of the first and second editions (1696 and 1712) of the *Gazetteer of Taiwan Prefecture*—both of which copied Lin nearly verbatim. Several other early Qing writers also copied Lin's lines on the ape-like "folk of high antiquity" in describing various hostile groups. One Kangxi author, for example, noted: "The Kuilei savages are about three or four feet tall. They climb trees, jumping and throwing things, as nimble as monkeys. They are all a nest-lodging, cave-dwelling, fur-eating, blood-drinking bunch. They do not know how to plow and plant. They are the folk of high antiquity."[30] The notion of the "folk of high antiquity" as an uncivilized, pre-agricultural people thus soon became a standard feature of the rhetoric of privation. Early Qing ethnographic descriptions further portrayed the "savage" as belligerent, bloodthirsty, and stupid; they were, on the whole, quite derogatory. Primitivist representations of the Taiwan indigenes served largely as a counterdiscourse against the dominant view of the Taiwan indigenes as culturally inferior.

Yu Yonghe and the Dual Vision of the Savages

The earliest Chinese literati to write about Taiwan's natives did not travel much beyond the core of Chinese settlement in the southwestern corner of the island and were therefore unfamiliar with the extent of cultural diversity among the island's indigenous people. These early writers and gazetteer compilers referred to the Taiwan indigenes in blanket terms like "Eastern Savage" or "native savage." Soon after the establishment of Qing rule on the island, however, literati became aware of the need to draw finer distinctions among the various indigenous groups on the island, some of which appeared more "wild" than others.

This process of differentiating between different groups of indigenes was already evident to some degree in Lin Qianguang's account, which describes the "savages" of the mountains as particularly bellicose. The notion of distinguishing between threatening and nonthreatening natives was made even more explicit in Yu Yonghe's *Small Sea Travelogue*, which records his ten-month expedition from the Taiwan prefectural capital in the south of the island to the sulfur springs of Beitou in the north. The text is composed principally in the form of a travel diary, with dated entries, and also includes some poetry. It thus contains extensive first-person narration, Yu's subjective responses to the people and the environment, and his opinions on colonial policy. These qualities distinguish Yu's work from Lin Qianguang's terse, impersonal geographic record. Yu's detailed descriptions of the early Taiwan frontier made *Small Sea Travelogue* one of the most celebrated and widely copied accounts of Taiwan.

Yu differentiated various groups of natives by selectively employing the rhetoric of privation and primitivism. During the course of his journey up the western coast of the island, Yu encountered a wide range of indigenous peoples, some of whom he regarded as vile and uncouth, and others whom he found fairly civilized. He also noted that whereas the indigenes dwelling close to the Chinese settlements on the plains were generally accommodating to the Chinese, those dwelling in the mountains were often hostile. To account for these differences, Yu constructed two categories: the "native savages" (*tufan*) and the "wild savages" (*yefan*).

Among the savages, there is a difference between native savages and wild savages. The wild savages live deep within the mountains, screened behind layered ranges of linked peaks that jut up into the Milky Way. The forest is so deep, and the bamboo thickets so dense that you cannot see the sky when you look up. Brambles and vines are [so tangled] that you cannot lift your foot. Since the Chaos of Creation, no ax has ever entered here. The wild savages live in its midst, dwelling in lairs and caves, drinking blood and eating fur. . . . The wild savages rely on their ferociousness and from time to time come out and plunder, burning huts and killing people, and then returning to their lairs. . . . They do not know to turn toward civilization (*xianghua*); they are really mere beasts![31]

Yu's primordial landscape of mountainous jungles untouched since the Creation is a fitting home for the "blood-drinking and fur-eating" and "cave-dwelling" "wild savages" who are little more than beasts. He represents both the landscape and its inhabitants as though they had remained static.[32] Even as he vilified the "wild savages," Yu, through the rhetoric of primitivism, romanticized the "native savages" of the plains. Drawing on the images of primitivism established by Chen Di, he continued: "Now, as for the nearby savages of the flatlands, in winter and summer they wear a single cloth, with coarse grain they can eat their fill. With no consciousness, no knowledge, no strivings, and no desires, they naturally roam in the world of Getian and Lord No-Cares."[33] Like Chen, Yu alluded to the Daoist classics in constructing an image of a primitive utopia where people are content with simple clothing and food. Yu's parallel construction "no consciousness, no knowledge, no strivings, and no desires" calls to mind the *Laozi*'s idealization of a people "without knowledge and without desire,"[34] and the phrase "naturally roam" (*ziyou*) calls to mind the *Zhuangzi*'s celebration of "free and easy wandering" (*xiaoyaoyou*). Finally, Yu echoed

Chen Di in calling the "plains savages" the people of Getian and Lord No-Cares. Thus, although Yu denied the coevalness of both the "wild" and the "native" savages, he represented them as inhabiting radically different pasts. Through such representations, a bifurcated image of the Taiwan indigenes—the "friendly savage" and the "hostile savage"—emerged. These opposing images would later be codified as the "cooked savage" and the "raw savage."

From Figurative Allusion to Historical Analogy

By the eighteenth century, the trope of the indigenes as the people of antiquity had become a cliché of ethnographic discourse, employed by travel writers and gazetteer compilers alike. Qing literati clearly regarded this trope as a useful framework for understanding the cultural difference of the Taiwan indigenes. In the eighteenth century, as writers on Taiwan employed tropes of anachronism with increasing frequency and variety, the character of these tropes changed. First, authors began to move away from figurative toward more literal historical analogies. They went beyond the old clichés of knotting strings and burrowing caves to document a wide range of specific customs that appeared to be analogues of ancient practices: divination techniques, the construction of tools, funerary customs, and so on. The accumulation of such analogies, particularly when assembled in local gazetteers, had the effect of adding weight to the notion of the Taiwan indigenes as the ancients. Second, in comparison to seventeenth-century accounts, eighteenth-century records display a shift toward the rhetoric of primitivism. Allusions to Peach Blossom Spring, for example, abound in eighteenth-century writings. The notion of Taiwan as a Peach Blossom Spring was perhaps particularly apt in Qing writings, since the island had served as a refuge for Ming loyalists fleeing the invading Qing (although, of course, this was never mentioned directly by Qing authors). The rhetoric of privation by no means disappears in eighteenth-century works, but references to "blood-drinking and fur-eating," and "cave-dwelling and nest-building" appear less frequently than in the earliest Qing accounts. This shift took place in large part because by the eighteenth century the indigenous people as a whole appeared less threatening and less strange to the Chinese, who therefore felt less need to demonize them.

The *Gazetteer of Zhuluo County* of 1717, edited by Zhou Zhong-xuan, exemplifies these trends. Zhou Zhongxuan was a native of Guizhou who served as magistrate of Zhuluo county during the 1710s and as acting magistrate for Taiwan county in 1722. During his term of service in Zhuluo, he oversaw the compilation of the first gazetteer of that county. The account of "savage customs" in this gazetteer differs both quantitatively and qualitatively from those of the Taiwan prefectural gazetteers of 1696 and 1712.[35] Zhou, moreover, emphasized the rhetoric of primitivism more than the two earlier compilers had. In example after example, he projected the indigenes back into an idealized past. In the section "Miscellaneous Customs," for instance, he remarked:

Husband and wife are mutually devoted. Even when they are wealthy, they do not have maids and concubines or boy servants. For their entire lives they never go out the village gate. They hold hands when walking and ride together in the same carriage. They do not know the bitterness of being separated in life. They do not steal. They know not of gambling or gaming. They spend their days planting and weaving, fishing and hunting, and collecting firewood. Their world is an unchiseled block of primeval Chaos.[36]

In yet another image of a primitive utopia, the people are content, carefree, and innocent of vice. "Unchiseled block of primeval Chaos" is an allusion to the *Zhuangzi*, where it is stated, "The people of antiquity lived amidst the primeval Chaos, finding peace and tranquility united with the world."[37] The passage refers to a natural society that has not yet been shaped by the rules and rituals of civilization. Like his seventeenth-century predecessors, Zhou connected the notion of utopia to a temporal displacement, an escape from the contemporary world. These images seemed commonplace by the eighteenth century, but what makes Zhou's gazetteer stand out is the frequency of such images.

Another noteworthy feature of Zhou's account is his attempt to counter the derogatory clichés of earlier accounts with empirical observations. For example, in recording the custom of drinking deer's blood, Zhou remarked "but they do not eat the fur," thus correcting the *Book of Rites* phrase "blood-drinking and fur-eating."[38] This skepticism toward the privative clichés popular in the earliest descriptions of the Taiwan indigenes characterizes the work of a great number of eighteenth-century writers. The effort to replace clichés with direct observation of customs was part of the general trend favoring empiricism in ethnographic writing in eighteenth-century Taiwan, a subject that I discuss further in Chapter 4.

Historical Analogy and Assimilation

The conceit of the Taiwan indigenes as the ancients proved useful for those Qing literati who argued for the ease of their assimilation into the Chinese empire. As Stevan Harrell has asserted, the notion that frontier peoples exist in an earlier stage of historical development suggests that civilizing them is simply a matter of bringing them forward in time. One of the earliest travel writers to make a strong case for the assimilability of the Taiwan indigenes was Yu Yonghe. Rejecting the argument that these people were merely "naked and tattooed savages who are not worth defending," he asserted that they possessed the potential to become "civilized" human beings. Yu supported this claim by drawing a historical analogy between the Taiwan indigenes and the Jingman barbarians of Chinese antiquity, who had long since been assimilated into the Chinese population.

If only we could civilize (*hua*) [the Taiwan indigenes] with rites and propriety and reform their customs with the *Classic of Poetry* (*Shijing*) and the *Classic of History* . . . how would they be any different from the people of China? In antiquity there [also] existed the custom of cropping the hair and tattooing the body among the Jingman, who lived in the close territory of Wu and Yue. Today this area has blossomed into a refuge for civilization.[39]

Here Yu set a developmental trajectory for the Taiwan indigenes based on historical analogy. By comparing the Taiwan indigenes to the tattooed and short-haired Jingman of antiquity, he suggested that the cultural privation signified by such practices is simply a historical stage. If the Jingman were able to be transformed into Chinese subjects, then so can the Taiwan indigenes.

Yu's analogy between the Taiwan indigenes and the Jingman was a significant move in another respect, for the Jingman dwelt in the southern borderlands of China. In associating the Taiwan indigenes with the Southern rather than the Eastern Barbarians, Yu set a precedent for an important shift in Qing ethnographic discourse: the gradual conceptual transformation of the Taiwan indigenes from eastern islanders to southern Chinese frontier tribes. This rhetorical move, which would serve to link the Taiwan indigenes more closely to China proper and the history of Chinese southward expansion, naturalized their incorporation into the Chinese empire. From Yu's time on, we find numerous comparisons of the Taiwan indigenes to the Man and Mai, ancient southern tribes, as well as to the Miao and the Yao, contemporary southern tribes.

For Yu, the key to the transformation of the Taiwan indigenes lay in education in the Confucian classics. Based on his belief in their capacity for moral transformation through education, Yu argued for the ease of assimilating the Taiwan indigenes: "At the longest it will take a hundred years, at the fastest, thirty."[40] Once transformed, the people of Taiwan would be no different from the people of China.

The Chinese term for "to civilize" (*hua*) literally means "to transform"; to civilize was to morally transform. According to the Confucian concept of transformation, exposure to Civilization and the authority of the ruler would bring about progressive moral improvement, as people learned moral principles and changed their behavior in accordance. The ideal of what Pamela Kyle Crossley has called "transformationalism" was central to Chinese culturalism, the notion that Confucian culture was a universally valid (and superior) Civilization, open to all who submitted to its transformative power. As such, the process of moral improvement could transform not only the ordinary Chinese but also barbarians.

The process by which barbarians were transformed was known as *xianghua*, "turning toward transformation/Civilization," or *laihua*, "coming to be transformed"—the idea being that the prestige of Civilization would inspire barbarians to come toward it and submit to transformation. In theory, once barbarians were morally transformed, they would no longer be barbarians; Chinese identity was therefore understood in cultural and moral terms.[41] As Crossley demonstrates in *The Translucent Mirror: History and Identity in Qing Imperial Ideology*, the ideal of transformationalism was central to Qing ideology under the Kangxi and Yongzheng (1723–35) emperors, forming the basis for the incorporation of various frontier peoples into the empire. More will be said about this subject in Chapter 4.

Early Qing policy in Taiwan was guided by this ideology of transformationalism. As John Shepherd has shown, the Qing court viewed the "civilizing" of the indigenes as an important means of extending state control.[42] Yet, the court approached this matter conservatively, seeking only to promote Confucian civic values and submission to constituted authority and not to enforce the wholesale assimilation of the indigenes. Cultural differences were tolerated as long as they did not threaten Qing control. The transformation of the Taiwan indigenes was understood as a gradual and long-term process. Therefore, the efforts to "civilize" the indigenes instituted by the Kangxi administration were limited and consisted primarily of educating youths in the Confucian classics (even then, the administration devoted very few funds to this cause). These educational efforts were considered a part of the general endeavor of raising the level of civilization on the island, among the Han settlers and the indigenes alike.

This conservative approach to "civilizing" the indigenes was bolstered by the conceit of the savages as the ancients, which supported the notion that the Taiwan indigenes were not absolutely different from the Chinese but simply farther behind them on the ladder of evolution. The historical metaphor thus served to domesticate the strangeness of Taiwan indigenes by placing them within a familiar trajectory of historical development and moral transformation.

The Rhetoric of Privation and Colonial Critiques

In *The Chinese World Order: Traditional China's Foreign Relations* (1968), John King Fairbank argued that traditional Chinese relations with non-Chinese peoples were colored by sinocentrism and the assumption of Chinese superiority.[43] Given this model, one would expect Chinese accounts of frontier peoples to be marked by an attitude of Han Chinese superiority. Indeed, this was the case in the majority of early Qing representations of the Taiwan indigenes, which depicted these people as uncivilized, brutish, and stupid creatures. Yet, Qing ethnographic writing was not uniformly chauvinistic, and a significant number of literati fashioned themselves as defenders of the indigenes. Yu Yonghe, for example, deplored the abuses that the natives had suffered, first at the hands of the Dutch and the Japanese, then at the hands of Koxinga's "lawless" men, and finally, at the hands of the Qing settlers. Qing literati objected to the exploitation of the indigenes on humanitarian grounds, as well as out of a Mencian concern for the well-being of imperial subjects. Frontier officials were also aware that maltreatment could provoke rebellion. They therefore perceived the behavior of greedy Han Chinese settlers, unscrupulous interpreters, and venal officials who "squeezed" the natives as a potential threat to frontier stability.

The rhetoric of primitivism provided a ready vehicle for Qing literati who wanted to criticize Han Chinese who took advantage of the "naïveté" of the Taiwan indigenes. Chen Di, for example, used the rhetoric of primitivism to censure Chinese traders who cheated the Taiwan indigenes with inferior goods and corrupted them by introducing them to worldly desires. Qing writers similarly deplored the abuse of the Taiwan indigenes by unscrupulous Han Chinese. By constructing the Taiwan indigenes as innocent and ingenuous victims of scheming and greedy Han Chinese, critics of colonial exploitation sought to take the moral high ground.

This was the strategy employed by Zhou Zhongxuan, who justified his calls for administrative reforms by appealing to the paternalistic ideology of the Qing state, which cast the emperor as the protector of the weak. During his term as acting magistrate of Taiwan county in 1722, Zhou used the rhetoric of primitivism to appeal to the governor-general in defense of the exploited indigenes: "The savage customs are simple and pure, remnants from remote antiquity. Ever since Chinese settlers mixed among them, the strong ones have cheated them."[44] Due to their simple natures, Zhou argued, the savages deserved special protection from Chinese encroachment and the exactions of Chinese tax collectors.

Thus, tropes of anachronism were so commonplace in Qing representations of the Taiwan indigenes that they even found their way into memorials and other policy communications. This is not surprising, since there were numerous linkages between travel writing and the Qing colonial administration. The authors of travel accounts were themselves frequently connected to the Qing colonial apparatus. Travel accounts were widely read by colonial officials and policymakers, and, as mentioned in the preceding chapter, they were a primary source for the Taiwan gazetteers. Through these gazetteers, the views of writers such as Chen Di, Lin Qianguang, and Yu Yonghe became familiar to colonial officials. Tropes that may have begun as literary allusions thereby became conventional elements of colonial discourse, part of the language of colonial policy debates.

Although such examples are numerous, overall, tropes of anachronism are not as commonplace in policy writings as they are in Qing travel accounts and gazetteers. Moreover, it is difficult to judge the degree to which policymakers were persuaded by this rhetoric, as opposed to economic and strategic arguments. More likely, the rhetoric of privation and primitivism simply provided writers the terms in which to couch their arguments. Nonetheless, as a counterbalance to Han Chinese chauvinism, the rhetoric of primitivism played a significant role in Qing colonial discourse, particularly as a vehicle for critiques of colonial exploitation.

An examination of tropes of anachronism in late imperial accounts of Taiwan suggests appreciable similarities between Chinese representations of non-Han indigenous peoples and Western anthropological constructions of the primitive through the denial of coevalness. Yet it also suggests differences between the two discourses. For example, Fabian asserts that "the history of our discipline [i.e., Western anthropology] reveals that such use of Time almost invariably is made for the purpose of distancing those who are observed from the Time of the observer."[45] In the Chinese case, however, the comparison of indigenous peoples to the ancients was also part of an inclusive discourse, used to make the case that they were worthy of membership in the Chinese empire. Moreover, whereas Western anthropological discourse, based as it is on the episteme of natural history, tends to privilege the notion of progress, late imperial Chinese travel writers were more inclined to privilege antiquity. Thus, the notion of history as degeneration from an idealized past figures more prominently in Chinese writings, and the denial of coevalness assumed a rather more ambiguous function than in Western anthropological discourse.

This chapter has demonstrated how, in late imperial accounts of Taiwan, the dual vision of history as both progress and degeneration led to the emergence of two opposing rhetorics—that of privation and that of primitivism. This ambiguity allowed writers to use the trope of the savages as ancients for a variety of ends: both to denigrate and to idealize the indigenes, and both to legitimate colonization and to critique colonial abuses. The seemingly oppositional rhetorics of privation and primitivism expressed not only the authors' conflicting attitudes of fear and admiration for the indigenous people of Taiwan but also ambivalence toward their own culture. The denigration of the savage is rooted in Chinese cultural chauvinism, and the idealization of the savage reveals a Chinese anxiety that material advancement might lead to moral degeneration. Travelers thus projected the virtues of antiquity onto the "primitives" of Taiwan in order to make self-reflective critiques of Chinese society. Because Qing writers used tropes of anachronism with such flexibility, we must attend to the context in which these tropes were deployed if we wish to determine their rhetorical effects.

The trope of the savages as the ancients would serve as the dominant trope in representations of the Taiwan indigenes into the late nineteenth century. In Chapter 5, I examine how the opposing rhetorics of privation and primitivism figured in the construction of the "raw" and "cooked" savages. The next chapter turns to the representation of Taiwan's landscape, also figured by many Qing travel writers as an anachronous space, a primeval landscape untouched by human hands.

CHAPTER 3

A Hidden Jade in a Ball of Mud

Landscape and Colonial Rhetoric

Since the Qing had not intended to acquire Taiwan permanently when it sent Shi Lang into battle, in annexing the island it became, in effect, an accidental colonizer rather than a colonizer by design.[1] The court continued to regard Taiwan with some ambivalence and did not embrace the idea of colonizing the island wholeheartedly. Even as official rhetoric celebrated the conquest of the island and the spread of civilization beyond the seas, the sentiment that Taiwan was nothing but a "ball of mud" lingered. Taiwan was "Wilderness," and Wilderness embodied all that was dreadful—poisonous miasmas, dangerous terrain that concealed hostile savages, and barren desolation that resisted cultivation.

The conviction that the burdens of governing Taiwan outweighed the benefits to be gained from colonizing it profoundly affected the court's formulation of Taiwan policy, as John Shepherd has shown.[2] Kangxi-era Taiwan policy was shaped mainly by the memory of the conflict with Ming loyalists; there was no desire to turn the island into an agricultural colony as the Dutch had done.[3] The foremost policy goal was to prevent Taiwan from reverting to a rebel base; the development of agriculture and trade was secondary. Hence, the court enacted a set of quarantine policies in 1684 that limited transportation and communication between the island and the mainland and restricted Han Chinese immigration to Taiwan.[4] The aim was to minimize conflict on the frontier by maintaining Taiwan's ethnic status quo and keeping vagrants and political rebels off the island. Rather than attempting to incorporate Taiwan wholesale into the empire, the court sought to cordon off the island and keep it somewhat isolated.

In fact, the Qing conquest of Taiwan was a partial conquest, for it brought only the western side of the island under Qing control. The Kangxi court had no interest in extending imperial control beyond the Central Mountain Range to the eastern side of the island, since the maintenance of the status quo was the order of the day. The court was, therefore, content to let this terrain remain beyond the pale and "off the map."[5]

Not all Qing literati agreed with the Kangxi court's quarantine policy. Some argued that the government should actively encourage the colonization of western Taiwan by Han Chinese settlers. Pro-colonization advocates differed from quarantine supporters in terms of their visions for Taiwan. Whereas those opposed to colonization were content to use Taiwan as a security "screen" for China's coastal provinces, proponents of colonization saw Taiwan as a potentially lucrative source of rice and sugar for the mainland market—material benefits that would offset the burden of transforming Taiwan into an agricultural colony.

With this debate in mind, Qing travel writers surveyed the frontier landscape. Looking at the land through "imperial eyes," they asked: Is Taiwan truly the barren and horrid wilderness of the Ming image, or is it the fertile paradise of promised bounty that Shi Lang claimed?[6] In their descriptions of the landscape, travel writers thus presupposed a project of transformation, one either doomed to fail or destined to turn Taiwan into a thriving agricultural colony. This chapter examines how representations of Taiwan's landscape evolved in the seventeenth and eighteenth centuries, as writers began to depict the open spaces of the frontier in terms not of desolation but of potential and opportunity.

An Impenetrable Wilderness

Kangxi-era travelers to Taiwan encountered a landscape dominated by mountains and dense jungle, with only small pockets of land on the western coastal plain reclaimed for agriculture. Following annexation, the Qing repatriation of rebel troops and civilians on the island caused Taiwan's Chinese population to drop from 100,000 to below 80,000. This depopulation had an adverse effect on agricultural production, and during the first decade of Qing rule sugar production remained below Dutch levels. Although the output of rice bounced back more rapidly, it, too, remained low. As part of the quarantine policies of 1684, the Qing banned rice exports from Taiwan in order to ensure the stability of the local rice supply. The frontier economy continued to be dominated by the deer trade, as it had been under the Dutch and the Zheng. Qing travel writers immediately seized on this point of difference between the island frontier and the agricultural economy of "China proper."

Early Kangxi representations of Taiwan's landscape largely confirmed the assumption that the island was not worth developing as an agricultural colony. The earliest accounts depict the scenery in terms of age-old images of frontier desolation. The first draft gazetteer of Taiwan, for example, represents Taiwan as an empty land:

The land is broad, but there are few people. The scene is utterly desolate. Outside of the puny prefectural city, it is all green grass and brown sand without end on the Northern and Southern Routes for as far as you can see. And so the countryside beyond the city walls is not called "countryside" but simply "grasslands."[7]

The distinction between "countryside" (*xiang*) and "grasslands" (*caodi*) is the distinction between land that has been put to productive use as farmland and uncultivated land in its wild state. Based on a deeply ingrained cultural assumption that agriculture was the foundation of civilization, Chinese literati took for granted that farmland was lovely and wasteland horrid. To "open" land and reclaim it for agriculture was to plant the seeds of civilization; "unopened" land signified the absence of civilizing influence. Travel writers perceived Taiwan's "unopened" deer grazing lands as a primitive, archaic environment that had never known the touch of civilizing hands.[8]

In the eyes of Qing literati, Taiwan's terrain fit neither the conventional model of the agrarian countryside nor that of the scenic landscape with picturesque mountains and waters.[9] One of Taiwan's first magistrates, Ji Qiguang, complained bitterly about the lack of scenic beauty on the island:

There are no wonders to show the traces of the gods and immortals. There are no scenic spots to be gazed on from towers and pavilions. Where there are mountains, they are obscured by overgrown weeds. Where there are waters, they are drowned out by crashing waves. It is a place where deer, boar, wildcats, and rats roam; where dragons, snakes, sea serpents, and vipers coil. This is nothing more than wilderness. If you are looking for natural landscape scenery, there is nothing at all.[10]

To Ji, the shaping hand of man was missing, leaving only nature in overabundance—vegetation obscured mountains, tumultuous waves disrupted tranquil waters, and wild animals roamed free. For Chinese literati, pristine land was equated not with purity and transcendent beauty but with chaos. In order for land to be good landscape, it had to be tamed and shaped. Early Qing travelers therefore saw little value in Taiwan's terrain, in terms of either productivity or aesthetics.

In addition to depicting frontier desolation, Qing travel writers wrote at length about the island's vigorous subtropical vegetation, in terms that highlighted the inhospitality of the topography. Descriptions of dense foliage, tangled vines, and thorny underbrush emphasized the impenetrability of the jungle. Many writers claimed that one could travel for days in the jungle without seeing the sky or sun. The jungle thus became a world of darkness and mystery, representing the dangers of the unknown and the unseen. Travelers described the island's vegetation as so uncontrolled that even the major roads were overrun with weeds. Yu Yonghe, for example, wrote this account of his arduous overland trek up Taiwan's western coast:

Looking out over the plain, there is nothing but weeds; the vigorous vegetation covers your head, and even the feeble vegetation comes up to your shoulders. When the cart passes through this growth, it is like being in the underworld. The tips of the grasses graze your face and cut your neck. The mosquitoes and flies suck your flesh like starving vultures and hungry tigers; it is impossible to shoo them away. The blazing sun beats down on you, and your neck and back are about to split open. You feel as if you have undergone the most extreme suffering and toil of the human world.[11]

For Yu, Taiwan's vegetation is more than impenetrable; it swallows the traveler whole. The environment is an overwhelming force inflicting all kinds of pain upon the traveler. Such representations fit the established image of Taiwan as a wild, uncivilized place. In particular, descriptions of Taiwan's plant life as tangled, thorny, gnarled, and growing in "horrid clumps" connoted chaos and disorder.

Despite the emphasis on Taiwan's flourishing vegetation, travel writers rarely represented this untamed growth as a measure of the land's productive potential. Rather, they expressed horror at the sight of such chaos. The uncontrolled growth of weeds, wild plants with no recognized value, was associated with waste and decay. Indeed, many writers were of the opinion that Taiwan's land was unsuited to agriculture.[12] Such reports of Taiwan's terrain corroborated the court's position that Taiwan was not worth developing as an agricultural colony.

The belief that Taiwan was unsuited for agriculture was driven in part by the assumption that land beyond the pale was endowed with inferior natural capacity. Environmental theories derived from classical texts suggested that immanent spatial energy (*qi*) was unevenly distributed among geographic regions. According to one school of thought, expressed by the Southern Song poet Chen Liang, only the Central Plain possessed the proper *qi* to support China's superior culture, whereas the energy of the hinterlands was "peripheral," and that of the distant lands "perverse and inferior."[13] Ming and Qing writers believed Taiwan to be heavily endowed with noxious *qi*. This *qi* was thought to produce miasmas, which emanated from the earth and water in the form of mists and caused deadly tropical diseases such as malaria. Qing travel writers constantly brooded over these dreaded miasmas and the generally noxious, or even lethal, character of the environment.[14]

In the minds of many Chinese travelers, such conditions—the impenetrable, tangled wilderness, the heat and the deadly miasmas—made Taiwan unfit for human habitation beyond the southwestern core carved out by generations of settlers. At several points in his journey over Taiwan's western coastal plain, Yu Yonghe characterized the terrain as "unfit for humans."[15] In describing his camp in the sulfur-mining region of Danshui, Yu provided a vivid depiction of a hostile terrain:

Going out of the hut, the weeds bury your shoulders, and the old trees are gnarled; it is indescribable. Horrid clumps of bamboo grow up in their midst. Within a foot of you not a thing can be seen. At night, cobras with their swollen necks make noises next to the pillows in every room. From time to time they snore like cows. They have the strength to swallow deer. Small snakes chase people and are as fast as flying arrows. At night, I don't dare go beyond the threshold of the house. The sea wind howls angrily; everything resounds. The forests and valleys shake and rock. The hut and bed are on the verge of collapsing. In the middle of the night the apes howl, sounding like ghosts crying. A single lamp flickers, and I sleep next to those who are on the verge of dying from malaria. What are Ziqing's remote frontier and Xinguo's marshes next to this?[16] Liu Zihou said: "Bozhou is not a place fit for humans to live." Let Zihou know of this place, and he would regard Bozhou as a paradise.[17]

With this dramatic gesture, Yu declared the Taiwan frontier to be even more dreadful than the historical Chinese frontiers in Inner Asia and on the southern borderlands. Every element of the environment, from the flora and fauna to the wind and sea, conspires to create a cacophonous atmosphere of terror.[18]

Remote areas of the frontier were also described as "no-man's-land" (*wuren zhi jing*). This phrase, literally "a land with no people" or an "uninhabited terrain," effectively erases the indigenous people from the landscape—a gesture repeated over and over in Qing representations of Taiwan. The trope of a no-man's-land is similar to the trope of "empty lands" described by Anne McClintock in *Imperial Leather: Race, Gender and Sexuality in the Colonial Contest*. As McClintock points out, the myth of "empty lands" effects a territorial appropriation "for if the land is virgin, colonized peoples cannot claim aboriginal territorial rights."[19] In Qing Taiwan, too, the idea that lands were uninhabited later paved the way for Han Chinese appropriation of indigenous lands.[20]

A Natural Bandits' Lair

Taiwan's impenetrable wilderness also provided cover for outlaws and headhunters. Indeed, Qing descriptions of the landscape reinforced the image of the island as a bandits' lair. Ji Qiguang, for example, depicted the environment as providing the perfect conditions for pirates and rebels to conceal themselves: "The rivers are deep and the forests dense. It is easy to hide away there."[21] Travel writers frequently wrote of outlaws and headhunters burrowing into the dense jungle as rats into a nest. The impenetrability of Taiwan's landscape was, therefore, associated with hidden dangers and lawlessness.

The Central Mountain Range, in particular, was perceived as a natural bandits' lair. With soaring peaks reaching as high as 13,200 feet and precipitous gorges, the Central Mountain Range formed an imposing presence on Taiwan's landscape. Descriptions of the Central Mountain Range as layered, deep, and impenetrable again played into fears that Taiwan's terrain served as a perfect hideaway. Early Qing writers frequently represented these mountains as a screen, with narrow passes and strategic defiles shielding rebels and bandits from the reach of Qing troops. These fears would later drive government policy concerning this terrain.

Since few Chinese dared to venture into the Central Mountain Range, Qing writers represented the "inner mountains," as this range was known, as a mysterious world unto itself.[22] Many early travelers figured this terrain as a primeval wilderness untouched since the beginning of time. Lin Qianguang, for example, wrote: "In the inner mountains there are large trees that date from the time of Creation."[23] To Yu Yonghe, the tangled state of the vegetation signified the primeval condition of the inner mountains: "The forest is so deep and the bamboo thickets so dense that you cannot see the sky. Brambles and vines are so tangled that you cannot lift a foot. Since the Chaos of Creation, no ax has ever entered here."[24] The trope of the inner mountains as an untouched, archaic landscape fostered the perception that Taiwan was, at its core, an utterly uncivilized, primitive place.

Fueling the notion that this land was pristine wilderness, Kangxi writers frequently used the phrase "human footsteps do not reach here" (*renji budao*) to describe the inner mountains. What they meant, of course, was that *Chinese* footsteps had not yet entered this terrain. Nonetheless, the use of this phrase promoted the conceit that this land was untouched ("virgin," to put it in Western terms) territory. Others called the inner mountains a no-man's-land.[25] Such figures of speech served at once to deny the presence of indigenous people on the landscape and to deny their full status as human beings.

Mapping Wilderness

Early Qing maps also represented Taiwan in terms of the visual iconography of wilderness. Perhaps the most widely circulated maps of the island were the woodblock prints contained in the local gazetteers. The primary function of these pictorial maps was to provide a qualitative understanding of the terrain to complement the quantitative descriptions contained in the text. Many of these maps depict Taiwan in terms of the visual equivalent of the trope of "empty lands." The map of Taiwan prefecture from the *Gazetteer of Taiwan Prefecture* of 1696, for example, depicts most of Taiwan's terrain as empty space.[26] The handful of landmarks that are depicted pictorially are Chinese and

Dutch. Although major rivers, ports, and indigenous villages along the coast are labeled, much of the land is represented as undifferentiated space.

The gazetteer's three county maps are even more starkly empty. In these maps, not a single feature of the natural landscape is labeled, and only the county seats and a few other landmarks are shown. The Fengshan county compound and the Zhuluo county compound (see Fig. 8), in particular, appear isolated on the empty landscape and dwarfed by towering mountains. Taiwan seems to be virtually uninhabited. Like travelers' descriptions of the terrain as uninhabited, the visual representation of "empty lands" served to erase the indigenous people from the landscape.

Of course, the emptiness of these early maps was partly a function of the lack of geographic knowledge about Taiwan during the Kangxi era. Yet the *Gazetteer of Taiwan Prefecture* maps seem almost to mark a step backward from the map in the *Gazetteer of Fujian Province* of 1684, on which nearly every mountain is labeled. Moreover, maps are not only records of geographic knowledge but also social constructions of space. And in this case, what gets left out—namely, the indigenous settlements on the island—is telling. In visual terms, the cartographic images of the *Gazetteer of Taiwan Prefecture* stand in sharp contradistinction to the images of mainland Fujian as depicted in the *Gazetteer of Fujian Province*. The empty space of the Taiwan prefectural map, for example, contrasts with the denseness of the Fujian province map (see Fig. 9), which is filled with landmarks. The close proximity of these landmarks, which represent prefectural and county seats, indicates the density of settlement in mainland Fujian. The individual prefectural maps in the *Gazetteer of Fujian Province* (see Fig. 10) are similarly characterized by denseness and by the prominence of government buildings. Indeed, the composition of these maps is dominated by architectural structures, with the landscape serving as a backdrop. Conversely, the Taiwan maps are dominated by landscape. The maps of the mainland prefectures are further characterized by their symmetry, an image of a civilized and well-ordered landscape.

In pointed contrast, early pictorial maps of Taiwan present images of a chaotic wilderness. A map from the *Gazetteer of Zhuluo County* (1717), for example, shows a landscape dominated by layered mountains, dense forests, and overgrown bamboo (see Fig. 11).[27] The

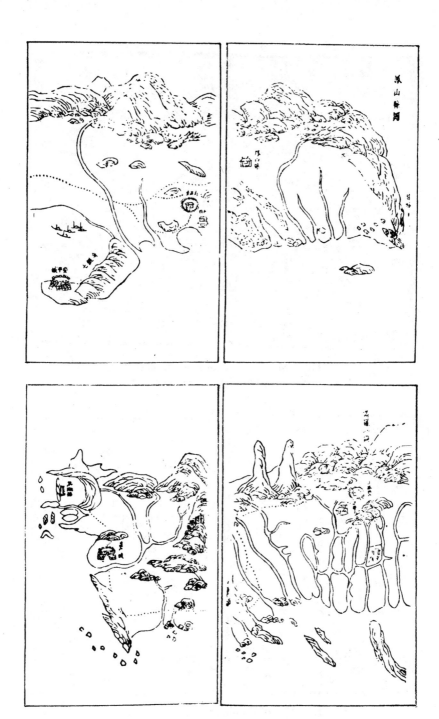

Fig. 8 Maps of (*top*) Fengshan county and (*bottom*) Zhuluo county
from the *Gazetteer of Taiwan Prefecture* (1696)

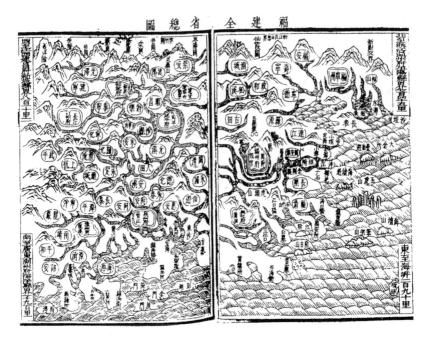

Fig. 9 Map of Fujian province from the
Gazetteer of Fujian Province (1684)

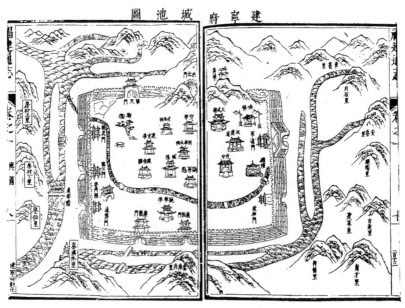

Fig. 10 Map of Jianning prefecture from the
Gazetteer of Fujian Province (1684)

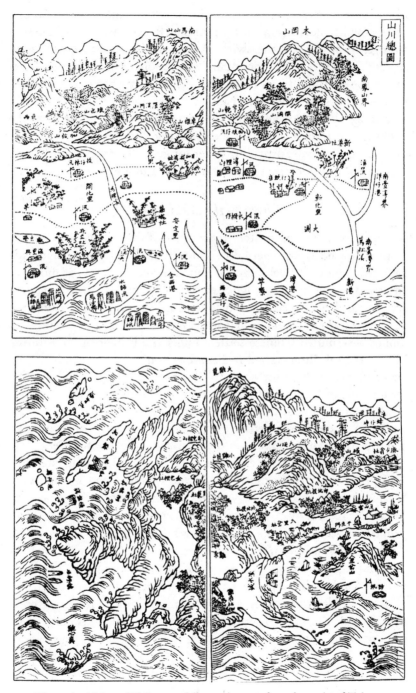

Fig. 11 (*top*) Map of Taiwan and (*bottom*) map of northern tip of Taiwan
from the *Gazetteer of Zhuluo County* (1717)

landscape becomes increasingly wild, less settled, and less open as one moves farther north (Fig. 11, bottom panel). An image of wildness is strongly projected by the swirling lines of the waves that meet up against the curves of the mountains and the sharp bends of the shoreline at the northern tip of the island. The density of swirling, crooked lines generates an image of chaos and wild energy.[28] Like travelers' descriptions of Taiwan's terrain, these pictorial images of the landscape as thickly forested and "strategically" (*xian*) layered (i.e., difficult to penetrate, providing cover for guerrilla troops) would have confirmed the notion that the island was a natural bandits' lair.

Clearing the Wilderness

Whereas early Kangxi writers represented Taiwan largely as an impenetrable wilderness, a very different picture of the island's landscape emerged from the travel essays of Lan Dingyuan, one of the most vociferous pro-colonization advocates of the Kangxi era. Lan Dingyuan accompanied his cousin, Commander Lan Tingzhen, on a campaign to suppress a local rebellion in Taiwan in 1721. Led by Zhu Yigui, who unified disgruntled Chinese settlers under the banner of "restore the Ming," the rebellion started in Fengshan county in the south of Taiwan and then spread northward to Zhuluo county. It was the first major uprising of Chinese settlers since the annexation of Taiwan, and it posed a serious threat to Qing rule on the island. The rebellion thus served to intensify the debate over the relative merits of quarantine and pro-colonization policies in the management of the frontier.

As Lan Tingzhen's secretary on the campaign, Lan Dingyuan had the opportunity to see much of Taiwan's terrain, and he afterward became known through his writings as something of an expert on Taiwan's geography.[29] Based on his experiences in Taiwan, Lan penned an account of the campaign against the rebels, *Record of the Pacification of Taiwan* (*Ping Tai ji*, 1723), and a collection of travel essays and other writings, *Record of an Eastern Campaign* (*Dongzheng ji*, 1721). Lan's policy opinions are often reflected in his landscape essays, where descriptions of scenery combine with musings on colonial affairs.[30] Lan's travel writing was thus colored by his colonial vision of transforming the island into an agricultural outpost of Chinese civilization.

Lan Dingyuan rejected the idea that Taiwan was unsuited for agricultural settlement because of its location beyond the seas, and he argued this point in a number of his writings. He proposed transforming Taiwan into a "bountiful paradise" by "opening the land and gathering subjects."[31] For Lan, Taiwan's wilderness embodied not desolation but productive potential.[32] Lan's travel writing is characterized by a tendency to project his vision beyond the landscape before him into the future; he saw Taiwan not simply as it was but as it might be. He imagined taming the wilderness by clearing the forest and burning the scrub, transforming wasteland into farmland.

In his travel essays, Lan Dingyuan presented a new picture of Taiwan's landscape; where earlier writers dwelt on the hostility of the terrain, Lan searched out the positive qualities of Taiwan's topography. Although he did note strategic aspects of the terrain—the dense vegetation that blocked roads, the deep mountains that served as a refuge for rebels—he counterbalanced these descriptions with praise for the lush greenery and the expansive plains. Indeed, he highlighted the broadness, flatness, and openness of the topography, qualities understood to be desirable in agricultural terms. Thus, where others wrote of tangled wilderness and poisonous miasmas, he wrote of open expanses and idyllic farm scenes; where others saw "abysmal mountains and parched earth," he saw "soaring mountains and fertile earth"; where others called Taiwan a "malarial land," he called the island a "bountiful paradise."[33]

A comparison of Yu Yonghe's description of the route from Zhuqian to Nankan and Lan Dingyuan's account of the same area, for example, yields sharp contrasts. Yu Yonghe found this place "not fit for humans"; Lan Dingyuan saw rich potential in the land.[34] Although he did observe that travelers considered this area a "dreaded route" because of occasional raids by headhunters, he also pointed out that the land was flat, open, and abundantly fertile. Surveying the landscape with a developer's gaze, Lan noted that the plains were crosscut with streams that could be used for irrigation if the land were converted into farmland. He imagined the nice profits to be made if the land were reclaimed: "It would be of great benefit to the subjects of northern Taiwan" (by which he meant the Han Chinese subjects).[35] Again, Lan projected his vision of the scene into the future.

Of all the sights he encountered on the frontier, idyllic farming scenes gave Lan the greatest pleasure. One such scene he found in the mountain villages of Shuishalian.[36]

Ahhh! To think that in the midst of the myriad mountains, there should be such a body of water. In the midst of these vast waters, there is this scenic spot. Floating fields are enough for the populace to be self-sufficient; [37] canoes come and go. . . . The man from Wuling rejoiced at entering Peach Blossom Spring; in the past I thought this might be a fable. But now that I have seen Shuishalian, I know that [Tao Qian] was truly not deceiving me.[38]

With these allusions to the famous Peach Blossom Spring—a mythical, primitive utopia described by the poet Tao Qian—Lan portrayed Shuishalian as the picture of pastoral tranquility; it is isolated from the world of public life, situated in a scenic landscape, and self-sufficient. Most important, it is a model of simple, agrarian society. Elsewhere, Lan figured Shuishalian as the fairy isle Penglai. He thus represented this spot in the inner mountains not as a dark world of goblins and half-human monsters but as a hidden utopia tucked away in the recesses of the frontier landscape.

Lan similarly praised Hebao island in Banxian, comparing its beauty to the celebrated West Lake in China and describing it as a kind of island paradise. He wrote:

All my life I have had an obsession with landscape. Every time I come across dense woods or ravines, strange peaks or weird rocks, clear streams or wide lakes, then I wander around and cannot bear to go back. . . . When I visited Hangzhou, I delighted in the West Lake. . . . [In Taiwan] the island-mountain Hebao is almost perfect. A village is built on the island-mountain, and water surrounds it on four sides. The fields are encircled by water, and skiffs moor in the shade of ancient trees; it is like being in the time before Fu Xi and Huang Di. Fishing and hunting, nothing is impossible. Why serve in the dusty world driven hastily by labors?[39]

Again, Lan constructed the landscape as a primitive utopia, comparing Hebao island to the world before the legendary sage kings Fu Xi and Huang Di, the golden age of carefree simplicity. Adopting the persona of a Daoist recluse, Lan described Hebao island as the perfect place to build a hut to retire from the dusty labors of public life.

Describing the beauty of these two scenic spots in fairly conventional literary terms, Lan domesticated the frontier landscape by transforming it into "countryside" (*xiang*): the setting of rural, agrarian life. Such selected sites served as models for his vision of taming Taiwan's landscape and converting wilderness into the "bountiful paradise" of farmland. Through his writings, Lan sought to convey that there were potential benefits to offset the burdens of colonizing Taiwan and to counter those who dismissed the island as a barren wilderness.

The landscape that Lan encountered was, of course, different from the terrain described decades earlier by travelers like Yu Yonghe and Ji Qiguang, who had complained of the lack of scenic spots. In the intervening years, Taiwan had undergone significant demographic and economic changes. By the beginning of the eighteenth century, Qing quarantine policies were being subverted by migrants from China's overpopulated southeastern coast who flocked to Taiwan in search of unopened land. These settlers came from four prefectures in China: Zhangzhou and Quanzhou in Fujian and Huizhou and Chaozhou in Guangdong (Canton). John Shepherd hypothesizes that by 1717 Taiwan's Han Chinese population exceeded 120,000.[40] By mid-century, the Han Chinese were the dominant ethnic group on the island. At the same time, the deer were becoming severely overhunted, and agriculture was beginning to replace deer hunting as the mainstay of the frontier economy.

As the growing Chinese settler population converted Taiwan's deer fields into farmland, they not only changed the face of the landscape but also brought pressure to bear on the Taiwan indigenes, who relied on deer hunting for their livelihood. Interethnic conflict caused by Han Chinese encroachment on indigenous lands soon became a major concern for the government. These demographic changes forced the Kangxi court to re-evaluate its policies. As John Shepherd writes: "Faced with an expanding and unruly frontier population, the government had to choose between two policies: withdrawing and containing the expanding settlement or tolerating its extension and fostering its control."[41]

Pro-colonization advocates and quarantine supporters differed in their assessments of the best means of asserting control over the frontier. Quarantine supporters sought to minimize the cost of frontier management by limiting the expansion of Han Chinese settlement. In contrast, pro-colonization advocates argued that the only way to ensure Qing control was to populate the frontier and encourage reclamation; with more land under cultivation, the agrarian tax base would expand and increase the revenues available to support the extension of the Qing civil and military presence on the island.

Those who sought to contain the Han Chinese population advocated the establishment of boundaries to keep settlers within the direct control of the existing administration. One proposal called for a boundary to be drawn at the Dajia River and for Han Chinese settlement to be restricted to the territory south of the river.[42] This boundary would protect indigenous lands from further Han Chinese encroachment and prevent unruly settlers from congregating beyond government control. Proponents of this approach argued that this was the most cost-effective way of avoiding interethnic conflict and maintaining order on the frontier.

Lan Dingyuan strongly opposed making these lands off-limits to Chinese settlers. In his opinion, the only way to assure stability on the frontier was to clear the wilderness and populate the empty lands; the quarantine approach simply left the frontier open to outlaws. Moreover, Lan implicitly believed that the land belonged to those who made the best use of it, which to him clearly meant those who would farm the land: to Lan, land that was not farmed was "wasted." Lan lamented the shame of such land in his "Record of the Zhuqian Plains":

It is fated to be opened [to settlers], a fact that human force cannot repress. What one ought to do, then, is to go along with this momentum and guide it for the better. How can the officials in charge be at ease with abandoning 100 *li* of rich and fertile land, a natural source of joy and profit on this earth, and letting it become a place that is a headache for the people, just because they do not want to be bothered with a troublesome task? If there are officials and defensive troops, then the people will go at land reclamation just as they are drawn to the towns and will set up thousands of homes. Without being recruited, they will come of their own accord; the threat from the savages will likewise disperse of its own accord without the need to drive them off.[43]

Lan again projected his colonial vision onto the landscape, constructing a pastoral scene of thousands of homes dotting the plains. He imagined Chinese villages replacing the indigenous presence on the land, which would disperse of its own accord. Lan cast this as an inevitable process, the destiny of the frontier, which human force cannot prevent. Lan's discourse is similar to the "rhetoric of appropriation" described by David Spurr in his *Rhetoric of Empire*:

It implicitly claims the territories surveyed as the colonizer's own; the colonizer speaks as an inheritor whose very vision is charged with racial ambition. Simultaneously, however, this proprietary vision covers itself. It effaces its own mark of appropriation by transforming it into the response to a putative appeal on the part of the colonized land and people. This appeal may take the form of chaos that calls for restoration of order, of absence that calls for affirming presence, of natural abundance that awaits the creative hand of technology. Colonial discourse thus transfers the locus of desire onto the colonized object itself.[44]

Indeed, in urging officials not to "abandon" (*qi*) the land, Lan transformed his appropriating desire into an appeal from the land for the affirming presence of Chinese farmers. The word *qi*, also meaning "to discard, reject, cast away, or neglect," carries strong negative connotations and implies a failure to fulfill a moral imperative. To abandon or neglect the land is to wrong it. Lan thus constructs frontier reclamation as a duty, shirked only by lazy officials who wish not to be bothered with a troublesome task. Lan's ideas about the development of the frontier bear some similarities to the European notion of the "white man's burden."

To make a space for his agrarian vision, Lan frequently represented Taiwan's plains as empty lands—denying the indigenous people's presence on the landscape even as he decried the threat they posed to settlers. As he wrote of Zhuqian, for example, "the land is broad and there are no people. Wild savages come and go." Elsewhere he justified the inevitability of land reclamation by arguing "where there is land, there cannot be no people."[45] Clearly, Lan Dingyuan did not quite regard Taiwan's indigenes as "people" (*ren*). Lan had little concern for the welfare of Taiwan's indigenous people, for he viewed them as lowly savages who were best driven off if the land were to live up to its full potential—an attitude I discuss further in subsequent chapters.

Like other pro-colonization advocates, Lan believed that the hostile nature of Taiwan's terrain could be easily transformed by the presence of Chinese settlers. He ardently opposed the suggestion that Taiwan's environment was ill-suited to Chinese people. As he wrote: "Previously Fengshan to the south and Zhuluo to the north were poisonous, miasmatic areas where county magistrates did not dare to go, yet now settlers are rushing [there] . . . like ducks taking to water"[46]—the image implied that Taiwan was a fitting, and even natural, environment for Chinese settlers.

Lan was not alone in arguing that the environment did not present an insurmountable obstacle to development. The *Gazetteer of Zhuluo County* of 1717, for example, contained an essay advocating frontier reclamation. Reminding readers that the once-miasmic lands of Fujian and Guangdong had long been settled and were now considered a "happy land," the author suggested that Taiwan would follow the same trajectory. He argued that the presence of settlers would naturally transform the environment: "When the *qi* of mountains and rivers is obstructed and pent up, it produces miasmas. If there are people there to organize and manage the landscape, then the *qi* will have an outlet, and what was once sealed will gradually open. This is a principle of natural law."[47]

As settlers cleared the frontier and built roads, he claimed, insects, snakes, and other horrid creatures would gradually be driven away, and noxious influences and pestilence would subside. Furthermore, sanitation and medicine would ameliorate the ill-effects of the environment. Wilderness can thus be shaped by human presence and transformed from something noxious into something productive. Through the image of harmful elements subsiding of their own accord, the author of this essay emphasized the ease of reclaiming the wilderness and rendered invisible the hard labor of clearing the frontier.

The author went on to compare the northern Taiwan frontier to a piece of jade contained within an uncut rock that goes unrecognized:

When jade is inside an uncut rock, travelers who pass it on the road will not even look twice at it. When they know that it is a jade, then everyone hopes to grab it. Today, the land between Banxian and Danshui is well irrigated and fertile. Its ports connect to any destination. Truly, it is a jade inside an uncut rock. If immigrants reclaim this land, and there is traffic back and forth between China, then everyone will know it is a jade.[48]

The metaphor of Taiwan as a hidden jade is a nice twist on the well-established image of the frontier wilderness as a ball of mud and suggests that its potential value could be realized only through human effort—by chiseling and cutting away at the wilderness so that the jade-green farmlands could emerge in their full brilliance and beauty.

This trope also belongs to the rhetoric of appropriation, for it casts the land as an undiscovered jewel waiting for someone to come along and recognize its value. The trope carries an implicit critique of the quarantine policy, which was grounded on the assumption that there was little value to be realized from colonizing Taiwan. The metaphor of the hidden jade was a fitting image for an island that would later be known as "Treasure Island" (*baodao*).

The theme of the virtuous gentleman recognizing value in an unappreciated piece of land was a well-established motif in Chinese travel literature, made most famous perhaps by the Tang dynasty essayist Liu Zongyuan. Lan Dingyuan would be praised by later travelers to Taiwan for his prescience in recognizing the potential of the Taiwan frontier: he was one who saw the jade in the ball of mud.

Lan Dingyuan's pro-colonization stance led him to disagree fiercely with the court's decision to tighten the quarantine restrictions in the wake of the Zhu Yigui rebellion. In 1722, Governor-General Manbao established an island-wide boundary running down the length of the island parallel to the Central Mountain Range. In order to prevent outlaws from taking refuge in the mountains, as they had during the rebellion, the boundary confined Chinese settlement to Taiwan's western coastal plains. As the governor-general decreed: "In the mountainous areas it is easy for villains to hide; thus we order that settlers living within ten *li* of the mountains be removed. From the north route to the south route, we must build a great wall and a deep trench as a permanent boundary; those who cross this boundary will be considered robbers and bandits."[49] The boundary was thus a response to the strategic difficulties presented by Taiwan's terrain. It also served to shelter indigenes living in the restricted terrain from further Han Chinese encroachment, an aspect of the boundary I discuss further in Chapter 4.

Toward a Pro-Colonization Policy

Lan Dingyuan's ideas found only a lukewarm reception during the Kangxi era, when the quarantine course held sway. But the Yongzheng emperor, who was more favorable to the active colonization of the frontiers, gave greater weight to Lan's policy suggestions and adopted a number of measures permitting the expansion of Han Chinese immigration and settlement on the island. To support this

expansion, the emperor extended the Qing civil and military admin-
istrations on the frontier. In 1723, a new county was established at
Zhanghua and a new subprefecture at Danshui (both measures that
Lan Dingyuan had advocated). The court also gradually liberalized the
rice-export policy in response to the increasing demand for Taiwanese
rice on China's overpopulated southeastern coast.

By the mid-eighteenth century, the new immigrants had opened
vast tracts of land for commercial rice and sugarcane production. Merchants exported Taiwanese rice and sugar to southern China, and
sugar to northern China, Japan, and Southeast Asia, earning huge
sums of Mexican silver dollars. Half a century of Chinese colonization
transformed Taiwan into one of the most important producers of rice
and sugar in Southeast Asia, a major shift from the deer-trade economy of the early Kangxi era. Han Chinese immigrants also assumed a
more important role in Taiwan's economy as commercial agricultural
production replaced the deerskin trade.

As Taiwan became a major supplier of rice to China's southeastern
coastal region, the island was no longer perceived solely as a breeding
ground for pestilence but also as a source of nourishment for the pov-
erty-stricken Chinese coast. Taiwan came to be regarded more and
more as a green farmland and well-ordered landscape and less as a wilderness where wild animals roamed free. As Lan Dingyuan's cousin
had predicted in the 1720s: "The wilderness of monsters, the remote
malarial land" was turning into "a civilized place of clothes and caps, a
rich and fertile paradise."[50] As China's coastal markets grew depen-
dent on Taiwanese rice and sugar, the island came to be better integrated with China proper. By the end of the century, Taiwan would
become known as the "Granary of China."

If eighteenth-century writers had debunked the naysayers' contention that Taiwan's land was not worth plowing, what of the native
people? Could the Qing make officials of them? Or were they indeed
naked and tattooed savages not worth defending?

CHAPTER 4

Debating Difference

Racial and Ethnical Discourses

When Censor Huang Shujing toured Taiwan after the Zhu Yigui rebellion, he was deeply impressed by the indigenous people. As he observed: "When I first arrived here, I saw [the natives] as bug-eyed
primitives, wild beings whose basic natures had not been refined by
Culture. But when I traveled through their territory and stayed in
their huts, I saw with my own eyes that in eating and in drinking, at
work and at rest, they are no different from the people of China."[1]
This firsthand experience inspired Huang to compile a comprehensive
account of the customs of the Taiwan indigenes and how they varied
from village to village, from south to north. He ordered Taiwan's
county magistrates to participate in the collection and classification of
ethnographic data and native songs and also combed the textual record
for information. The final product was a substantial work entitled *An
Investigation of Savage Customs in Six Categories (Fansu liukao)*, so
called because Huang chose six categories of investigation: housing,
eating and drinking, clothing and ornaments, marriage, mourning and
burial, and tools. Anything that did not fit into one of these categories
was placed under "miscellaneous."

Like other frontier officials, Huang Shujing understood the importance of reliable and precise information about the native people and
their customs. Just as knowledge of the terrain was essential for ruling
the colonized population, so was ethnographic knowledge. The need
for accurate and comprehensive ethnographic information became
particularly evident during the Zhu Yigui rebellion, when certain native villages sheltered the rebels, whereas others provided troops to

the Qing army. From the perspective of the eighteenth century, the earliest Qing ethnographic accounts were too brief, too sensationalist, and unreliable, often imparting little more than clichéd images of "savages." To answer the needs of local officials in Taiwan, Huang Shujing (a practitioner of evidential scholarship) aimed to produce an account that would be empirical, detailed, systematic, and comprehensive. Huang's *Investigation* was widely praised in his own time and is still considered the best Qing ethnography of the Taiwan indigenes.

But Huang Shujing was interested in more than just collecting ethnographic information about the Taiwan indigenes; he also sought to make a larger point with his *Investigation*. As he wrote in his preface:

This work will make known the everlasting glory of our dynasty, which shines over all under Heaven, extending even to people in this remote corner of the sea. Those in charge of protecting this place should tremblingly obey the imperial policies and instructions and wholeheartedly protect the welfare of the savages. They must not say that they are of a different race and therefore not aid them.[2]

Huang's preface touches on one of the most controversial issues regarding Taiwan for Qing literati: Were the Taiwan indigenes of a different race (*yilei*), or were they "no different from the people of China"? This question was not simply academic, for it touched on a larger matter—What was the place of the Taiwan indigenes within the Qing empire? Detractors of annexation had suggested that they had no place; that they were "naked and tattooed savages not worth defending" and that "we could not even make officials out of them." In contrast, Shi Lang made a case for their inclusion in the empire: "Since this land has entered the map," he argued, "the native savages and the subjects are alike all considered children."[3] Shi Lang thus appealed to the paternalistic ideology of the Qing emperorship, which claimed "all under Heaven" as children of the emperor and equally deserving of imperial protection.

The question whether the Taiwan indigenes could ever be considered full subjects (*min*) of the empire was a difficult one, and even after annexation Qing writers continued to exclude them from this category. In the Ming conception, the Chinese domain was defined not only by territorial boundaries but also by difference from the barbarians that surrounded it. Chinese science defined five cardinal directions: east, west, south, north, and center. China, the Middle Kingdom, lay at the center, and the barbarians lay in the four directions. Maps such as the "Unified Map of Chinese and Barbarians" represented the Chinese domain surrounded by barbarians in the four directions (see Fig. 4, p. 39). For the most part, the territorial and cultural boundaries of the Chinese domain were coterminous, since those who dwelt outside the physical borders of China, the land of ritual and righteousness (*liyi zhi bang*), were, by definition, barbarians.

With the Manchu conquest of China and the Qing expansion of the empire beyond its Ming borders, however, the boundaries between Chinese and barbarians were set into flux. And the distinctions between inner and outer no longer seemed so clear. Just as the annexation of land "beyond the seas" challenged the Ming territorial conception of the Chinese domain, so did the incorporation of "savages" into the empire challenge the conception of China as the realm of civilized people. Qing literati thus faced the task of defining a new relationship between Chinese and barbarian.

To Qing literati, there were obvious cultural differences between the Han Chinese and the Taiwan indigenes; the harder question was: Were these people *essentially* different from the Chinese? In addressing this question, literati considered the relative importance of a number of factors—physical characteristics, human nature (*xing*), and customs—in constituting the difference between Chinese and savage. They also considered the potential of Culture (i.e., Chinese civilization) to transform the indigenes into proper Chinese subjects. Qing literati expressed a wide range of opinions on these issues. There were those like Huang Shujing who saw an essential identity between Chinese and savage and, on the opposite end of the spectrum, those like Lan Dingyuan, who saw an essential alterity.

In this chapter, I argue that Qing discourse on the Taiwan indigenes falls into two broad categories: "racialist discourse" and "ethnical discourse." As I mentioned in the Introduction, I define racialist discourse roughly as discourse that focuses on physical differences and innate differences in human nature (*xing*). Racialist discourse further constructs difference as categorical and absolute, along the lines of the distinction between animals and humans. Ethnical discourse is, in very general terms, discourse that focuses on cultural differences and that constructs difference as a matter of degree while emphasizing certain human universals. This chapter examines the conflict between these two discourses in seventeenth- and eighteenth-century writings on the Taiwan indigenes. In the next chapter, I discuss the Qing subdivision of Taiwan's natives into "raw savages" and "cooked savages," a phenomenon that further complicated views of the indigenes.

The Formosans

Modern anthropologists consider the indigenous people of Taiwan, or Formosans, to be Malayo-Polynesian, or Austronesian, although their origins are a matter of debate.[4] When the Dutch arrived on the island in 1624, they found the Formosans living in independent villages that varied in size from a few thousand to less than a hundred. There was intermarriage and trade between these villages, as well as warfare and vendetta killings. Although villages entered into temporary alliances against common enemies in times of war, they were never united under a kingdom or other political entity.

Using ethnolinguistic criteria, anthropologists have classed these villages into broad groupings. Various proposals have been put forth concerning the precise number of these groups and their names, and disputes continue to arise among anthropologists, linguists, and activists concerning the criteria for groupings. Taiwan's Government Information Office officially lists eleven major groups in Taiwan: Ami, Atayal, Bunun, Kavalan, Paiwan, Rukai, Puyuma, Saisiyat, Tao, Tsou, and Thao. One thing is clear, however: these ethnolinguistic groups were neither social entities nor political units nor self-identified "ethnic groups" in Qing Taiwan. These groupings, or "tribes," are the constructions of modern anthropologists as well as the state.[5]

According to anthropologists, the Formosans lived mainly by the swidden cultivation of millet and rice and by hunting deer and wild boar. They also grew crops such as taro and yams or collected them from the wild. Before the arrival of the Dutch, they had no plow agriculture. Plentiful fish and game diminished the attractiveness of intensive agriculture, and farming was mainly women's work.[6] By the sixteenth century, the Formosans were trading actively with Chinese and Japanese seafarers. They supplied Chinese traders with deerskins, horns, and venison in exchange for salt, cloth, porcelain, rice, iron, and other goods. Formosan traders also dealt in rattans and medicinal herbs gathered in the forests, as well as sulfur, used by the Chinese in the manufacture of gunpowder.

Today, approximately 430,000 people are officially identified as "Taiwan's Indigenous Peoples."[7] "Indigenous rights" and land restoration have become vital, and often explosive, political issues. The question of the place of the indigenous peoples within the nation is still a difficult one: Are they simply one ethnic group among many in multiethnic Taiwan? Or are they the original and authentic Taiwanese, the rightful owners of the island?

Racialist Discourse

When the Qing conquered Taiwan, the Kangxi emperor noted that the local population was made up of "soldiers, as well as natives (*turen*), and Blacks (*heiren*). They are not of a single race (*zhonglei*). And none are civilized." The emperor's suggestion for dealing with this disparate population was straightforward: "Terrorize with force those who respond to force; embrace with benevolence those who respond to benevolence."[8]

Although the emperor seems to have had a fuzzy understanding of Taiwan's ethnic composition ("Blacks" is possibly a reference to the indigenes or to the Black slaves of the Dutch who lived on the island in the seventeenth century), he set a precedent for conceptualizing the island's diverse population as different *zhonglei*/races. This idea figured prominently in the earliest Qing writings on Taiwan, particularly the earliest local gazetteers. The section on customs in the *Gazetteer of Taiwan Prefecture* of 1696, for example, opens with this statement: "In the past, Taiwan was home to a breed (*zhong*) of forehead-carving, black-toothed, cropped-haired, tattooed [people]."[9] As such, these early sources employed what I am calling "racialist discourse."

I identify terms such as *zhong* (seed, class, breed, type), *lei* (category, kind, type, species), *zu* (lineage, tribe, stock), and *qun* (herd, flock, group) with racialist discourse, for Qing writers employed these terms to express categorical distinctions between groups of people such as the Han and the Taiwan indigenes.[10] Moreover, these terms possess nuances of meaning similar to various Western historical concepts of race—race as species, race as tribe or stock, and race as type.

Of course, these *particular concepts* did not exist in seventeenth- and eighteenth-century China, and I do not mean to suggest that they did. Nonetheless, the Chinese concepts embodied in the terms *zhong, lei, zu,* and *qun* do bear comparison with Western constructs of race.[11] These terms were often used in conjunction with other terms like *bie* (separate, other, distinguish, discriminate) or *yi* (strange, different, alien) to form compounds such as *yilei, yizhong,* or *biezhong,* all of which convey the idea that the other is categorically different.

PHYSICAL DIFFERENCE
AS A MARKER OF RACE

Physical appearance was one criterion for identifying people as *yilei*. When the *Gazetteer of Taiwan Prefecture* described the Taiwan indigenes as a separate breed, for example, it identified them as such by their strange and monstrous appearance, as a black-toothed and tattooed people. The notion of physical difference as a distinguishing characteristic of a population had precedents in older accounts of island natives. The Song dynasty *Historical Investigations of Public Affairs* (*Wenxian tongkao*) record of Pisheye (which Huang Shujing speculated was an early name for Taiwan) described the people thus: "Their language is incomprehensible. They are naked and their eyes are glaring, almost as if they were not of the human race (*fei renlei*)."[12] The *History of the Sui* (*Suishu*) account of Liuqiu, another island that Qing writers frequently identified with Taiwan, similarly emphasized the physical difference of the natives: "The people have deep eyes and long noses; they somewhat resemble [literally: are of the same category as] Tartars."[13] In both cases, the physical appearance of the island natives served to establish them as *yilei*: either as not of the human category or as belonging to the Tartar category. Both descriptions are examples of racialist discourse, for they emphasize physical difference as a defining characteristic of a people as well as categorical difference.

For Qing travel writers, physical appearance was a key index of the alterity of the Taiwan indigenes, although they did not distinguish what we might consider innate traits from acquired physical characteristics. Early Kangxi writers, in particular, found the appearance of the Taiwan indigenes to be strange and, at times, frightening. They were particularly struck by the natives' nakedness, their exotic adornments (like feathers and huge earrings), and their tattoos. Such visual differences in physical appearance marked a clear boundary between the savages and the Han Chinese, who wore the clothes, shoes, and hats of "civilized people." In the eyes of Qing literati, these differences in appearance were also indices of cultural inferiority.

Qing travelers regarded certain aspects of the indigenes' appearance as monstrous or even "inhuman."[14] Tattoos, for example, lent the savages a hideous and threatening mien. As Yu Yonghe wrote in his travelogue: "The savage cart drivers I saw were all covered with black tattoos. On their backs were the outstretched wings of birds. From their shoulders to their navels, they had net patterns cut in slanting strokes. On each shoulder there was the likeness of a human head, revolting and terrifying."[15]

Qing writers often noted the "round" and "deep" eyes of the indigenes. Just as nineteenth-century Western racial theorists often singled out the "slant" eye as the most distinctive feature of the "Mongoloid" race, so did many Qing writers fix on round eyes as the characteristic feature of the Taiwan "savages." Qing writers often described their eyes as "staring," which carried connotations of primitive ignorance, or as "glaring," which emphasized their ferocious appearance. Loose hair was associated with brutishness and even bestiality. Blackness, whether of skin or teeth, was associated with vileness and ugliness—as in the phrase "vile and black" (*louhei*). The *Gazetteer of Zhuluo County*, for example, bluntly characterized the natives of the county as "ugly and weird looking and . . . black."[16] Other authors expressed disgust at the sight of natives with scabby skin that showed the ravages of ringworm or revulsion at the "stink" of the natives. Overall, ugliness could be read as an index of moral inferiority because of the association between repugnance (*e*) and evilness.(*e*). I discuss the association between physical appearance and moral qualities further in Chapter 6.

Aside from appearance, early Qing texts also constructed the physical difference between Han Chinese and the Taiwan indigenes in terms of physical capacities. Travel writers and gazetteers alike claimed that the natives were able to run as fast as galloping horses, were impervious to weapons, and had tremendous endurance. Qing literati also claimed that indigenous women were able to return to physical labor immediately after childbirth.

Yet, overall, Qing texts paid less attention to matters of physical appearance and constitution than to cultural difference. Huang Shujing, for example, did not include physical appearance among his six categories of investigation. Among the Taiwan gazetteers, only the *Gazetteer of Zhuluo County* of 1717 devoted an entire subsection of its "savage customs" entry to "appearance" (*zhuangmao*). And although Qing writers did comment on the strange (or not so strange) appearance of the indigenes, they never developed a taxonomy of the savage physical "type." Where the savage body became most important was in ethnographic illustrations, a subject I discuss in Chapter 6.

HUMAN NATURE AS AN INDEX OF DIFFERENCE

More important for establishing the Taiwan indigenes as *yilei* was the claim that they possessed a distinct human nature (*xing*). The *Gazetteer of Taiwan Prefecture* of 1696 opened its "savage customs" section with the declaration "The native savages are different in nature from our people."[17] The statement established an immediate categorical difference between the people of China and the Taiwan indigenes.

The concept of an inborn nature, endowed by Heaven, was an important Chinese philosophical construct. The two most important classical statements on the subject were made by the philosophers Mencius and Xunzi. Mencius claimed that human nature is essentially good; Xunzi took the opposing position that human nature is essentially evil. From these basic claims the philosophers developed complex arguments concerning morality, education, and other related issues that would become central to Chinese intellectual history. For our purposes, suffice it to note that Mencius believed that humanity and morality are rooted in man's inborn nature: education serves to help man "preserve" and "nurture" his original nature, which is easily "lost" or "destroyed." In contrast, Xunzi argued that desires and hatred stem from man's inborn nature, which must therefore be curbed and reformed by education and ritual principles (*li*).

Both Mencius and Xunzi constructed their arguments about human nature as universal. Arguing that human nature distinguishes us from animals such as dogs and oxen (each of which has its own distinct nature), Mencius asserted that the universality of human nature is evident in the unity of tastes and moral sensibilities:

Men's mouths agree in having the same relishes; their ears agree in enjoying the same sounds; their eyes agree in recognizing the same beauty.

Shall their minds alone be without that which they similarly approve? What is it, then, of which they similarly approve? I say it is the principles of reason (*li*) and of righteousness (*yi*).[18]

Xunzi also identified certain human universals:

All men possess one and the same nature: when hungry, they desire food; when cold, they desire to be warm; when exhausted from toil, they desire rest; and they all desire benefit and hate harm. Such is the nature that men are born possessing.[19]

In discussing the nature of the savages, Qing writers alluded to both the Mencian and the Xunzian arguments concerning the universal aspects of human nature.

Yet other classic texts asserted that human nature differed from place to place. The *Book of Rites*, for example, states: "The people of the five regions—the middle states [China], the Rong, the Yi, and the other [people]—all have their various natures, which cannot be altered."[20] This passage established a precedent for regarding barbarians as different from the Chinese in their essential human natures; it also established a precedent for regarding human nature as immutable, fixed according to place of birth. Along similar lines, the *Chronicle of Zuo* declared that "if he is not of our kind (*zulei*), he is sure to have a different mind (*xin*)."[21] Like the passage from the *Book of Rites*, this statement supported the notion of incommensurate moral differences between Chinese and barbarians, and it became another locus classicus of racialist discourse.

The idea that Chinese and barbarians differed in their essential human natures was a central tenet of racialist discourse, tantamount to suggesting they were a different species: indeed, xenophobic Chinese writers often denigrated non-Chinese others by suggesting that they possessed the natures of dogs or goats. The notion that barbarians were endowed with distinct human natures implied that they possessed a different moral sensibility from the Chinese.

The issue of human nature was a focal point of Qing discourse on the Taiwan indigenes, as writers debated whether they shared a common human nature with the Chinese. The idea that the Taiwan indigenes possessed a distinct human nature had been proposed by numerous Chinese writers since Chen Di, who wrote: "By nature they are brave and like to fight."[22] Lin Qianguang, whose account of the Taiwan indigenes served as the basic source for the earliest gazetteers, similarly called the Taiwan indigenes a "stubborn and stupid people" who "by nature like to kill people."[23] These writers constructed the Taiwan savages as inherently belligerent and murderous. This view of savage nature suggested that the Taiwan indigenes would be naturally hostile to Qing rule and Chinese settlement of the island.

The local gazetteers were more explicit about the notion that the nature of the savage was fundamentally different from that of the Chinese. The *Gazetteer of Zhuluo County* of 1717 went so far as to assert that cultural differences between the Taiwan indigenes and the Han Chinese were the product of differences in inborn natures: "The [low and crude] customs of the savages accord with their natural dispositions (*xing*)." Therefore, the gazetteer argued, "You cannot say they are no different from the people of China."[24] The contention that the savages possessed a distinct human nature was fundamental to the construction of these people as *yilei*.

ENVIRONMENTAL DETERMINISM
AND HUMAN DIFFERENCE

The *Gazetteer of Zhuluo County* of 1717 emphasized yet another explanation for the fundamental alterity of the savage and the Chinese—environmental differences. This gazetteer opened its "savage customs" section by stating, "The livelihoods of the people are variously endowed by the forces of Yin and Yang," and then continued, "Across the sea on the furthest frontier, where the land is remote and the *qi* is obstructed and perverse, is it not fitting that the customs are low and crude?"[25] The association between crude customs and obstructed or perverse *qi* draws on a tradition of environmental determinism that dates to Chinese antiquity.

In various theories of environmental determinism, the earthly ethers, or *qi*, were held responsible for everything from local customs and behavior to the physical constitution and human nature of the people. As the *Book of Rites* stated, "The bodily capacities of the people are sure to be according to the sky and earthly influences."[26] The commentator Zheng Xuan (127–200) glossed this passage as meaning that the local *diqi* (earthly ethers) determined differences in the natural constitution of barbarians.[27] Since earthly ethers varied from place to place—superior in some places, inferior in others—each place would naturally have its own type of people and its own customs. The earthly ethers of China, especially the Central Plain, were considered superior and had given rise to Chinese civilization. Thus, the *Gazetteer of Zhuluo County* suggests that crude customs are fitting for the remote and isolated land of Taiwan, with its inferior earthly ethers. There is also a correspondence in Qing writings between descriptions of Taiwan's *qi* as obstructed and perverse (*wan*) and characterizations of the natives as stubborn and stupid (*wan*).

Theories of environmental determinism received perhaps their clearest articulation from the Qing philosopher Wang Fuzhi (1619–92), an infamous anti-Manchu critic. Basing his arguments on the idea that *qi* is the fundamental creative force of the universe, Wang theorized that geographic location ultimately determined the fundamental difference between Chinese and barbarians. The central region, or "divine region" (*shenqu*), was the territory of the Chinese people. In contrast, "north of the deserts, west of the Yellow River, south of Annam, east of the sea, the ether is different, and people have a different essence, nature produces different things."[28] Wang also theorized that those born in different places, with their different atmospheres, would, as a result, naturally follow different customs. For all these reasons, Wang argued that a strict categorical (*lei*) distinction must be drawn between Chinese and barbarian. As James Millward has demonstrated, despite the fact that Wang's writings were suppressed until the late Qing because of their anti-Manchu content, many of his central tenets—including the idea of a strict categorical distinction between Chinese and non-Chinese and the idea that environmental factors determined the difference between the Chinese and those outside of China proper—were familiar to Qing literati, since they were reworkings of traditional ideas.[29]

Among the Qing literati who traveled to Taiwan were many who espoused such ideas of environmental determinism and asserted a direct connection between the habitat of the Taiwan indigenes and their natural dispositions or behavior. In particular, many attributed the "lascivious" behavior of the local populace to the hot and humid subtropical climate. There were also those who believed that different customs were suited to different places, a belief that led them to adopt a position of cultural relativism. Yet, many also believed that changes in the landscape could transform the local earthly ethers, changing both the weather and the character of the native populace. Therefore, ideas about environmental determinism were not necessarily associated only with racialist discourse. I explore these ideas further in the next chapter.

Ethnical Discourse

Even though the earliest Taiwan gazetteers asserted that the Taiwan indigenes were "different in nature" from the Chinese, not all Kangxi literati agreed with this position. Among the more vociferous dissenters was Yu Yonghe, who rejected out of hand the notion that the Taiwan indigenes were essentially different from the Chinese in either body or inborn nature:

People discriminate against (*qishi*) them on the grounds that they are of a different race (*yilei*). They see them without clothing and say, "They do not know cold." They see them walking in the rain and sleeping under the dew and say, "They do not get sick." They see them running for long distances with heavy loads and say, "They really have endurance." Ai! Are they not also human?! Look at their limbs, their torsos, their skin and bones; in what way are they not human, so that you say these things? You cannot gallop a horse all night; you cannot harness an ox crookedly; otherwise, these creatures will get sick. If oxen and horses are this way, how much the more so for people? . . . Enjoying fullness and warmth, suffering from hunger and cold, hating labor and delighting in idleness and pleasure, this is human nature. You may consider these people different, but what need is there to consider their nature different? The benevolent gentleman will know not to reject my words.[30]

Drawing on Xunzi's arguments concerning the universal aspects of human nature, Yu Yonghe asserted that the savages and the Chinese share a common human nature: both desire fullness, warmth, and rest. On this ground, he exhorted others not to consider the savages different in their inborn natures. Yu also argued that the humanity of the savages is evident in their bodies, which are fundamentally human in "limbs, torsos, skin, and bones." Earlier in his account, Yu had remarked that the indigenes who frequented the Chinese markets "are not very strange in appearance. Only their two eyes are round and deep and staring. This sets them apart slightly."[31] For Yu, these limited differences, while distinguishing the savages from the Han Chinese, were less significant than the essential flesh-and-bone similarities of all humans. Emphasizing these basic commonalities of body and human nature, Yu rejected the notion that the savages are *yilei*.

Huang Shujing similarly appealed to the notion of a universal human nature in making his case that the indigenes were "no different from the people of China."[32] As he wrote in his travelogue: "I asked [the natives] why they were barefooted. They said: 'It is not that we enjoy it; it is just that we do not have shoes.' From this we can see that human nature is the same everywhere."[33] Like Yu Yonghe, Huang alluded to the Xunzian argument for certain basic human desires—for comfort, for warmth, and for freedom from pain—to make a case for a universal human nature.[34]

Huang further asserted that the respectful and friendly demeanor of the natives he encountered on his tour of inspection was evidence that "their natural human nature has not been diluted. How could it be that they are different in their Heaven-conferred nature?"[35] Here Huang adopted a basically Mencian view of human nature: that is, the "undiluted" character of human nature is fundamentally good, containing within it the roots of courtesy, modesty, and morality. To argue that the indigenes and the Chinese shared a common human nature was therefore to argue that both groups were endowed with the same moral capacity.

On these grounds, both Yu and Huang argued for the fundamental educability of the indigenes. Yu Yonghe asserted that education in the Confucian classics and training in ritual etiquette could transform the indigenes into proper subjects of the empire. He argued, "At the longest, it would take one hundred years, and at the fastest, thirty years, to see their customs change and see them comply with the rites and teachings. How would they be any different from the people of China?"[36] Again, Yu insisted that there is no essential difference between the savages and the Chinese. To bolster his case for the ease of assimilating the indigenes, Yu pointed out that the same process had taken place on other southern frontiers of China in the past, places now regarded as centers of Chinese civilization and learning.[37] Yu was thus confident that the savages would one day be full subjects of the empire.

Huang Shujing similarly argued that Confucian education could transform the wild savages into civilized human beings. In contrast to writers like Lin Qianguang and Lan Dingyuan who dismissed the Taiwan indigenes as a "stupid and stubborn" people, Huang noted that local teachers considered native children intelligent and suggested that it was only the heavy corvée burden that hindered their progress in learning the classics. Huang therefore urged local officials to rectify their governance and improve efforts in education so that one day Chinese and barbarians would be unified.[38]

The writings of Yu Yonghe and Huang Shujing exemplify "ethnical discourse." Denying any categorical difference between Chinese and savage, both writers emphasized certain human universals, particularly the idea of a common human nature. They furthermore de-emphasized the import of physical differences between Chinese and savage. For both Yu and Huang, the primary difference between the Chinese and the savage was cultural, a product of nurture and not nature.

Human Difference and Imperial Ideology

Although there is nothing inherently prejudicial in the assertion that a group of people are *yilei*, in Qing discourse on Taiwan the concept of *yilei* was generally associated with denigration, much as the English verb "to discriminate" connotes negative racial discrimination. The very concept of *lei* (classes or categories) implies incommensurate differences, fundamental incompatibility between things. *Lei* denotes the essential distinction between man and animals, birds and beasts, or humans and the supernatural. Indeed, by association with other denigrating phrases such as *fei renlei* (not of the human race) or *chulei* (belonging to the order of beasts), the term *yilei* possesses connotations that are analogous to the Western construct of race as species. In short, to label the other *yilei* can be to imply that the other is less human than beast-like.

The idea of categorizing peoples as *yilei* was at odds with Qing imperial ideology, which sought to downplay the strict distinction between Chinese and barbarians (*Huayi zhi fen*)—a distinction that formed the philosophical basis for anti-Manchu sentiment and opposition to Qing emperorship as barbarian rule. As Pamela Kyle Crossley has demonstrated, to refute this opposition, the Kangxi and Yongzheng emperors embraced the "transformationalist" ideals set forth in classic Confucian texts as their official creed. According to the Confucian concept of moral transformation, exposure to Civilization and the moral authority of the ruler would bring about the progressive moral improvement of all human beings, as they learned moral principles and changed their behavior in accordance. Crossley argues:

"The Kangxi and Yongzheng emperors, aware that there were literati who argued that the Qing rulers were irremediably barbaric and their rule incorrigibly illegitimate, were inclined to rely upon this tenet to maintain that they, too—both the Aisin Gioro imperial lineage and the Manchus—had been morally transformed, and their rule was just and benevolent."[39]

As mentioned in Chapter 2, the ideal of transformationalism was central to Chinese culturalism, a universalist ideology. To insist on an essential distinction between Chinese and barbarian was to go against the "fundamental Confucian ideal of cultural transformation of populations and moral transformation of individuals."[40] Indeed, as the Yongzheng emperor would contend in an edict of 1730, the fundamental categorical distinction in natural law was not between Chinese and barbarian but between people and animals.

As both Yu Yonghe and Huang Shujing recognized, racialist discourse was incongruous with the Confucian ideal of transformationalism, for the claim that barbarians possessed distinct inborn natures, or fixed moral characters, suggested that they were unassimilable.[41] Several leading anti-Manchu thinkers of the Ming-Qing transition espoused the notion of an essential difference between Chinese and barbarian based on human nature. The ardent Ming loyalist Gu Yanwu (1613–82), for example, advocated that barbarians and Chinese be separated into distinct spheres, where each could live in accordance with their inborn character.[42]

Ethnical discourse, in contrast, was far more compatible with Qing imperial ideology. The insistence on the essential humanity of the savages, in both body and nature, was in keeping with the emphasis on the human/animal distinction over the Chinese/barbarian distinction. The notion of a universal human nature, moreover, supported the ideal of the cultural transformation of populations: if the savages were no different in their human natures, then it stood to reason that they, too, were educable—a point that both Yu and Huang argued. Indeed, as discussed in Chapter 2, Qing policy was based on the assumption of the fundamental educability of the Taiwan indigenes and guided by the ideology of transformationalism.

In addition to the ideal of transformationalism, the ideal of imperial paternalism was fundamental to Qing ideology. This ideal was encapsulated in the image of the benevolent emperor who took all under Heaven as his children—a ubiquitous image in Qing writings on Taiwan from Shi Lang's annexation memorial to the local gazetteers and Huang Shujing's *Investigation*. Racialist discourse did not necessarily preclude the use of the inclusive paternalistic rhetoric of Qing imperialism. The *Gazetteer of Zhuluo County*, for example, stated: "Even though the [people of the empire] are different races (*zhonglei*), in the eyes of the emperor all are given consideration."[43] In this formulation, the Qing emperor is a unifying center and casts his benevolent gaze over the various and different races of the empire.

The 1720s saw a gradual discursive shift in the Taiwan gazetteers. Whereas the claim that "the native savages differ in nature from our people" headed the discussion of savage customs in the first two editions of the *Gazetteer of Taiwan Prefecture* (1696, 1712), by the publication of the first *Gazetteer of Fengshan County* (1720), the wording had been changed to read "The *customs* of the native savages are *not the same* as those of the Han Chinese" (italics added).[44] The subtle change in wording ("nature" versus "customs," and "different" versus "not the same as") marks a shift away from racialist discourse toward ethnical discourse. The *Gazetteer of Taiwan Prefecture* of 1742 eliminated the original phrase entirely and opened instead with a passage from Chen Di's *Record*. In turn, the *Gazetteer of Taiwan Prefecture* of 1747 gave voice to the debate on human nature by presenting quotes from both sides of the issue. Although the gazetteers gradually moved away from stating absolutely that the savages were different in nature from the Chinese, the debate on inborn nature remained open among Qing literati into the late nineteenth century.

Views of the Indigenes and Policy

As is evident from this brief survey, Qing literati held different opinions of the Taiwan indigenes. These different views informed their positions on various aspects of Qing Taiwan policy, particularly education, corvée, and land rights.

Both Yu Yonghe and Huang Shujing were highly critical of Han Chinese exploitation of the indigenes. Indeed, Yu penned his defense of the fundamental humanity of the indigenes in order to censure those who "discriminated" against (literally, considered differently) them—Chinese monopoly traders, interpreters, and, most of all, the "village bullies," who had been on Taiwan since the Koxinga era. Yu criticized "this lot" for taking advantage of the "naïveté" of the indigenes for personal gain by exacting labor, property, excessive taxes, and sexual favors from them. To Yu, it was the notion that the indigenes were *yilei* that led these people to treat them as beasts of burden rather than as human beings, behavior unbefitting the "benevolent gentleman."

Huang Shujing similarly criticized Han Chinese abuses of the indigenes, especially the burden caused by excessive corvée demands, and he often expressed sympathy for their plight. One practice he particularly objected to was the endless requisition of oxcarts and native porters, a practice that petty officials and soldiers often abused. On his tours of inspection, Huang made a point of paying his native sedan bearers with money and tobacco and for his accommodations in tribal lodges with tobacco and cloth.

Both Yu and Huang belonged to a school of thought that saw Han Chinese settlers as the source of frontier conflict. Their critiques demonstrate the complexity of ethnic interaction in Qing Taiwan, which was not a simple matter of colonizers versus colonized. Given the island's history as a stronghold of Ming loyalists, the Qing state did not trust the Han Chinese settlers to be loyal to the regime. Instead, the Qing pursued a divide-and-conquer strategy, mobilizing the indigenes to aid in the suppression of Han rebellions on the island and Chinese troops to suppress native rebellions. Governmental tours of inspection of the island were always conducted by a pair of supervising censors, one Manchu and one Han Chinese. As John Shepherd has shown, Qing statecraft on the Taiwan frontier was a matter of balancing the various interests of the Qing state, the Han settlers, and the indigenous peoples.[45] In this equation, it was the interests of the state that came first.

Given these conditions, Chinese officials did not always favor the interests of Han Chinese settlers over those of the indigenous people. Those who supported the quarantine policies were often apt to perceive unruly Han Chinese settlers as the source of problems on the frontier. Hence Qing literati often championed the interests of the indigenous people, particularly when it came to preserving their livelihoods, a fundamental issue of the Mencian statecraft practiced by the Qing state.

This concern for the preservation of livelihoods led Huang Shujing to support the drawing of the so-called savage boundary (*fanjie*) in 1722. As mentioned in the preceding chapter, this boundary was drawn in the wake of the Zhu Yigui rebellion, primarily in order to maintain tighter control over the expanding and unruly Han Chinese settler population. Reclamation of land and harvesting of timber and rattan beyond the boundary were forbidden to settlers, and those who crossed the boundary were to be penalized. As such, the boundary had a secondary function of protecting tribal lands within the cordon from Han Chinese encroachment, thereby preventing the escalation of interethnic conflict. In 1750 and again in 1760, the Qing redrew the boundary line, to define the boundary in places where it had not been clearly articulated (especially in northern Taiwan) and to accommodate ever-expanding Han Chinese settlement (see Color Plate 4).

Huang Shujing perceived the protective function to be an important justification for the boundary, for he blamed frontier unrest on greedy Han Chinese settlers who incited skirmishes by encroaching on the indigenes' land, stealing their game, and entering the mountains to cut rattan and timber. He therefore spoke of the boundary as a means of restricting illicit encroachment by Han Chinese. As interethnic conflict increased in the mid-eighteenth century because of the expansion of the Han Chinese population, the protective function of the boundary assumed pre-eminence. The boundary also had a third function: to prevent hostile tribes from coming out of the mountains and attacking Han settlers. The boundary thus worked two ways—to keep settlers out and to keep the indigenes in.

In sharp contrast to Huang Shujing, Lan Dingyuan fiercely opposed the boundary policy, as mentioned in the preceding chapter. To a pro-colonization advocate like Lan, the interests of Han Chinese settlers were paramount, and he viewed the boundary as an impediment to the development of Taiwan as an agricultural colony. Lan rejected Huang's argument that interethnic conflict was caused by Han Chinese encroachment on tribal territory. In Lan's eyes, it was the savages who were the root of frontier unrest, for it was in their "wild natures" to kill and take heads. Whereas Huang argued that the indigenes needed protection from rapacious Han Chinese, Lan argued that the Han Chinese needed protection from ferocious, bloodthirsty savages. But the boundary was not an effective means of achieving this goal: "You may keep the settlers out, but you will never be able to keep the savages in."[46]

Lan conveyed some of these sentiments in a poem he composed for Huang Shujing. In this poem, Lan wrote of the ignorant and fierce character of the savages and the need to tame them in order to make them "forget their savagery." He lamented the loss of arable lands for Chinese settlers and spoke of the boundary as a "retreat and avoidance." He concluded that the establishment of the boundary would "cause irreparable harm."[47]

Lan Dingyuan's views on the Taiwan indigenes were connected to his views on the land; he regarded the Taiwan indigenes primarily as an obstacle to land reclamation. In both his travel writings and his policy statements, Lan represented the Taiwan indigenes in derogatory terms. In contrast to Huang Shujing, he considered the indigenes to be fundamentally different, indeed inferior, to the Chinese. The "native savages" were "stubborn and stupid," "ignorant and foolish," and even "repugnant." At times he also likened them to animals.

Indeed, Lan Dingyuan regarded the Taiwan indigenes as natural beasts of burden. He objected to efforts to relieve the indigenes of excessive corvée: "This will make the native savages gradually dissatisfied with their lot and unwilling to render their services. They will try to compare themselves with the Han Chinese in everything and hope to do as they do in China. This will bring about unspeakable damage."[48] In Lan Dingyuan's mind, the savages were inferior in status to the Han Chinese, and it was important to preserve this distinction. In contrast to Huang Shujing, the savages deserved differential treatment for Lan Dingyuan precisely because of their fundamental alterity.

Lan saw the Taiwan indigenes not only as essentially different from the Chinese but also as fundamentally in opposition to them. The theme of a "savage threat" is ubiquitous in Lan's writings, and he harped on their belligerence, ferocity, and propensity for rebellion. In his travel essays, the savages were constantly a dangerous yet unseen presence, lurking at the edges of the landscapes that he painted in such glowing colors. The open plains and secluded mountain spots Lan described are alluring, but the looming threat of headhunters makes travelers wary and settlers nervous and spoils the beauty of the scenic landscape.[49] One of his chief complaints about traveling in Taiwan is that the savages mar his "bountiful paradise."

Although he sometimes attempted to disguise this sentiment, Lan essentially saw no room for the Taiwan indigenes in his vision of Taiwan as a Chinese countryside; hence, he sought either to eradicate them or to make them disappear through assimilation. Lan was unusual among Taiwan travel writers in that he did not include an ethnographic account among his writings. In contrast to Yu Yonghe, Huang Shujing, and other travelers who took an avid interest in recording the "strange customs" of the Taiwan indigenes, Lan displayed little interest in ethnography, although he did have much to say about the Taiwan indigenes from a policy perspective and he took care to record the types of weapons they used and their methods of warfare.

Just as Lan thought that the only way to deal with frontier land was to settle it and transform wilderness into farmland, so he thought that the only way to deal with the indigenes was to aggressively assimilate them, transforming them into Chinese subjects and making them "forget to be savages." Aside from "civilizing" the indigenes, Lan also frequently spoke of "taming" them, implying that they were like animals that needed to be whipped into submission. He also advocated more drastic measures. Whereas Huang Shujing sought to deal with interethnic violence by separating the two groups physically, Lan coolly suggested, "counter killing with killing."[50]

Boundaries and Ethnic Groups

Although the 1722 boundary was established for purposes of frontier management rather than as an ideological act, the boundary served to reify the distinction between Han Chinese and savage. Indeed, alternative names for the boundary were the "subject-savage boundary," and the "Han-savage boundary," both of which conveyed the symbolic function of the boundary as a divider between the two constituencies. It is thus somewhat ironic that Huang Shujing, who objected to drawing categorical distinctions between Han and indigene, staunchly supported the establishment of a boundary that literally drew a line separating the two. Since crossing the boundary was prohibited by law, the "subject-savage boundary" had the effect of marking a legal distinction between the two groups and restricting physical movement and residency on the basis of ethnicity. The institution of the boundary thus played a significant role in the construction of ethnicity on the Taiwan frontier.[51]

The articulation of ethnic distinctions through physical boundaries was not unique to the Taiwan frontier; rather, it was a long-established Chinese practice—as John Shepherd has pointed out. The Great Wall is the most famous example, but there were numerous Qing examples as well. In Manchu territory, the Qing built the Willow Palisade, a dense barrier of trees paralleled by a trench, to prevent Han Chinese settlers from entering Manchu tribal lands.[52] Both the Willow Palisade and the Taiwan Savage Boundary demonstrate the intimate connection between ethnicity and land rights on the Qing frontiers, with ethnic identity rooted in territorial claims.

The division between Han Chinese and savage was illustrated on many eighteenth-century maps of Taiwan. One of the most famous is the Qianlong-era *Map of the "Subject-Savage Boundary"* (*Minfan jietu*, 1760, Color Plate 5), which depicts both the original boundary line (drawn in red) and the revised boundary of 1750 (drawn in blue).[53] Land beyond the boundary is marked "restricted land," or "restricted land, wastelands." Visually, these lines demarcate savage territory from Chinese territory and serve as a symbolic boundary between the two ethnic groups of Han Chinese and savage, between civilization and the realm beyond the pale. The depiction of two lines, in red and blue, shows that these boundaries were shifting and not absolute.

Indeed, while Qing literati argued over the theoretical question of whether the Han Chinese and the savages were separate "breeds," in practice, the distinction between Chinese and savage was formulated as less of a clear line than a continuum. This notion of a continuum between Chinese and savage was articulated through the concept of "raw and cooked" savages, the subject of the next chapter.

CHAPTER 5

The Raw and the Cooked

Classifying Taiwan's
Land and Natives

In objecting to the "Savage Boundary," Lan Dingyuan declared: "If we could open their lands and gather our subjects there, then the [savage] threat would subside of its own accord. In time, the raw savages would be transformed into cooked savages. And in more time, it would become a district of registered, taxpaying households."[1] Like other writers of his time, Lan Dingyuan divided the Taiwan indigenes into two categories: "raw savages" (*shengfan*) and "cooked savages" (*shufan*). The Qing practice of classifying the Taiwan indigenes into two distinct groups would have lasting influence on the ethnological classification of the Formosans. The Japanese colonists of Taiwan (1895–1945) initially adopted the Chinese categories of "raw savages" and "cooked savages" and later replaced them with the terms "high mountain tribes" and "plains tribes." The Chinese Nationalist (KMT) government, which took possession of Taiwan following Japan's defeat in World War II, in turn divided the island natives into "mountain brethren" (*shandi tongbao*) and "plains tribes" (*pingpuzu*). Today, Taiwan's indigenous people are categorized as "mountain aborigines" (*gaoshanzu*) and "plains aborigines" (*pingpuzu*).

The modern construction of "mountain aborigines" and "plains aborigines" as distinct ethnic groups thus has its roots in the Qing construction of the "raw" and "cooked" savages. Many in Taiwan today take for granted that the ancestors of the mountain aborigines were the Qing dynasty's "raw" aborigines, and the ancestors of the plains aborigines were the "cooked" aborigines. Yet, as Qing references to "raw savages of the plains" make clear, the territorialization of the "raw savages" in the mountains (and the concomitant territorialization of the "cooked savages" on the plains) was a gradual, historical process. Moreover, the Qing understood the distinction between the raw and the cooked as a fluid and shifting boundary, one without the primordial associations of ethnic boundaries. Groups that were raw in one historical period might become cooked at a later date. Indeed, as is evident from Lan Dingyuan's statement, Qing literati regarded the transformation of the raw into the cooked as a desirable phenomenon. For the Qing, "raw" and "cooked" were not ethnic designations in the manner that "mountain aborigines" and "plains aborigines" are today.

Indeed, the terms "raw" and "cooked" were applied not only to the indigenous peoples but also to the land. This overlap demonstrates the intimate connection between frontier land and native peoples in Qing colonial discourse. This chapter analyzes how the concepts of raw and cooked were constructed in Qing representations of the Taiwan frontier. The first part examines the various ways Qing writers constructed the "raw savage" and the "cooked savage." I argue that Qing concepts of the raw and the cooked captured the complex intersection of ideas about acculturation, political submission, and habitat. I further examine how representations of Taiwan's landscape informed Qing constructions of ethnic difference and how the association between the raw and mountain terrain, on one hand, and the cooked and plains land, on the other hand, developed, leading to the eventual conflation of raw/mountain and cooked/plains. The second part examines cartographic representations of the division of Taiwan into raw terrain and cooked terrain. This chapter demonstrates how Qing ideas about "cooking" the landscape and "cooking" the natives were intertwined.

Part I: Raw and Cooked Others

The classification of non-Han frontier peoples as "raw" (*sheng*) and "cooked" (*shu*) dates back at least to the Song dynasty. *Sheng* and *shu* express a host of binary concepts, not only raw and cooked, but also unripe and ripe, unworked and worked (as metal or stone), wild and tamed, unplowed and plowed, strange and familiar.[2] Most of these paired terms fit into the nature/culture binary that Claude Lévi-Strauss posited as a universal of human thought in his *The Raw and the Cooked*.[3] All these terms imply a process of transformation from one state into the other. In *The Discourse of Race in Modern China*, Frank Dikötter suggests that the classifications "raw barbarians" and "cooked barbarians" derived from the distinction between those who ate their food raw and those who ate their food cooked; those who ate raw meat being considered the most barbarous.[4] But, as Stephen West points out, the contexts in which these terms appear in Chinese sources make clear that "raw" and "cooked" do not refer to literal acts of eating but instead are used in a figurative sense.[5] What is it, then, that made a barbarian raw or cooked?

Premodern sources offer no universal definition of the terms; rather, writers on various frontiers offered different explanations in the cases of different peoples such as the Miao, the Lao, the Wa, and the Jurchens.[6] The concepts of the raw and the cooked cannot be separated from the historical contexts in which they were employed, for the manner in which the raw and the cooked were defined reflected specific political and economic circumstances, specific types of interaction between Chinese and non-Chinese peoples. In the case of Taiwan, the concepts of raw and cooked were embedded in the context of Taiwan's colonial history under the Qing. As Liu Liangbi, compiler of the *Gazetteer of Taiwan Prefecture* of 1742, wrote: "In the past Taiwan was inhabited by native savages. After annexation to the imperial domain, then there was a distinction between the raw and the cooked."[7] In other words, the distinction between the raw and the cooked arose out of the colonial encounter and was not inherent in the savages themselves.

The concepts of the raw and the cooked are produced in what Mary Louise Pratt calls the "contact zone": that is, "the space of colonial encounters, the space in which peoples geographically and historically separated come into contact with each other and establish ongoing relations, usually involving conditions of coercion, radical inequality, and intractable conflict."[8] As products of the contact zone, the concepts of the raw and the cooked embody the relation of non-Chinese others to the Chinese imperial state and its dominant culture: one kind of relation in the case of the raw, and another in the case of the cooked. Taiwan's contact zone was characterized not only by coercion, inequality, and conflict but also by negotiation, co-optation, and accommodation. The concepts of the raw and the cooked expressed all these dynamics. As the nature of Taiwan's contact zone evolved from the seventeenth to the nineteenth century, so, too, did Qing understandings of the "raw savage" and "cooked savage."

DEFINING THE RAW AND
COOKED IN TAIWAN

As is evident from Chapter 2, the earliest Chinese literati to write about Taiwan's natives did not employ the terms "raw savage" and "cooked savage." Rather, they referred to the Taiwan indigenes in blanket terms like "Eastern Savage" or "native savage."[9] But with the establishment of Qing rule on the island, writers began to perceive a need to draw finer distinctions among the various indigenous groups on the island. They were particularly concerned with distinguishing those who had submitted to Qing control from potentially hostile groups. They also sought to distinguish those villages that had already become somewhat acculturated to Chinese ways during the Zheng era from those that "kept to their old ways." Writers therefore began to employ a variety of terms to convey these distinctions.[10]

In 1951, Chang Yao-ch'i proposed three stages for the history of Chinese appellations for the Taiwan indigenes. In the first stage, the natives were classed as "wild" or "native" by the degree of their acculturation to Chinese culture. In the second stage, the natives were classed as "raw" or "cooked" depending on whether they had submitted to Qing control. In the third stage, the natives were classed as "mountain" or "plains" according to where they lived.[11] Although I find Chang's stages to be too neat and oversimplified to apply to Qing sources, his outline does capture the general trends in the classification of the Taiwan indigenes. I would argue, however, that ideas about acculturation, political submission, and habitat were never as distinct as Chang suggests but were, rather, intertwined.

By the end of the Kangxi period, the terms "raw savage" and "cooked savage" were widely used in the literature on Taiwan. Yet, there was no unanimous definition of these terms. Perhaps the earliest quasi-official definition was offered by the editor of the *Gazetteer of Zhuluo County* of 1717, who wrote, "Those who pay taxes are called cooked savages. Those who have not yet submitted to civilization are called raw savages or wild savages."[12] This author defined the raw and the cooked in terms of their relation to the Qing state: those who had submitted to Qing control were "cooked" and those who had not submitted (*weiguihua*) were "raw," or wild. Later gazetteer writers similarly defined the "cooked" as those who paid taxes and performed corvée: in essence, being "cooked" was a matter of fulfilling one's duties as a subject of the empire.

The issue of taxes was an important one, for the Chinese imperial state considered those who paid taxes "good subjects" (*liangmin*) and those who evaded taxes bandits.[13] Historically, officials on China's borderlands worried that Han Chinese farmers would escape beyond state control into "barbarian" territory in order to avoid taxation. Such Chinese were known as *Hanjian*, traitorous or false Chinese. Those who crossed the boundaries into barbarian territory permanently, in effect, "went native." After generations, their descendants ceased to be Han Chinese. As early as the Tang dynasty, there were cases of tribal peoples (especially on China's southern borders) whose ancestors were said to have been Han.

Yet, taxpaying could not serve as the sole criterion for defining the raw and the cooked in Taiwan. Several Qing writers expressed an awareness that this criterion was problematic. In 1697, Yu Yonghe had noted the existence of groups who, "although they are not wild savages, do not pay taxes."[14] As late as the nineteenth century, a subprefect for savage affairs, Deng Chuan'an (fl. 1830), conversely noted the existence of a number of groups that the gazetteers listed as part of taxpaying districts, but that were, in his opinion, still "unsubmitted" (*weiguihua*). He wrote: "I'm afraid that there must still be many places like this where the raw and cooked savages are mixed together. If one does not pass through these areas personally, one cannot ascertain the facts."[15] These contradictions indicate that although the criterion of taxpaying may have been a convenient guide for bureaucrats, it did not tell the whole story.

In travel writing, Qing literati were more apt to articulate the distinction between raw and cooked in cultural terms. Lu Zhiyu, who traveled to Taiwan in the early years following annexation, offered this definition of the raw and the cooked in his travel account: "Among their tribes are raw savages and cooked savages. What are the raw? Those who do not mix among the Han and who cannot communicate in our language. What are the cooked? Those who live in mixed settlements of Han and savage and who speak our language."[16] In this case, the meanings of *sheng* and *shu* are closer to "unfamiliar" and "familiar"; the two groups are defined in cultural or linguistic terms and in terms of their interaction with Han Chinese settlers. Other Qing sources also defined the cooked savages as those who lived close to, or mixed among, Han Chinese settlers.

Kangxi-era definitions of the raw and the cooked, therefore, included not only political but also cultural criteria.[17] Such criteria were not unrelated, as the ambiguity of the Chinese term *hua* indicates. Literally "transformation;" the term gave rise to a number of interrelated concepts: *guihua*, for example, means submission to the Chinese state; *wenhua*, culture; and *jiaohua*, to civilize. Chinese literati assumed a theoretical relation between submission to Chinese political authority and submission to cultural transformation. Indeed, a euphemism for submitting to Qing rule was "submitting to civilization" (*fu jiaohua*). Even though it did not always prove true in practice, Qing literati in Taiwan were familiar with the ideal that moral and cultural transformation (*jiaohua*) would naturally follow from political submission (*guihua*), even if only by a slow, evolutionary process.

The theoretical intersection between political submission and acculturation is embodied in the concepts of the raw and the cooked. In ideal terms, the cooked savages—those who had undergone transformation— would be both loyal and civilized. Thus, the two terms "cooked savage" and "civilized/submitted savage" (*huafan*) were sometimes used interchangeably in Qing writings. Conversely, raw savages—those who had not yet undergone transformation from their original state—had submitted neither to the state nor to civilization. Thus, the term "raw savage" was often used synonymously with "wild savage." The fact that real life rarely mirrors ideals led to the contradictions noted by Yu Yonghe, Deng Chuan'an, and other Qing writers.

THE WILD AND THE TAME

Another important function of classifying the indigenes as raw or cooked was to distinguish hostile groups from the amenable. As the Qing administration in Taiwan was all too well aware, political submission could not be measured in terms of tax payment alone: the propensity for rebellion and violence also had to be considered. (This was true of Han Chinese settlers as well.) As the Qing expanded their ethnographic knowledge of the Taiwan indigenes during the eighteenth century, the gazetteers called not only for an understanding of the diversity of native customs (Huang Shujing's project) but also for greater precision in identifying hostile and violent groups. As the *Gazetteer of Taiwan Prefecture* of 1747 noted: "The raw and the cooked differ in terms of tameness and perversity. The savages of north and south also differ in terms of strength and weakness."[18] In this context, the meanings of "raw" and "cooked" are closer to "wild" and "tame."

Indeed, as Qing writers began to construct the Taiwan indigenes as two distinct groups, negative traits that had formerly been associated with the "Taiwan savages" as a whole began to be mapped on to the wild, or raw savages.[19] Whereas early texts claimed, for example, that the savages "by nature like to kill," or were "stubborn and stupid," now writers attributed these characteristics to the raw savages alone. Headhunting, a notorious practice that the earliest sources had associated with the natives of Taiwan and other Pacific islands, also came to be seen as a raw savage practice.

By the early eighteenth century, travel writers increasingly emphasized the violent and murderous behavior of the raw savages. The expansion of the Han Chinese population at this time caused an escalation of conflict between Chinese settlers and the indigenes over land and other resources. Hostile indigenes were thus becoming a real threat to the safety of Han Chinese settlers. Although some writers blamed interethnic conflict on troublemaking Han Chinese settlers, many Qing literati attributed the belligerence of the raw savages to their inherently bloodthirsty natures.

Lan Dingyuan, for example, declared that headhunting was set in the "wild natures" of the raw savages and was in no way a reaction to provocation by Han Chinese settlers. Lan wrote: "The raw savages kill people. In Taiwan there are often incidents. Even though this lot have the appearance of humans, they have absolutely no human principles."[20] Lan thus constructed the raw savages as bestial in nature, lacking the moral sense that restrains humans from indiscriminate killing. He therefore regarded them as human in a physical sense alone. Even Huang Shujing, who objected to considering the savages a separate breed (*yilei*), made an exception for the raw savages of Kuilei mountain, of whom he wrote: "Fierce and intractable and fond of kill-ing, they really are another breed beyond the pale."[21] Numerous other sources also labeled the raw savages *yilei*. Being *yilei* was thus associ-ated with ferocity, intractability, and bloodthirstiness.

Others portrayed the raw savages as naturally rebellious and greedy:

The raw savages of Taiwan, by habit, like to rebel. When they are not content, then they come out of the mountains to plunder and kill traders and subjects. . . . It is hard to satisfy their greed. . . . Moreover, it is their custom to kill people in order to display their martial bravery. They cut off the heads of those they have killed, scrape off the skin and flesh, boil them up, and paint them with gold.[22]

As Qing writers constructed belligerence and ferocity as signal charac-teristics of "rawness," raw savage hostility toward Han Chinese set-tlers became more than a matter of a refusal to submit to Qing rule; it was an expression of their wild natures.[23]

The notion that the raw savages were murderous by nature enabled writers like Lan Dingyuan to justify the use of force to suppress them: "Counter killing with killing; use savagery to subdue the savages. At-tack them and make them afraid; pacify them and make them tame."[24] The idea of "taming" the savages contrasted sharply with the idea of "transforming" them; where the goal of transformation was the moral improvement of the savages (in a Confucian sense), the goal of taming them was simply to secure their subordination. This notion also sug-gested that, like animals, the raw savages had to be subdued by force. Qing writers thus spoke either of "transforming" or of "taming" the raw savages—depending on their own viewpoint and the circum-stances of the moment.

In juxtaposition to the raw savages, the cooked savages—submissive, pacific, and harmless—appeared much more benign. In-deed, travel writers often described the cooked savages not as perpe-trators of violence but as victims of raw savage headhunters them-selves. The raw savages thereby served as a foil against which images of the cooked savages as tame and friendly natives emerged.[25] Qing writers thus projected their fears of the ethnic other onto the raw while constructing the cooked as unthreatening.[26]

THE RAW AND THE COOKED AS STAGES
OF CULTURAL DEVELOPMENT

The concepts of raw and cooked can also be related to Chinese ideas about the historical stages of human development. As discussed in Chapter 2, the Chinese story of the evolution of civilization established several distinct stages of historical development marked by the introduction of particular technologies. A key dividing line in this historical trajectory was the invention of plow agriculture.

As the images of the raw and the cooked savages began to diverge in the eighteenth century, Qing writers increasingly reserved the rhetoric of privation, associated with the most brutish stage of antiquity, for representations of the raw savages. Whereas early Kangxi-era writers had declared the "Taiwan savages" as a whole to be "blood-drinkers and fur-eaters" or "cave-dwellers and nest-builders," literati now depicted only the raw savages in such terms.[27] The cooked savages, in contrast, were frequently portrayed in terms of the rhetoric of primitivism, as innocent beings who embraced the virtues of the simple and natural life. The raw savages came to be associated with the privative aspects of high antiquity, and the cooked savages with the idealized aspects of antiquity.

Lan Dingyuan's explanation of the differences between the raw savages and the cooked savages demonstrates how these two types were associated with different stages of development, the raw being more backward than the cooked.

Among the native savages of Taiwan there are two kinds: raw and cooked. Those who live deep in the mountains and who have not submitted to civilization are raw savages. All of them cover their bodies with deerskins, and they plant taro roots in the mountains. Their strength lies in their ability with bow and arrow, pike and spear. . . . Those who live on the plains mixed [among the Han Chinese], who obey the law, and who perform corvée are the cooked savages. They are contented at farming with plow and hoe, no different from the [Chinese] subjects. Their only difference lies in their hair, which is long in back and cropped at the front, their pierced ears and tattooed mouths, and their clothing and adornment.[28]

Numerous other Qing writers followed this pattern of representing the raw savages as hunters or primitive farmers and the cooked savages as more advanced agriculturists. The cooked savages were thus sandwiched between the raw savages and the Chinese on the ladder of cultural and material evolution; although not coeval with the Chinese, they were, nonetheless, more advanced than the raw savages, having given up such brutish practices as "eating fur and drinking blood" and headhunting and having learned to build huts, weave cloth, and plow the land. Thus, the concepts of the raw and the cooked were tied to the concept of historical stages of cultural development.

Such representations of the cooked savages reflected changes that were taking place among the Taiwan indigenes during the eighteenth century. When Huang Shujing traveled through Taiwan in 1722, he noted many aspects of cultural change among the cooked savages. More and more of these people were taking up farming, using Chinese tools and techniques, in large part because of the dwindling deer population. Increasing numbers of youths were becoming proficient in the Confucian classics. And clothing styles were coming to resemble Chinese styles—trousers and, on special occasions, even hats and shoes.[29] Such changes inspired eighteenth-century writers to praise the cooked savages for leading Taiwan's transformation from a "land of naked, tattooed savages" to a "place of caps and belts" (*guandai zhi qu*).[30]

TERRITORIAL ASSOCIATIONS OF THE RAW AND THE COOKED

Lan Dingyuan's definition of the raw and the cooked makes evident another important trend in eighteenth-century representations of the Taiwan indigenes—the tendency to associate these two groups with different habitats. He located the raw "deep in the mountains" and the cooked on the plains, mixed among Han Chinese settlers. By the nineteenth century, the association between the raw and mountain terrain, on one hand, and the cooked and the plains, on the other hand, had become so naturalized that the paired terms "raw savage" and "cooked savage" were often taken as equivalent to "mountain savage" and "plains savage," respectively. How did Qing writers move from administrative and cultural definitions of the raw and the cooked to a territorial definition?[31]

Of course, there appears to be an obvious empirical explanation: that is, raw savages lived in the mountains, and cooked savages lived on the plains. Yet, as Chang Yao-ch'i pointed out as early as 1951, this explanation is not entirely satisfying since even Kangxi-era writers knew of the existence of "raw savages" on Taiwan's eastern coastal plains. There were also mountain villages like Shuishalian, which had submitted and entered the tax registers as early as 1694. Moreover, numerous "raw" villages had joined the ranks of the "cooked" over time by submitting to Qing rule. I argue that intersections between Qing ideas about landscape and inhabitants were a significant factor in the development of a territorial definition of the raw and the cooked.

In Qing writings on Taiwan, both mountains and forests represent a particular typology of landscape, as discussed in Chapter 3. Commonly described in terms such as *xian* (strategic, dangerous), *zu* (blocked, obstructed), and *chong* (layered), mountains were associated with qualities such as impenetrability, strategic fastness, and danger. Forests, too—especially the Taiwanese jungle with its tangled, dense, and thorny vegetation—were associated with qualities of impenetrability, darkness, and mystery. Such terrain seemed to provide the perfect hiding ground for bandits and headhunters, screening them in strategic fastness. The association between hiding and vegetation is underscored by the fact that a number of Chinese words for "hide" or "conceal" (*bi, cang, meng*) contain the grass radical.

Qing writers made frequent reference to savages hiding themselves in the underbrush, taking cover in the jungle, lurking to ambush those who wandered into the mountain forests. They also wrote of hostile savages skulking away into the bush like rats to their nest. Travel writers claimed that the Taiwan indigenes were uniquely able to penetrate the dense jungle and disappear without a trace. As mentioned in Chapter 3, the fear of the dangers represented by Taiwan's mountain forests constituted a major theme of Qing writing about the island.

Even before the firm establishment of the categories of raw and cooked, travel writers followed a pattern of associating Taiwan's mountain jungles with fearsome, belligerent, and even monstrous beings. Lin Qianguang, for example, noted: "As one goes deeper into the mountains, the people have the appearance of apes, being smaller than three feet tall. When they see people, they climb into the treetops. If people want to capture them, then they draw their bows and confront them."[32]

The *Gazetteer of Taiwan Prefecture* of 1696 also recorded the existence of monstrous people and demonic spirits in the mountains: "In the deep mountains where wheel tracks rarely reach, there live people with human bodies and animal faces. . . . Hobgoblins of the trees and rocks and spirits of the hills and waters also come and go. It is truly another world."[33] Several sources told of "chicken-footed savages" who lived in the mountains—people who supposedly had claws for feet.[34] Many writers lamented the fact that the fear of the mountain forest, with its monsters, spirits, and wild savages, prevented Han Chinese from obtaining natural resources such as wild tea, fruits, and rattan.[35]

In contrast, Qing writers associated the plains with qualities such as openness and transparency. The land was more easily surveyed and thus easier to control than mountainous terrain.[36] Therefore, whereas the mountains were coded as threatening in Qing writings on Taiwan, the plains were depicted as safe and benign. If the mountain forests provided cover for headhunters, then the open plains made them vulnerable. As Lan Dingyuan wrote in *Record of an Eastern Campaign*, "The places where the raw savages move must be dense forest or brambled thickets where they can hide themselves. When they come to fields on the plains, then they shrink back, not daring to cross."[37] Another source noted of the headhunters who took cover in the mountain forests, "If you chase them out onto the open flat lands, then they lose their advantage."[38] Just as it was dangerous for the Chinese and docile "cooked savages" to enter the forests, it was dangerous for forest dwellers to venture onto the plains.[39]

Furthermore, in Qing Taiwan the plains were associated with sedentary agriculture and hence civilization, and the mountains with hunting and gathering, considered primitive economic activities. Taiwan's western coastal plains had been the primary site of Chinese settlement since the Dutch colonists of Taiwan first recruited Chinese farmers in the seventeenth century. After annexation, more and more of this land was converted into farmland. Lands that had been "opened," or reclaimed for agriculture, had been transformed from their natural state—in essence, "cooked." In contrast, Qing texts represented Taiwan's mountains as raw wilderness; as Yu Yonghe put it, "untouched since the Chaos of Creation."[40] This raw wilderness was the habitat of those who lived in darkness and privation, wearing animal skins, dwelling in caves, and hunting wild game. Therefore, the construction of the open plains as the domain of the cooked savages and the mountain wilderness as the domain of the raw savages seemed fitting.

THE "SAVAGE BOUNDARY"

The distinction between the mountain-dwelling raw savages and the plains-dwelling cooked savages was given physical expression with the establishment of the "savage boundary" in 1722.[41] Drawn along the foothills of the Central Mountain Range and marked with stones or trenches known as "earth-oxen," the physical boundary of the "earth-oxen redline," as it was sometimes known, divided Taiwan's mountains from its coastal plains. Despite the fact that some territory claimed by the cooked savages actually fell beyond the boundary, the boundary soon came to be known as the "raw savage boundary" (*shengfan jie*). Theoretically, the boundary placed the raw savages on one side of the line and the cooked savages and the Han Chinese on the other side.[42]

Therefore, in much Qing literature on Taiwan the pertinent distinction is not necessarily between Han and savage but between the plains-dwellers—Han Chinese and cooked savages—and mountain-dwellers—raw savages and Han Chinese outlaws. Indeed, as representations of the raw savages and the cooked savages diverged, Qing writers began to construct the cooked savages as closer to Chinese subjects. Several eighteenth-century sources described the cooked savages as "no different" from or "just like" subjects, a category from which they were generally excluded during the early years of Qing rule. The *Gazetteer of Taiwan Prefecture* of 1747 went so far as to declare: "The cooked savages live mixed among the gentry and commoners. They pay taxes and perform corvée and are therefore also subjects."[43] One alternative name for the boundary, "subject-savage boundary," articulated the division between taxpaying subjects and those beyond Qing rule, thereby reinforcing the position of the cooked savages as "equivalent to" subjects.

A precedent for the boundary line was the "Miao walls" built by the Ming in 1615 to separate the cooked Miao from the raw Miao in southwestern China. Yet unlike the Miao, the Taiwan indigenes were never defined as raw or cooked based on their location inside or outside the wall. This was due to the fact that the primary function of the "Han-savage boundary" of 1722 was to divide the Han Chinese and the raw savages and not the raw and the cooked savages. Nonetheless, the boundary effectively territorialized the raw savages in the mountains and the cooked savages on the plains.

As these associations became naturalized, more and more Qing writers began to offer territorial definitions of the raw ("faraway in the inner mountains") and the cooked savages ("nearby on the plains" or "mixed among Han Chinese").[44] The territorialization of the raw savages in the mountains drew on well-established images of this terrain as secluded, impenetrable, and dangerous. The introduction of the term "submitted raw savage" (*guihua shengfan*) in the mid-eighteenth century reinforced the shift away from using submission as the primary criterion for classifying the raw savages and the cooked savages (although it was never entirely abandoned) toward emphasizing territorial and cultural criteria.[45]

COOKING

Since the possibility of transformation is inherent in the concepts of *sheng* and *shu*, the distinction between raw savages and cooked savages was never absolutely fixed; as Wu Ziguang would point out in the early nineteenth century, "The cooked savages of today were raw savages in years past."[46] In order to effect the transformation from raw to cooked, from unripe to ripe, from unworked to worked, there had to be agent of transformation. Qing literati in Taiwan offered various ideas about what this agent of transformation might be.

Many travel writers saw the transformation of Taiwan's wilderness landscape as the key to transforming the nature of the populace. As Yu Yonghe proposed: "If we could burn the swamps and mountains and flatten the blocked defiles, then after a few decades we would be able to transform the thorny thickets into level roads and transform the descendants of [the mythical dog] Panhu into good subjects."[47] Yu's vision of transforming Taiwan's natives is based on the view that there is a correspondence between a landscape and its inhabitants. He proposed to cook the landscape by transforming the chaos of wilderness into the artful arrangement of civilization in order to cook the people: if they could replace the nasty and obstructed qualities of the landscape with openness and light, then they could do the same for the natives. By analogy, as the brambles and thorns were transformed into level and smooth (*tan*) roads, so, too, would the natives be made peaceful and satisfied (*tan*).

Lan Dingyuan also regarded the clearing of the wilderness as the means of transforming the natives, although he understood this process in a less figurative sense than Yu Yonghe. Lan advocated burning the vigorous weeds and dense brambles of the mountain forests in order to deprive the savages of hiding places. He further proposed converting Taiwan's wastelands into fields, which, he noted, the raw savages dared not cross. Land reclamation was thus his solution to the question of how to cook the raw savages.

If the brambles and thorns are opened day by day, then all the troubles will subside of their own accord. There is nothing better than allowing the subjects to reclaim land. When the savages hear the sounds of guns and cannons, they run away frightened, and for days they do not dare to come out. By this means, we can subdue the savages with savagery and induce them to submit and be tamed. After they have been induced for a long time, then more and more of them will gradually be transformed, until all the raw savages have become cooked.[48]

Like Yu Yonghe, Lan Dingyuan sought to eliminate the nasty and tangled elements of the landscape, "opening" the land in order to civilize the natives. For both Yu and Lan, the conversion of the landscape from the raw state of wilderness into "cooked land" (*shudi*) paralleled the conversion of the natives from the raw state of savagery. But Lan proposed to clear the wilderness not for the beneficial and uplifting effect it would have on the natives but in order to rid Chinese settlers of "troubles." Eliminating the habitat of the raw savages would eliminate the threat they posed to Chinese settlers. The frightful sounds of guns and cannons would induce the raw savages to submit and be tamed. Firepower was thus Lan's agent of transformation. Lan believed that the aggressive colonization of Taiwan would not only transform the raw savages into cooked savages but also, in time, transform the cooked savages into "human subjects" (*renmin*).

The notion that changes in the landscape could effect changes among the populace drew on ideas about correspondences among the climate, the environment, and human customs. In fact, the very word for customs, *fengsu*, with its root in *feng* (wind), suggests the connection between customs and environmental factors.[49] This connection was demonstrated by the fact that gazetteers conventionally categorized customs under the general heading *fengtu zhi*, a heading that also included information on the local climate, seasonal activities, wind and tidal patterns, and natural products—all things produced from the land. The *Gazetteer of Taiwan Prefecture* of 1742 explained how the environmental factors of different geographic locations affected customs: "All land can be divided into hard and soft, dry and wet. *Qi* can be divided into yin and yang, fair and foul. The climate follows these conditions. Thus the formation of customs is also variously produced from the land and cannot be altered. Therefore, the customs and habits found in the five directions are not the same."[50] This type of environmental determinism reinforced the assumption that wilderness produced base and rude customs and that miasmic land could not sustain civilization.

Yet geography did not have to be destiny, for Qing literati also believed that the moral influence of the emperor had the power to effect changes in the environment and climate, thereby bringing about changes in customs. As the *Gazetteer of Zhuluo County* stated: "The transformations of *qi* in Heaven and earth, follow the emperor's movements of them. . . . As the emperor's transformations are daily renewed, so the transformations of *qi* are daily changing."[51] The emperor possessed this influence because of correspondences between the forces of Heaven above and the power of the emperor (as the Son of Heaven) on earth. Since local earthly *qi* affected the development of local customs, changes in the transformations of *qi* would naturally produce changes in local customs. The *Gazetteer of Taiwan Prefecture* of 1742 asserted that the beneficial cosmic influence of the emperor had wrought changes on the "land of tattooed and black-toothed [beings]," "transforming wilderness into civilization and lifting the dark obscurity to reveal clear brightness."[52] Thus, environmental, climatic, and cultural changes went hand in hand.

These changes in climate and customs could also be effected by human modifications of the landscape, as both Yu and Lan suggested. Acts of ordering the natural landscape—reclaiming wastelands, establishing a prefecture and counties, building roads—translated into ordering the social landscape: as the chaos of wilderness was set in order, so, too, would the natives be tamed. Thus Lan argued that opening Taiwan's land would naturally transform the raw savages into cooked savages and the cooked savages into good subjects, turning Taiwan into a land of "taxpaying households."

Shen Qiyuan, acting prefect of Taiwan in 1729 and, like Lan, an advocate of colonization, proposed good governance as the agent of transformation. With proper Confucian government, he argued, "we can transform the immigrants into settled locals, transform the cooked savages into Han people, and transform the raw savages into cooked savages."[53] Shen thus envisioned a hierarchy of transformation, from raw to cooked, from cooked to Han, and, for the Han Chinese, from frontier immigrants to a rooted local society resembling that of mainland China. Shen was unusual among the writers of his time for suggesting that the cooked savages could be transformed into Han Chinese—not "good subjects" or "people of China" but Han Chinese. For Shen, then, cooking not only involved the moral transformation of "civilization" but also the ethnic transformation of "Hanization" (*Hanhua*).

The concept of *Hanhua* was linked to, but also distinct from, the concept of *jiaohua*, becoming civilized. The complicated and oftentimes confusing relationship between the two terms indicates the changing meaning of being Chinese under the Qing. Historically, *jiaohua* meant primarily the adoption of Confucian morality and principles of social hierarchy. The study of the Chinese classics was an important step in this process. *Hanhua* meant the adoption of specifically Han customs. During the Ming, when China was defined as a territorially bounded entity centered on the Han Chinese people, the concepts of *jiaohua* and *Hanhua* were understood to be largely synonymous. Under the Manchu Qing dynasty, however, this was no longer the case, as Han Chinese culture was redefined more narrowly as the particular culture of the Han Chinese people. It was therefore possible to be civilized without being Hanized. Indeed, eighteenth-century policy on the Taiwan frontier followed precisely this principle, advocating the civilizing, *jiaohua*, of the indigenes but not Hanization.[54] Moreover, aspects of becoming civilized under the Qing—for example, the adoption of the queue—involved "Manchuization."[55] Being civilized thus encompassed a broader scope of cultural practices in the high Qing than it had under the Ming. As I demonstrate below, the multicultural ideology of the Qing dynasty made room for the accommodation of non-Han cultures under the umbrella of Chinese civilization. In the formulation of Taiwan policy, those who favored the quarantine approach were content with a gradual pace of cultural change among the Taiwan indigenes; pro-colonization advocates, in contrast, favored a more rapid pace.

Theoretically, the trajectory of change could proceed only in one direction—from raw to cooked. Yet, there was also the dangerous possibility of the cooked reverting to the raw, joining with the raw savages in raids and rebellions (just as there was a possibility of good Han subjects becoming *Hanjian*). As John Shepherd notes, anxiety over cooked savages "going wild" first surfaced in official reports from the Yongzheng era, when there was increasing pressure on tribal lands.[56] The threat drove the formulation of new policies to protect their land rights in the 1730s, since the "raw boundary" of 1722 did little to shield tribal territory on the plains from Han Chinese encroachment. The question of land rights on the plains became urgent in the Qianlong period, for Han Chinese settlement was expanding at a furious pace. As the Qianlong court grew increasingly anxious about interethnic conflict on Taiwan, the emperor overturned many pro-colonization policies of the Yongzheng era and sought to return once more to the quarantine approach of the Kangxi era.[57] Yet times had changed, and the growth of the Han Chinese settler population made it even more difficult for the court to balance the interests of the Han Chinese and the indigenous people.

When the raw savage boundary was redrawn in 1760, the quarantine line was pushed back into the foothills, creating a new class of land between the old "earth-oxen redline" and the new boundary. The government allotted these lands to the cooked savages, creating a buffer zone between the raw savages and the Han Chinese. In the words of one Qing writer, the new boundary system served to "keep the raw savages inside, the Han subjects outside, and the cooked savages in between to separate them."[58] The cooked savages assumed a new status, sandwiched between the raw savages and the Han. The role of the cooked savages as a buffer would be institutionalized with the establishment of "savage military colonies" in the foothills after the Lin Shuangwen Rebellion of 1786–88, the second major settler rebellion on the island. The "savage military colonists" (*tunfan*) would later play a vital role in assisting the Qing in campaigns against unruly raw savages.

In many ways, their territorial location in a buffer zone signified the liminal position of the cooked savages—theoretically on their way to becoming Chinese subjects (or, perhaps, even Han Chinese), but still in danger of "going wild" and reverting back to the raw. Indeed, one definition of "cooked barbarians" (*shuyi*), offered by noted Qing geographer Wei Yuan was: "Those who occupy an intermediary position between barbarians and Han are cooked barbarians."[59] The cooked savages/barbarians were neither fully Han nor fully other, but a third and ambivalent category produced in contact zones. Mid-eighteenth-century descriptions of Taiwan's cooked savages as "just like" subjects simultaneously emphasized their similarity and highlighted their difference from the Han Chinese.

Part II: The Cartographic Representation of Raw and Cooked Taiwan

Since the terrain that fell outside the "raw savage" boundary did not come under Qing administrative control, this area soon became known not only as "beyond the boundary" (*jiewai*) but also as "beyond the pale." Taiwan was thereby effectively divided down the middle, split between "cooked territory" (*shujing*) and "raw territory" (*shengjing*). The distinction between raw and cooked territory was not only a distinction between unplowed (*shengdi*) and plowed land but also a distinction between a domain of savagery and the domain of civilized, or semi-civilized peoples, as well as a distinction between terrain beyond Qing control and Qing-controlled territory. In splitting the island down the middle, the 1722 boundary policy made official the role of the Central Mountain Range as a barrier. In fact, since the terrain beyond the Central Mountain Range had never been under Qing control, these mountains had served as an unofficial dividing line ever since annexation.[60] Where once the Taiwan Strait had served as the symbolic boundary between the Chinese empire and the realm beyond the pale, after annexation the Central Mountain Range assumed that function.

Kangxi maps depicted the Central Mountain Range as such a barrier. As mentioned above, early Qing maps of Taiwan showed the island not from a bird's-eye view but from the perspective of the China coast (see Color Plate 3). As a result, these maps showed only the western side of the island, with the Central Mountain Range on the horizon line. This cartographic convention supported the notion that the eastern side of the island had "not yet entered the map" (*weiru bantu*). Moreover, many early Qing maps marked certain of these mountains with the phrase "human footsteps do not enter here" (see Color Plate 3), signifying that this terrain was utterly outside civilization.[61] The tall mountains on the horizon line thus served visually as a barrier, marking the back edge of Taiwan. This visual representation fit early Qing descriptions of the island as "facing the seas and backed by mountains" or "rimmed by mountains," as if the eastern coast did not exist.

The handful of extant early Qing maps of Taiwan's eastern half, known as the "Transmontane Territory" (*shanhou, houshan*),[62] reinforced the notion that this terrain was raw wilderness.[63] The *Gazetteer of Zhuluo County*, one of the few early gazetteers to provide a map of eastern Taiwan, includes eighteen pages of maps of the western side of the island, but only four pages of the Transmontane Territory (Fig. 12). The visual iconography of wilderness, evident on the map of western Taiwan, is even more exaggerated on the map of the Transmontane Territory. This map projects an image of an unsettled landscape dominated by nature. Indigenous villages are vaguely denoted on the lowlands with labels such as "thirty-six villages of Gemalan." Pictorially, however, the hilly mounds surrounded by bamboo that suggest the locations of these villages blend into the natural landscape. Enormous waves pound the shores, reinforcing the sense of desolation and wildness of the eastern side of the island. These fierce waves further suggest the inaccessibility of the eastern coast.[64]

Like the other early maps of Taiwan's eastern coast, this map reflects the lack of geographic information about the terrain behind the mountains. Indeed, many Qing writers were unclear as to what lay beyond the Central Mountain Range: some wrote that there was only sea; others claimed that behind the mountains were simply more mountains; still others asserted that there were arable plains; and yet others declared that there was simply no way of knowing.

The fact that Qing pictorial maps of Taiwan conventionally showed only the western side of the island created an image of Taiwan as a kind of half-island—as if Taiwan consisted only of the western alluvial plains and the foothills of the Central Mountain Range (see Color Plate 3). Labeled "maps of Taiwan," such cartographic images created a certain ambiguity concerning the name "Taiwan." Was "Taiwan" simply that part of the island that came under Qing control or the entire island?

This ambiguity was reinforced by cartographic representations of Taiwan as an island split between Qing territory and savage territory. Eighteenth-century maps such as the *Map of the "Subject-Savage Boundary"* (Color Fig. 5) illustrate this division of Taiwan's terrain.[65] The

Fig. 12 Map of the Transmontane Territory,
Gazetteer of Zhuluo County (1717)

image of Taiwan as a divided island was projected most explicitly on maps that showed Taiwan from a bird's-eye view, enabling both sides of the island to be seen at once. In this regard, the cartographic image produced as a result of the Jesuit survey of the island was enormously influential.

The Jesuit survey of Taiwan was part of the overall survey of the Qing empire carried out by French Jesuits at the behest of the Kangxi emperor. Employing Western cartographic technology and consulting Chinese geographic sources, the Jesuits conducted the most comprehensive survey of the empire that had ever been undertaken. The survey of Taiwan was carried out by three cartographers, who spent the year 1714–15 surveying the island, traveling from the northern tip of Taiwan to the south. From this survey, the Jesuits constructed a map of the entire island, which was then included in the Kangxi-Jesuit Atlas.

The Kangxi-Jesuit Atlas went beyond any other Chinese maps in representing the frontiers, not only Taiwan but also the northwestern frontiers. Nonetheless, the limitations of the atlas demonstrate that early Qing geographic knowledge of the frontiers was still far from comprehensive. Many areas that could not be surveyed in detail were left blank, including the eastern coast of Taiwan and much of Mongolia and Manchuria. As the Qing extended its control over the frontiers, as new territories "entered the map," these cartographic blanks would be filled in.[66] The extension of Qing mapping was therefore directly related to imperial expansionism.

Like their European counterparts, the Qing employed cartography in the service of empire building. Within the context of Qing imperialism—attempts to "unify" the conquered Chinese empire and to consolidate control on the frontiers—the atlas served both vital strategic and symbolic ends. As Peter Perdue has demonstrated, the various stages in the production of the Kangxi-Jesuit Atlas reveal its intimate connection to strategic concerns.[67] In addition, concerted attempts were made after the completion of the atlas to extend the map into strategically important areas in Tibet and Inner Asia. To this end, the Qianlong emperor sponsored an updated and expanded atlas, which was finished in 1760.

The Kangxi-Jesuit Atlas was at once a vital strategic tool for exercising control over the empire and directing troop movements and a symbolic representation of the extensiveness of the Qing empire. Of-

ficially titled the *Map of a Complete View of Imperial Territory*, the atlas provided a bird's-eye view of the entire empire, satisfying the emperor's desire to "be able to see all parts of the empire at a glance."[68]
The possession of the atlas was thus an expression of the imperial
power of survey (*chenglan*).

This dual purpose is revealed in the two models of the atlas that
were produced on the basis of the Jesuit survey—one strictly for court
consumption and one for more general consumption.[69] The *Map of a
Complete View*, first presented to the emperor in 1718, included lati
tude and longitude lines and precise cartographic detail. Because of its
strategic value, this version was restricted to use by the court and
high-ranking officials. A popular version of the atlas, which was less
detailed and less precise (it did not include longitude and latitude lines)
was published in the imperial encyclopedia, *A Complete Collection of
Books and Illustrations, Past and Present* (*Gujin tushu jicheng*) in 1728.
Although this version of the map was less useful in strategic terms, it
was nonetheless significant in ideological and political terms, for it
made the Jesuit cartographic representation of the empire available to
a wider audience of Qing elites.

The Kangxi-Jesuit Atlas and the Qianlong update did much to produce a new spatial image of an expanded Qing empire. These large-
scale maps projected an image of a unified Qing terrain that stretched
beyond the seas into Taiwan, beyond the wall into Mongol territory,
and later (after 1759) beyond the passes into Xinjiang. With frontier
regions that could not be surveyed in detail left blank, the atlas conveyed a very different sense of the limits of the Chinese empire. This
was not the Ming image of an empire tightly bounded by natural geographic features but one that extended into fuzzy, empty space, an
empire with elastic boundaries that was continuing to stretch.

Although the Kangxi-Jesuit Atlas itself was available only to a small
number of high-ranking officials, the cartographic image of the Chinese
domain produced by this atlas cast its influence beyond the court (and
as far afield as Europe).[70] Not only was this cartographic image reproduced in the *Complete Collection of Books and Illustrations*, but it also
informed the production of several other important Qing maps, including those in the comprehensive gazetteers. Through such reproductions, the Jesuit-produced cartographic image of the Qing empire
helped to construct a new spatial image of the imperial realm in the

minds of elites. Local maps, such as the provincial gazetteer maps, also made use of the new geographic information provided by the Jesuit survey. Therefore, despite the fact that Chinese cartographers did not adopt Jesuit principles and methods until the late nineteenth century, as Cordell Yee has argued, the cartographic images produced by the Jesuits did influence eighteenth-century Qing mapmakers, who reworked and adapted Jesuit maps to Chinese forms, sometimes even pictorial forms.[71]

Certainly, the Jesuit survey did much to revolutionize the mapping of Taiwan. Whereas earlier maps of the empire, such as Cai Fangbing's map (see Chapter 1), had depicted Taiwan as a small circle, the Jesuit map and those modeled after it showed Taiwan truer to scale as a long, sweet-potato-like form (see Fig. 13). And whereas earlier maps of Taiwan, such as the Fujian provincial gazetteer maps, had conventionally shown the island from the perspective of the Chinese coast, as a horizontal landmass, the Jesuit map was the first to orient Taiwan vertically and to depict the island from a bird's-eye view. The Jesuit map also depicted the topography of the island with much greater precision. The map is quite detailed, demonstrating extensive knowledge of Taiwan's major ports, rivers, and mountains.

As Xia Liming demonstrates in his *History of the Development of Maps of Taiwan During the Qing Dynasty* (*Qingdai Taiwan ditu yanbianshi*), the Jesuit map of Taiwan served as one of the basic models for Qing maps of Taiwan until the nineteenth century.[72] The Jesuit cartographic image of the island (minus lines of longitude and latitude) informed numerous important maps of Taiwan, including those in not only the *Complete Collection of Books and Illustrations* but also the *Gazetteer of Fujian Province* of 1737 (see Fig. 14) and the *Comprehensive Gazetteer of the Great Qing Realm* of 1746. It also informed the cartographic representation of Taiwan in the prefectural gazetteers beginning in 1742, although the planimetric image of the Jesuit map was reinterpreted in a more conventional Chinese pictorial form, and the island was reoriented as a horizontal image. Through such reworkings, Jesuit cartography indirectly influenced the way in which Qing literati perceived the spatial image of Taiwan and its geographic features. This hints at the intriguing relationship between technology and visual culture, an important topic for future research.

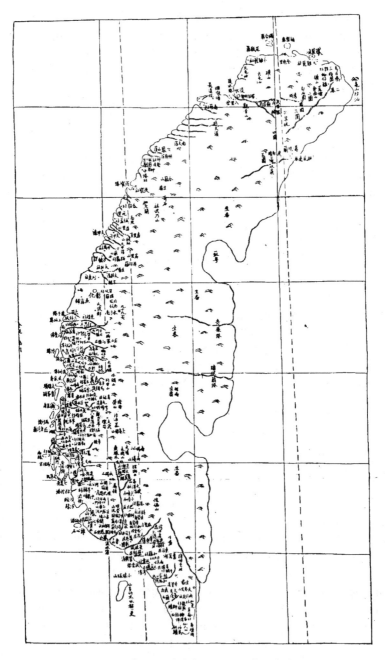

Fig. 13 "Carte chinoise de l'île Formose d'après les travaux
des Jésuites" from C. Imbault-Huart, *L'île Formose—
Histoire et Description* (1893)

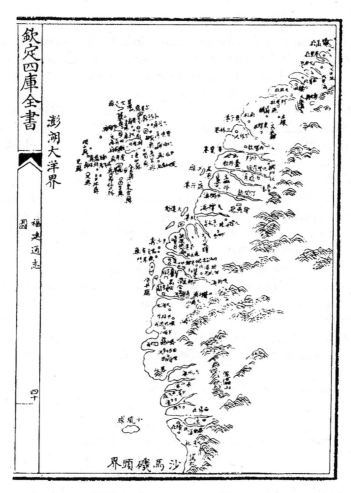

Fig. 14 Map of Taiwan from *Gazetteer of Fujian Province* (1737)

As reproduced in the *Complete Collection of Books and Illustrations*, the Jesuit map projects an image of the island sharply divided between "cooked territory" and wilderness. This map shows the western side of Taiwan in great detail, with bays and rivers and mountains labeled in Chinese. The map depicts major landmarks, including Taiwan's prefectural and county seats, military posts, important Chinese settlements, and a number of indigenous villages, giving the western side of the island a degree of visual density. Beyond the western coastal plains, however, the map gives few landmarks, reflecting the limits of both Chinese and Jesuit knowledge of the island. The Central Mountain Range is depicted pictorially as a dense cluster of mountains running down the right-hand edge of the island. A select number of placenames are marked among these mountains, but for the most part this area is unlabeled. Beyond the mountain range, the map fades off into empty space with no indication of habitation or significant landmarks on the eastern coast. The map is vague about the island's boundary on the eastern side and provides no visual representation of the eastern shoreline. With the eastern half of Taiwan a cartographic blank, this map once again supported the notion that Taiwan was bounded by the Central Mountain Range.

Numerous maps based on the Kangxi-Jesuit Atlas, including the Qianlong-period *Comprehensive Geographic Map of the Great Qing* (*Da Qing yitong yutu*, 1789), created an even more explicit image of an island divided between "cooked territory" and "savage territory" (*fanjing*) by marking the terrain beyond the Central Mountain Range with the words "raw savages" in several locations running from north to south (see, for example, Fig. 13). Again, a contrast is established between the densely settled western coast and the virtually empty Central Mountain Range and eastern coast, which have few landmarks other than mountains. What is left off the map is just as significant as what is on the map.[73]

All these maps reinforced the spatial image of Taiwan as a divided island, with anything beyond the Central Mountain Range literally off the map. Thus, the Kangxi-Jesuit Atlas and its reproductions, although marking a radical departure from earlier conventions of mapping Taiwan, confirmed the image of Taiwan as a half-island. The construction of Taiwan's Central Mountain Range as the boundary between the Chinese domain and the realm beyond the pale reinforced the new conception of Taiwan as a hedgerow for China. But the cartographic representation of eastern Taiwan as a savage wilderness that had not "entered the map" would have serious political ramifications in the nineteenth century.

CHAPTER 6

Picturing Savagery

Visual Representations of

Racial Difference

In 1751, the Qianlong emperor issued an imperial edict:

Our dynasty has unified the vast terrain that lies within the frontiers. The various barbarians, inner and outer, have submitted and turned toward civilization. Each of them has a different costume and appearance. We order the governors-general and provincial governors along the frontiers to have illustrations made copying the likeness of the clothing and ornaments of the Miao, Yao, Li, and Zhuang under their jurisdiction, as well as of the outer barbarians and savages, and to submit these illustrations to the Grand Council, that they may be compiled and arranged for imperial survey. Thereby will be displayed the abundance of Our meetings with kings (wanghui).[1]

With this decree, the Qianlong emperor ordered his officials to compile the *Qing Imperial Tribute Illustrations* (*Huang Qing zhigong tu*) so that he might survey the peoples of his empire and his "tributary" states. The commissioning of this work reflected not only the Qianlong emperor's desire to display "the abundance of Our meetings with kings" but also his interest in racial classification. The *Tribute Illustrations* was only one of several projects of ethnographic collecting sponsored by this emperor. As Pamela Kyle Crossley has demonstrated, imperially sponsored works of ethnographic documentation such as the *Researches on Manchu Origins* (*Manzhou yuanliu kao*) represented the emperor's desire to form a "rigid taxonomy of culturally-distinct races within the empire."[2] This desire was born of the emperor's conviction that such classification would bring order to the multiethnic, multicultural, and multilingual empire created by Qing expansionism, which reached its height during his reign. Ethnographic projects like the *Tribute Illustrations* both represented the diversity of the Qing realm and provided a means of classifying and thereby symbolically ordering this diversity.[3] As was the case with the Qing *Comprehensive Gazetteers*, frontier officials played a vital role in the production of the *Tribute Illustrations*.

In response to the emperor's order, local officials in Taiwan produced illustrations of the various "savages" under their jurisdiction; the following year, the governor-general of Fujian-Zhejiang submitted fourteen pictures of Taiwan's "raw and cooked savages" to the Grand Council.[4] These pictures were but a handful of the numerous illustrations of the Taiwan indigenes produced during the Qing to satisfy a more general interest in visually documenting the strange people and customs of the frontier.[5] Such images were commissioned by traveling officials or gazetteer compilers who valued ethnographic illustrations (*fengsutu*), as well as maps, as important sources of geographic information and hence as aids for frontier administration.[6] According to one Taiwan gazetteer, it was common practice for frontier officials to commission both maps and ethnographic illustrations "in order to aid in the investigation of the terrain."[7] In some cases, frontier officials submitted ethnographic illustrations, just as they did maps, for imperial inspection. As this chapter shows, these pictures bore a close relation to the practice of ethnographic recording.

The production of ethnographic illustrations demonstrates the importance of visual knowledge to Qing understandings of race/ethnicity on the Taiwan frontier. These pictures were an important supplement to Qing ethnographic texts, which focused on customs and devoted little space to descriptions of physical difference. Drawing heavily on ethnographic texts for their subject matter and annotations, these illustrations contained little that was new in the way of information. Instead, much as Qing pictorial maps provided a qualitative understanding of the terrain to complement the quantitative data contained in texts, these illustrations essentially served to answer a fundamental question: What did the natives look like? In ethnographic illustrations, we find the bodies that are largely missing from Qing ethnographic writing about the Taiwan indigenes. An analysis of ethnographic illustrations thus provides a fuller understanding of how Qing literati apprehended racial/ethnic difference. This chapter examines how the *Tribute Illustrations* and other ethnographic illustrations of the Taiwan indigenes served to visualize the idea of racial difference.[8]

In *Colonial Desire: Hybridity in Theory, Culture and Race*, Robert Young argues that from their inception Western concepts of race developed together with concepts of culture. Even nineteenth-century "scientific" theories of race, which appear on the surface to be about biology, genetics, and physical difference, were always simultaneously theories of cultural difference. The concept of race was significant primarily as it accounted for differences in intelligence and moral capacity, differences that in turn naturalized social and political hierarchies. Racial theorists argued that the superiority of Western civilization proved the superiority of the White race and that the "failure" of Africa to produce great civilizations attested to the inferiority of the Black race. (The potential problem of Egypt was explained away by Nott's proposal that Egyptians were Caucasians.) As Young shows, without culture, race is little more than a meaningless set of physical traits. At the same time, Young argues, nineteenth-century theories of culture, especially "national cultures," cannot be separated from notions of race. Thus, "race" and "culture" were intertwined in a complex and subtle manner that continues to affect our thinking about race and ethnicity today.[9]

I would argue that Qing constructions of racial difference also implicitly merged ideas about physical difference with ideas about cultural and moral difference.[10] This is perhaps most readily evident in ethnographic illustrations; in these pictorial representations, native dress, adornment, and bodies manifest cultural difference. Artists also employed various conventions to express differences in inborn nature through representations of the human figure. In this chapter, I discuss several examples of the pictorial representation of the Taiwan indigenes in order to demonstrate how notions of physical difference, cultural difference, and differences of inborn nature intersected in Qing constructions of race/ethnicity.

Representing Savage Customs

The earliest extant ethnographic illustrations of the Taiwan indigenes are the woodblock-print illustrations in the *Gazetteer of Zhuluo County* of 1717 (Figs. 15–23). Like the maps found in gazetteers, these illustrations were meant to be viewed in conjunction with the textual descriptions recorded in the gazetteer. As the editor declared, the pictures were intended to provide a "general impression" of the appearances of the "savages" and their customs through "likeness in form" (*xingsi*).[11] The editor claimed that these pictures were based on first-hand knowledge of the "cooked savages"; the "raw savages" were excluded from representation since Chinese explorers had not yet been able to observe their customs directly. As a vehicle for readers to visualize the Taiwan indigenes, these illustrations served to produce ethnic difference through the display of strange customs and strange bodies.[12]

The ten gazetteer illustrations are arranged so that they form a rough sequence of seasonal activities. Beginning with the annual roof-raising, the illustrations progress through the planting of seedlings, harvesting, the storing of crops in the granary, the harvest festival and drinking party, pounding the grain, deer hunting, fishing, and picking betel nuts. These customs are presented in a timeless, ahistorical framework in the visual equivalent of the ethnographic present. The particular customs selected for illustration are meant to be understood as "typical scenes," representative of "[cooked] savage customs" in the county as a whole.

The illustrations are loosely modeled on the genre of "illustrations of tilling and weaving" (*gengzhi tu*), which was originally inspired by a set of verses on this theme composed during the Song dynasty. As suggested by the genre's name, these pictures illustrate the various stages in the production of rice and silk, two of premodern China's most important economic activities. Tilling and weaving were also considered the "proper" occupations for ordinary men and women, respectively, in Chinese agrarian civilization. The illustrations thus present an idealized picture of Chinese agrarian life for literati viewers. This genre regained popularity during the Qing, as both the Kangxi and the Qianlong emperors commissioned sets of these illustrations, from which woodblock-printed editions were made and

Figs. 15 (*left*) "Raising the Roof" and 16 (*right*) "Planting Seedlings"
from the *Gazetteer of Zhuluo County* (1717)

Figs. 17 (*left*) "Ascending the Threshing Floor" and 18 (*right*) "Festival"
from the *Gazetteer of Zhuluo County* (1717)

Figs. 19 *(left)* "Drinking Party" and 20 *(right)* "Pounding Rice"
from the *Gazetteer of Zhuluo County* (1717)

Figs. 21 *(left)* "Hunting Deer" and 22 *(right)* "Fishing"
from the *Gazetteer of Zhuluo County* (1717)

Fig. 23 "Picking Betel Nuts" from the
Gazetteer of Zhuluo County (1717)

disseminated. The initial prints of the Kangxi *Imperially Commissioned Illustrations of Tilling and Weaving* (*Yuzhi gengzhi tu*) were produced in 1696; several other printings followed.[13]

Although modeled on this genre, the illustrations of "savage customs" in the *Gazetteer of Zhuluo County* differ in important ways that highlight the primitiveness of the Taiwan indigenes. First, these illustrations show the indigenes engaged not only in the orthodox occupation of farming[14] but also in a variety of "primitive" economic activities: hunting deer with bow and arrow, spearing fish in the rivers, and scaling tall palms to pick betel nuts. Second, whereas the *Illustrations of Tilling and Weaving* show a strict gender segregation, with men tilling and women weaving, the illustrations of the Taiwan indigenes show men and women working together in the fields and carousing together at village festivals and drinking parties. For Chinese literati, this lack of gender segregation clearly signified the savages' ignorance of "civilized" propriety. Third, the exotic costumes of the Taiwan indigenes, with their loincloths, leg wrappings, giant earrings, armloads of bracelets, and feathers in their hair, signify their ethnic difference.[15]

Perhaps most notably, the near nakedness of the "savage" bodies contrasts sharply with the depiction of the Han Chinese subjects in the *Illustrations of Tilling and Weaving*. The gazetteer's "Planting Seedlings" (Fig. 16), for example, is closely modeled on the same scene from *Illustrations of Tilling and Weaving*; only the relative nudity of the indigenes stands in sharp contrast to the Han Chinese farmers—a clear sign of their primitiveness.[16] The depiction of bare-breasted women in several illustrations not only signifies their "uncivilized" character but also caters to the established Chinese notion of non-Han women of southern climes as sexually promiscuous and uninhibited. The large, bare feet of the indigenous women further signal their difference from Han Chinese women, who typically had bound feet. Such pictures rendered the "savage" female body available to the voyeuristic colonial gaze, a subject to which I return in Chapter 7.

Scenes such as "Drinking Party" (Fig. 19) reinforced images of Taiwan as a savage island.[17] The picture depicts a disorderly scenario of several figures seated on the ground outside a hut drinking rice wine from enormous bowls, which are also placed on the ground. The male figures are half-naked, despite the presence of a woman. With arms and legs flying every which way, these figures present a lively but unruly scene. This picture fit the well-established image of the Taiwan savages as "fond of drink" disseminated by Chinese travel writing.[18] Such "typical" scenes confirmed the low place of the Taiwan savages on the Chinese scale of civilization.

Illustrated Ethnographic Albums

Qing imperial expansionism also brought new prominence to another pictorial genre, the illustrated ethnographic album.[19] Several frontier officials stationed in Taiwan made reference in their travel writings to commissioning such albums.[20] The Manchu official Liu-shi-qi, who served in Taiwan as a censor from 1744 to 1747, wrote, for example:[21]

In the course of my duties, I toured around and inquired after customs and strange products. I saw all kinds of unusual and weird things that have never been seen in China proper. It was then that I began to believe that the world is so vast that there is nothing it does not contain. In my spare time from official duty, I ordered a painter to make illustrations of things that I had seen and heard. Although he could only capture a small part, the suitability of the products and the exoticness of the customs are enough to demonstrate the extensive reach of civilization.[22]

The paintings commissioned by Liu-shi-qi were bound in two albums: the *Illustrations of Taiwan's Savage Villages* (*Taiwan fanshe tu*) and the *Illustrations of Taiwan's Flora and Fauna* (*Taihai caifeng tu*). In declaring that the pictures would demonstrate "the extensive reach of civilization," Liu-shi-qi indicated that the purpose of these illustrations was not only to document the customs of the Taiwan indigenes but also to glorify Qing expansionism. Liu-shi-qi had originally planned to submit this painted album to the emperor upon his return to China, but he was dismissed from office on charges of corruption and was therefore never able to make this presentation. Instead, he kept the album as a souvenir to show his friends at home in the capital.

According to Tu Cheng-sheng, there are five kinds of illustrated albums of the Taiwan indigenes extant, some of which were produced in multiple copies by the artists' studios.[23] *Illustrations of Taiwan's Savage Villages* (Color Plates 6–9) is perhaps the most famous of these. The Academia Sinica's copy of Liu-shi-qi's ethnographic album contains seventeen illustrations and one map. The album leaves are painted in color on paper, and each leaf carries short explanatory textual notes. In addition to these notes, Liu-shi-qi composed an explanatory text, which provided more detailed information about the customs illustrated in the album. Another outstanding example is the album painted by Chen Bishen around 1770 (Color Plates 10–12), which contains eighteen illustrations of customs, eleven illustrations of plants, and three illustrations of animals.[24] Again, the album leaves are painted in color on paper, with annotations penned in the margin. In addition to the albums studied by Tu, there is evidence of other examples in private collections and of others that appear to have been lost. Due to this limitation of sources, any conclusions we draw about this genre can only be tentative.

These illustrated albums relate to a genre known in English as "Miao albums" and in Chinese, "Miao Man tu" (Illustrations of the southern barbarians) or "Bai Miao tu" (Illustrations of the hundred barbarians).[25] This genre arose in the early eighteenth century and became popular with collectors (Chinese, Japanese, and Western) in the nineteenth and twentieth centuries. The albums typically consist of painted illustrations in color on either silk or paper, accompanied by brief textual explanations. Hundreds of such albums were produced in the Qing. They range in quality from very luxurious editions, exquisitely painted, with elaborate brocade covers, to low-end editions. A variety of southern locales, including Guizhou, Yunnan, Hunan, Guangdong, Hainan Island, and Sichuan, were illustrated in these albums.[26]

In *Qing Colonial Enterprise: Ethnography and Cartography in Early Modern China*, Laura Hostetler argues that Miao albums were originally designed to educate frontier officials about the habits and customs of various non-Han groups on China's southern frontiers.[27] They were also used to help officials distinguish the various groups of the region, since they illustrated the distinctive characteristics and costumes of each group.[28] According to Hostetler, as the genre evolved, the albums became prized as art objects.[29]

Statements by Liu-shi-qi and other frontier officials in Taiwan demonstrate that, as early as the eighteenth century, illustrated ethnographic albums were also valued as souvenirs, designed to impress viewers with the exotic sites of the frontier.[30] In addition, artists in China produced pictures copied from such sources (or based on their imaginations) to cater to literati curiosity about exotic people and locales. A set of four hanging scrolls depicting the Taiwan indigenes produced by the artist Xu Shu around 1820, for example, each an assemblage of vignettes copied from ethnographic albums, indicates that ethnographic illustrations were used for decorative as well as educational purposes.[31] Through such illustrations, the "Taiwan savages" became objects not only of imperial survey but also of entertainment for armchair travelers who marveled at the picturesque images of primitives. Such pictures of the exotic other confirmed the viewers' own sense of being civilized.

A conventional repertoire of typical scenes, which would have been readily perceived by Chinese literati as exotic and primitive, soon emerged in the illustrated albums of Taiwan. This repertoire included economic activities such as "plowing and planting," "planting taro" (Color Plate 8), harvesting (Fig. 17), "pounding rice" (Fig. 20), "hunting deer" (Fig. 21), "fishing" (Fig. 22), and "weaving cloth" (Color Plate 6). It also included scenes, such as "running contests" and "capturing wild oxen" (Color Plate 10), depicting the special skills for which the indigenes were known. Many scenes featured practices Chinese literati considered especially exotic or primitive: "tattooing," "the nose flute" (Color Plate 11), "baby hammocks," and "monkey-style picking" (that is, climbing trees like monkeys and picking betel nuts; Color Plate 7 and Fig. 23). Other customs favored for illustration were "welcoming the bride," "raising the roof" (Fig. 15), "savage festival" (Color Plate 12 and Fig. 18), and "drinking party" (Color Plate 11 and Fig. 19). The albums might also include vignettes that did not represent "original" customs but scenes that had been codified by Qing literati as typical of Taiwan frontier life: "traveling by oxcart," "crossing the stream," "guarding the passes," and "the watchtowers." Some albums included illustrations, like "sugar production" (Color Plate 9) and "village schoolteachers," that portrayed the local Han Chinese. The captions assure the viewer that the scenes depict "typical practices," emblematic of savage culture and frontier life.

The scenes depicted in albums like the *Illustrations of Taiwan's Savage Villages* reflected established Chinese images of Taiwan as a land of unsophisticated savages. In "Monkey-Style Picking" (Color Plate 7), for example, both the image and the title reinforce the Chinese conception of the Taiwan indigenes as primitive and animal-like.[32] The figures are depicted high in the trees, moving easily from tree to tree with the agility of monkeys.[33] This picture stands in particular contrast to the relative technological sophistication depicted in Liu-shi-qi's illustration of Han Chinese sugar production, where water buffalo are harnessed to a machine that grinds the sugarcane (Color Plate 9).[34] Like the *Gazetteer of Zhuluo County* illustrations, such pictures confirmed the low place of the indigenes on the scale of cultural development.

The difference and the lure of Taiwan was represented perhaps most vividly in the image of "dancing natives," a subject widely featured in illustrations of the Taiwan indigenes.[35] Chen Bishen's album, for example, depicts a group of colorfully dressed women dancing in a circle to the beat of a gong and the swaying of feathered banners in the scene "Savage Festival" (Color Plate 12).[36] The dancing in this picture represents the performance of "primitiveness," a scene that Qing travel writers observed with fascination. Numerous stereotypes associated with the Taiwan indigenes—that they were carefree and happy, fond of drink, and given to sensuality and childlike pleasures—came together in this image. "Dancing natives" thus soon became a standard visual trope of primitivism, a trope also commonly found in the Miao albums.[37]

Primitivism and Privation in
Pictorial Representation

Overall, Liu-shi-qi's album presents a picturesque image of the Taiwan indigenes as simple, rural folk. Liu-shi-qi's colleague, Censor Fan Xian, praised the pictures for evoking the atmosphere of "illustrations of the 'Airs of Bin'" (*Binfengtu*), a genre of illustrations of pastoral poems from the *Classic of Poetry* that depicted the ancients engaged in farming and other rural activities.[38] In alluding to this genre, Liu-shi-qi's album employs a visual equivalent of the rhetoric of primitivism and projects the indigenes back into a simple and idyllic past.[39]

This visual primitivism is most evident in the album's illustrations of the cooked savages, which constitute the majority of the illustrations. Although the cooked savages are represented with primitive technologies—the bow and arrow, simple hoes and plows, rudimentary looms, and crude rafts—they appear carefree and at ease. Scenes of strife and physical violence, often featured in Miao albums, are entirely absent. The figures are painted as pleasant in aspect, their exotic dress and adornment notwithstanding. The artist has placed the figures in picturesque settings that lend a lyrical mood to the pictures; palms and banana trees, the conventional stuff of tropical southern scenery, enhance the exotic atmosphere.

Although the artist employed the visual iconography of primitivism in the representation of the cooked savages, in the representation of the raw savages he employed the visual equivalent of the rhetoric of privation (Color Plate 8). The raw savages wear animal skins and sport cropped hair (*yipi duanfa*), customs associated with a brutish past. In addition, the artist represented the raw savages "living in the wilderness" (*yeju*), in the rugged terrain of the mountains. Painted in drab colors, this terrain contrasts sharply with the idyllic, pastoral landscapes that form the backdrops for the illustrations of the cooked savages. Further signifying the privation of the raw savages, the artist portrayed them planting taro in the mountains without the aid of plows, a practice indexing the low level of their cultural development. Visual tropes of privation are also evident in numerous Miao albums, where some of the ruder groups are portrayed in terms of various metonyms for privation and savagery: long hair hanging loose (*pifa*), wearing animal skins (*yipi*), or living in caves (*xuechu*).

Just as Qing literati employed the rhetoric of privation and primitivism to distinguish raw and cooked savages, then, Qing artists employed the visual equivalents of privation and primitivism to the same end. Owing in large part to their focus on the cooked savages (whose customs were easier to observe), the extant ethnographic illustrations of Taiwan (excluding any held in private collections) are dominated by visual primitivism. On the whole, these albums, most of which date from the eighteenth century, project an image of a people who could readily be civilized and incorporated into the empire.

Representing Physical Difference

Like the illustrations from the *Gazetteer of Zhuluo County*, Liu-shi-qi's album illustrations serve to produce racial difference through the display of savage bodies. The most prominent characteristic of the savage body is, again, its relative nakedness: bareheaded and barefooted, wearing nothing but a loincloth, the cooked savage male stands in sharp contrast to the clothed, capped, and shod (and hence civilized) Chinese subject. His pierced ears, large hoop earrings, and bracelets also set him apart from the Han Chinese man. The cooked savage women, with their large, bare feet and exotic headgear, are implicitly contrasted with bound-footed Han Chinese women.[40]

Other visual signs of difference in these pictures include the savages' dark skin, round eyes, and lack of facial hair, features that Qing writers identified as distinguishing these people from the Han Chinese. The artist of Liu-shi-qi's album depicted the savages with the "bug-eyed" or "staring" look that Qing literati equated with primitive ignorance and truculence. Furthermore, the artist has portrayed the raw savages as more physically distinct from the Han Chinese, with darker skin and rounder eyes, than the cooked savages. Thus, their greater cultural difference from the Han Chinese is expressed visually in terms of their greater physical difference, the less civilized raw savages being represented as further removed from Han Chinese normative ideals of physical appearance than the cooked savages.

The articulation of cultural otherness through physical strangeness was a well-established convention in Chinese pictorial representations of foreigners. The *Illustrated Record of Strange Countries* (*Yiyu tuzhi*,

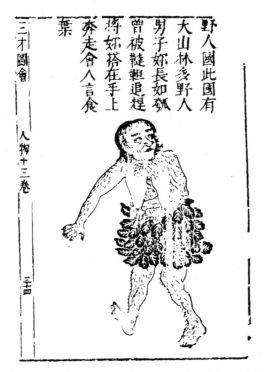

Fig. 24 Figure from the "Country of Wild People"
from Wang Qi's *Pictorial Compendium of
the Three Powers* (1607)

ca. 1430), for example, which provided a model for the great Ming encyclopedia, *The Pictorial Compendium of the Three Powers* (*Sancai tuhui*, 1607), demonstrates quite explicitly the urge to represent foreigners as physically distinct from the Chinese. Foreign peoples are
depicted with extremely hairy bodies, impossibly long limbs, or as
enormously fat. Some are hermaphrodites of sorts. The figure from
the "Country of Wild People" (Fig. 24), for example, is a man with
long, flowing hair, hairy legs, and pendulous breasts. In addition, this
work contains numerous examples of half-human, half-animal beings
from various mythical countries.[41] The strangeness of foreign peoples
is represented through the strangeness of their bodies.

The notion that cultural differences are embodied in the human
figure, although evident in ethnographic illustrations of the Taiwan
indigenes, is even more apparent in the Qing *Tribute Illustrations*.

The Taiwan Savage in
the Qing Tribute Illustrations

The *Tribute Illustrations* was an ambitious project to catalog the enormous variety of peoples assigned the status of "barbarians" (inner and outer) by the Qing.[42] Taking over a decade to complete, this work contains more than 300 pictures of non-Han peoples within the Qing empire, as well as peoples from numerous Asian and European countries. Each group is represented by a pair of figures, male and female, displayed like specimens against a blank ground. Each pair represents a distinct type, with a distinct appearance and costume, and distinct customs. Many of the figures hold some kind of representative object—a local product, an animal, a tool, a weapon, an instrument, and so forth—associated with the local culture. These material artifacts constitute signs of identity, along with the "native" costumes worn by the figures. The illustrations are annotated with brief texts giving information on a range of subjects: customs, a group's physical characteristics, their inborn nature, proclivities, local geographic information, trade information.[43] But the recording of ethnographic information in the *Tribute Illustrations* was secondary and far from comprehensive; the primary purpose of this collection was the visual representation of these peoples.[44]

The Qing *Tribute Illustrations* was produced in several forms: a woodblock print version published in 1761; a set of four scrolls painted by the court painter Xie Sui, completed between 1761 and 1775; a *Siku quanshu* edition published in 1790; and a final version published in 1805.[45] Xie Sui's version of the *Tribute Illustrations* is a stunning pictorial work; painted in color on silk, it depicts a magnificent array of figures rendered in fine detail, with elaborate and brilliantly colored costumes.[46] Like the modern Miss World pageant, where a dazzling array of national difference is presented through the display of ethnic dress, these scrolls made manifest the spectacle of ethnic diversity. This impressive collection fulfilled the Qianlong emperor's desire to use the *Tribute Illustrations* to display his prestige as the ruler of an empire accepting tribute from all corners of the world.[47]

Since illustrations of non-Han peoples residing within the empire constitute over two-thirds of the *Tribute Illustrations*, this work cata-

logues primarily the extensive diversity of peoples brought under
Qing rule by the imperial expansionism that reached its peak under
the Qianlong emperor. Among those represented are various types of
"savages" from Taiwan; there are thirteen groups depicted, based on
the models provided the Grand Council by the governor-general of
Fujian-Zhejiang. Despite the fact that the prototypes for the *Tribute
Illustrations* were supposedly based on firsthand observation, it is my
opinion that the final illustrations are heavily informed by artistic
imagination and pictorial conventions for representing barbarians.
The pictures thus reveal a great deal about Qing imaginative conceptions of savagery.

Embodying Savagery

The various Taiwan indigenes depicted in the *Tribute Illustrations* are
classified both by administrative divisions and by the categories of raw
and cooked. The entries begin with the cooked savages of Taiwan
county, turn south to Fengshan county, then north to Zhuluo
county, Zhanghua county, and finally Danshui subprefecture. The
submitted raw savages follow, again in sequence from south to north.
Last are the raw savages of the inner mountains. The illustrations thus
proceed from the most civilized specimens through increasing degrees
of savagery; in tandem, the figures visually turn increasingly savage
and belligerent in appearance as we progress from the cooked to
the raw.

In each of the thirteen illustrations, the differences between the
savage body and the civilized body are emphasized. The strategy for
representing savage bodies in this work, especially male bodies, is
similar to Chinese pictorial conventions for representing what art historian Craig Clunas calls "the ugly bodies of the poor." Clunas writes
that the bodies of the urban poor in works such as Zhou Chen's *Beg-
gars and Street Characters* (1516) are "distinguished by their relative nudity and above all by their lack of verticality. The poor bend forward
whether burdened by disease and want or stooped in toil over their
tools, in contrast with figures who are both decently clothed and
dominantly erect in posture [e.g., Chinese elites]."[48]

Similarly, the bodies of the Taiwan savages in the *Tribute Illustrations* are represented in varying degrees as underclothed, undisci-

Fig. 25 Cooked savages of Fengshan county, Taiwan,
from *Qing Imperial Tribute Illustrations* (ca. 1751)

plined, and coarse. Often, the figure is represented with legs spread apart and torso hunched over. The feet are bare and heads uncovered. The muscles of the male savages are drawn in an exaggerated fashion, as are facial lines—all to emphasize the grotesqueness of these figures. The strongly delineated muscles of the savage male are very much reminiscent of Chinese pictures of bandits or demons, figures whose musculature distinguishes them from the Chinese elites with their soft and languid limbs.

That savagery is a matter of degree becomes clear when we compare the cooked savages of Fengshan county (Fig. 25) to the raw savages of the inner mountains of Zhanghua county (Fig. 26).[49] The cooked savages of Fengshan stand relatively erect and are clothed except for the feet and head. Their hair is pulled back neatly in a bun and their facial expressions are open and pleasing. Their brightly colored costumes are a combination of pale purple, blue, red, green, and brown. Although their costumes are exotic, these figures do not appear to be too far removed from civilization.

Fig. 26 Raw savages of Zhanghua county, Taiwan,
from *Qing Imperial Tribute Illustrations* (ca. 1751)

In contrast, the male raw savage of Zhanghua is the embodiment of the grotesque and the terrible. He is drawn in a demonlike stance, with one leg raised, holding a spear in one hand as though ready to strike. This figure is depicted nearly naked, with bulging and rippling muscles. His hair is loose (a sign of wildness), and he sports a number of feathers in his headband. This figure presents quite a threatening mien, for he not only holds a sword but carries two knives at his waist. The expression on his face is grotesque and contorted. Reinforcing the bellicose appearance of this figure, the scant costume he wears at his waist is a blazing, fiery red. His female counterpart is noticeably less fierce, although her exposed midriff signifies her relative savagery.[50]

This picture draws on the visual iconography of savagery established by such works as the *Illustrated Record of Strange Countries*. In particular, it bears a strong resemblance to the *Illustrated Record*'s depiction of the man-eating, demonic Raksha (Fig. 27).[51] The Raksha is

Fig. 27   Raksha from Ning Xian Wang (attr.),
Illustrated Record of Strange Countries (ca. 1430),
FC.246.5 (reproduced by permission of the
Syndics of Cambridge University Library)

drawn with the same rippling musculature, the same bulging eyes and ferocious expression; he is posed in a similar stance to the raw savage of Zhanghua, with a spear in the right hand, and his left hand outstretched. The *Illustrated Record* describes these Rakshas as ferocious man-eaters, so fierce that none dare set foot in their country. Both these figures, the Raksha and the raw savage, further resemble Chinese representations of the demon-queller, Zhong Kui. Employing the pictorial conventions for representing demonic beings, the *Tribute Illustrations* portrays the raw savage of the inner mountains as monstrous in appearance.

The visual representations of the cooked savages of Fengshan and the raw savages of Zhanghua correspond to the textual descriptions of each group. The text describes the Fengshan subjects as "good at plowing and planting. They grow fragrant rice. The men cover their bodies

朝
鮮
國
夷
官

Fig. 28 Korean gentleman from *Qing Imperial
Tribute Illustrations* (ca. 1751)

with deer hide; some wear a blanket like a cape. The women wear
blouses and skirts."[52] These people are thus associated with both agriculture and clothing, important indices of civilization for Chinese literati. "The raw savages of the inner mountains," on the other hand,
"live in the deep mountains and hidden valleys—places where human
footsteps seldom reach. They dwell in nests and caves, eating fur and
drinking blood. They are naked and fear neither the cold of winter
nor the heat of summer. . . . When they meet people from China
proper, they immediately attack them with spears."[53]

Described in terms of the rhetoric of privation discussed in Chapter
2, the raw savage is depicted as both utterly uncivilized and hostile.
The artist's depiction of the physical appearances of the cooked savage
and the raw savage can thus be read as a reflection of their relative levels of civilization. In particular, the grotesqueness of the raw savage is
associated with both cultural backwardness and belligerence.

Thus, racial difference as visualized in the *Tribute Illustrations* can be read as the embodiment of cultural difference; that is, the relative concepts of "civilized," "barbaric," and "savage" are variously embodied in the human figures. At one end of the spectrum is the Korean gentleman (Fig. 28), the first figure in the collection.[54] Perhaps considered the most "civilized" of all the barbarians, the Korean gentleman is not much different from the ideal Qing gentleman except for his lack of a queue. He is fully clothed, capped, and shod and stands erect with one hand to his bosom. The expression on his face, which is painted a pallid white, is placid. At the other end of the spectrum, we have figures such as the raw savage of Zhanghua (Fig. 26), whose difference from the civilized person is highlighted in every possible way, figures that resemble demons more than men. In between various figures embody relative degrees of barbarism. The visual distinctions the artist has drawn between the raw and the cooked savages raise the intriguing possibility that physical transformation could accompany the cultural transformation from raw to cooked.

Representing Inborn Nature

If physical appearance can be read as the outward manifestation of cultural difference, it can also be read as the outward manifestation of inborn nature. The raw savages of Danshui (Fig. 29), for example, who are described as unyielding, cruel, and fierce by nature, are portrayed as particularly monstrous in appearance.[55] Again drawing on the visual iconography of savagery, the artist has represented this figure with rippling muscles, loose hair, bulging eyes, and a fierce, contorted face. Demonstrating his ferocity, he is posed in a warlike stance, long knife in one hand and barbed spear raised in the other. The physical repulsiveness or ugliness (*e*) of this figure becomes an index of moral repulsiveness, of an evil (*e*) nature. In contrast, the tamed and submitted cooked savages are represented as outwardly pliant and even, in the case of the cooked savages of Taiwan county (Fig. 30), for example, submissive in bearing. Thus countenance serves as an index to a people's nature.[56]

The same strategy of representation is frequently employed in the Miao albums. In *Pictures and Explanations of the Barbarians of Yunnan* (*Dianyi tushuo*), held by the Academia Sinica, for example, the "Wild

Fig. 29 Raw savages of Danshui, Taiwan, from
Qing Imperial Tribute Illustrations (ca. 1751)

People" (*Yeren*) are depicted with the musculature, bulging eyes, and fierce expressions characteristic of the visual iconography of savagery. The artist has also given them unruly beards and fantastic eyebrows that accentuate their ferocious miens.[57] The annotation describes these people as belligerent and ferocious by nature.[58] Another notoriously fierce group, the Jiexie (Color Plate 13), is similarly depicted as monstrous in appearance and resembles Buddhist depictions of the demons of hell.[59] Indeed, one function of the Miao albums, as described by Laura Hostetler, was to distinguish between groups that were docile and those that were belligerent in nature. As stated in one album preface quoted by Hostetler, "Their customs are, of course, distinct, and their natures, consequently, can also be distinguished."[60] The visual embodiment of inborn nature through illustration was one means of signifying such differences.

Fig. 30 Cooked savages of Taiwan county, Taiwan, from
Qing Imperial Tribute Illustrations (ca. 1751)

Adding Bodies to the Picture

If we compare Qing ethnographic descriptions and illustrations, we
find that whereas the physical aspects of racial difference play a relatively small role in Qing ethnographic discourse about the Taiwan indigenes, in the realm of *tu*, "racial difference" is clearly visualized. In
travel accounts of Taiwan, writers devote relatively little attention to
the physical appearance of the indigenous people. They occasionally
mention in passing that the indigenous people have large eyes or dark
skin, or that the women are fair, but there is no systematic effort to
develop a physical typology of the savage. Gazetteers also devote relatively little space to physical appearance (*zhuangmao*).

In pictures we find the bodies that are missing from Qing ethnographic discourse about the Taiwan indigenes. In both ethnographic
illustrations and the *Tribute Illustrations*, it is quite clear visually that

the body of the savage is distinct from the body of the civilized Han Chinese. The physical differences pictured in the *Tribute Illustrations* can be read as the embodiment of cultural difference. The Taiwan indigenes, for example, clearly display on their bodies the visual signs of savagery—nakedness, tattoos, piercings, bulging muscles, and belligerent postures. In contrast, the Korean gentleman is the embodiment of civilization—clothed, placid, and erect in posture. The cultural differences between the savage and the civilized are thus visualized in physical terms. Physical appearance also serves as an index to inborn nature, for savagery and belligerence could be read through physiognomy: the moral qualities of good (*shan*) and evil (*e*) being revealed through a pleasant (*shan*) or ugly (*e*) aspect. Thus, in combination Qing ethnographic illustrations and ethnographic writing bear witness that physical difference, cultural difference, and differences in inborn nature were intertwined in Qing conceptions of racial/ethnic difference.

CHAPTER 7

An Island of Women

The Discourse of Gender

On Ming and Qing maps it is not unusual to find the Kingdom of Women located in the seas to the southeast of China (see Color Plate 2).[1] If early Qing travelers to Taiwan imagined that they had discovered a living museum of antiquity, they perhaps also imagined that they had stumbled upon this Chinese equivalent of the land of the Amazons. Encountering a realm with female tribal heads, uxorilocal marriage, and matrilineal inheritance, these travelers noted with astonishment that native custom gave precedence to the female sex. As in the Kingdom of Women, it appeared, on this island it was the women who took the lead and the men who followed. "The savages value woman and undervalue man" (*zhongnü qingnan*) became a commonplace of Qing ethnographic writing on the Taiwan indigenes. As a direct inversion of the Confucian patriarchal maxim "value man and undervalue woman" (*zhongnan qingnü*), this expression captured the utter alterity of Taiwan in Chinese eyes. The anomalous gender roles of the indigenous peoples became one of the most popular topics in Qing travel writing on Taiwan. Writers exhibited a particular fascination with the habits of the "savage woman." Women and their daily activities were also a favorite subject for ethnographic illustration (see Color Plate 6 and Figs. 17, 20). Female sex roles attracted this intense interest not only because they appeared strange in and of themselves, but also because they served as a marker of the strangeness of Taiwan as a whole. The discourse of gender was thus central to Qing colonial representations of Taiwan's "savagery."

Indeed, gender and ethnicity were closely intertwined in premodern Chinese ethnographic discourse. At least as far back as the Six Dynasties (222–589), the trope of gender inversion (the reversal of normative sex roles) was used to represent foreignness in both historical and literary texts. Kingdoms of Women were widely recorded in geographic texts such as the ancient *Classic of Mountains and Seas*, as well as in the dynastic histories and travel accounts. Such lands also became a favorite subject of fiction, the most famous Qing example being the nineteenth-century satiric novel, *Flowers in the Mirror* (*Jinghua yuan*). The trope of gender inversion was particularly popular in accounts of the region now known as Southeast Asia and (in the late Qing) of America and Europe. In such writings, the discourse of gender became a means of demarcating the "civilized" from the "barbarian" or "savage." The rigidity of sex roles in Confucian ideology meant that deviations from normative definitions of femininity and masculinity were readily interpreted as signs of barbarism. Other gendered tropes, such as hypermasculinization and hyperfeminization, were also employed to establish the alterity of non-Chinese groups. Such tropes were particularly popular in literary forms such as frontier poetry.

In Qing colonial discourse, gendered or sexualized tropes are employed not only as a means of signifying the otherness of the colonial subject but also quite often as a form of denigration. Thus, gender functions much as it does in the European discourses of discovery and colonialism—to express relations of domination and subordination. A critical point of difference, however, is that Qing colonial discourse does not represent the colonized land itself as metaphorically feminine or as virgin. Exploration and conquest, in turn, are not figured as sexualized acts of penetration and possession. Qing travel writers did, however, represent colonial expansion as a masculine quest for sexual experience, a trope that postcolonial scholars have identified as a major theme of Western imperialist writings. Colonial relations, too, are sexualized in their textual representations: colonial power and ethnic prestige are symbolized by the sexual license of Chinese men vis-à-vis native women. Thus, in terms of gender, Qing colonial discourse exhibits considerable overlap with European colonial discourses but is yet not entirely parallel. An examination of gender dynamics in Taiwan travel literature reveals that insights from Western colonial theory can provide useful tools of analysis, but that the particular gendered tropes of this literature derive from within the Chinese literary tradition.

The uses of gender as a metaphor for conceptualizing inequality or as a means of signifying relationships of power have been extensively theorized by postcolonial critics, anthropologists, and feminist scholars. Gender appears to be a particularly apt metaphor for colonial discourse because it expresses both difference and hierarchy. The link between gender and the construction of the "other" has been widely noted since Edward Said's *Orientalism*. Said posited that in European representations of the Orient from the late eighteenth century onward, the Oriental subject is gendered feminine (weak, subordinated, irrational, lascivious) in contrast to the normative Western self, which is gendered masculine (strong, dominant, rational, continent). As such, there is a structural equivalence between male and female, major and minor. In the China field, anthropologists such as Dru Gladney, Stevan Harrell, and Louisa Schein have found parallels to Western Orientalism in Chinese representations of non-Han minority peoples as a feminized and subordinated other to the Han majority.[2] Other recent scholarship, such as that of Ann Stoler, Anne McClintock, and Susan Morgan, challenges the oversimplification of Said's paradigm and calls attention to colonial women's differential experiences of gender politics.[3] Much of the newer scholarship adopts an intersectional approach, examining the connections of race, gender, class, and sexuality. Further elaborating the intersections between gender and ethnicity, Sau-ling Wong has written of the "ethnicizing of gender"— essentially the reverse phenomenon of Orientalism's "gendering" of ethnicity. Wong describes the "ethnicizing of gender" as the "attribution of allegedly natural ethnic essences such as 'Chineseness' or 'Americanness' to 'masculine' and 'feminine' behavior."[4] In the case of Qing travel literature we see a similar attribution of "civilized" and "barbaric" to "masculine" and "feminine" behaviors. The intersections of gender and ethnicity (or race) are thus varied and multidimensional.

This chapter examines the representation of the "savage woman" in Qing travel accounts of Taiwan and the linkages between gender and ethnicity in Qing colonial discourse. My central argument is that gender inversion is fundamental to the construction of the ethnic difference of Taiwan indigenes. One aspect of this inversion, the feminization of the indigenous men, may be regarded as a means of expressing the subordinate status of the colonized subject. However, it is less the feminization of the men than the anomalous roles of women that pre-occupy Chinese travel writers. This fascination stems in large part, I would argue, from their desire to imagine "another world." Taiwan frequently served as a projection of this desire in travel literature, whether as a world of the past, a world of marvels, or a "kingdom of women."

The savage woman not only symbolized difference to Chinese observers but was also a pivotal figure in the representation of colonial relations: colonial dominance was frequently represented in terms of Han Chinese access to indigenous women. Qing writings thus typically hypersexualized the savage woman, depicting her as more erotic, more promiscuous, than the Chinese woman. Intermarriage between Han Chinese settlers and indigenous Taiwanese eventually became a source of contention in frontier society, with women serving as a kind of contested terrain for the colonizers and colonized. At the same time, intermarriage between Han settlers and indigenous women was an important vehicle for transcultural exchange in colonial Taiwan: a two-way process of acculturation.

At other times, the discourse of gender in the travel literature was less about Taiwan itself than about the internal concerns of Qing society, in particular, the changing roles of women. As I demonstrate through a comparative analysis of fictional and ethnographic representations of various non-Chinese women, the idealization of the foreign woman became a common trope for self-reflexive critiques of Chinese society, in both travel literature and fiction. In this mode, the foreign woman serves as a projection for Confucian ideals perceived to be losing their hold in China. The figure of the savage woman, then, could serve a variety of rhetorical purposes, often opposing, depending on the needs of the travel writer.

Reading Gender Inversion

Certain practices emerged as indices of gender inversion in the literature: uxorilocal marriage, the "preference" for female children, matrilineal inheritance, the sexual assertiveness of women, the sexual division of labor, the absence of postpartum seclusion, and the fact that women were not sequestered. Although the existence of female tribal heads among certain groups represented an obvious inversion of the Chinese norm of male rulership, it was the domestic roles of native women that became the focus of attention in the travel accounts. Chinese writers theorized that it was the savage woman's position in the family that accounted for her social dominance. There is little discussion of women's roles in indigenous political or religious life, aside from occasional references to "female local chiefs."

According to modern anthropologists, the indigenous groups of Taiwan employed a variety of marriage and inheritance systems prior to Chinese colonization. The Siraya of the southwest region, the core of Dutch and Chinese settlement, practiced uxorilocal marriage and matrilineal inheritance. The rest of the groups on the western coast practiced virilocal and ambilocal marriage and a variety of inheritance patterns (patrilineal, ambilineal, and bilateral).[5] Groups on the eastern coast practiced matrilineal inheritance. The majority of Qing writers, however, tended to lump the various indigenous groups together as "savages." They generally characterized these "savages" as a gynocentric people who "valued woman and undervalued man."[6] Chinese sensationalism may have been a major factor in this stereotyping in the literature. In addition, Qing ethnographic representation tends to establish the identity of a group by fixing on its "unique" or "strange" features. My task here, as throughout this work, is not to establish the accuracy of Qing descriptions of indigenous Taiwanese society but to analyze their representational strategies.

Chinese travel writers may have been predisposed to view Taiwan as a gynocentric society in part because of the familiarity of tales of Kingdoms of Women (much as Sir Walter Raleigh was predisposed to find the Amazons in South America). Various Chinese geographic works, for example, Song author Zhao Rugua's *Record of the Various Barbarians* (*Zhufan zhi*), located Kingdoms of Women in the general vicinity of Taiwan, Japan, or the Malay archipelago. Such works may have planted the notion of connections between Taiwan and a Kingdom of Women in the minds of Chinese travelers. Certainly these legends of "matriarchal lands" must have colored their perceptions of indigenous Taiwanese gender roles.

Qing representations of the Taiwan indigenes were also influenced by a pattern of regional stereotyping in both literary and historical materials. By the Tang dynasty, a pattern of feminizing the southern borderlands and masculinizing the northern frontiers had been firmly established in the Chinese literary tradition. The south was associated with sensuality, languor, literary refinement, femininity, and female promiscuity; the north with barrenness, ruggedness, martial valor, and machismo. This divide between hyperfeminized southerners (peoples such as the Miao and the Dai), on the one hand, and hypermasculinized northerners (the Mongols and Jurchens), on the other hand, means that the simple structural equation male : female :: major : minor is untenable. Rather, Han Chinese writers configured their others in terms of polarized opposites of sexual excess, centering the Han self as the norm. To Qing literati, Taiwan seemed to fit neatly into preexisting images of "southern barbarians" as matriarchal types. Writers often borrowed tropes from earlier accounts of the Miao, the Lao, and even the natives of Siam to describe the indigenous peoples of Taiwan. The hypersexualization of Taiwan's indigenous women could also be fit into this larger pattern of stereotypes about the south. This gendering of the south as feminine thus forms an important context for reading Qing representations of the "savage woman" of Taiwan.

"Value Woman and Undervalue Man"

Descriptions of uxorilocal marriage and matrilineal descent among the Taiwan indigenes commonly invoked the notion of inversion. The earliest Chinese account of native marriage practices can be found in Chen Di's *Record of the Eastern Savages*:

The girl hears [the suitor's music] and admits him to stay the night. Before daylight he straightaway departs, without seeing the girl's parents. From this time on, he must come in the dark and leave with the dawn when the stars are out, for months and years without any change. When a child is born, she for the first time goes to the man's home and [brings him back to her home] to be welcomed as a son-in-law, as [the Chinese] welcome a new bride, and the son-in-law for the first time sees the girl's parents. He then lives in her home and supports her parents for the rest of their lives, and his own parents can no longer regard him as their son. Therefore they are much happier at the birth of a girl than of a boy, in view of the fact that a girl will continue the family line, whereas a boy is not sufficient to establish the family succession.[7]

This passage clearly represents an interpretation of native customs through the lens of Chinese gender ideology. Chen Di employed the discourse of inversion in likening the savage bridegroom to the Chinese bride. The phrase "to be welcomed as a son-in-law, as [the

Chinese] welcome a new bride" sets up the equation "savage man = Chinese woman." At the end of Chen's description, he delivered what would become one of the quintessential formulations of gender inversion among the Taiwan savages: "they are much happier at the birth of a girl than of a boy." This inversion of normative Chinese values serves as a basic index of the difference between Chinese and savage. Rather than simply marveling at the strange nature of this inversion, however, Chen provided a rationale for the difference in values. Since it is the savage women who assume the function of continuing the family succession (an all-important role in Chinese culture), daughters, and not sons, become the privileged progeny. In identifying the inheritance system as the root of the strange gender hierarchy, Chen represents the reversal of gender privilege as a product of social convention and economic relations. Such an explanation serves at once to distance the savages (they are matrilineal; we are patrilineal) and to normalize them (they, like us, value the sex that assures the continuation of the family line).

Following Chen Di, discussions of marital customs and their effects on the gender hierarchy became a standard element of descriptions of indigenous customs. Yu Yonghe provided this account of native courtship:

In marriage they have no go-betweens; when the girls are grown, their parents have them live separately in a hut. All the youths who wish to find a mate come along, playing their nose-flutes and mouth-organs. When a youth gets the girl to harmonize with him, he goes in and fornicates with her. After they fornicate, he goes home of his own accord. After a long time, the girl picks the one she loves and "holds hands" with him. The "hand-holding" is to make public the private commitment. The next day, the girl tells her family and invites the "hand-holding" youth to come to her home. He knocks out the two top bicuspids to give to the girl, and she also knocks out two teeth to give to the boy. They set a date to go to the wife's house to marry, and for the rest of his life he lives at the wife's residence. . . . The parents are not able to keep their son. Therefore, after one or two generations the grandchild does not know his ancestors; the savages have no family names.[8]

Highlighting female agency in mate selection, Yu painted a vivid picture of the "sexual assertiveness" of the savage woman, an image that would have been most shocking to Chinese audiences for whom arranged marriage was the norm. For Yu, gender inversion signaled the disruption of the entire kinship system, leading the savages to forget their own ancestors. The notion that the indigenes did not recognize their ancestors was another indication of their savagery, of their animal-like existence, since for Chinese, ancestor-worship was one of the cornerstones of civilization.

Other writers decried the "subordination" of the savage male by uxorilocal marriage practices, viewing the husbands as debased and emasculated.[9] To these authors, uxorilocal marriage was not simply different and strange but contemptible. The equivalence drawn in Chinese eyes between the savage groom and the Chinese bride provided an impetus for this interpretation of gender relations. That is, the notion of inversion, of a "mirror world," conditioned Chinese understandings of gender relations that differed from the Confucian norm.

The feminization of the indigenous male in Chinese sources may have initially been based on a structural similarity between their roles and the role of the Chinese wife; however, this feminization went beyond external metaphor to include the idea that there were shared features between the savage male and the female gender. The lack of facial hair among indigenous men was one characteristic that led Chinese observers to comment that the savage male was woman-like in his cosmetic habits. Others remarked that the beardless savage male was perhaps a natural eunuch. In either case, the absence of facial hair signified his minor status.

Industrious Women and Idle Men

The inversion of gender was also represented in the travel literature by descriptions of the sexual division of labor. Numerous Chinese observers expressed surprise at the fact that it was the indigenous women, and not the men, who were engaged in agricultural production. This perceived reversal of sex roles was interpreted by the Chinese as female "industriousness" and male "idleness," since Chinese literati did not recognize the male occupation of hunting as "productive" activity. As Lin Qianguang declared: "All the tilling is done by the wife; the husband, on the other hand, stays at home waiting to be fed."[10] This image of the man's childlike dependence on his wife's labor recurred frequently in the literature, providing yet another rationale in Chinese eyes for female dominance in savage society.

This traditional sexual division of labor proved to be an obstacle for both the Dutch and the Chinese colonizers of Taiwan in their efforts to convert the island into a commercial agricultural economy. John Shepherd describes the difficulties the Dutch and Chinese faced in convincing indigenous men to give up hunting and take up sedentary agriculture as a primary occupation: "For them, farming had two major drawbacks: first, according to the traditional sexual division of labor, it was women's work; second, it was labor-intensive drudgery."[11] Both the Dutch and the Chinese, therefore, were forced to import Chinese labor in order to sustain commercial agricultural development.

By the nineteenth century, the dominance of the female gender had become so much a part of the popular imagery of Taiwan that certain writers even attributed the stereotype of the supremely capable wife to the Han Chinese women on the island.

The South as a Realm of Women

The depiction of Taiwan as a matriarchal land can be regarded as part of a long tradition of southern exoticism in classical Chinese literature. The ancient poetic tradition of the *Songs of the South* (*Chuci*) established an association between the south, female goddesses, and eroticism that was to be replayed throughout Chinese literary history. The legend of Xi Shi, a beauty from the southern region of Yue who was used to seduce the king of the rival kingdom of Wu, further mythologized the south as a region of sensuality and female beauty. The stereotype of the sensuous south was perhaps most firmly established by the poetic tradition of the Six Dynasties. It was during this time that "lotus-picking songs" (*cailian qu*) portraying young girls of the southern Jiangnan region came to represent the sensual image of the south and its waterways.

Historical and pseudo-historical accounts of non-Han peoples of the southern regions were another source of this stereotype. Historical works such as the *History of the Han* (*Hanshu*), for example, noted that it was the custom in various southern regions for women to bathe openly in streams. The Dai became particularly famous for this custom, an image that remains popular among PRC tourists today.[12]

Indeed, the hypersexualization of non-Han in southern China has maintained a certain consistency over the centuries.

Female dominance, or gender inversion, was another favorite motif of accounts about "southern barbarians," both in histories and anomaly accounts. The entry on "The Lao Women" from the *Accounts Widely Gathered in the Taiping Era* (*Taiping guangji*), for example, focuses on gender inversion as its central point of interest.

In the south there are Lao women. They give birth to children and then get up. Their husbands lie in bed. Their diets are exactly the same as a nursing mother. They do not protect their pregnant women in the least. When the women go into labor, they give birth on the spot. They do not suffer in the least. They prepare food and gather firewood as usual. It is also said that according to Yue custom, if a wife gives birth to a child, after three days, she bathes in the stream. When she returns, she prepares gruel to feed her husband. The husband bundles the infant in the bedclothes and sits up in bed. They call him the "parturient husband." Their inversion is to such a degree.[13]

Ming and Qing gazetteer descriptions of groups such as the Miao, for example, followed a similar pattern of emphasizing female dominance or sexual assertiveness. In a study of Ming and Qing representations of the Miao, Norma Diamond found that

the Miao album pictures and gazetteer texts highlight wherever possible the occurrence of reversal of proper gender roles: among the Nong Miao men are expected to care for infants, among the Bafan Miao women do most of the agricultural work, and in several groups men and women join together in farming, raiding the fields of others (presumably Han settlers) or hunting.[14]

Travel accounts of foreign lands south of China's borders similarly employed the trope of gender inversion. Ma Huan's account of the naval expeditions of the eunuch admiral Zheng He, for example, noted anomalous gender roles in several Southeast Asian and South Asian countries. He wrote of Thailand, for instance:

It is their custom that all affairs are managed by their wives. From the king to the common people, whenever there are matters which require thought and deliberation—punishments light and heavy, trading transactions great and small—they all follow the decisions of their wives, [for] the mental capacity of the wives certainly exceeds that of the men.[15]

Ma Huan furthermore characterized Thai women as "promiscuous," a common stereotype of Southeast Asian women in Chinese travel accounts from at least the Yuan dynasty onward.

This feminization of the south was contrasted with the masculinization of the northern frontiers in both literary and historical sources. These gendered stereotypes were influenced by several factors: the existence of matrilineal customs among southern "barbarians"; the association of northern "barbarians" with warfare; theories of environmental determinism of human character (the environment of the north being rugged and that of the south being wet and fertile); and the relative strength of the expansionist northern dynasties vis-à-vis the overrefined and declining southern dynasties during the Six Dynasties era. These stereotypes were further developed in Tang literary treatments of the northern frontiers and the southern borderlands. The southern male was in effect emasculated not only by the empowerment of the southern female but also as part of a general feminization of the region. The feminization of southern peoples and the masculinization of northern peoples served to center the ideal Han Chinese self of the "central plains" as a privileged norm. A similar phenomenon can be seen in British colonial representations of the northern Indian Sikhs as martial/masculine and southern Indian peoples as sensual/feminine.[16]

The feminization of the Taiwan indigenes should thus not be understood simply as part of a general case of feminizing the other, but as part of this particular economy of regional stereotypes within the Chinese literary tradition. In describing the Taiwan indigenes as matriarchal, travelers were likely to have been influenced by the familiarity of images of female dominance in the south. Indeed, travel writers frequently compared the "savages" of Taiwan to the Southern Man "barbarians" or to "the people of Wu and Yue" in southern China. This is not surprising given the fact that the various Chinese ethnonyms for southern peoples, such as "Miao," "Lao" and "Man," although perhaps originally referring to specific ethnic groups, came to be commonly used to refer to "southern barbarians" in general. Thus, characteristics attributed to any particular group could be mapped on to other groups as part of the general stereotype of the "southern barbarian." In making the comparison between the Taiwan indigenes and China's historical "southern barbarians," Qing writers effectively recast the once-obscure island of "Eastern Savages" as part of China's sensuous and feminine southland, eminently familiar to readers of China's poetic tradition from the Tang on.[17]

The image of Taiwan as part of the exotic/erotic southland was promoted by descriptions of female bathers, native sexual habits, and feminine beauty. Yu Yonghe, for example, frequently included notes in his travelogue about the physical appearance (and indeed sexual attractiveness) of the women whom he encountered. His diary entry for one day has the note "of the savage women that we saw, many were fair-skinned and beautiful."[18] On another day he observed: "there were also three young girls working with mortar and pestle. One of them was rather attractive. They appeared in front of outsiders naked, but their composure was dignified."[19] Although there is frequent reference in the literature to both male and female nudity (nakedness in general being a sign of impropriety and thus cultural inferiority), it is only the savage woman's lack of shame concerning nudity that receives comment from the travel writers. Since one of the chief markers of proper femininity in Chinese culture was the shrouding of the body, the savage woman's lack of modesty must have appeared to Chinese observers as particularly strange and offensive.

It is partly for this reason that travel writers expressed great interest in the bathing habits of indigene women, noting in particular the frequency and openness of this practice. Censor Lui-shi-qi went so far as to devote an entire entry of his travel account to the topic "Bathing in the Stream." His description explicitly eroticizes the act of bathing by linking it with play, flirtation, and voyeurism. The objectification of women is particularly apparent in Qing ethnographic illustrations in which women are often depicted in festival dress or bare-breasted (Color Plate 12, Figs. 17, 18, 20).

The image of Taiwan as a land of exotic sensuality was perhaps most promoted by descriptions of native courtship and marriage practices. A standard favorite in the Taiwan literature was the anecdote about youths sealing partnerships with young girls based on their ability to harmonize with them on the mouth organ: "to harmonize" being a pun on "to couple." For a Chinese audience, such anecdotes were reminiscent of poetic motifs in the ancient *Classic of Poetry* and thus conjured up images of a primitive past. At the same time, the notion that the savages lacked an understanding of sexual propriety signaled their uncivilized status.

The absence of the segregation of the sexes and proscriptions against physical contact—a taboo signified in Chinese society by the Confucian precept "in giving and receiving men and women do not touch [hands]"—were again marks of a lack of sexual propriety in savage society. Travel writers frequently remarked that savage men and women would sit together "mixed," or "without order." Other Qing travelers saw an opportunity to indulge in voyeurism and other behavior taboo in their own society. Censor Lui-shi-qi, for example, made this note under the heading of "Suckling the Child" in his travel account: "The savages have no taboos against contact between male and female. When the savage woman nurses her child, those who see will play and tease from the side. She will be very pleased, thinking that people adore her child. Even if one touches her breast she will not prevent it."[20] The savage woman's body thus formed a direct contrast to the proper Chinese female body, which ideally remained out of sight and beyond touch. Such details added a titillating element to ethnographic description and bolstered the image of Taiwan as a fantasy island where Chinese men had free license to dally with the native women.

Intermarriage: The Role
of Woman in Transculturation

The notion that Chinese men had easy access to the savage woman's body fed into the representation of Chinese colonial prestige in travel writing. Interethnic marriage or sexual relations served in numerous narratives as a means to represent the ethnic hierarchy of the colonial society, calling attention to the unequal balance of power between Chinese and indigene. As an object of Han Chinese sexual desire, the "savage woman" became a site for the contestation of power between colonizer and colonized. Yu Yonghe, for example, observed of the Chinese on the island, "They take the savage women as their wives and concubines. Whatever is demanded of them, they must comply; if they make a mistake, they must take a flogging. And yet the savages do not hate them greatly."[21] Yu furthermore represented the accessibility of native women to Chinese as a product of ethnic privilege:

Should the guests take liberties with them [the women], they do not get angry. A husband, seeing a guest becoming intimate with his wife, is very pleased, saying that his wife is really charming, and that therefore Chinese like her. . . . However, should one of their own people fornicate with [a man's wife], then he will take his bow and arrows, search out the adulterer, and shoot him dead. But he will not hold it against his wife.[22]

Such anecdotes portray the indigenes as clearly subordinated to the Chinese, supplying women and labor without animosity. The cuckolded husband is even said to interpret Chinese intimacy with his wife as a compliment, as proof of her exceptional qualities. For a Qing audience, such an anecdote could serve to confirm the superior status of the Chinese vis-à-vis the colonized natives.

Other travel writers contradicted Yu's claim regarding the liberties allowed Chinese men by recording conflicts between Han settlers and the local populace over such relations. Indeed, as rates of intermarriage increased during the Qing, owing to an unfavorable sex-ratio among the Han settlers, the Chinese demand for indigenous women came to be seen as a source of ethnic conflict by the administration.[23] After a local revolt, the Qing administration prohibited intermarriage between Han Chinese men and indigenous women in 1737. In terms of the legal code, this prohibition was subsumed under the statutes concerning the "savage boundary" and, like other aspects of the quarantine policy, was intended to maintain the ethnic status quo and thereby prevent interethnic conflict.[24]

Like the other boundary laws, the prohibition against intermarriage served to reinforce the ethnic distinctions between Han Chinese and indigene. The wording of an elaboration of the statute in 1834 indicates that the central concern of the law was not intermarriage per se but the improper crossing of the ethnic divide by Han Chinese men and the attendant threat that they might "go native." The law stipulated severe punishments for Chinese men who "loosened their queue, changed their costume, and married raw savage women."[25] A lesser penalty was stipulated for Chinese men who married raw savage women but maintained their queues and their Chinese costume. In the eyes of the Qing law, those who went native by adopting indigenous clothing and flouted Qing custom by loosening their queues clearly signaled their status as disloyal *Hanjian* who sought to live beyond Qing law. Intermarriage implied a similar danger but was viewed as less problematic when markers of Han Chinese (clothing) and Qing (queue) identity were maintained.

Plate 1 Illustrated Scroll of a Tour of Inspection of Taiwan, detail (Qing) (reproduced by permission of National Museum of Chinese History)

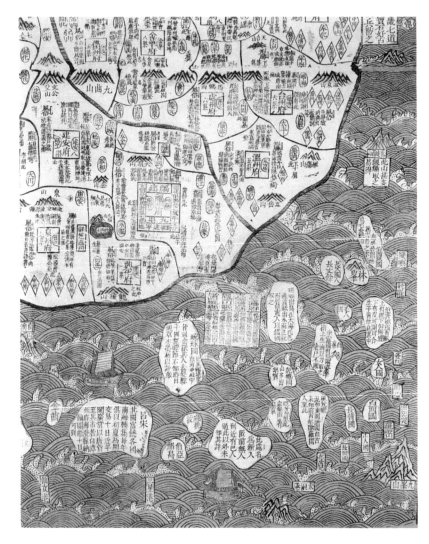

Plate 2 Chinese world map, detail (1743) from The British Library (15406.a.28)
(reproduced by permission of The British Library)

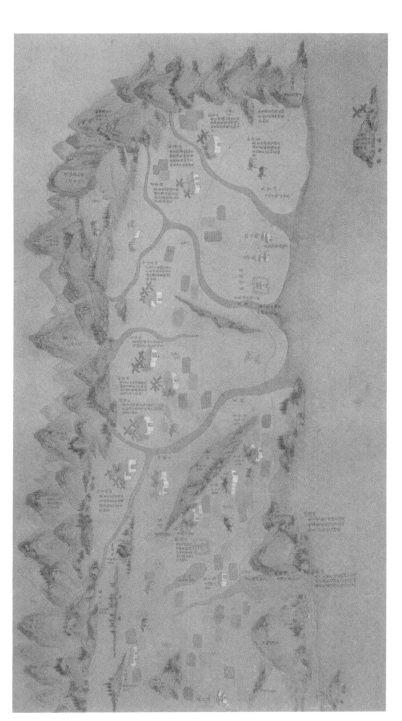

Plate 3 Huang Shujing (attr.), *A Map of Taiwan's Savage Villages*, detail (Kangxi era) (reproduced by permission of National Taiwan Museum) (*Continues on next two pages*)

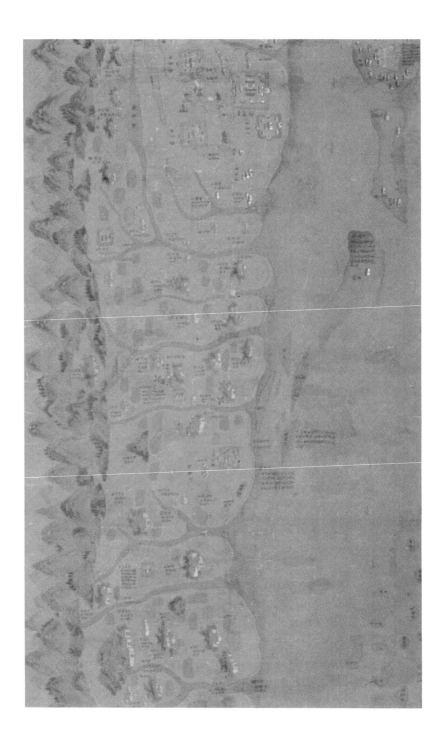

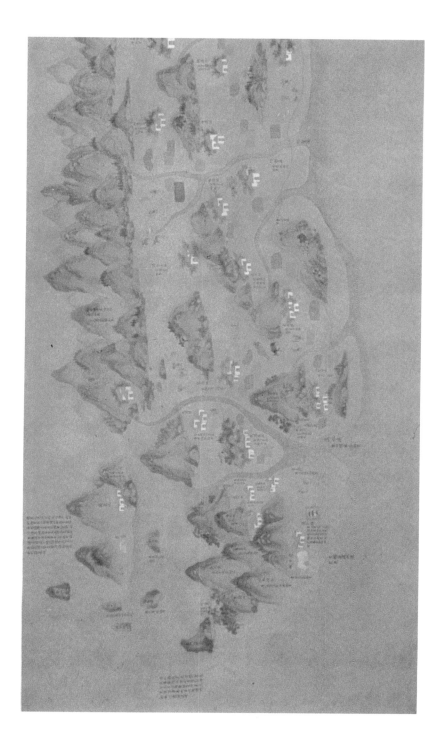

Plate 4 Map of Taiwan showing the Savage Boundary lines of 1750 (red) and 1760 (blue) (reproduced by permission from Ka Chih-ming, *Fan toujia*, p. 176).

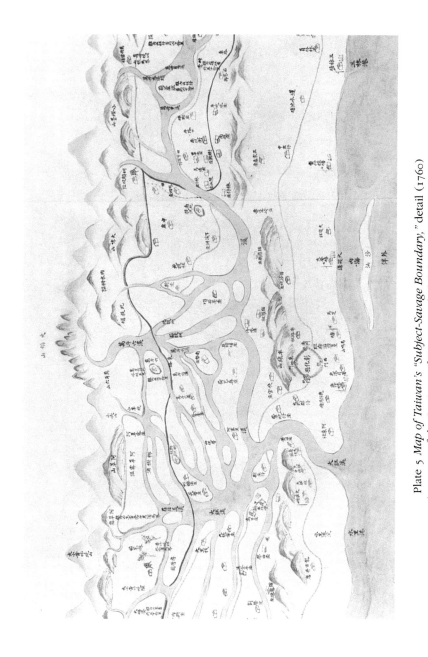

Plate 5 *Map of Taiwan's "Subject-Savage Boundary,"* detail (1760)
(courtesy of the Institute of History and Philology, Academia Sinica)

Plate 6 "Weaving" from Liu-shi-qi's *Illustrations of Taiwan's Savage Villages* (1745)
(courtesy of the Institute of History and Philology, Academia Sinica)

Plate 7 "Monkey-Style Picking" from Liu-shi-qi's *Illustrations of Taiwan's Savage Villages* (1745) (courtesy of the Institute of History and Philology, Academia Sinica)

種芋

鳳邑生番內山不知耕
種在於山間劃土種芋
每熟刈地為墢以火
墢之即播垂雲貿稅
出而食焉以為長久之
得

Plate 8 "Planting Taro" from Liu-shi-qi's *Illustrations of Taiwan's Savage Villages* (1745) (courtesy of the Institute of History and Philology, Academia Sinica)

Plate 9 "Sugar Production" from Liu-shi-qi's *Illustrations of Taiwan's Savage Villages* (1745) (courtesy of the Institute of History and Philology, Academia Sinica)

Plate 10 "Catching Wild Oxen" from Chen Bishen's *Illustrations of Savage Customs* (ca. 1770) (reproduced by permission of National Museum of Chinese History)

Plate 11 "Drinking Party, Nose Flutes" from Chen Bishen's *Illustrations of Savage Customs* (ca. 1770) (reproduced by permission of National Museum of Chinese History)

Plate 12 "Savage Festival" from Chen Bishen's *Illustrations of Savage Customs*
(ca. 1770) (reproduced by permission of National Museum
of Chinese History)

Plate 13 Picture of Jiexie from *Pictures and Explanations of the Barbarians of Yunnan* (Qing) (courtesy of the Institute of History and Philology, Academia Sinica)

Plate 14 Illustration of "Raw Savages Celebrate by Drinking from a Dripping Head" from *A Qing Album of Ethnographic Illustrations of Taiwan* (1875) (courtesy of the National Palace Museum, Beijing)

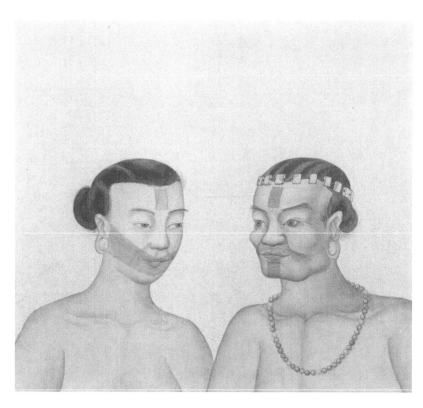

Plate 15 Illustration of "The Physical Appearance of the Bellicose Savages of Taipei" from *A Qing Album of Ethnographic Illustrations of Taiwan* (1875) (courtesy of the National Palace Museum, Beijing)

Although the law was intended to uphold ethnic distinctions on the frontier, unlike nineteenth-century American "antimiscegenation" laws, the Qing statute was not based on fears of "racial amalgamation."[26] Nor did it cast Han-indigene marriage as a sexual crime (again, the statute was classed under regulations concerning "border crossings," showing once more the conceptual links between territorial and ethnic boundaries). Despite the fact that the Qing deemed it expedient to limit intermarriage during this period in order to stabilize Han-indigene relations, there were apparently no social prohibitions against such couplings. Shepherd found that "the Chinese perceived no racial divide between Han and aborigines that would impede the ability of aborigines to acquire Chinese status characteristics or deny legitimacy to mixed marriages and their offspring."[27]

In fact, intermarriage between Han Chinese and indigene could even be perceived as beneficial by officials who advocated an assimilationist colonial policy.[28] One local official, for example, argued, "With marriage and social intercourse, there will be no separation between the savages and the people. If the officials do not segregate them as a different race (*zhong*), then after some time they will naturally assimilate (*hua*)."[29] As wives, then, indigenous women could be regarded as key vehicles for transculturation.[30] Indeed, anthropologist Melissa Brown has argued that during the Qing "intermarriage was the primary mechanism for introducing and spreading Chinese values and practices into Aborigine communities."[31] Although the phenomenon has been less well studied, intermarriage may also have been an important mechanism for introducing indigenous practices into Chinese communities, as indicated by the fears expressed in the 1834 law. Antonio Tavares's work provides evidence of the "indigenization" of individual Han Chinese men who married into native communities.[32]

The wording of the Qing statute on intermarriage presumed that these nuptials took the form of Han Chinese men "taking" (*qu*) indigenous women in marriage. The law is silent on the matter of indigenous men marrying Han Chinese women and on indigenous women "receiving" (*zhao*) Han Chinese men as uxorilocal husbands, rendering these possibilities all but invisible. The intersection of ethnic and gender privilege in the colonial context is thus inscribed into the subtext of the law.

The Lady Baozhu: Crossing
Between Genders and Ethnicities

Examples of Han women marrying indigene men were comparatively rare, at least until the late Qing.[33] There are few mentions of such marriages in the Qing travel literature other than the fascinating legend of Baozhu, a Han Chinese courtesan who became the female chieftain of an indigenous tribe. One nineteenth-century traveler, Ding Shaoyi, reconstructed the identity of this mysterious figure by relating two items from the local lore, one concerning a female chieftain and one concerning the Chinese consort of a local chief.

Prefect Deng Chuan'an of Fuliang says in his *Measuring the Sea with a Calabash*: "During the Jiaqing period [1796–1821], the female chieftain (*tuguan*) Baozhu made herself up like an aristocratic lady of China. In her administration, she followed the law. Someone sent the officials a memorial [stating that her tribe] followed the law obediently and respectfully, not killing people, not rebelling. Even though this place is beyond the pale, how is it different from China proper?" Legend has it that during the Zhu Yigui rebellion, the chief of the Beinanmi, Wenji, decided to get a beauty for his consort. There was a courtesan in Taiwan city who heard of this with delight and volunteered to go. The savages value women to begin with, and since the chieftain got a courtesan, he doted on her to the extreme, doing whatever she commanded. Then they got rid of their old customs and were civilized with the rites and laws of China. Therefore the seventy odd villages of the Beinanmi are the most orderly, and their customs were long different from those of the other savages. "Baozhu" is not like a savage woman's name. Perhaps this so-called female chieftain was after all a prostitute.[34]

The equation of Baozhu and the Han courtesan is based on one central point of coincidence, the woman's role in initiating the assimilation of her tribe to Chinese culture. The equivalence is facilitated by the liminality of both women: one a savage who resembles a Chinese; one a Chinese who resembles a savage. This allows Ding to speculate that they must be one and the same person.

By crossing ethnic boundaries to live among the savages, this figure "Baozhu" was able to take advantage of both the gender inversion in savage society and the superior status of her ethnicity to elevate her standing: in other words, she placed herself in a position in which both her femininity and her Chineseness were valued. The story thus nicely demonstrates that in certain cases it is ethnicity that brings privilege, and in other cases, it is gender. In dramatically rising from the station of a prostitute to a chieftain, Baozhu crossed not only ethnic boundaries but also status lines, "dressing herself up like an aristocratic lady of China." Baozhu's identity thus remained in a liminal state, between the savage and the civilized, between the lowly and the noble, between the matriarchal and the patriarchal. It is from this liminality, this ambiguous status, that Baozhu derived her power. The figure of Baozhu serves as a metaphor for the unique culture produced in the contact zone of the frontier; in "giving up" her Chineseness, Baozhu induces the savages to "give up" their savagery.[35] By straddling the insider/outsider opposition, by becoming a "hybrid," Baozhu in effect obliterates this opposition. As Ding's source, Deng Chuan'an, phrased it: "Even though this place is beyond the pale, how is it different from China proper?" In being placed at this point of cultural transference, on the cusp between different ethnicities and different gender ideologies, the figure of Baozhu illustrates how ethnicity and gender combine variously in the constitution of power.

Gender Inversion and the
Critique of Chinese Womanhood

Although I have examined the phenomenon of gender inversion mainly as a means of signifying the strangeness of the other, gender inversion could also be employed as a rhetorical device, often in a self-reflexive critique of Chinese mores. This device is generally linked to the mode of primitivism, in which the "less civilized" other is seen as a repository of values associated with a more virtuous, simple past. The status of the foreign woman as other made her a figure on which not only undesirable but also idealized traits could be projected. As an idealized other, the foreign woman serves as a foil against which to contrast the flaws of Chinese womanhood.

This technique is employed in a Qing vernacular story about a merchant's travels to Vietnam. Entitled "On a Journey to Vietnam a Jade Horse Miniature Is Exchanged for Crimson Velvet" ("Zou

Annan yuma huan xingrong," ca. 1661), the story uses the exotic setting of Vietnam to deliver a moral lesson about the laxity of contemporary Chinese women. Two of the central devices employed to establish the foreignness of Vietnam are the familiar tropes of gender
inversion and hypersexualization. In particular, it is the violation of
Chinese norms of gender segregation that captures the attention of the
narrator. However, a satirical twist in the narrator's rhetoric shifts the
story into the mode of self-reflexive critique. While proclaiming Vietnamese women to be inferior in their customs and lax in their sense of
public propriety, the narrator reveals his true object of criticism to be
Chinese womanhood. A description of the public bathing habits of
Vietnamese women becomes an opportunity to deride Chinese
women for their hypocrisy.

[The Vietnamese women] cannot measure up to our Chinese women,
who close the door so tightly when they take a bath that no breeze gets
through and furthermore insist that the maid stand outside the window
for fear that someone will peep on them. But these women's false pre-
tenses are really just a big show. Just look at our women of the south, all
day they go touring in the mountains or by the waters, visiting temples,
leaning on gates and standing in doorways, going to plays or societies;
they let the public see their powdered faces. And yet they want to criticize the shortcomings of men! Commenting and laughing at the looks of
passersby, they do not know how to cherish the "face" of the family. But
if the breeze so much as lifts up their skirts to reveal a bit of leg, or if they
are feeding a baby and their breast is exposed, or if they are going to the
toilet and their "thing" is exposed, they make a hundred gestures to cover
this and conceal that, and put on airs of distress. They do not know that
"face" and the body are one: if they want to cherish the body they should
cherish "face"; if they want to conceal the body, they should cover the
"face." The ancients said it well: "If the fence is secure, the dogs will not
get in." If you had not let outsiders see your face, how would they think
of violating your body?[36]

Although the Vietnamese are portrayed as less civilized because of
their lack of gender segregation, the real critique in this passage is
aimed at the moral degeneracy of Chinese women. Indeed, the narrator reveals at the conclusion that his dominant didactic concern is not
the violation of gender norms by Vietnamese women but the trans-
gressions of Chinese women. The structure of the story allows the au-

thor to simultaneously indulge in exotic fantasy and advocate greater conservatism in gender roles.

The nineteenth-century literatus Wu Ziguang employed a similar self-reflexive critique by idealizing the indigenous women of Taiwan as paragons of ancient simplicity and virtue.

Their clothing is all frugal and plain . . . and they have a profound understanding of the proprieties of antiquity. Moreover, they do not use cosmetics, just like the Lady of Guo [Yang Guifei's sister] who feared being stained with color. They do not paint their eyebrows: even if they had the brush of Zhang Chang, they would not use it.[37] Their manners are far superior in virtue to those of Chinese women.[38]

Wu claimed that it was the savages rather than the women of China who maintained the proprieties of Chinese antiquity. The women of China, he implied, have conversely become degenerate and frivolous. Rather than seeing an inversion of gender in the foreign culture, Wu projected a hyperrealization of Chinese gender ideals.

The idealization of the foreign woman as a foil to contemporary Chinese womanhood may have expressed an anxiety concerning the new social roles for women emerging during the late Ming and Qing.[39] Confucian ideals that were no longer upheld by Chinese women were thus projected onto foreign women. A particularly poignant example of this move appears in the famous account of the Qing massacre at Yangzhou, "A Record of Ten Days in Yangzhou" ("Yangzhou shiri ji," 1645). At one point in this piece, a Manchu soldier derides Chinese women for failing to demonstrate the chaste resolve of Korean women in the face of rape. The lesser commitment to Confucian strictures for female chastity is thus read as a symptom of the degeneration of Chinese society as a whole—an accusation that serves as a justification for the Manchu invasion. In all these examples, the association of particular sex roles with "civilization" and "barbarism" is turned on its head and used as a device to critique Chinese society, as "civilized" trades places with "barbaric."

The most famous Qing example of this type of gender play is Li Ruzhen's celebrated novel, *Flowers in the Mirror*. In this work, Li created a number of fantastically learned foreign female characters whose understanding of the Confucian classics far surpasses that of the average Chinese male. Throughout the novel, female literary talent is given an aura of glamour, and it is implied that China would be well served by the development of such talents among the female population. Li Ruzhen furthermore employed gender inversion in the Kingdom of Women episode of this novel, to satirize, and thereby denaturalize, Chinese sex roles. In particular, he called into question the humanity of practices such as footbinding. Through both satire and utopian vision, Li Ruzhen presented an idealized model of accomplished (albeit still Confucian) femininity, embodied in the women of fabulous countries.

Whether through the idealization of the foreign woman or through inversion, gender serves as a ready vehicle for the expression of ethnic alterity in Qing travel accounts. The linkage between gender and ethnicity is particularly strong because the difference that is built into gender can readily be converted into the difference of the foreign, and vice versa. The particular objectification of women in Qing ethnographic writing furthermore meant that Woman became a stand-in for the other. Thus, the strangeness of the "savage" woman of Taiwan represented the strangeness of her culture as a whole. The native woman also served as a mediator between colonizer and colonized, and as such became a figure through which relations of desire, domination, and exchange were expressed. The multiplicity of gendered images demonstrates, moreover, that the linkages between gender and ethnicity are not simply based on a direct metaphoric equivalence, the analogy Chinese : savage :: male : female. This is particularly true within the colonial or crosscultural context, where gender itself is already racialized, or ethnicized, creating an instability around the terms of gender. Therefore, although feminization may be a form of denigration, not all women are denigrated. What it meant to be a Han Chinese woman in colonial Taiwan was vastly different from what it meant to be an indigene woman, as the legend of Baozhu so nicely illustrates. Moreover, although the discourse of gender was central to the construction of ethnic difference in Qing travel writing, this discourse could also be employed as a vehicle for comment on concerns internal to Chinese society. Qing representations of "savage" gender relations thus in large measure reflected Chinese interests and cannot be read as reliable observations of indigenous life.

Modern-Day Manifestations
of Colonial Gender Discourse

The figure of the indigenous "mountain woman" (*shandi funü*) has continued to play a special role in modern Taiwan, being used to represent in many ways the "face" of indigenous culture to outside observers. The continuities between Qing and modern discourse are aptly demonstrated in a media article from the 1960s entitled "Aborigine Women of [Taiwan] Province March Toward the Realm of Civilization," which touts the achievements of the KMT in modernizing indigenous lifestyles.[40] The author, Yang Baiyuan, not only employed many of the old tropes of gender inversion but also argued that because of the vital role played by women in the matrilineal indigenous societies, governmental efforts at "civilizing" the indigenes must be directed primarily at the women. Indigenous women are thus again expected to serve as vehicles for the transmission of Chinese culture.

The discourse of hypersexualization has also continued to be employed, with some very real consequences for indigenous women—namely, their commodification in the tourism and sex industries. Photographs of indigenous women in traditional dress grace government tourist brochures. Costumed women are available for photo-ops with Chinese and Western tourists at all the major sightseeing areas, and, of course, no tour of Wulai or Taroko Gorge would be complete without a show of dancing indigenous girls. Indigenous women also constitute a major part of the sex industry and sex tourism in Taiwan and are disproportionately represented in illegal under-age prostitution. Poverty is a driving force behind this phenomenon. Also at play, however, are stereotypes about the indigenes' propensity for heavy drinking, which are used to justify the "natural" suitability of indigenous women as bar hostesses and nightclub entertainers. In the 1980s, the feminist and indigenous rights movements in Taiwan began generating greater social awareness of discriminatory attitudes toward indigenous women, and some of the older colonialist discourse has been discredited. It remains to be seen what new images will emerge.

CHAPTER 8

Fashioning Chinese Origins

Nineteenth-Century Ethnohistoriography

The question of the origins of the Taiwan indigenes had plagued Chinese literati since the earliest encounters. Even before Qing colonization of the island, Chen Di declared the origins of the Taiwan indigenes unknowable because of their absence from the Chinese histories, and the majority of Qing writers followed this line.[1] From the first, however, others speculated about the origins of these people. Their hypotheses, some fantastic, generally traced the Taiwan indigenes to China in some fashion. Yu Yonghe, for example, suggested that they were descended from Jin refugees who had fled China after the Yuan takeover and subsequently forgotten their origins.[2] Xu Huaizu proposed that they were the descendants of the five hundred boys and girls taken overseas by the magician whom the first Qin emperor had sent in search of the fairy isle Penglai.[3] Yet, these various hypotheses remained nothing more than speculations, and the problem of the Taiwan indigenes' origins went unsolved.

In the nineteenth century, literatus Deng Chuan'an composed an essay suggesting that the Taiwan indigenes were the living ancestors of the Chinese: "A Discourse on the Resemblance of Savage Customs to Those of Antiquity" ("Fansu jingu shuo").[4] In this essay, Deng used the methodology of evidential scholarship to compare the customs of the savages systematically with those of the ancients. Although Zhou Zhongxuan and other eighteenth-century writers had noted numerous congruences in the customs of the two groups, they had never attempted a rigorous analysis of these correspondences. In applying the methodology of evidential research to the study of indigenous customs in Taiwan, nineteenth-century literati like Deng Chuan'an turned the historical metaphor into a serious paradigm for ethno-historical research. For these evidential scholars, Taiwan was a living museum in which they could conduct empirical investigations of antiquity.

Nineteenth-century travelers to Taiwan were what Ali Behdad calls "belated travelers."[5] By this time, there was an abundance of texts about Taiwan, and the dominant textual tropes had been established. Travelers arrived on Taiwan with the baggage of expectations shaped by reading about the island, expectations that in turn informed their own writings.[6] The nineteenth-century writers who expected to encounter a living museum in Taiwan sought to go beyond the ethnographic documentation that had engaged eighteenth-century writers by turning to comparative ethnohistory. Comparative ethnohistory allowed them to develop interpretive paradigms for ethnographic data that on the whole tended to naturalize the incorporation of Taiwan into the Chinese empire. The rhetorical purpose of Deng's scholarly exercise, for example, was to diminish the difference between the Chinese and the savages by establishing their hypothetical common origins in the culture of Chinese antiquity. This chapter examines the work of two authors who attempted to domesticate the strangeness of savagery by extending the metaphor of the savages as ancestors into the domain of comparative ethnohistory.

Evidential Scholarship and the Search for Antiquity in the Wilderness

A native of Jiangxi who served in Taiwan as a subprefect for savage affairs (*lifan tongzhi*) from 1822 to 1830, Deng Chuan'an was inspired by the aphorism "When propriety is lost in China, search for it in the wilderness" to research the customs of the Taiwan indigenes. His concern with moral degeneration in Chinese society was motivated by his involvement with the evidential scholarship movement.

Emerging in the seventeenth and eighteenth centuries as an intellectual rejection of the Neo-Confucian orthodoxy, evidential research was a mode of empirical philological analysis aimed at verifying or refuting received interpretations of classical texts. Skeptical of the unquestioned authority of the Confucian classics, evidential scholars emphasized empirical research, precise scholarship, and rigorous analysis as the means of validating knowledge. Evidential research gained popularity among the literati elite in the Qing because many scholars blamed the fall of the Ming in 1644 on the moral decline engendered by Neo-Confucian distortions of the true meanings of the classics. Qing evidential scholars sought to rectify this moral degeneration by recovering the original meanings of the ancient sage-kings through philological analysis. The call for a "return to antiquity" (*fugu*) thus became a call for the renewal of society.[7]

The methodology of evidential research influenced a wide range of disciplines in the Qing: phonology, etymology, paleography, epigraphy, history, geography, and even mathematics became vehicles for reconstructing and reconnecting with antiquity. Comparative ethnohistory, too, was called on to serve similar ends. For Deng Chuan'an and others who followed him in Taiwan, the study of indigenous customs as analogues to, or survivals of, ancient customs lent itself to the evidential scholar's project of reconstructing the past and recovering antiquity.

The influence of evidential scholarship on Deng's "Discourse" is apparent, for Deng went beyond historical allusion to search for precise textual evidence to support his analogies. Fanciful references to Lord No-Cares and Getian are absent from this essay; rather, Deng took the notion that indigenous customs represent survivals or derivations from ancient Chinese practices seriously. The moral agenda of the evidential scholarship movement is also evident in "Discourse," for Deng not only offered his material as a resource for general research on antiquity (*kaogu*) but also suggested that the savages pointed the way for the restoration of antiquity.

By emphasizing the influence of evidential scholarship on Deng, I do not wish to suggest that "Discourse" is the product solely of Qing intellectual trends. In conceptualizing the customs of the indigenes as remnants or survivals from antiquity, Deng drew on the precedents of two early works that collate observed folk practices with historical textual records: Ying Shao's (fl. 189–194) *Comprehensive Account of Folkways* (*Fengsu tongyi*) and Ren Fang's (460–508) *Narratives of the Marvelous* (*Shuyi ji*). As Robert Campany argues in his study of Six Dynasties anomaly accounts (*zhiguai*), the hermeneutic of these two works is founded on the Confucian idealization of the past as an age of perfect virtue and the paradigm of history as a process of cultural degeneration.

The collection of local folkways, then, is justified by the notion that they represent remnants of archaic customs.[8] Through the collation of folkways with texts, Ying Shao sought both to find a missing link to the exemplary past and to demonstrate how far current practices have deviated from their original forms. In the chapter "Mistaken Rites" ("Qian li"), for example, Ying compared the performance of local rites in his own time with accounts from the classics in order to correct contemporary practice by critiquing its deficiencies.

Ren Fang shared Ying Shao's basic methodology of collecting folkways, but he differed from his precursor in that he did not grant the old texts absolute authority. Instead, he corrected practices and texts against one another: that is, he interpreted local customs as survivals of practices recorded in texts such as the *Records of the Grand Historian*, the *History of the Han*, and the *Classic of Mountains and Seas*, and at the same time he used contemporary analogues to corroborate the historical records.[9] It is this methodology of comparing texts and practices that Deng Chuan'an applied to the study of Taiwanese indigenous folkways.

Deng opened his essay by laying out examples of resemblances between the customs of the indigenes and those of antiquity. He began with the primitive economic system and then discussed marriage, dress, and other customs. Deng traced the origins of these customs to Chinese antiquity and thus established a single lineage of descent for the Chinese and the Taiwan indigenes. His paradigm of one historical path has two implications. First, by denying the indigenes a separate history, it domesticated the savages and legitimated the Qing colonization of Taiwan. Second, it established that the Chinese classics can be used to talk about savage customs and vice versa. Deng wrote:

In antiquity when they traded, they simply exchanged what they had for what they lacked. It was only after the introduction of merchant tariffs that they began to measure weights by the principles of the treasury and monetary system established by Taigong of the Zhou.[10] In the beginning there were no coins, neither spade-shaped nor knife-shaped.[11] Now money has become a national treasure and cannot be circulated outside the borders. . . . [Money] does not circulate among the raw savages. [Chinese] interpreters take products that the savages need and enter the mountains to farm taxes.[12] These products are nothing more than provisions and daily necessities. The savages do not value strange objects and despise practical objects; therefore the raw savages are easily satisfied.

Those tribes that pay taxes are "submitted tribes" (*guihua she*); the tribes that do not pay taxes are wild savages. How can the raw savages pay taxes? It is only by means of the interpreter, who submits taxes to the administration from what he obtains by tax farming. Officials never do site inspections in the savage territory where the interpreters trade with the wild savages, taking risks for the sake of profit. Therefore, although the taxes paid by the cooked savages are the *suan* tax of the Han and the *yong* tax of the Tang, the taxes of the raw savages are still the merchant tariffs of the *Ritual of Zhou*. Since when have they sent tribute outside their borders?

They cannot communicate in their language with those outside their borders; how could they understand writing? If one side has a credit in trading, they use knotted strings in place of promissory notes. When the amount is paid back as arranged, then the knot is untied. This is an example of how their customs resemble those of high antiquity.

The populace is divided into savages and Han Chinese. The Han always exploit the savages. The savages are divided into inner and outer. The inner can pacify the outer. For example, in the past She'a village in Shuishalian was populated by raw savages. I know not how they were inveigled by the Han, who then seized their land and depopulated their village. As for the fertile soil of Puli village, it was truly coveted by the Han.[13] The Han provided the cooked savages with goods, and in the end they were able to obtain the land and clear it. The two groups lived mixed together without mutual suspicion. Wei Jiang of the Spring and Autumn period had a discourse on "conciliating the Rong," in which he stated that [the Rong] "are fond of exchanging land for goods. Their lands can be purchased."[14] It is really true!

In this first section, Deng constructed the indigenes as preservers of the admirable aspects of antiquity. He compared the trading practices of the raw savages to the simple barter system of the ancients as described in the *Mencius*. According to the *Mencius*, barter was abandoned and merchant tariffs adopted as a result of human avarice and the lack of contentment with the simple life. Deng also used the familiar image of knotting strings as an example of how savage customs resemble those of antiquity. Like Chen Di and other authors, he employed the rhetoric of primitivism for a self-reflexive critique, contrasting the simple virtues of the savages with the materialism and greed of Chinese society since the invention of money. He further condemned the Han Chinese for exploiting the natives and taking advantage of their primitive naïveté to appropriate their lands. Deng's ethnohistorical researches thus point to a vision of history in which the material development of civilization has been accompanied by moral decline.

Where Deng differed from Chen Di was in his attempt to establish a single model of cultural evolution through precise comparative ethnohistory. For him, the raw savages and the cooked savages are emblematic of different historical stages of his evolutionary model: in the matter of taxes, for example, the raw savages exemplify Zhou practices, and the cooked savages Han and Tang practices. Taiwan thus offers the Chinese literatus a window onto the march of history—with the raw savages representing high antiquity, the cooked savages late antiquity, and the Han Chinese civilization at its most evolved.

In collating indigenous customs against textual accounts of antiquity, Deng assumed that the Chinese textual tradition had a comprehensive explanatory power, even regarding seemingly strange customs and events on a distant frontier. For example, he found the key to understanding the indigenes' loss of land rights in a passage from the *Chronicle of Zuo* describing the Rong of antiquity.[15] By linking their customs to the Chinese histories, Deng once again domesticated the strange and legitimated the place of the Taiwan indigenes within the Chinese empire.

Deng continued his efforts to normalize savage customs—even seemingly aberrant customs—in the next section of his essay. Qing travel writers conventionally regarded the practice of uxorilocal marriage as a sign of the strangeness of indigenous culture. Deng instead traced this custom back to its Chinese origins in order to demonstrate that it was a part of the Chinese past, albeit a degraded part.[16]

Jia Yi [200–168 B.C.] said: "Among the people of Qin, poor families with swarthy sons would marry them out as uxorilocal sons-in-law." The "Biographies of the Wits and Humorists" in the *Records of the Grand Historian* says: "Chunyu Kun was an uxorilocal son-in-law from Qi." So [the ancients] thought that uxorilocal sons-in-law were base. The men who, according to savage custom, marry uxorilocally are just like women [in China] who marry virilocally. Obedient and dutiful, they do not dare to take their own initiative; such is the degree to which they are debased. As for the divorcing of wives in antiquity, the custom is clearly set forth in the *Book of Rites*.[17] Today it is no longer practiced. Only the savages maintain this custom. Taking a wife is called "holding hands"; divorcing a wife is called "dropping hands." When they do not get along, they divorce. Is this not like the ancient way?

Wearing animal skins and letting the hair hang loose—these are really the customs of the Rong [barbarians of middle antiquity]. Now as for the people of high antiquity, they also wore feathers and skins and were in the wilderness. . . . [Among the raw savages of Shuishalian] the men wear red on top and bottom, also like the crimson leather gaiters from the *Chronicle of Zuo*.[18] Now that I have seen the nobility of the leather military costumes, I am moved to think that this is the legacy that continues the heritage of military merit.

In this passage, Deng moved away from the rhetoric of primitivism and adjusted his judgments of customs to match those provided by the histories. In keeping with the methodology of evidential research, he used precise textual evidence to demonstrate that the ancients considered the custom of uxorilocal marriage debased: it then follows that the savage customs must also be debased. His attitude toward the red leg gaiters of the Shuishalian natives is similarly shaped by textual precedent. Deng fancied that these costumes were survivals from the Spring and Autumn period as described in the *Chronicle of Zuo*, and he praised the natives for preserving a noble heritage. In this manner, Deng's ethnographic observations become empirical evidence for a reconstruction of the past.

In the next passage of the essay, Deng demonstrated even more vividly how Taiwan can serve as a living museum for observing the past.

The way they cut their hair is different from shaving the head and wearing the queue. The *Chronicle of Zuo* related that at the battle of Ailing, because of the shortness of hair in Wu, Gongsun Hui of Qi commanded his followers to bring back their heads strung on eight-foot lengths of rope.[19] Today in Anli village, the women cut their front hair into short bangs covering the forehead.[20] Among the wild savages outside the boundaries of Zhaolan, the men also cut their hair and wear it loose. So I know what short hair is really like. But the savages only cut the hair on the front of the head, leaving the other half long to make a bun, unlike the people of Wu, who cut all their hair.

A visit to Anli village provided Deng the opportunity to witness first-hand the cropped hairstyle described in historical accounts: in viewing the indigenes, he envisioned the likeness of ancient figures. Deng did not, however, grant historical imagination precedence over the methodology of evidential research: he aimed for precision in his comparison and was careful to distinguish the Wu, who were said to cut all their hair, from the Taiwan indigenes, who only cropped the front.

He played text off against firsthand experience, letting the one supplement the other.

Deng was not alone in using empirical observations of the Taiwan indigenes to confirm material recorded in the ancient texts. As early as the seventeenth century, Chen Xueyi, an associate of Chen Di, described how reading Chen's *Record of the Eastern Savages* had led him to overcome his skepticism toward the histories:

When I read the ancient histories, those that talk about the times of Fuxi or Shennong all tell of people who wore grass and ate wood. I privately thought that these records had been passed down from so long ago that their descriptions now seemed a bit far-fetched. How could you really believe them? It is only now after I have read *Record of the Eastern Savages* that I believe that these words were not fabrications. . . . The Eastern Savages are only a few days' travel from our Quanzhou [in Fujian], but their nakedness and their custom of knotting ropes for accounting are no different from what was recorded in the ancient histories.[21]

For Chen Xueyi, historical analogy served not to normalize savage customs but to confirm the existence of such customs in Chinese antiquity. He questioned the authority of classical texts because of their distance from his own age and instead granted authority to an eyewitness account. The privileging of experiential knowledge made Taiwan an important site for travel writers, since the island provided a microcosm of the past close at hand. The importance of experiential knowledge is further demonstrated in the next section of Deng's essay, where he relied on his own observations to elucidate obscure points in the classics.

The *Classic of Poetry* says: "His granary, his bin." The commentary explains that "the bin is a chassis of a chariot."[22] Having observed the way the savages of Shuili village build huts as granaries and store grain in rectangular bins, piling up several bins to make one granary, I would conjecture that perhaps in antiquity there were bins smaller than granaries, and that perhaps "bin" [in the *Classic of Poetry* line] does not refer to the sidebars of chariots; we cannot know.[23]

Deng based his philological inquiry into the meaning of a term from the *Classic of Poetry* on material evidence gathered in Taiwan. One important aim of evidential research was to find evidence to elucidate obscurities and lacunae in the classical texts and thus to clarify the Confucian tradition. A key text in this tradition was the *Classic of*

Poetry, which was said to have been edited as an ethical guide by Confucius himself. Trusting his own observations, Deng challenged the orthodox gloss on this line of poetry. This move was possible because he had already set up a correspondence between savage Taiwan and Chinese antiquity at the beginning of his essay. Taking this correspondence for granted, Deng envisioned that just as the past illuminates contemporary practice, so can contemporary practice illuminate the past. Just as the past grants meaning and order to what appears to be strange or incomprehensible in the present, so, too, does the present render the past comprehensible.

In the spirit of evidential research, Deng Chuan'an looked at the past not simply for its own sake but also for the sake of his own age. Accordingly, he asserted that a moral lesson could be learned from comparing contemporary practice and the classics:

The "Quli" chapter of the *Book of Rites* says: "In sharing food, do not rub the hands." The notes explain, "Rub" means "rubbing together." The *Book of Rites* says: "Eating with the hands." The *Book of Rites* also says, "Shoes should not be worn into the hall," and "They did not have their feet bare at any sacrifices, whether in the room or in the hall. But at banquets they might have their shoes off." Therefore, when Chushi Shengzi of Wei went to the banquet in his socks, he angered the duke.[24] Thus, in antiquity when they ascended the hall or went to banquets, they took barefootedness as a sign of respect. How can you say that the savages are fierce and wild, then, simply on account of the fact that they are barefooted, or the fact that the raw savages eat with their hands rather than with spoons or chopsticks?

Here, Deng made a plea for tolerance of cultural differences. In his view, Chinese contempt for indigenous Taiwanese customs stems from an imperfect understanding of antiquity. His ethnohistorical comparisons remind the reader: do not despise the savages, for they are simply behaving as we did in the past. The historical metaphor thus serves to diminish ethnic difference, again by establishing a single lineage of descent for the Chinese people and the Taiwan indigenes.[25] In the end, Deng directed his critique at those Chinese who failed to understand that the ancients regarded barefootedness as a sign of respect or that the *Book of Rites* prescribed etiquette for the proper way to eat with the hands. It was this lack of understanding that Deng aimed to rectify through his project of ethnohistorical collecting.

Having established through textual proofs that the indigenes are corollaries of the ancients, Deng concluded by lamenting the degeneration of Chinese civilization.

Alas! Since antiquity, in the alternations of substance (*zhi*) and form (*wen*), precedent has been replaced by innovation. Form and ornamentation (*wen*) day by day grow ascendant, whereas substance and plainness (*zhi*) daily recede.[26] By what means can we return to the origin and perfect the ancient (*fanben xiugu*)? By searching for the ten in one thousand, the one in a hundred of the lacunae in the ancient texts? Unexpectedly, in searching overseas, in examining the wilderness, because the customs there are rude, one can find the most original propriety (*li*). The classics and commentaries variously tell what came at the end or the beginning, and they have discrepancies as well as agreements. Often [the commentaries] make forced interpretations in order to extend their arguments. Even though I deserve only to be compared to the unwise and ignorant, this work can provide material for those who investigate antiquity![27]

In this concluding passage Deng made explicit his vision of history as a dual process of material progress and moral degeneration. He then addressed the dilemma of how to return society to its origins and restore moral order. Since the Chinese classics and their orthodox commentaries are filled with lacunae, they no longer provide an adequate link to the exemplary past. The only way to return to origins, Deng suggests, is by learning from primitive culture. Deng's claim that the rude customs of the wilderness provide the key for recovering the original propriety of antiquity is based on a phrase from the *History of the Later Han*: "When propriety is lost in China, search for it in the wilderness."[28] The wilderness thus assumes an important function as a repository for all that has been lost in China through the process of civilization.

Wu Ziguang's Supplement to the Comprehensive Account of Folkways

Deng Chuan'an was an important model for Wu Ziguang (fl. 1875), who, approximately a generation later, wrote an ethnographic essay patterned after "Discourse." Wu Ziguang was originally a native of Guangdong who immigrated to Taiwan with his father during the Daoguang (1821–50) period. Unlike the authors we have considered so far, Wu settled permanently on the island. He even served for a period of time as an instructor of indigenous pupils in the local schools of Anli. His writings thus demonstrate a higher degree of familiarity with the island and its indigenous people, particularly those of the Anli area. Wu's "Record of the Customs of Savage Tribes" ("Ji fan-she fengsu"), completed sometime before 1875, is a detailed work of ethnohistoriography that correlates the customs of both "raw" and "cooked" savages with similar customs recorded in classical texts. Wu found historical analogies for a wide range of cultural practices and items of material culture—including funerary rites, medicine, costume, wine, and meat. Wu Ziguang framed this essay as a sequel or supplement to the works of Deng Chuan'an and Ying Shao:

> The Prefect Sir Deng Chuan'an wrote the "Discourse on the Resemblance of Savage Customs to Those of Antiquity" . . . in the hope of making people return to origins and go back to antiquity. . . . Now I have stayed in Anli tribal village for several years and rejoice in the fact that they, being unconscious and natural, have many customs from before the time of Fuxi and Huangdi. By what means can we exhort people to imitate them in order to return to high antiquity? I have written a comprehensive account of the folkways of the savage tribes as an addendum to Ying Shao's *Comprehensive Account of Folkways*.[29]

Wu pushed the logic of Deng Chuan'an's essay and overtly claimed that his ethnography of the indigenes was intended as a lesson for the Chinese, who must reform their customs in accord with the ways of antiquity. The sinocentric rhetoric so prevalent in much Chinese writing on non-Chinese peoples is here reversed: it is not that the savages need to conform to Chinese customs in order to be civilized but that Chinese must imitate the savages in order to regain a pure moral state. Like Ying Shao's investigation of local folk customs in China, Wu's investigation into savage customs was intended to rectify contemporary Chinese mores.

In "Record of the Customs of Savage Tribes," Wu adopted an evidential research approach to ethnohistory—drawing on etymologies, genealogies, proofs, phonology, and *zhengming* (the rectification of names). For example, he stated:

> In the inner mountains, there are beautiful savage women. However, the customs of tattooing the foreheads and chiseling the teeth have not changed for hundreds of generations. Note that forehead means brow;

that is, the upper part of the face. See Xu Shen's *Shuowen* [*jiezi*] and the *Erya*. As for tattooing the forehead, they carve the brow and pour in red and green dye. See the notes on "The Hereditary House of Yue" in the *Records of the Grand Historian*. The only difference is that in antiquity they carved on the top of the brow, while the savages carve on the two cheeks.[30]

In addition to the *Records of the Grand Historian*, Wu referred to a variety of texts to find precedents for indigenous customs—the *Ritual of Zhou*, the *History of the Han*, the *Songs of the South*, the *Spring and Autumn Annals* (*Chunqiu*), the *Chronicle of Zuo*, and the *Book of Rites*. A theme that runs throughout his essay is that contemporary customs are imperfect survivals, or remnants, from the past. Like Ying Shao, he was interested in how contemporary practice deviated from ancient custom:

According to ancient ritual, when a person died, [the mourners] would take a piece of clothing up on the roof and call out [the name of the deceased], crying out for the person to return. This was how they called the soul. In antiquity they practiced this custom at the time of death. In contrast, the savages practice this at the time of memorial rites. There is only a slight difference here.[31]

Although indigenous customs diverged from ancient ritual texts, Wu did not advocate that they be rectified in accord with ancient practice; rather, he was concerned with the rectification of contemporary Chinese mores. Wu's essay sets forth the same claim made by Deng Chuan'an: propriety, which has been lost among the Chinese, can now be found among the savages, who have yet to be corrupted by modernity.

The writings of Deng Chuan'an and Wu Ziguang, widely read by nineteenth-century travelers to Taiwan, demonstrate that comparison of the Taiwan indigenes to the ancients of China could work as part of an inclusive discourse. Whereas the earliest literati travelers to Taiwan used the trope of the savages as the ancients primarily to signify the strangeness of the Taiwan indigenes through temporal distancing, these nineteenth-century authors sought to domesticate the otherness of the Taiwan indigenes by incorporating them, as living ancestors of the Chinese, into the larger scheme of Chinese history. By proposing the Taiwan indigenes as a lost link of sorts between the moderns and the ancients, they tied the island natives more closely to the people of "China proper."

Interlude 2

Over the course of the eighteenth century, Taiwan was transformed from a trade entrepôt into an agricultural colony of Chinese settlers. By 1777, the Han Chinese population on the island had grown to nearly 800,000, approximately an eightfold increase since annexation. The settler population was concentrated on the western coastal plains, where the indigenous population seems to have remained fairly constant at around 40,000.[1] Whereas in the late seventeenth century Qing Taiwan policy had been shaped by external considerations, namely Western and Japanese interest in the island, policy in the eighteenth century largely focused on the domestic considerations of empire and the cross-strait trade in rice and sugar.

By the second half of the nineteenth century, however, the global perspective on Taiwan re-emerged with a new wave of Western, and then Japanese, imperial activity in the region. Once again, Taiwan's location along the sealanes linking China, Japan, and the Philippines would cause the island to become the focus of interest from various trading powers as well as individual adventurers. The late nineteenth century was an era of territorial concessions and unequal treaties for China. In 1860, the Treaty of Peking forced the opening of treaty ports in Taiwan at Danshui in the north and at Anping in the south. This wrought a radical transformation in Taiwan's economy in the second half of the nineteenth century. Whereas the production of rice and sugar for the mainland market had been the mainstay of Taiwan's economy since the mid-eighteenth century, within a decade after the opening of these treaty ports a flourishing international trade had converted Taiwan into a highly commercialized agricultural producer for the global market.

The opening of the treaty ports boosted the demand for sugar and created new markets for Taiwanese tea and camphor. Although tea had long been cultivated on a limited scale in Taiwan, primarily for local use, the opening of trade with the West expanded the market for tea phenomenally. Americans developed a taste for "Formosa Oolong," and French connoisseurs esteemed "Oriental Beauty." If eighteenth-century Taiwan had been the Granary of China, it was now a land of Green Gold. Similarly, trade with the West expanded the market for Taiwan's camphor (a traditional medicinal ingredient and aromatic), particularly in the late 1880s after Western chemists discovered new uses for the substance. Among the new applications, camphor's use in the manufacture of smokeless gunpowder and celluloid generated great demand for the substance in the West.[2] By the 1890s, Taiwan had become the source of two-thirds of the world's camphor supply.

The new profitability of these products and the integration of Taiwan into global markets heightened foreign interest in Taiwan. Beginning in the mid-nineteenth century, various Western powers and individual adventurers had flirted with the idea of colonizing eastern Taiwan, which remained beyond effective Qing control. Commodore Matthew Perry, for example, submitted a proposal to make Taiwan an American protectorate in 1854.[3] Late nineteenth-century Taiwan once more became a site of international contestation, as it had been in the seventeenth century. What was new this time around was the emergence of so-called new imperialism, that is, modern industrial imperialism. The players, too, had changed: instead of the Portuguese, Dutch, Spanish, and Japanese daimyo, China now faced competition from the British, French, Americans, and a modernizing, centralized Japanese state. Instead of deerskins and sugar, traders now desired Taiwan's tea, camphor, and coal. In the age of treaty ports, Qing Taiwan policy would have to be formulated with an awareness of this new global context.

CHAPTER 9

'Opening the Mountains and Pacifying the Savages'

In November 1871, a raging storm shipwrecked a trading vessel from the Ryukyus (present-day Okinawa) on a remote corner of Taiwan's southeastern coast; fifty-four of the sixty-nine sailors were slaughtered by the "savages" of nearby Mudan village. This, in a nutshell, was the infamous "Mudanshe Incident," an affair that would have repercussions far beyond the small islands of Taiwan and the Ryukyus and that would precipitate Taiwan's transformation into a full-fledged province of China.

When the shipwreck survivors returned to their homeland, local officials brought the atrocities to the attention of authorities in Tokyo. Using the affair as a chance to move forward with plans to annex the Ryukyus, Japan agreed to intervene on the condition that the territory be incorporated into the Japanese empire. In 1872, Japanese officials took the case to the Qing capital and demanded reparations on behalf of their new imperial subjects. The Qing refused to accept responsibility for the actions of the Mudan natives on the grounds that their territory lay beyond the Savage Boundary and was therefore not under Qing jurisdiction (see Color Plate 4). The court had used this logic before to deny responsibility for other shipwrecks off the island's eastern coast and southern tip (a region known in English sources as "Aboriginal Formosa"). After the wreck of the U.S.S. *Rover* in 1867, for example, the Chinese disclaimed accountability for the slaughter of the crew on the grounds that "the Americans were not murdered in Chinese territory, or on Chinese seas, but in a region occupied by savage tribes. . . . The savage region does not come within the limits of our jurisdiction."[1] The matter was further complicated in the case of the "Mudanshe Incident" by the Qing court's refusal to recognize Japanese sovereignty over the Ryukyus (Ch. Liuqiu). Since China had long considered this territory a tributary state, the Qing argued that Japan had no right to interfere in this case. The dispute lasted until 1874, when the Japanese decided to take matters into their own hands and dispatched a punitive expedition to Taiwan's "savage territory."

This action sent a message to the Qing court (as well as to the Western trading nations, which were watching these developments with intense interest) that if the Qing would not assert its authority over the inhabitants of "savage Taiwan," then others would certainly do so. The Qing court, it seems, had talked itself into a rhetorical trap: if "savage territory" was not "Qing territory," then what was to prevent Japan, or any other imperial power, from laying claim to it? As Robert Eskildsen demonstrates, this possibility had, in fact, already been broached to Chinese authorities by American Consul Charles LeGendre in the negotiations over the *Rover* Incident.[2] LeGendre threatened that the foreign occupation of Aboriginal Formosa "would be the first step in the direction of a policy of violence that might ultimately end in the dismemberment of the Chinese empire or at least its humiliation."[3] With LeGendre serving as adviser to the Japanese on the "Taiwan Expedition," it is no surprise that the Qing regarded the Japanese action as a direct challenge to Chinese sovereignty over Taiwan and hence as a threat to long-term Chinese coastal security.

Finally realizing the dangers of the ambiguity surrounding Taiwan's sovereignty, the Qing reversed the position it had maintained since the *Rover* Incident and declared that all of Taiwan and its inhabitants were, in fact, under Chinese authority. In order to support this claim (which U.S. Consul James Davidson remarked was clearly "an after-thought"),[4] the court agreed to indemnify Japan. The Qing further acknowledged Japanese sovereignty over the Ryukyus and thus ended this crisis in Sino-Japanese relations.

The Mudanshe Incident and the Japanese expedition thrust Taiwan into the international spotlight. The British, French, and Americans (shipwrecked crews from all these nations had suffered similar depredations in Aboriginal Formosa) had watched eagerly to see whether the Japanese expedition into "savage territory" would constitute an act of war against China. In China, the affair prompted the first serious empirewide debate on the issue of China's "self-strengthening," the modernization efforts intended to bolster China's position in the international "survival of the fittest."[5] This watershed made clear that the island the Kangxi emperor had once dismissed as a remote ball of mud beyond the sea now lay at the crosscurrents of international trade and politics.

In the wake of the Japanese expedition, the Qing court instituted a new policy of "Opening the Mountains and Pacifying the Savages" (*kaishan fufan*)—a 180-degree turnaround from the quarantine approach that dominated the seventeenth and eighteenth centuries. The goal of this aggressive colonization policy was to assert formal Qing control over the "savage territory" that lay beyond the Qing boundary line and finally bring the entire island "onto the map." The new slogan of the era, "Divide Not Savage and Han" (*wufen fan yu Han*), heralded the eradication of the old Savage Boundary and a new determination to make imperial subjects of the savages. The Opening and Pacifying policy signaled the Qing court's resolve to definitively transform Taiwan from a savage island into Chinese territory.[6]

The decision to Open the Mountains and Pacify the Savages was motivated by two factors: the Qing court's need to assert sovereignty over the strategically vulnerable island and Taiwan's new economic importance. In the second half of the nineteenth century, Taiwan became a major international exporter of tea, sugar, and camphor. Far from being a "drain on the imperial treasury," Taiwan was now a rich source of commodities in global demand. Western traders and adventurers were increasingly taking an interest in the island, "drooling" over it, in Chinese terms. The Qing realized that Taiwan was a valuable possession, worth every effort to keep it out of the hands of others.[7]

In this chapter, I examine the changing images of Taiwan's landscape and indigenous people in the era of Opening the Mountains and Pacifying the Savages through a reading of Luo Dachun's *Diary of Taiwan's Naval Defense and Opening the Mountains* (*Taiwan haifang bing kaishan riji*, 1875) and related texts. I also discuss the renewed importance of the image of Taiwan as a fence for the Chinese domain. Initially introduced in the annexation debate of 1683, this image re-emerged in the late nineteenth century as the international integration of markets and the spread of Western imperialism made it clear that Taiwan had to be viewed in a global perspective once again. Finally, I demonstrate how the Qing reconfigured Taiwan's position within the empire as it moved to colonize the entire island and firmly establish Taiwan as an integral part of the Chinese realm on a par with the other provinces.

From "Granary of China" to Land of "Green Gold"

In the second half of the nineteenth century, we see a marked shift in representations of Taiwan's landscape. Late eighteenth- and early nineteenth-century literati constructed Taiwan as a divided land, split between Qing-controlled Taiwan—sometimes referred to as "cooked territory"—and "raw savage territory." In their eyes, all that was lovely about the island's landscape was located in "cooked territory," where the wasteland had been "opened" and converted into "good farmland." It was here that Chinese settlers had revealed the jade within the ball of mud by clearing the wilderness of ugly brown weeds and planting lustrous green fields of sugarcane and rice. In sharp contrast, Qing literati considered the territory beyond the Savage Boundary a miasmic wilderness. Despite the fact that it proved impossible to stop illegal Han Chinese settlement of land beyond the boundary, eighteenth- and early nineteenth-century literati continued to refer to this area as "unopened" terrain where "human footsteps rarely reached." Quarantined off from "cooked territory," this land still appeared remote, politically and culturally, from the Chinese empire. On the whole, Qing literati in Taiwan were perfectly content to let it remain that way.

These literati took for granted that Taiwan's plains were the most desirable land on the island: on these open and flat lands could be sown the seeds of plow agriculture and civilization. Taiwan's mountainous forests, in contrast, they considered a horrid and dangerous place; impenetrable, dark, and forbidding, this terrain of tangled brambles and prickly bamboo epitomized wilderness and savagery. Qing writers associated this terrain with lurking savages and bandits, deadly disease, monsters, and ghosts. In the eighteenth century, even the rumors of gold and jade were not enough to induce more than a handful of adventurers to risk the perils of the Inner Mountains. As the *Gazetteer of Zhuluo County* stated: "Even though there may be those who would search for wondrous and exotic things, who [among them] would dare brave the monsters and step into no-man's-land?"[8]

By the late nineteenth century, however, a new image of Taiwan's Inner Mountains had emerged. Qing literati began viewing the lands in "savage terrain" as the cream of the island's land. Some figured the Inner Mountains as brimming with "rare treasures and extraordinary jewels." Forested mountains long characterized as "dense" or "impenetrable" were now praised by travel writers as a splendid vision of "abundant" kingfisher green on the vista. Writers claimed that the Inner Mountains were a "Heavenly storehouse" of natural resources. As one anonymous nineteenth-century author declared: "The land behind the mountains is fertile and suited for farmland. The landscape is clear and lovely, not inferior to the West Lake [in China]. It is rich in products such as coal, sulfur, camphor, the five metals, timber, etc. . . . Foreigners are drooling over it."[9] The language of desire had entered literati representations of Taiwan's Inner Mountains. And it was desire reflected in foreign eyes.

The new images of Taiwan's landscape owed much to the dramatic changes in the island's economy produced by the opening of treaty ports to foreign trade. The integration of Taiwan into the international market made tea and camphor production tremendously profitable and had an enormous impact on land use in Taiwan. During the time when the island served as the "Granary of China," Taiwan's plains lands, where the primary crops were rice and sugar, were the most valued. For historical and topographic reasons, rice and sugar production was concentrated in the southwest of Taiwan. In contrast, tea was grown in the uplands, plateaus, and valleys of the northern third of Taiwan, with its cooler climate. Taiwan's mountains, in particular, provided an ideal environment for growing tea, since tea grown at higher elevations is considered more fragrant, "high mountain tea" being especially prized. Camphor, too, was a product of Taiwan's forests. Taiwan's uplands were now valued as never before.

As tea and camphor became lucrative sources of income, the mountain forests came to be regarded not solely as a source of disease and mortal danger but also as a font of riches worth risking one's life for.

Mountain mists, once considered the source of miasmas, now bestowed a dewy taste to tea leaves—and a dewy touch to the cheeks of young girl tea-pickers. Among the famous Taiwan teas are varieties with names such as "Wind and Fog" and "Dew of the Mountains." Praise for tea and admiration of tea-pickers emerged as a new topos of travel writing. Similarly, the "primeval" trees of the forest, once considered a symbol of the chaos of wilderness, were now a marvelous boon for camphor makers, who felled the giant trees and reduced them to the chips from which camphor was distilled.

The new economic value of Taiwan's uplands and the desire to find unsettled frontier land led Han Chinese settlers to flock to northern Taiwan in ever greater numbers and resulted in a significant demographic shift over the course of the nineteenth century. At the beginning of the century, the overwhelming majority (70 percent) of Taiwan's Han Chinese lived in southern Taiwan; by the late nineteenth century, nearly one-third of Taiwan's Han Chinese lived in northern Taiwan, and over a quarter lived in central Taiwan.[10] Migrants to northern Taiwan came from the south of the island, as well as from the mainland, many from famous tea-growing districts in Fujian. What was once regarded as a desolate frontier, a "no-man's-land," was now a magnet for entrepreneurial Han Chinese. Moreover, in the late 1860s, officials began to promote the development of coal and gold mining in the mountains of northern Taiwan. As the number of settlers in this region increased, they began to press ever farther into the mountains in search of land and natural resources.

Thus, although the Mudanshe Incident provided the immediate impetus for asserting Qing control over the rest of the island, the new value of Taiwan's mountain lands in the treaty port era also provided an economic incentive for opening the mountains. At long last, the Qing court perceived the benefits of fully colonizing the island as outweighing the burdens.

The new appreciation of Taiwan's mountain lands led Qing literati to see the "raw savages" in a new light—not as a danger to be kept quarantined behind a barricade but as an impediment to development. (This, of course, was exactly how Lan Dingyuan had seen them in the early eighteenth century.) The intensified economic exploitation of Taiwan's uplands and forests after 1860 resulted in the escalation of conflict between Han Chinese and the native inhabitants. Camphor gatherers crossing over into tribal lands to fell trees frequently lost their lives (and heads) to raw savage headhunters. Qing officials calculated that if the mountains were to be opened and the protective barrier taken down, the raw savages who stood in the way of progress would have to be "pacified." Hence, the two-pronged campaign to Open the Mountains and Pacify the Savages. The move to "pacify the savages" was also in part a response to external demands that the Qing exercise jurisdiction over the inhabitants of Aboriginal Formosa and so prevent future assaults on foreign navigators.[11]

The policy of Opening the Mountains and Pacifying the Savages was initiated by Shen Baozhen, Taiwan's first self-strengthener. Shen's primary goal was to ensure Taiwan's naval security by extending Qing control over all the island, and he understood Opening and Pacifying within this context. The opening of the mountains was to be achieved by clearing the forests, building roads into the mountains, extending the civil and military administration, and recruiting Han Chinese immigrants to settle the land and establish villages. The pacification of the savages was to be achieved through punitive campaigns to force their submission to Qing rule, as well as through efforts to "civilize" them. At designated geographic centers of pacification, Shen established Confucian schools to instruct the raw savages. His program also included the settlement of Han Chinese immigrants among the indigenes—perhaps on the Confucian theory that "if the gentleman lives among them, what barbarism would there be?" In order to strengthen Qing administrative control on the island, Shen proposed dividing Taiwan into two prefectures—Taiwan and Taipei. Established in 1875, the new prefecture of Taipei was given jurisdiction over the northern third of the island, an area that had gained greater economic importance during this time. Although his tenure on the island was brief (1874–75), Shen laid out the basic outline for the Opening and Pacifying campaign.

Shen's right-hand man, Luo Dachun, composed a diary narrating the progress of the new colonization program in its early phase. This work, *A Diary of Taiwan's Naval Defense and Opening the Mountains*, records Luo's experiences in opening mountain roads along Taiwan's northern route in 1874–75.[12] Written in the unembellished language of the military man, the diary provides a vivid picture of the campaign to tame the wilderness and subdue the savages.

Taming the Wilderness

In Luo's diary, northern Taiwan's Transmontane Territory is both a trove of riches and potential fecundity and a horrid wilderness. Luo identified northern Taiwan as the source of the island's most valuable products: in his estimation, coal, indigo, tea, and camphor. He predicted that mining would one day be more profitable than farming and make the land long dismissed as "wilderness mountains" enormously valuable. Luo further described the land of Taiwan's eastern coast as ideal for farming—flat, open, and underpopulated. Like Lan Dingyuan, Luo extended his vision of the landscape into the future; as did Lan, he often saw the good qualities of the landscape underneath the surface of wilderness. Describing a section of Taiwan's eastern coast, Luo wrote: "Even though the wild weeds are over a foot high, the landscape is clean and rich, full of vitality."[13] He envisioned charming villages filling up the empty landscape and farmers unleashing the potential of the land, transforming it into "good fields." Assessing the abundance of natural resources and fertile farmland, Luo Dachun called northeastern Taiwan the "cream" (*jinghua*) of the island's land.

Yet all the treasures of this region—the fertile plains of the eastern coast, which could be converted into farmland; the coal of northern Taiwan's mountains, which promised large profits; the tea and camphor produced by industrious settlers; and the rumored deposits of gold and silver ore—all this lay in Luo's distant vision of the landscape. What lay close at hand in his account of opening mountain roads and battling savages was a wilderness filled with nastiness: miasmas that sickened his soldiers, an ominous darkness that shielded the enemy, and the impenetrable, tangled vegetation of the jungle that his troops dreaded to enter. Luo's account contains one particularly vivid description of the hardships faced by soldiers:

Although the route was no more than several dozen miles, it was extraordinarily wild and strategically fast. Cliffs towered overhead; dry gullies sank far down below. All the mountains faced north, and the sunlight could not penetrate. Ancient trees were a miserable green, and the cold wind howled angrily. The soldiers looked at each other and went pale. There was nothing for it but to stop.[14]

The image of the mountain forest as a hiding place for hostile savages and Chinese bandits (and, in the worst-case scenario, foreign forces) looms large in Luo's diary. He writes of savages lying in wait in the dense jungle during the day and emerging to attack at night, and of soldiers ambushed by natives lurking unseen in the tall grasses or perched high in the trees "like apes." He represents the savages as an invisible but ever-present threat. "When we advance, they disappear; when we retreat, they reappear."[15] On every page of his diary, the landscape seems to work in concert with its inhabitants to resist Qing forces.

Luo's aim in opening the mountains was to eradicate this threat; clearing the wilderness and replacing impenetrable jungle with roads and farmland would eliminate the enemy's hiding places. Luo thus represented the campaign against the savages as a simultaneous effort to clear the wilderness. As he wrote of his work in opening roads: "All along the route we clipped and shaved everything clean, so that the thorny ones [savages] would have nowhere to skulk."[16] Luo's choice of the words "clip" and "shave" is interesting in this context, for these words connote the queue, the Manchu hairstyle of a shaved pate and long braid, which the Qing imposed on Chinese men when they conquered China and which they were now attempting to impose on the raw savages. Elsewhere, Luo described "clipping and opening" the weeds, cutting brambles, and burning grasses—all measures designed to bring order to the chaos of the wilderness and to deprive the savages of places from which to ambush. As we saw in eighteenth-century accounts, there was a link between taming the landscape and taming the natives.

The Bellicose Savage

Even as new images of Taiwan's landscape were emerging in the nineteenth century, old images of the "savages" were being revived. Reflecting the intensified conflict between raw savages and Han Chinese, especially woodsmen, late nineteenth-century sources are full of references to savage attacks and murders. As it had been in the seventeenth century, headhunting once again became a major theme of the literature. The cannibalization of shipwrecked sailors also re-emerged as a favorite topic—except this time, the victims were mainly Western and Japanese sailors.

In texts of the Opening and Pacifying period, one figure comes to the fore—the bellicose savage (*xiongfan*). The very name conjures up the heightened tension of this time. Shen Baozhen offered this definition:

There are dozens of types of raw savages. Overall, they can be placed in three categories: those from Mudanshe and other villages who plunder and kill for a living and who are brave and fearless of death are called "bellicose savages"; those from the region of Beinan and Puli who live near the Han subjects and who somewhat understand human nature are called "good savages" (*liangfan*); those from Doushi and other villages in northern Taiwan, who carve their foreheads and tattoo their faces, who hunt people like game, and whom even the village savages fear are called "bellicose savages of the character *wang*" (*wangzi xiongfan*). So we may speak generally about pacifying the savages, but in reality there are these differences among them.[17]

The division of the raw savages into "good savages" and "bellicose savages" was a crucial means of distinguishing those raw savages amenable to Qing rule from those hostile to it. Only those opposed to it required "pacification."

This subdivision of the raw savages mirrored the earlier division into the categories of raw and cooked. Just as eighteenth-century writers had once mapped the negative traits of savagery, namely, cultural backwardness and belligerence, onto the raw savages, now writers mapped the more fearsome and repulsive traits of rawness onto the bellicose savages. Although the raw savages in general were still associated with privation, the bellicose savages came to embody the most reprehensible aspect of savagery—bloodthirstiness. Alternative names for the bellicose savage included "cruel savage" (*hanfan*) and "ferocious savage" (*qiangfan*).

The bellicose savage features prominently in Luo's diary. On nearly every page bellicose savages lurk in the jungle, ambush Qing soldiers, kill Han settlers, or engage in headhunting. Page after page, the impression of the savages' ferocity and bloodthirstiness becomes overwhelming. Whereas earlier travel writing had generally set headhunting at a distance—as something the writer had "heard" but not "seen"—Luo's diary provides rare eyewitness descriptions of the spoils of headhunting.

Our troops split up to invade their lairs. There were several hundred grass huts but not a single person. In front of each hut, we saw skulls, old and fresh. Some huts had as many as over one hundred; even those with the fewest had several dozens. The foul stench was overwhelming. Taking advantage of the winds, we set fires and burned their village. Only then did the savage troops disperse.[18]

Luo's uncanny village of the dead is empty of human inhabitants and peopled only by skulls. Adding to the gruesome sight of thousands of severed heads is the overwhelmingly foul stench of rotting flesh carried on the wind. The horror of the scene makes the Qing soldiers' torching of the village appear as an act of cleansing. Such portraits of the bellicose savages as despicable, subhuman headhunters who lived among the filth and stench of carrion legitimated the violent "pacification" in the eyes of Qing literati.

Racialist discourse played a central role in the construction of the bellicose savage and, to a lesser degree, in the construction of the raw savage in general. Writers focused on physical differences and differences in inborn nature in representing the bellicose savage as categorically other, as *yilei*. Authors paid relatively little attention to their customs, aside from dismissing them as "repulsive," and the clichés of privation stood in for empirical ethnographic observations. In this respect, the literature of the Opening and Pacifying era stands in sharp contrast to Deng Chuan'an's and Wu Ziguang's methodical evidential research approach to documenting raw savage customs.

Fang Junyi, for example, gave this description of the raw savages in his *Brief Account of the Soldiers' Pacification of Taiwan's Savage Villages* (*Zhunjun pingding Taiwan fanshe jilüe*, 1874):

The raw savages come and go [in the deep jungle], hunting animals for food, drinking blood and eating fur, living in caves and dwelling in wilderness, with the beasts of the forest as their companions. They are the color of dirt, absolutely not of the human race. They can penetrate cliffs and climb trees with the nimbleness of monkeys. They lie in wait in strategic passes with their weapons. They consider killing people to be macho. When they have killed a person, they cut off the head and display it.[19]

Fang's association of physical blackness with categorical otherness is a typical move of racialist discourse. The characterization of the raw savages as "not of the human race" also belongs to this discourse. This passage further illustrates the convergence of racialist discourse with the rhetoric of privation and its denigrating impulse; it is replete with the privative clichés of savagery, like "drinking blood and eating fur," that were so popular in early Kangxi representations of Taiwan's indigenes. Primitivism, which had figured so prominently in Deng Chuan'an's work, disappears entirely from the literature of Opening and Pacifying.

Aside from dark skin, writers singled out bulging or deep eyes and flat faces as characteristic features of the raw savages. Some wrote that the raw savages had the bodies of monstrous giants; others, that they had the bodies of dwarves. In general, authors tended to attribute to them physical characteristics that fell below the mark of Chinese ideals of physical beauty, that were strange, ugly, or vulgar. To Qing literati, the physical hideousness or repulsiveness of the raw savages was an outward manifestation of their moral reprehensibility.

One late nineteenth-century author, Kuang Qizhao, suggested a physical distinction between two groups of raw savages, the "plains raw savages" (pingpu shengfan) and "mountain cave raw savages" (yanxue shengfan). He described the former as "tall, with an admirable physique. They are strong warriors who imitate the clothing of the cooked savages and even have a writing system." In contrast, the "mountain cave raw savages" are "vulgar and black in appearance, and dwarf-like in size. They live by hunting. The men and women wear no clothing."[20] The differences between the two classes of raw savages are measured both in terms of relative levels of cultural development and in terms of physical attractiveness, according to normative Chinese ideals.[21]

The tendency to link privation and belligerence with physical hideousness or deformity found its most extreme expression in the representation of the bellicose savages as monsters, often half-human, half-animal. Huang Fengchang's Account of Taiwan's Raw and Cooked Savages (Taiwan shengshufan jishi, 1875), for example, contains this colorful anecdote, which is reminiscent of pre-Qing stories of cannibal islands in the China Seas:

A ship came from Japan, sailing by the mountains behind Keelung. The wind ceased, and the ship was seized by an eastward current. They were shipwrecked on a reef. There were seventy-five people on board, but none knew where they were. Four people went ashore to seek directions. They saw creatures of a separate breed galloping toward them. These creatures captured a Japanese sailor and ate him. The other three fled and bumped into a man in the scrub. They spoke with him and discovered he was a native of Quanzhou [in Fujian]. They took him back to their ship, where they reported the incident of the monsters that had cannibalized their companion. The Chinese man said, "Those are not monsters. They are a separate breed of raw savages. They have snake heads and hideously beastlike bodies. They can fly-walk . . . all my companions have been cannibalized. Only I am left alive."[22]

This anecdote was inspired no doubt by the Mudanshe Incident and the countless other shipwrecks of the nineteenth century. Such stories of attacks on shipwrecked sailors spread among naval crews far and wide and brought international notoriety to the "cannibals" of eastern Taiwan.[23]

The construction of the raw savages as cannibalistic monsters reflected the heightened fear of hostile indigenes during this time. The figure of the half-human, half-animal monster can be read as a metaphor for the notion that the raw savages are not fully human, culturally or morally. The dehumanization of the bellicose savages was also manifest in the prevalence of animal imagery in the literature. Luo Dachun and other contemporaneous writers frequently figured the bellicose savages as animals: galloping like horses, scurrying away like scared rats, climbing trees like monkeys, flying through the jungle like birds, or hiding in caves like tigers. This dehumanization of the bellicose savages served to legitimate the Qing military campaign against them.

Also indicative of the resurgence of racialist discourse was the emphasis on the notion that the inborn nature of the raw savages differed from that of the Chinese. Late nineteenth-century writers most commonly characterized the nature of the raw, or bellicose savages as "wild," "fond of killing," or "hard and unyielding." One reason for this renewed focus on inborn nature in the literature of the Opening and Pacifying era is that military strategists considered an understanding of the enemy's nature essential. Thus Luo Dachun classified the various groups he encountered on the pacification campaign according to a typology of inborn natures, as wild, fickle and untrustworthy, bellicose, cowardly, and so on.[24]

The idea that the raw savages (or subclasses thereof) were endowed with aggressive and unyielding wild natures lent support to the view that they could not be transformed by education alone. Rather, force and repression were required to tame them. As Luo Dachun explained: "When those with wilderness natures first come into the corral of law, they must first be bound with firm rules. Only then can you slowly give them a gradual grinding and polishing."[25] Writers of the Opening and Pacifying period spoke not only of "transforming" the raw savages but increasingly of "taming" them or "making them compliant." Moreover, in contrast to earlier writers who spoke of the savages "coming to be transformed," these writers more often referred to the raw savages as "surrendering." We thus see a militarization of the rhetoric in texts of this era.

Representations of the raw savages, and the bellicose savages in particular, as ferocious, bloodthirsty, and wild in nature legitimated the notion that these people needed to be "pacified," by violence if necessary. Luo's diary contains numerous episodes of soldiers setting fire to native villages in order to "strike fear in the savages' hearts," as he explained. Such extreme measures of "pacification" doubtless appeared justified to Qing readers in light of the countless incidents he recorded of Han Chinese and foreigners attacked or killed by bellicose savages.

These images of the raw savages were also manifest in visual representations from this era. As Tu Cheng-sheng has demonstrated, during the Opening and Pacifying campaign, Shen Baozhen commissioned one of his men to take charge of producing a set of ethnographic illustrations depicting the various tribes of Taiwan.[26] The illustrations in this album, held by the National Palace Museum, Beijing, are markedly different from those in Liu-shi-qi's album from the eighteenth century, which was dominated by visual tropes of primitivism. In contrast, this album is rife with images of privation and belligerence: in addition to illustrations of "cave dwelling" and other archaic practices, there are numerous scenes of violent battles, drunken brawls, attacks on Chinese settlers, and the infamous practice of headhunting. One illustration, for example, portrays a dance of victory after a headhunting raid, with the hero triumphantly brandishing a Chinese head. Another depicts a celebratory feast at which the headhunters drink wine poured through a severed head, in a brazen display of depravity and bloodthirstiness (Color Plate 14). In both illustrations, the representation of the raw savages as dark-skinned, tattooed, and naked but for loincloths underscores not only their cultural but also their physical difference from the Han Chinese. These physical differences are further highlighted in a number of leaves devoted to the "appearance" (zhuangmao) of various groups, including the notorious "Bellicose Savages of the Character 'Wang,'" who are shown naked from the bust up, with exotically tattooed faces and large holes through their earlobes—embodying the visual iconography of savagery (Color Plate 15). As with the literature of the Opening and Pacifying era, the visual representation of the raw savages in this album evinced a distinct turn away from primitivism toward privation and an emphasis on racial difference.

Shoring Up the Hedgerow

The figure of Taiwan as China's hedgerow, first suggested during the annexation debate, regained prominence after the Mudanshe Incident. But it was now coupled with an anxiety that the hedgerow might be breached. To eighteenth-century writers, Taiwan's Central Mountain Range, with its towering, screen-like massif, represented the physical embodiment of the concept of Taiwan as a barricade. In contrast, late nineteenth-century writers predicted that if foreign powers were to claim Taiwan's eastern coast as their own, then even the imposing barrier of the Central Mountain Range and the hedgerow of dense jungle could not prevent them from one day taking all of the island. Qing officials now realized that the fence would have to be constructed out of naval defense.

Shen Baozhen and Luo Dachun argued that opening the mountains was imperative for naval defense. By cutting roads through the wilderness, they could ensure that Qing forces had easy access to Taiwan's eastern coast, thereby strengthening the island's defenses. Without this ability to penetrate the mountains, the Qing could never secure eastern Taiwan, leaving the terrain wide open to the drooling foreigners who had already taken Vietnam, India, and Singapore. Luo Dachun cautioned that if the Transmontane Territory were lost, then the Cismontane Territory, too, would eventually fall to foreigners.[27] And if Taiwan were lost, then the naval defense of China would be endangered. As Luo warned, "Once the hedgerow is breached, then the poison of vipers and lizards will one day enter through our back and penetrate our heart."[28] Using anatomical imagery, he represented Taiwan as the back of the Qing empire and China proper as the heart, a figure that suggested a close integration of the two as one body. As a part of the Chinese geo-body, Taiwan had to be kept safe from the penetration of foreign imperialism.

The image of drooling foreigners runs like a thread through Luo's diary. Foreigners were a threat that was at once distant and close at hand, for he saw them from time to time in the course of his expeditions through Taiwan's mountains. In particular, Luo noted missionaries establishing parishes among the "raw savages." He represented this activity as a danger, not so much because of the advance of Christianity but because of the potential for Western powers to make allies of their converts. Luo's fears were heightened when he glimpsed missionaries drawing maps of the "savage terrain." He read these carto-graphic efforts as a signal of foreign intent to take possession of the terrain—with missionaries acting as agents of Western imperialism. For Luo, as for other late Qing literati, the links between the study of geography, especially cartography, and imperial ambition were abun-dantly clear. Numerous late nineteenth-century authors portrayed the Qing as racing against the West to expand geographic knowledge of Taiwan's eastern side. This race lent urgency to the project of docu-menting and mapping "savage terrain," an area that the Qing had been content to leave terra incognita for centuries.

Luo's assessment of the danger foreign powers (Western and Japa-nese) posed to Taiwan led him to embrace the idea of fully coloniz-ing the island. Drawing on the rhetoric of the annexation debate of 1683, he argued for the wisdom of extending Qing control into "savage territory":

People say that the territory is a remote and isolated wilderness. They say that if we had the land, it would not be worth taxing; that if we had the people, they would not be worth pacifying. They say that it would be best to leave it as is. . . . I disagree. . . . The Cismontane Territory has been on the map for ages. In the past, the cooked savages were just like the raw savages of today. If the raw savages of yesteryear could be cooked, then what is to prevent the raw savages of today from being cooked?[29]

Criticizing proponents of the old quarantine policy, Luo praised Lan Dingyuan's perspicacity in advocating the aggressive colonization of Taiwan at several points in his diary. In Luo's assessment, the only way to ensure the long-term success of opening the mountains was to colonize the land with Han Chinese settlers. He pointed out that just as Han Chinese immigrants had long ago subverted the restrictions on crossing the Taiwan Strait, so had Han Chinese in search of camphor, timber, rattan, palm, and deer subverted the "raw savage boundary" in recent years. Painting Han Chinese colonization as an unstoppable tide, he argued that it was high time to do away with the old quaran-tine approach and lift the Savage Boundary. In advocating the full-fledged Chinese colonization of the island, Luo Dachun made clear that he envisioned Taiwan as a domain for Chinese subjects.

Divide Not Savage and Han

The vision of "all Taiwan" (*quan Tai*) as a Chinese territory was widely shared by Qing literati writing on Taiwan. Shen Baozhen spoke of the Opening and Pacifying campaign not only as a measure to secure Taiwan's naval defense but also as a mandate to transform savage Taiwan into a civilized Chinese domain. As he put it, "Take their land, and prefecture and county it; take the savage masses, and cap and clothe them."[30] The aim was to create a Taiwan in which there was no divide, administratively or culturally, between Han Chinese and savage.

To "prefecture and county" the land meant to draw administrative divisions on the landscape, set up yamens encircled by city walls, establish military colonies, and found walled villages with Chinese settlers. The building of city and village walls was important not only as a means of strengthening security but also as a symbolic gesture of civilizing the terrain; Chinese literati had long regarded the lack of city walls as a sign of Taiwan's primitiveness. In tandem with these efforts, the government would support the conversion of the newly cleared wilderness into farmland through irrigation projects and grants of oxen. In short, Shen's vision for the land was to transform it into a Chinese countryside. Another late nineteenth-century writer, Wu Guangliang, even proposed changing the indigenes' *she*, "tribal villages," into *zhuang*, "[Chinese] villages." As he explained: "In China proper, the places where the commoners live are all called such-and-such hamlet (*cun*), or such-and-such village (*zhuang*); there is nothing called a *she*."[31] All these measures were part of the effort to eliminate distinctions between the Han Chinese and the savages: or more accurately, to eliminate what was distinct about indigenous culture and make savage Taiwan over into something resembling China proper.

To "clothe and cap" the savages meant to change the "naked savages" into civilized subjects of the Qing empire. Along with making over the terrain, Shen planned major reforms for the indigenous populace. Although much of Shen's agenda was pragmatic, intended to rationalize the regulation of the indigenous villages and bring the administration of "raw territory" in line with the administration of "cooked territory," it also included a significant cultural component. Shen aimed to civilize the savages by teaching them "proper" Han

Chinese customs and language and to make farmers of them, fixing them in "proper" occupations. He further included in his agenda the broad mandate to "change their customs." Pacification was thus not limited to a military campaign to force the savages' submission; it was also a campaign to assimilate them.

The new policy therefore signified a major departure from the established policy of gradual cultural change. The old policy had been predicated on the theory that the indigenes could be slowly (and voluntarily) transformed over time through exposure to Civilization and the moral authority of the emperor. In contrast, the new policy envisioned the rapid acculturation of the indigenes: they were to immediately discard their "disgusting customs" and adopt "proper" customs. Shen did not advocate "transforming" indigenous customs but "changing" (*bian*) them, a word that connotes sudden and radical change—as in *biange*, "revolution," or *tianbian*, a sudden change of weather. The aggressive colonization of the land was to be matched by the aggressive acculturation of the natives. The acceptance of certain aspects of cultural change was made a condition of surrender: Luo Dachun's terms of surrender included adopting the queue, ending headhunting, and establishing an officially recognized tribal head.

This radical departure from the old cultural policy was necessitated by the new Qing determination to make the savages into "Chinese subjects." This aspect of late nineteenth-century policy was formulated with the uncomfortable awareness of foreigners "drooling" over "savage territory." Qing officials determined that if eastern Taiwan were to be accepted as "Chinese terrain," it would have to be peopled by "Chinese subjects." This notion was in part a product of the negotiations over the *Rover* Incident and the Japanese Taiwan Expedition, during which time LeGendre and others proposed that "international law" would recognize Chinese sovereignty over Taiwan only on the condition that they "civilize" the savages.[32] Although the Qing refused to accept the universal claims of (Western) "international law," its actions in Taiwan were no doubt partially influenced by knowledge of this discourse (a subject that I discuss further in the Epilogue). Doing away with the old vision of gradually transforming the raw savages into cooked savages and the cooked savages into subjects, the "pacifiers" sought to transform the raw savages directly into Chinese subjects—and to do so within a relatively short span of time. Only by instituting such rapid change could the ideal of "Divide not savage and Han" be realized.

The rhetoric of the time expressed the new resolve to transform the savages immediately into subjects. Whereas Yu Yonghe and Lan Ding-yuan had envisioned cooking the savages through the rather abstract process of reclaiming the wilderness and setting into motion a gradual metamorphosis of environment and populace, writers now proposed very concrete measures: "seven items to civilize the savages," "eight items," even "thirty-two items," and so on.[33]

A discursive shift can also be seen in the mode of representing the indigenes. Whereas the dominant trope since Chen Di's time had been the savages as the ancients, the dominant trope was now the savages as children. The idea of imperial subjects as children of the emperor had, of course, always been a fundamental element of Qing imperial discourse. But in writings of the Opening and Pacifying era, this conceit took on a new prominence. The Chinese phrase for the subjects as "children," *chizi*, conjures up a more vivid image than the English equivalent—an image of red, naked infants. This image suggests the infant's absolute lack of socialization at the moment when it enters "raw" and naked into the world. It also connotes a precious innocence unsullied by human corruption. The term thus implies an equivalence between nature and the infant/savage. The image further suggests the vulnerability of the newborn, who must rely entirely on the benevolence of the emperor. Again, colonial rhetoric disguises its true face, casting the indigenes as helpless infants who need the protection and guidance of parents (a Chinese term for local officials was "father and mother officials" [*fumu guan*]).

Indeed, late nineteenth-century authors set forth their suggestions for reforming indigenous culture in the condescending tone of parents telling off silly children: "They must learn to wear raincapes, in order not to get soaked by rain; they must learn to wear sunhats, in order not to be tanned by the sun."[34] Literati also exhorted the indigenes to wash their faces, to take medicine when sick, to eat with utensils and not their hands, to stop drinking alcohol, and to establish friendly relations with their neighbors, as well as to save food for times of hunger, to produce cloth for future use, and to regulate hunting so as not to neglect their crops. Qing literati believed that these lessons would change the indigenes from primitive children who did not possess the foresight to plan for the future into mature, civilized adults.[35]

Literati suggestions for reforming indigenous culture reveal much about what they considered fundamental to becoming a civilized Chinese subject. One classic name for China was "the land of ritual and righteousness." Accordingly, the transformation of the savages into Chinese subjects was to begin with the learning of Confucian ritual and ethical principles. As the foundation of Confucian morality, the indigenes were to be taught the Five Bonds: the bonds between ruler and official, parent and child, husband and wife, elder brother and younger brother, and between friends. The institution of these bonds would teach the principles of loyalty to the ruler, filial piety, proper gender distinctions, the hierarchy between senior and junior, and good relations between neighboring villages—all principles Chinese literati perceived to be lacking in savage society.[36]

Since education in the Chinese classics was the vehicle for imposing these norms, Qing literati sought to compel the indigenes to learn the Chinese language, and to select youths to be taught literacy in classical Chinese. The indigenes were further urged to adopt the Chinese calendar and to follow Chinese seasonal rituals. In doing so, they would be raised up from a people who "knotted strings" to a people who possessed writing and the calendar.

Another metonym for civilization was "a land of clothes and caps." Indeed, Chinese literati regarded the adoption of clothing as a cornerstone of the civilizing project: as Shen Baozhen termed it, the "clothing and capping" of the savages. Clothing was of central importance, for it marked the distinction between man and beasts. As one late nineteenth-century literatus put it: "The savages must no longer go naked like animals, but must wear clothes in order to enter the human race."[37] Similarly, Qing official Wang Kaitai emphasized the adoption of clothes as a primary means of becoming both human and Chinese.

Do not divide savage and Han Chinese. Make them civilized as one body. The birds and the beasts have feathers and fur; people should have clothes and caps. The savages are in the middle of the frontier wilderness, and they suffer from a lack of linen and silk. Therefore, the men and women are bareheaded and naked. How can they not feel shame?[38]

To wear clothing was to distinguish oneself from the animals. Therefore, proper clothing was made of woven cloth, not feathers, furs, or skins, the "coats" of animals. Wang also emphasized the importance of clothing for instilling the feeling of shame, one of the basic elements of Confucian morality. To complete their transformation from "naked beings," Qing literati urged the raw savages to stop tattooing and to adopt the queue.

The Qing imposed the queue on raw savage males mainly as an act symbolizing their submission to the Manchu regime. The court had already ordered the cooked savages to adopt the queue in 1758. By the nineteenth century, Qing writers took the queue as a distinguishing feature separating the raw and cooked savages. Qing official Shi Mi, for example, explained: "One may distinguish those who are sincere in submitting from those who are not sincere by whether they wear the queue. Those who do not wear the queue harbor a mind to rebel. Those who wear the queue have already reformed into cooked savages."[39] The imposition of the queue was also a means of eliminating the "crude" practices of wearing loose hair or cropping the hair. The admiration that Deng Chuan'an and Wu Ziguang had felt for such ancient practices was gone. Late nineteenth-century literati further spoke of imposing the queue on savage males in order to clearly articulate gender distinctions.

Indeed, an essential element of the civilizing program was to right gender inversion. Whereas Qing literati since Chen Di had regarded gender inversion as an index of the strangeness of savage culture, literati now proposed concrete measures to bring the indigenes in line with normative Confucian gender roles. The elimination of gender inversion was to begin with the institution of "proper" marriages—virilocal marriages arranged by matchmakers with the permission of the parents. Free divorce was to be ended, as was promiscuity. "Proper" terms of kinship, which distinguished maternal from paternal relatives, were to be adopted. Patrilineal descent was to be instituted by compelling the indigenes to take Chinese-style surnames and mandating that children take the surnames of their fathers. In short, the indigenes were to "value man and undervalue woman." Furthermore, gender distinctions were to be made clear in matters such as clothing and hairstyle, with men adopting the queue and women tying their hair in buns. Men and women were no longer to sit together at meals and festivals and were not to share eating utensils. The savages were to take up appropriately gendered occupations—men farming and women weaving. Through such measures, savage society would come to resemble Chinese society, the model for civilized society.

All these diverse cultural mandates were unified under the overall conception of bringing order to the chaos of savage society through establishing proper distinctions (*fenbie*). Thus literati urged the savages to "distinguish" the five Confucian bonds, to "distinguish" Chinese-style surnames, to "distinguish" proper kinship relations, to "distinguish" proper terms of address (in order to clarify relations of kinship and hierarchy), to "distinguish" monthly rituals and the passage of the years, to "distinguish" humans from animals (by wearing clothes), and to "distinguish" the two genders.[40] The establishment of order was also to be achieved through prohibitions, most important, the prohibition of headhunting and vendetta killings.

The literati who proposed these various measures declared that such changes were necessary to make the savages understand "human feelings." They thus conceptualized the civilizing program carried out in the name of "pacifying the savages" as a means of transforming the animal-like savages into proper human beings. The final result would be, as Wang Kaitai put it, "No division between savage and Han. Glorious for 10,000 years!"[41]

The campaign to transform the raw savages into proper subjects of the Qing empire demonstrates that the boundary between *min* and non-*min*, which was the central legal distinction on the Taiwan frontier, could shift over time and was not defined by race. Although frontier laws, such as those governing the boundary line, taxes, corvée, and intermarriage, served to mark distinctions between different ethnic/racial groups on the island, they did not preclude *fan* from gaining status as *min* solely on the basis of race/ethnicity. If *fan* (savage) and *min* (subject) had been fundamentally opposed in early Qing rhetoric, by the late nineteenth century the concept of *fanmin* (savage subject) had entered colonial discourse.

Savage Terrain Enters the Map

Just as the savages and Han Chinese were to come together as one body, the two sides of Taiwan were to come together as one terrain. Qing literati had long regarded eastern Taiwan as "off the map." By the late nineteenth century, this idea was so firmly ingrained that it would seem only natural for the Qing court to abjure all responsibility for atrocities committed in "savage territory." In asserting their sovereignty over "all Taiwan," the Qing were compelled to reconfigure this established conception of Taiwan.

The paradigm of Taiwan as only half "on the map," set into place through institutional structures like the Subject-Savage Boundary, was reinforced through cartographic representations of the island. As mentioned in Chapter 5, the Jesuit map of Taiwan, through its widespread reproduction in various forms, did much to produce the spatial image of a divided Taiwan, in Europe as in China (see Fig. 13, p. 146).[42] The earliest public Chinese version of the Jesuit map appeared in the imperial encyclopedia, *A Complete Collection of Books and Illustrations, Past and Present*, of 1728. This map shows Taiwan from a bird's-eye view, presenting a sharp visual contrast between the western side of the island, which is dense with landmarks, and the eastern side, which is entirely devoid of landmarks and fades off into empty space beyond the Central Mountain Range. The fact that the eastern coastline is not drawn in signifies the lack of geographic knowledge about this side of the island and furthermore conveys the impression that this area is beyond the pale.[43]

The *Comprehensive Geographic Map of the Great Qing* of 1789, which is also based on the Jesuit model, even more explicitly represents Taiwan as a divided island, with the words "raw savages" running down the length of the island to demarcate "raw savage terrain."[44] Cartographers followed this convention into the late nineteenth century. The "Map of Taiwan Prefecture" from the *Comprehensive Gazetteer of the Great Qing Realm* of 1842 (Fig. 31), for example, depicts Taiwan with the eastern side marked: "The eastern terrain is all territory of the raw savages of the Inner Mountains."[45] Beyond this label, the map simply fades off into empty space. On all these maps, the boundary between the Qing domain and the realm beyond the pale slices through the island. Such cartographic images helped to impress in the minds of Qing literati the notion that the eastern side of Taiwan had "not yet entered the map."[46]

In order to support the endeavor to make eastern Taiwan "enter the map" in the wake of the Mudanshe Incident, the Qing stepped up efforts to map the terrain. During the Opening and Pacifying campaign, Taiwan Circuit Intendant Xia Xianlun spent one year surveying Taiwan's Inner Mountains from south to north, crossing through much of "no-man's-land." Under his direction, a set of twelve maps

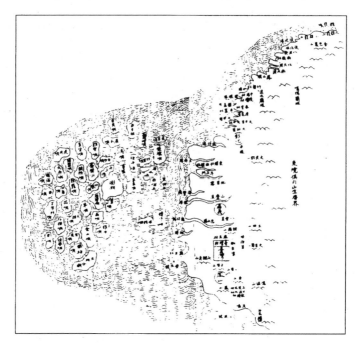

Fig. 31· "Map of Taiwan Prefecture" from the *Comprehensive Gazetteer of the Great Qing Realm* (1842)

was produced, which Xia later published as *Maps of Taiwan with Explanations* (*Taiwan yutu bingshuo*, preface dated 1879). In his preface, Xia explicitly linked mapping to conquest.

The ancients had histories on their right and maps (*tu*) on their left, granting equal importance to visualizing and perusing (*guanlan*). When [Han dynasty general] Xiao He entered the passes, the first thing he did was to collect maps and written records. Without maps, one cannot have comprehensive knowledge of all the roads and their obstacles, of the terrain and its strategic passes.[47]

Xia's contribution to Opening and Pacifying was therefore to map terrain that the existing gazetteers had "dismissed as wilderness and not investigated."[48] Xia further wrote in the body of the text that "only since the commencement of Opening and Pacifying in 1875 have we begun to be able to get and record maps."[49] As maps facilitated conquest, conquest facilitated mapping.

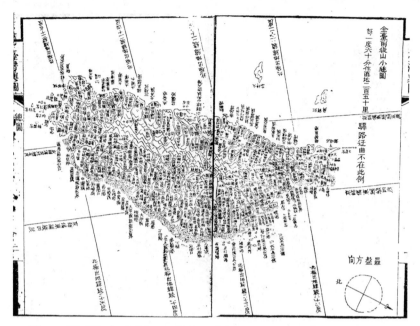

Fig. 32 Xia Xianlun's "General Map of the Cismontane and Transmontane
Territory" from *Maps of Taiwan with Explanations* (1879)

The first map in this groundbreaking collection was a "General
Map of the Cismontane and Transmontane Territory" ("Qianhoushan
zongtu").[50] This map (Fig. 32) at last showed both sides of the island
with equal density. It projects an image of eastern Taiwan not as an
empty wilderness but as a terrain that had been "prefectured and
countied." The Central Mountain Range is no longer represented as
an insurmountable obstacle between the two halves of the island;
rather, it is sandwiched between the coasts like a very thin layer of
jelly. By putting eastern Taiwan firmly on the map, this work represents a radical departure from the *Comprehensive Geographic Map of
the Great Qing* model, which had been reproduced as late as 1863 in the
*Qing Imperial Comprehensive Geographic Map of China and Foreign
Lands* (*Huang-chao Zhongwai yitong yutu*).[51] The collection also includes a "General Map of the Transmontane Territory" ("Houshan
zongtu"), which shows the topography of the eastern coast in a combined planimetric/pictorial perspective (Fig. 33).[52]

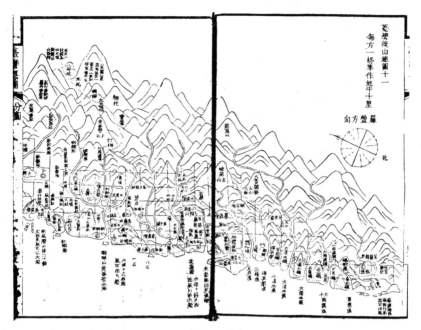

Fig. 33 Xia Xianlun's "General Map of the Transmontane Territory"
from *Maps of Taiwan with Explanations* (1879)

Xia's collection was only one of a number of atlases of "all Taiwan"
produced in the late nineteenth century. Such cartographic representations of the island promoted a new spatial image of the once-divided
Taiwan as a unified Qing terrain, an image reinforced by the label "all
Taiwan" (*quan Tai*). Travelogues composed following the Opening
and Pacifying campaign similarly employed the phrase "all Taiwan" in
their titles. The adoption of this term followed on its use in official
discourse to assert Chinese sovereignty over both sides of the island.
At long last, the entire island had "entered the map."

Taiwan Becomes a Province

A second major international crisis precipitated the promotion of
Taiwan to provincial status: this time it was the French naval block-
ade of 1884–85. Unlike the Japanese punitive expedition of 1874, the
French action against Taiwan was not a direct result of events on
the island itself but a byproduct of the Sino-French War of 1884. The
French decided, upon conclusion of this hostility, to attempt to seize

Taiwan in order to guarantee the payment of the indemnity promised them by the Qing government. The Qing dispatched Liu Mingchuan, Taiwan's most famous self-strengthener, to the island to ward off the French threat. The battle with the French extended from August 1884 to July 1885; during this time French naval forces instituted a six-month blockade of northern Taiwan. In the end, France was defeated, and Liu proclaimed Taiwan's champion.

The crisis prompted Liu Mingchuan to further Taiwan's self-strengthening by modernizing the island's infrastructure and economy and by revamping the island's administrative structure. In 1885, the Qing court authorized the promotion of Taiwan from a prefecture of Fujian province to a province in its own right, a move that various literati had been calling for throughout the Opening and Pacifying period. Liu Mingchuan oversaw this dramatic administrative change, serving simultaneously as governor of Fujian and governor of Taiwan during the transition period. To accord with the new administrative structure, Liu divided the island into three prefectures: Tainan, Taiwan, and Taipei. The eastern coast was designated a separate administrative department, Taidong. Liu transferred the site of Taiwan's new provincial capital from Tainan (the site of Taiwan's original prefectural capital) to central Taiwan, alienating the entrenched elites in the south. Eventually, the northern city of Taipei, designated the temporary provincial capital while the new capital was under construction, became the permanent capital. The locus of Taiwan's political power (but not cultural prestige) thereby shifted from the south to the north.

As governor of Taiwan, Liu Mingchuan did much to modernize the island. He conducted a major cadastral survey and land tax reform and carried out numerous technological innovations, including building a railway, setting down cable and telegraph lines, establishing modern coal mining, and creating a steamship line. Liu is also famous for his costly and aggressive military campaigns against unsubmissive indigenes; between 1884 and 1891, Liu conducted more than forty such punitive expeditions.[53] The successes and failures of Liu's program of self-strengthening have been extensively analyzed by various scholars and do not bear repeating here.[54] I touch on them briefly simply to note the importance of Liu Mingchuan in Taiwan's history.

The complex transition period would take until 1887, when Taiwan officially achieved the rank of a Chinese province, reflecting its new importance within the Qing empire. The process of making Taiwan a province paralleled the conversion of Central Asian Xinjiang into a province in 1884. The elevation of these formerly "remote" frontier territories—one "beyond the seas" (*haiwai*) and one "beyond the passes" (*guanwai*)—to provincial status was a move to tie the strategically important peripheral regions more closely to China proper. This signaled a new Qing determination to construct a more tightly integrated empire, envisioned as "the center and outer as one family" (*Zhongwai yijia*). In both Taiwan and Xinjiang, the promotion to provincehood was accompanied by administrative reforms, the promotion of Han Chinese immigration, and intensified efforts to educate (and thereby assimilate) the indigenous people—all measures aimed at making the frontiers more "Chinese." This process, which James Millward refers to as the "domestication of empire," was in large part a response to the growing pressures of foreign imperialism in the late nineteenth century.[55] This change in the conception of empire is signified in texts of the time by the increasing use of the term "China" (*Zhongguo*) instead of "Qing empire" (*Da Qing*).

Taiwan would enjoy its new identity until 1895, when the Treaty of Shimonoseki, which ended the Sino-Japanese War, officially ceded the island to the Japanese. Thus ended Taiwan's brief career as a "Chinese province."

CONCLUSION

Taiwan as a Lost Part
of 'My China'

At some time in the early 1930s, a writer named Chi Zhizheng sat down and composed a new preface to his *Travelogue of All Taiwan* (*Quan Tai youji*), which he had written decades earlier on the eve of Taiwan's cession to Japan. Reflecting back on his Taiwan sojourn, he wrote:

I was in Taiwan for three years. Whenever I passed through any territory, I would first survey the conditions of the terrain and then pronounce which places would flourish in the future and which places, although flourishing today, would decline in the future. I hear that the Japanese have developed those places I had once predicted would flourish. Alas! My China possessed a territory that had the potential to flourish, but China was never able to develop it. In the end, it is foreigners who have developed this terrain. Does this not hurt?! Is this not cause for regret?! How I blame those officials who severed our nation's territory to end the [Sino-Japanese] war! . . . Now this territory no longer belongs to us, and my travel account, too, is rendered useless. Nonetheless, since my account survives, hundreds of years from now when patriotic men of my nation read it, they will know that some time ago our China originally possessed this beautiful land, and that, in misfortune, it was lost and became foreign territory (*yiyu*). Some may cry in anguish, shedding tears and thinking thrice on it. I am already eighty years old. When I think back to the Taiwan of forty years ago, before it was severed, I can still see the flourishing and bustling scene before my eyes. Today, I take up my pen and write this preface to this account. Still I cannot stop this flood of old tears. Alas![1]

Chi Zhizheng's grief at the loss of Taiwan, as expressed here, is a far cry from the Kangxi emperor's declaration that it would be "no loss" to abandon the island. Chi's nostalgic preface thus reveals how dramatically Chinese perceptions of Taiwan had changed in the intervening centuries. Once dismissed as a "ball of mud," Taiwan was now cherished as a "beautiful land"; once dreaded as a miasmic and remote wilderness, Taiwan was now regarded as a "flourishing and bustling" cosmopolitan place. Whereas the Kangxi emperor had once seen Taiwan as "of no consequence to us," Chi Zhizheng lamented Taiwan's cession as the "severing of our nation's territory."[2] Chi's grief demonstrates the profound transformation since the late seventeenth century in the conception of the perimeters of the Chinese domain—a domain he witnessed metamorphose from the Qing empire into a republican nation, *My China*.

From a Chinese Realm to a
Multicultural Empire

The Ming conception of China was of a domain defined both by natural geographic borders and by the cultural boundaries between the civilized Chinese and surrounding barbarians. Qing expansionism established an imperial domain that surpassed these territorial boundaries and encompassed Han Chinese and various frontier peoples. The expansion of the Qing empire was a gradual process that took place under the Kangxi, Yongzheng, and Qianlong emperors, the great emperors of the High Qing era. Through various wars of conquest, these emperors added Taiwan, a substantial part of Central Asia, Mongolia, and Tibet to the empire. This imperial expansionism thereby displaced both China (as a territory centered on the Central Plain) and the Han Chinese from the center of the empire.

In place of the Ming paradigm of the Chinese empire, the Qianlong emperor articulated a new vision of the empire as a great unity (*datong*) of five domains: Manchu, Mongol, Han, Tibetan, and Muslim. Unifying these diverse sectors of the empire was the Qing emperor, who personified the power of the Qing imperial house. The status of these five "culture blocs" as the principal sectors of the Qing empire was signified through the use of Manchu, Mongolian, Chinese, Tibetan, and Turki/Arabic for multilingual imperial inscriptions on the many gates, stelae, and monuments erected during the Qing.[3]

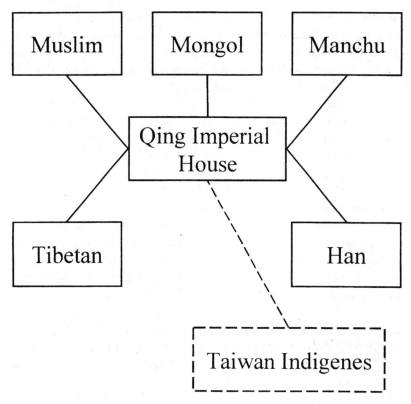

Fig. 34 Proposed supplement to James Millward's diagram of the Qianlong emperor's vision of the empire (drawn by Charles Robert Broderick III after Millward, *Beyond the Pass*, p. 201, fig. 9)

In this new imperial ideology, the emperor's universality was manifest not through his embodiment of Confucian Civilization, as it had been in previous dynasties, but through his capacity to rule impartially over his diverse subjects. "Chinese Culture" did not occupy a privileged position within this scheme of the empire as a "great unity"; rather, the Han constituted one bloc among five. James Millward has argued that the "Chinese World Order" model of concentric rings centered on Chinese Civilization, popularized by John King Fairbank, must be replaced for the Qing by a new model in which the five major culture blocs occupy parallel positions centered on the Qing imperial house (see Fig. 34).[4] At the center of this structure, which he calls "Five Nations, Under Heaven," is not an abstract "Chinese Civilization" but the person of the Qing emperor, who turned a different face to each sector of his empire. As James Hevia and others have demonstrated, the Qianlong emperor was simultaneously the Chinese Son of Heaven; the Khan of Khans; the cakravartin king; the overlord of Mongolia, Xinjiang, Qinghai, and Tibet; the pacifier of Taiwan, Yunnan, Vietnam, Burma, and the Zungars and Gurkhas; the incarnate bodhisattva Manjusri; and head of the Aisin Gioro, the dominant clan among the Manchus.[5] The universality of the emperor was thus dramatized through his embodiment of cultural pluralism.

The paradigm of the empire as "Five Nations, Under Heaven" was articulated through a variety of imperially sponsored projects. These endeavors included the great multilingual encyclopedic glossary, the *Imperial Glossary of the Five Dynastic Scripts*; massive translations of the Tibetan Buddhist canon; and various other geographic, ethnographic, and historiographic works.[6] The vision of the Qing empire as a great unity was also articulated through architectural projects such as the Qianlong emperor's replicas, built in Rehe, of the Tibetan palaces of the Dalai Lama and Panchen Lama, the Manchu palace complex at Mukden, and the tents erected at Rehe to receive Mongol and Turkic lords.[7] Such works symbolized the multifaceted nature of Qing emperorship, which transcended linguistic, cultural, and religious differences.

The Qianlong emperor may have transcended such differences, but he did not seek to diminish them. In this respect, the Qianlong emperor's orientation toward cultural difference departed from that of his predecessor. As Pamela Kyle Crossley writes in *A Translucent Mirror: History and Identity in Qing Imperial Ideology*: "For the Yongzheng emperor, the erosion of cultural differences (and the achievement of a morally correct world) is the mission of the ruler. For the Qianlong emperor, the clarification of cultural differences, and subsequent proof of the universal competence of the emperorship, is the mission of the ruler."[8]

In seeking to clarify rather than erode cultural differences, the Qianlong emperor rejected the Yongzheng ideology of transformationalism. Although the Qianlong emperor demanded the submission of the "Five Nations" to imperial authority, he did not seek to compel these groups to "come to be transformed." Thus, as James Millward emphasizes, the Qianlong emperor's vision of a "great unity" was no melting pot.[9] Qianlong ideology emphasized instead the delineation of strict boundaries between the empire's primary cultural blocs. The state established administrative structures, laws, and land policies to support the maintenance of these boundaries, often through the physical segregation of groups.

Contemporary scholars have characterized the Manchus, Han Chinese, Mongols, Tibetans, and East Turkestanis as "linguistic or ethnic blocs," "nations" (Millward), "constituencies" (Crossley), and "races" (Crossley).[10] There is probably no perfect English word to describe these groups of people, and any choice is bound to be controversial.[11] Whatever term one chooses, it is important to note that the Qianlong emperor's vision of the empire as Five Nations, Under Heaven was predicated on a conception of these five groups as culturally integral descent-groups, each distinct from the others. In ideal terms, each group (race/nation/constituency) had its own language, its own customs, its own genealogy, and its own history: all of which, it might be added, were Qing constructions. As Pamela Kyle Crossley has demonstrated, the Qianlong emperor had a vested interest in the cultural integrity of these groups and sought to ensure an "orderly congruence of race to custom."[12] For the emperor, congruence was a means of bringing order to the diversity of a multilingual, multicultural, and multiethnic empire.

The Place of the Taiwan Indigenes
Within the Multicultural Qing Empire

Notably absent from this scheme of Five Nations (as well as from many contemporary accounts of Qing imperialism) were the Taiwan indigenes. They, like the Yao and the Miao of southwestern China and various other frontier peoples, were not considered principal constituencies in the new vision of empire. Thus, despite the fact that they were the "emperor's children," symbolically they were not recognized as cultural blocs of the empire. This difference in status is partially signified by the fact that whereas references to the East Turkestanis and Mongols as "dog-Muslims" and "barbarians" were excised from Qing official discourse after the incorporation of their territories, Qing officials continued to refer to the Taiwan indigenes as "savages" (a derogatory and imprecise term).[13] Nor did Qing official discourse censor references to the Taiwan indigenes as animals. If the Qing emperor was an impartial ruler over diverse peoples, then why accord different status to different peoples within the empire?

The answer lies in a combination of cultural and political factors that made the Taiwan indigenes superfluous to the "great unity." Pamela Kyle Crossley asserts that the Manchus, Mongols, Han Chinese, Tibetans, and East Turkestanis assumed their status because they "all had a relationship to the emperor informed by the historical role of their ancestors in the creation and development of the [Qing] state."[14] Unlike these Five Nations, the Taiwan indigenes had played no such historical role. Nor did the Taiwan indigenes ever present a substantial challenge to Qing control over the empire; they were never regarded as competitors for pre-eminence in the region, as were the Mongols, for example. The Qing therefore had no reason to seek an alliance with the Taiwan indigenes, nor to grant them partnership in the empire.[15]

Furthermore, the Taiwan indigenes did not constitute a "nation" in the eyes of the Qing. They had no centralized leadership—no king, no prince, no khan—but were simply disparate tribes with no recognized leader to speak for them as a body. Qing literati regarded this lack as a measure of the indigenes' primitiveness. In military terms, the absence of a centralized leadership and organized army enabled the Qing to effectively employ a divide-and-conquer strategy on Taiwan.

There was also a vast difference in the cultural status the Qing accorded the Taiwan indigenes and the Five Nations. The Taiwan indigenes had no written language, no history, and no genealogy, all key elements in the construction of the Five Nations as "races" or "constituencies." Genealogy, in particular, as Crossley has argued, was a fundamental premise of the "racial thinking that [was] glorified in the Qianlong era"[16] and played a central role in the construction of particular groups as "races/nations." Furthermore, Qing literati considered their customs anachronous; unlike Tibetan Buddhism, for example, they appeared to be irrelevant to modern Qing society (other than as a vehicle for primitivist critiques).

In contrast to the Five Nations, the Taiwan indigenes were not recipients of imperial efforts to codify their "culture" as an integral entity. Even in Huang Shujing's *Investigations of Savage Customs in Six Categories*, the most exhaustive and precise Qing source on the subject, "savage customs" are nothing more than a collection of variable practices that differ from village to village, with no orthodox standard, no historically authoritative model. The Qianlong emperor sponsored no dictionaries of the "savage language," no grand multilingual gazetteers on the scale of the *Imperially Commissioned Unified Language Gazetteer of the Western Regions* (*Xiyu tongwen zhi*, 1763), a geographic and genealogical dictionary in Manchu, Chinese, Mongolian, Tibetan, and Turki/Arabic. There were no scholarly researches into the Taiwan indigenes' origins (which were declared "unknown") or their ethnohistorical development (their customs were declared "timeless," unchanged since Creation). There was no tracing of their genealogy (an impossible task, for they had no surnames and no records of their ancestors). Without a codified language, without a history, without a genealogy, in short, without a formalized "heritage," the Taiwan indigenes could hardly constitute a *zu* (race/nation/constituency). They were nothing more than scattered tribes of savages in the eyes of the Qing.

Thus, in terms of Qianlong ideology, the Taiwan indigenes shared in the emperor's "impartial love," but they were not partners in empire. Whereas Qianlong ethnic policy worked to support the maintenance of strict boundaries dividing the empire's five major cultural blocs, it did not always do so on the Taiwan frontier. Although certain policies did serve to delineate the distinctions between Han Chinese and indigene, other policies were assimilationist in character.

Upon ascending the throne, the Qianlong emperor began to roll back the aggressive colonization policies of the Yongzheng era and to reinstate the quarantining of the Taiwan frontier by tightening restrictions on Han Chinese immigration and land reclamation. The Qianlong emperor decreed a series of regulations to clarify the boundary lines and protect tribal lands from Han Chinese encroachment. There were also attempts to return illegally reclaimed land to the indigenes. These measures were taken largely in response to a number of revolts on the island. But they also reflected the colonial administration's concern for the increasing impoverishment of the Taiwan indigenes with the decline of the deer trade and the expansion of Han Chinese settlement.[17] In general terms, these land policies resemble those adopted by the Qing on other frontiers, such as Manchuria and Mongolia.[18]

In addition to land policies that separated the Han Chinese and the Taiwan indigenes, Qing officials banned intermarriage between Han Chinese men and indigenous women in 1737. In the 1760s, officials further proposed that Han Chinese who crossed over the boundary line to live among the natives be arrested.[19] Like the restrictions on Han Chinese immigration, these measures aimed to freeze the ethnic status quo on Taiwan and to physically separate Han Chinese and indigene. Although the ultimate goal of such quarantine policies was to prevent interethnic conflict, they also had the effect of reinforcing the distinctions, especially spatial, between the two groups. Furthermore, the Qianlong emperor established a separate office, the Subprefecture for Savage Affairs, to deal specifically with the indigenes. Ka Chih-ming has argued that before the nineteenth century, the Qing state had a vested interest in preserving the differences among Han Chinese, cooked savages, and raw savages in order to maintain their rule on the island through "ethnic politics."[20]

Certainly, all these measures can be regarded as institutional efforts to clarify the distinctions between Han Chinese and indigene. Yet, these efforts stopped short of delineating a cultural boundary between these two groups, along the lines of the boundaries between Han and Manchu or Han and Muslim. Instead, there was much in Qianlong policy that could be regarded as assimilationist. Of course, to say that Qianlong policy was assimilationist is to beg the question: assimilationist to what? to Han Chinese culture? or to Manchu culture? Qing attempts to "cook" the Taiwan indigenes appear to be a mixed menu of Confucianization, Hanization, and Manchuization—all aimed at gradually making the cooked savages resemble the other "subjects" of Taiwan.

The Qianlong period marked the high point of the establishment of Confucian schools for indigenous boys—the main vehicle for the Confucianization of the Taiwan indigenes. These boys were not only taught Confucian ethics but also encouraged to wear Han Chinese-style clothing and to adopt the Manchu-style queue. The Confucian schools also promoted the Chinese language, both spoken and written. No effort was made, as had been made under the Dutch, to develop a writing system for the indigenous languages.

Furthermore, in 1758, the administration effected a number of measures to change "cooked savage" customs to accord with those of "subjects"; they were to take Chinese-style surnames, and the males were to adopt the queue (which many had already voluntarily done). Many indigenes took (or were given) the surname Pan, the Chinese character *fan* (savage) with the addition of the water radical.[21] These regulations were intended not to clarify the distinctions between Han Chinese and indigene but conversely to diminish them.

Moreover, the local gazetteers of the Qianlong era were full of transformationalist rhetoric: praise for the emperor for transforming a "land of tattoos and black teeth into a land of clothes and caps" and for "bestowing the shining light of transformation" on the indigenes.[22] Literati, officials and nonofficials alike, still called on the indigenes to "turn toward transformation/civilization." Guided by the goal of transforming raw savages into cooked savages, and cooked savages into subjects, literati encouraged the Taiwan indigenes to gradually emulate Han Chinese customs and to adopt the Chinese "way of life" by learning plow agriculture and studying the Confucian classics.

It appears, then, that Qianlong ideology did not champion the preservation of the Taiwan indigenes' cultural integrity, as it did in the case of the Five Nations. The land rights of the Taiwan indigenes were to be preserved as best as possible—in the interests of frontier stability as well as native welfare—but their customs, it seems, were to be gradually "transformed." Some even argued that the Taiwan indigenes ought to be transformed into Han Chinese. Thus, although Crossley argues that the Qianlong emperor eschewed the ideology of transformationalism, this ideology still had relevance on the Taiwan frontier. In contrast to the Five Nations, who, despite their differences, were all fully cooked cultural entities in the eyes of the Qing, the Taiwan "savages" had come into the Qing empire raw. Therefore, although the Qianlong emperor may have rejected transformationalism as a philosophical premise, especially where the Manchus were concerned, in the case of the Taiwan indigenes transformationalism still had a role to play. Thus, the cultural status of various peoples affected policy orientation on the different frontiers of the multicultural Qing empire.

In order to make a place for the Taiwan indigenes, I would supplement James Millward's diagram of the Qianlong emperor's vision of the empire by adding a box in a second tier beyond the five major cultural blocs of the "great unity" (Fig. 34).[23] This position signifies both the secondary status of the Taiwan indigenes within the empire and Taiwan's physical location within Qing imagined geography.

Eighteenth-century Qing literati conceived of Taiwan as a periphery of the empire. The island was a fence for the Chinese domain, the border between China proper and the realm beyond the pale. Qing literati also spoke of Taiwan as lying on the boundary between the Chinese and barbarians (*Huayi zhi jiao*). As a hedgerow, Taiwan was crucial to the defense of the Qing domain, but it was not integral to that which it protected. Thus, despite the fact that Taiwan had "entered the map," it still occupied a liminal position within the Qing empire, straddling the fence between inner and outer.

The Taiwan indigenes were similarly neither fully incorporated into the empire nor fully outside it. The raw savages were beyond Qing jurisdiction; the cooked savages were administratively subjects of the empire, but discursively they were frequently distinguished from "subjects." Even the Qianlong emperor made this distinction when he declared that "in our imperial benevolence, the subjects (*min*) and savages (*fan*) are alike our children. There is no basis for discrimination."[24] Their status as subjects was thus somewhat ambiguous. It would not be until the late nineteenth century that the Qing would move to definitively establish the "savages" as full subjects of the empire.

From a Qing Empire
Back to a Chinese Empire

In the second half of the nineteenth century, the Qing frontiers, from Central Asia to Manchuria to Mongolia to Taiwan, were alike subject to a process that James Millward refers to as the "domestication of empire": that is, massive Han Chinese immigration and colonization of land; the extension of Chinese-style administrative structures; and increased efforts to establish Confucian free schools and promote literacy in the Chinese language.[25] These measures heralded the transformation of the Qing empire into a Chinese empire.[26] This change resulted in part from the increasing influence of Han Chinese officials at the Qing court after the suppression of the Taiping Rebellion (1850–64). It also reflected the court's determination to integrate the empire more tightly in order better to face the mounting pressure of foreign imperialism. As Pamela Kyle Crossley has argued, post-Taiping court rhetoric stressed hierarchy, conformity, harmony, and cultural uniformity.[27] The pluralism of the earlier Qianlong era was replaced by intensive efforts to "Hanize" the diverse peoples and vast terrain of the empire.[28]

In Taiwan, the "domestication of empire" took the form of the campaign to Open the Mountains and Pacify the Savages. This campaign aimed to transform the final frontier of Taiwan's wilderness into a copy of the Chinese agrarian landscape and the last of the "raw savages" into proper "Chinese subjects." It also aimed to assert Qing sovereignty over the entire island of Taiwan. Content for centuries to let half the island rest beyond the Savage Boundary and "off the map," the Qing were compelled to make this move by the Japanese challenge to Qing sovereignty over "savage Taiwan." It was not until 1875, then, that all of Taiwan entered the Qing map. And not until 1887, after the Sino-French War, that Taiwan officially become a province of China.

The Island Severed from the Chinese Body

Early Qing writers spoke of Taiwan "entering the map"; Chinese nationalists, however, did not speak of Taiwan "exiting the map" after the Treaty of Shimonoseki.[29] Rather, as with Chi Zhizheng, the outraged scholars and officials who protested the signing of the treaty spoke of Taiwan being "severed" (*ge*) from China, as a limb from the body.[30] The Chinese word *ge* means "to cut, to hack, to sever, to rupture." It is a term often associated with flesh as in butchery or in surgery; it is also associated with wounds and trauma as in beheading and castration. *Ge* implies a dividing or diminishing of the whole, a radical and dramatic rupture. To speak of Taiwan as "severed" from China is thus to conceive of the island as an integral part of the Chinese domain, as "sovereign territory," to use a modern term. The image of Taiwan as part of the body of China connotes a far tighter integration of the two than the image of the island as a hedgerow for the Chinese domain. It implies that the whole is rendered incomplete by the cutting off of this piece of the Chinese geo-body. The act of severing leaves a scar, a constant reminder of the pain of the knife. And so, Chi Zhizheng wept old tears, forty years after the cession of Taiwan to Japan.

The scar that was left when Japan annexed Taiwan was temporarily healed when China—this time the Republic of China—once again took possession of the island following World War II. But the wound would be opened four years later by the Chinese Civil War. With the victory of the Chinese Communists (CCP) imminent, the Chinese Nationalists (KMT) packed up their government, army, and many of the treasures of the Qing imperial collections and fled to Taiwan, establishing a provisional government of the Republic of China on the island.

It was out of this history of the Chinese Civil War that the current Taiwan issue emerged, with the KMT declaring the provisional government on Taiwan the legitimate government of "Free China," and the PRC staking its claim over the "renegade province" of Taiwan. In order to bolster the legitimacy of these claims, both sides promoted the historically inaccurate contention that Taiwan has been "a part of China" since antiquity and effectively erased the rich history of the Qing colonization of the island. This Chinese nationalist discourse (both the KMT and the CCP varieties) has naturalized the idea that Taiwan is an inalienable part of China's sovereign territory, a sacred part of the Chinese geo-body—a notion that first emerged from the protests over Taiwan's cession to Japan. The success of this discourse can be measured by the disappearance from the Chinese collective memory of the pre-Qing conviction that Taiwan was "beyond the pale."

In Taiwan's gradual transformation from "savage island" into "Chinese province," we see the profound changes in the imagined geography of the Chinese domain wrought by Qing expansionism. In the contemporary construction of Taiwan as a renegade province that must be "reunified" with the mainland in order to restore China's territorial integrity, we see the lasting impact of Qing expansionism on the imagined (and imaginary) geography of the modern Chinese nation-state.[31]

On the Impossibility of a Postcolonial
Theory of Taiwan

"Colonialism: the word's immediate associations are with intrusions, conquest, economic exploitation and the domination of indigenous peoples by European men." Nicholas Thomas begins his book *Colonialism's Culture: Anthropology, Travel and Government* with this simple assertion.[1] Thomas draws a caricature of our commonsense understanding of colonialism in order to critique it as narrow and inadequate for a full appreciation of the plural and particularized expressions of colonialism. As Thomas eloquently demonstrates, despite the attempts of theorists to move away from monolithic and essentialist characterizations of colonialism, it has proved difficult to displace the general assumptions attached to this word. Indeed, similar associations surround the word "imperialism." Although Thomas's book does much to move us beyond this oversimplified picture of colonialism, one fundamental assumption remains unchallenged in his call for a "pluralized field of colonial narratives."[2] And that is the assumption that colonizers were European men.

In the Introduction I asked what difference it makes if we treat Qing expansionism as "imperialism" or "colonialism." Here I pose the reverse question: What difference does it make if we refuse to consider the possibility of Qing "imperialism"? If we call the Qing an empire without "imperialism"?

In *Becoming "Japanese,"* Leo Ching argues that the absence of the decolonization process in the breakup of the Japanese empire has prevented both Taiwan and Japan from addressing their colonial relationship and its legacy.³ I argue that a similar "absence of decolonization" determines contemporary China-Taiwan affairs. In this case, however, the lack of decolonization has been occasioned not so much by the conditions under which the empire was dismantled but by the failure to acknowledge the very existence of Qing imperialism. Decolonization is thus rendered impossible by the refusal to name the historical relation between China and Taiwan as "colonial"; how can we speak of decolonization if there was no colonization? This double lack of decolonization (from Japan and China) precludes the possibility of Taiwan's postcoloniality.

As Liao Ping-hui and others have pointed out, the development of postcolonial theory in Taiwan has been hindered by the failure to reach any agreement on *when* Taiwan can be said to have entered the postcolonial phase: Was it with the end of Japanese rule in 1945? With the end of martial law and the KMT's "internal colonial" rule in 1987? Or is Taiwan still under American "neocolonial" rule? If Taiwan is not truly "postcolonial," can it possibly have postcolonial theory? Hence the problematic of Taiwan's postcoloniality is conditioned at once by a lack of decolonization and a continual re-colonization. On either score, Taiwan's postcoloniality is rendered "impossible."⁴

By turning the lens of colonial discourse studies on the China-Taiwan relation, this book asks how we might understand China's claim to Taiwan in the light of a deferred decolonization. What if we were to understand the China-Taiwan issue not simply as a "leftover" from the Chinese Civil War, as the PRC asserts, but also as a "leftover" from the history of Qing imperialism? How might our perspective on this issue change if we were to name the Qing presence on Taiwan "colonial"?

The very idea of "national reunification" between China and Taiwan is predicated on the denial of Qing imperialism. Hence the PRC has a vested interest in maintaining the idea that imperialism was solely the doing of European men. In official PRC accounts of Qing history, Qing expansionism is never spoken of as "imperialism"; rather, it is recast as "national unification" (*tongyi*). A wholly different beast from predatory and aggressive "imperialism," "national unification" implies a benign and natural process whereby the "domestic nationalities" came together (*tuanjie*) to form a unified China. Whereas "imperialism" involved the foreign conquest of culturally distinct peoples, "unification" occurred between (uniformly Chinese) majority and minority peoples. The homogenizing tendency of this discourse, which constructs frontier peoples as "Chinese" while masking the process by which they became Chinese, deflects the possibility of Qing "imperialism." Qing expansionism becomes an "internal affair," off-limits to meddling, "imperialist" Western critics.

If the concept of "national unification" naturalizes the PRC's claim to most of the territory incorporated under Qing expansionism, "Qing imperialism," or "colonialism," would denaturalize these claims. In other words, if we were to characterize the Qing occupation of Taiwan as a colonial conquest, then we would have to consider not only the question of "reunification" but also the question of Taiwan's decolonization.[5]

The erasure of Qing imperialism is further effected by PRC scholars' insistence that Qing expansionism be studied under the rubric of "frontier studies" (*bianjiangxue*) and not "imperial studies" or "colonial studies." In contrast to Western colonial studies, which has tended to be critical in nature since Said's *Orientalism* (1978), PRC frontier studies, a flourishing field since the 1980s, has been generally positive in its historical assessment of Qing expansionism. James Millward's review of this field has shown that the agenda of frontier studies is, in the words of PRC scholars, "to make widely known the traditional patriotism of the Chinese (*Zhonghua*) nationalities," to protect "sovereignty over national territory," and to strengthen "the unity of domestic nationalities."[6] These statements reveal how frontier studies serve as a pre-emptive defense against both internal and external pressures for decolonization of the former Qing frontiers by promoting the ideology of "national unification" at home and abroad. The methodology of frontier studies also diverges from that of colonial studies: frontier studies is highly empirical and focuses primarily on history, statecraft, and economics. "Discourse" and the politics of representation are not subjects for frontier studies.

The constitution of frontier studies as a field distinct from colonial studies not only ensures that Qing expansionism is not spoken of in the same breath as Western "imperialism" but also forecloses the possibility of conversations across the disciplinary divide, forecloses the possibility of shared theoretical and political concerns. China thereby avoids the uncomfortable position of having to speak not only as a victim of imperialism but also as a past perpetrator. Qing expansionism remains "glorious," unlike "shameful" Western imperialism: national unification the apple to imperialism's orange. In problematizing the distinction between "national unification" and "imperialism," I do not mean to deny the very real suffering of the Chinese people caused by Western and Japanese imperialism. What I wish to suggest is the possibility that our preoccupation with this victimization blinds us to other forms of historical oppression.

Taiwanese nationalists are not necessarily more open to talking of Qing imperialism/colonialism. There are some who argue that the Qing rule of Taiwan cannot be considered "colonial" in the same sense that Japanese rule was "colonial," for it was not "external" or "foreign." This argument is implicitly Han-Chinese-centric, for it presumes the perspective of the Han Chinese settlers of Taiwan. From the hypothetical perspective of the Taiwan indigenes, I would argue that Qing rule was every bit as "external" as Japanese colonial rule and the earlier Dutch presence on the island. In each case, foreign invaders claimed indigenous lands and subjugated indigenous peoples in the name of "civilization." This is not to homogenize the very different historical experiences of the Taiwan indigenes under Dutch, Japanese, and Qing rule but to question what it means when we refuse to label one set of invaders "colonizers." Ironically, the refusal to acknowledge Qing "colonialism" naturalizes the idea of Taiwan's "return" (*guang-fu*) to the Chinese motherland, which not only supports the push for "reunification" but also legitimizes the KMT's rule of Taiwan as the "Republic of China" from 1949 to 2000.

By recognizing the colonial nature of the historical Chinese presence on Taiwan, we enable the extension of postcolonial critiques to the treatment of the Taiwan indigenes by Han Chinese. We also call into question the Han-centric construction of the modern "Taiwanese" identity and related terms like *Taiwanren* (Taiwanese people) and *Taiwanhua* (Taiwanese language), which privilege the Minnan (Hokkien)-speaking descendants of immigrants from Fujian. Even recent attempts to decenter this ethnic/linguistic group from "Taiwaneseness" and move toward a pluralist construct of Taiwanese identity are often unconsciously Han-centric: witness, for example, the public address system of Taipei's new Mass Rapid Transit (MRT) system, which announces station stops in Mandarin Chinese, Hokkien, Hakka, and

English. This is a gesture of inclusiveness toward Taiwan's post-1949 mainland Chinese immigrants and Hakka residents (not to mention tourists). However, the absence of any indigenous languages in this system effects the erasure of the Taiwan indigenes from the new multilingual Taiwanese identity, as well as from the modern, MRT-riding public. This oversight is a symptom of the preoccupation in Taiwanese nationalist discourse since 1949 on the ethnic conflict between "mainlanders" and "Taiwanese."[7]

Western scholars have also shied away from talking of Qing "imperialism" or "colonialism" until fairly recently. Indeed, Peter Perdue's statement in a special issue on Manchu colonialism in *The International History Review* (June 1998) that "the Qing empire of China was a colonial empire that ruled over a diverse collection of peoples with separate identities and deserves comparison with other empires" served as a conceptual challenge both to the China field and to comparative historians. One ground for objecting to the term "Qing imperialism" is the argument that Qing expansionism does not fit the model of European imperialism. This brings us back to the assumption that imperialism was a singularly Western phenomenon. Theorists sometimes admit Japan as the single example of a non-Western imperial power. But as Leo Ching has shown, there is still some reluctance even then to accepting Japan as a "true" imperialist.[8] Qing imperialism, it would seem, faces a similar prospect of "inauthenticity."

Yet as I pointed out in the Introduction, there is no universally accepted model of "European imperialism." And as historian Robert Hind has argued, "There is no foreseeable prospect of securing a generally acceptable redefinition of colonialism and imperialism."[9] Indeed, most recent theoretical work has been devoted to demonstrating how the construct of "European imperialism/colonialism" is overly homogenizing, reductionist, and essentialist. In light of this, we must pause to consider how much the objection to the idea of "Qing imperialism" stems from the presumption that this phenomenon is by definition essentially different, *must* be different, by virtue of its Chineseness. This problematic is similar to that faced by Leo Ching in his endeavor to study Japanese imperialism. Here I would echo Ching's assertion that "I want to stress the need to be cognizant of our complacency in redefining and essentializing imperialism and colonialism as solely a 'Western' problematic in Euro-American academia."[10] I also want to stress the need to be cognizant of our complacency in accepting Chinese characterizations of Qing expansionism as so fundamentally different that the concepts of "imperialism" or "colonial discourse" cannot be used to study it.

It would be safer, of course, to call the Qing simply an "empire" or "imperium" and Taiwan a "frontier" with "ethnic" minorities and to avoid controversial words like "imperialism," "colonialism," and "race" entirely. But by consigning the study of Qing expansionism to the rubric of frontier studies or to the study of "empire," while reserving studies of imperialism and colonial discourse for the "real" (European) imperialists, we further reify the methodological and intellectual, even moral, gap between China studies and colonial studies.

In the same spirit, I have resisted describing Qing expansionism as "internal colonialism," a concept that has been productively applied to analyses of ethnic relations in the PRC.[11] I find the model of internal colonialism unsuitable for the study of Qing expansionism in several respects. First, the concept of internal colonialism is theoretically derived from analogies. Although there are various theses of internal colonialism, what they share in common is the idea that there are close parallels between relations that have developed *within* countries and the metropole-colony relationship: that is, the situation of ethnic minorities within a single nation-state is analogous to the situation of colonized peoples under colonialism. Thus, internal colonialism has been used to theorize, for example, the condition of Black ghettos within the United States and the Irish in Britain.[12] The applications of the concept generally presuppose the existence of a modern, industrial nation-state. Thus, whereas the position of Taiwan indigenes within modern Taiwan's political economy might be characterized as internal colonialism, I would argue that this concept does not adequately describe Qing expansionism. Second, we must attend to the ways in which the paradigm of internal colonialism is complicit with the PRC discourse of national unification. The term internal colonialism implies that the conquest and incorporation of frontier regions like Taiwan and Tibet were a process that happened domestically within China, a notion that reinforces the ahistorical conception of the Qing frontiers as essentially "Chinese." The concept of internal colonialism thereby becomes an unwitting ally both to the homogenizing discourse of national unification and to a Western racialism that similarly sees Qing expansionism as something that the Chinese did internally (read: to other fellow Orientals)—and for this reason was fundamentally unlike Western imperialism, which involved racial difference.[13]

As stated in the Introduction, I do not wish to deny the specificity of the historical experience of European imperialism between 1880 and 1914, a period sometimes referred to as "classical imperialism." Nor do I wish to embrace a universal definition of imperialism as a transhistorical, global phenomenon found in every place and every time. What I seek to do instead in insisting on Qing imperialism/colonialism is to *open a space* for multiple forms of imperialisms and colonialisms, so that their historically particular and local manifestations can be discussed within the shared framework of postcolonial concerns. I pose this opening of space as an alternative to closing off the dialogue from the outset on the a priori assumption that "Western" and "Eastern" imperialisms are *necessarily* different. I wish to find the middle ground between the right-wing "sameness" of universal racism and the liberal privileging of "difference," which in this case ironically reinforces the notion that "West is West, and East is East." It is therefore to challenge the implicit assumptions underlying the overly homogenizing construct of "Western imperialism" and the overly particularizing construct of "national reunification" that I have strategically deployed the terms "imperialism" and "colonialism" in this study. As Thomas alerts us, we are working "around a contradiction: colonialism is something that needs to be theorized and discussed, but discussion may be obstructed if we assume that the word relates to any meaningful category or totality."[14] By suspending this assumption, we may perhaps begin a dialogue.

In walking the fine line between narrowly restrictive definitions of imperialism that do not allow us to consider non-Western examples and overly general definitions that generate only banal insights, I have resisted offering an alternative model of imperialism/colonialism that would encompass both European and Qing imperialisms. To do so would only be to set up another idealized and static model that would do little to promote our understanding of either. What I propose to do instead is to suggest the possibility of *meeting points* between Western and Chinese colonial discourses.

One such meeting point or encounter took place at the boundary between Qing China and Aboriginal Formosa in 1867. In the course of negotiations with the Qing over the wreck of the U.S.S. *Rover* off of "aboriginal" Taiwan, U.S. consul Charles LeGendre composed a letter to the "Governor of Formosa" in which he declared:

For if you admit that such territory has never been explored, you admit also that it can be seized by the first power that will find it to its interest to occupy it in advance of you, and that power shall acquire an indisputable right to its possession as the Spaniards did when they discovered the New World, or as you did yourselves when you first implanted your colonies on the western shores of the Island. So you perceive the view we take of the native tribes of Formosa is that they should not be treated as independent, nor regarded as the owners of the soil they respectively live on; but that China has a right to that same soil because it occupies it at its leisure. In fact this doctrine seems to have been adopted by your Government. . . . And, in this [the colonization of western Taiwan], they only confirm, de facto, the rightness of the law I have quoted before and in virtue of which superior races, since the origin of the world, have, by degrees, substituted their civilization for that of an inferior one. The Chinese divide and parcel out the land of the natives of Formosa and grant it to their subjects as they need it, *exactly as if it had been vacant and unoccupied land*.[15] (Italics added)

Setting aside for the moment the rhetorical agenda of LeGendre's letter, we can identify some meeting points between Western and Chinese colonial discourse in this passage. LeGendre lays out a few basic assumptions here: that the world is divided into superior and inferior races; that superior races can be equated with civilization; that the civilized powers have the right to take possession of "unexplored" land they "discover"; that they have the power to *define* such land as "unexplored"; that superior races can treat the land of inferior races exactly as if it were vacant and unoccupied land; that the superior races are justified in "civilizing" the inferior races. All these assumptions regarding race and sovereignty issues are epitomized in the trope of "empty lands," a trope that we saw also played a vital role in Qing colonial discourse regarding Taiwan. Indeed, in LeGendre's assumptions we might recognize the essential discursive features not only of Western imperialist logic but of Qing imperialist logic as well. LeGendre himself sought to persuade his Chinese counterparts of this meeting point by arguing that the Qing occupation of western Taiwan had historically proceeded according to the principle that he outlined: "this doctrine seems to have been adopted by your Government." LeGendre was, of course, trying to find common ideological ground with Chinese negotiators in the interests of persuading them to adopt his agenda, and we cannot take his statements at face value. But if we can also recognize such commonalities without losing sight of the specificities (LeGendre's "rights" and "laws" and the trope of "discovery" have no counterparts in Chinese colonial discourse), then we will go a long way toward reconfiguring truly global critiques of colonialism.

Such meeting points are important not because they allow us to uncover a universal logic of imperialism, but because they disrupt our fundamental presumption that colonizers were European men and "the rest" the colonized. If LeGendre recognized the Chinese as fellow (if lesser) imperialists—indeed his memoirs talk at length about the Chinese "colonists" of Taiwan—and Ding Shaoyi recognized European colonists in North America as fellow "civilizers" of "savagery," then perhaps the fixation on imperialism as a uniquely Western phenomenon is a relatively recent one. Truly global critiques of colonialism must take into account colonial relations and their legacies of cultural hegemony in all contexts, rather than turning a blind eye to the cases where Europeans were not the perpetrators. This is not to homogenize or essentialize all colonizers: clearly there were important historical differences as well as continuities in the Dutch, Qing, Japanese, and Nationalist Chinese occupations of Taiwan, for example. But we must be conscious of the consequences when we label certain of these occupations "colonial" and refuse to apply the label to others.

For me, the questioning of imperialism/colonialism as a singularly Western phenomenon is primarily an issue of who can enter the conversation and from what point of entry. Up until now discussions of imperialism/colonialism (even the *mea culpa* variety) in cultural studies have tended to be structured around the dichotomy of the West/colonizer and the non-West/colonized. Non-Western voices have thus generally sat at the table as victims/critics. Within certain strands of postcolonial discourse, this is often a privileged position: it does little to disrupt our image of a powerful, if at times recalcitrant, West and a victimized or dominated "rest."

Therefore, I argue that the study of Qing imperialism is important not simply because we are adding another regionally specific case to the already long list of colonizers, nor because such a study can show us what is "missing" (from Western colonial theory) or what is "different" (about Qing imperialism). It is important precisely because it destabilizes the dichotomy between the West/colonizers and the non-West/colonized, a dichotomy that has largely continued to structure our commonsense perception of global power configurations and cultural differences well past the end of formal imperial rule.

Appendixes

APPENDIX A

Excerpts from Yu Yonghe's Small Sea Travelogue

The translated excerpts are from Yu Yonghe's Small Sea Travelogue (Pihai jiyou), written in 1697. Yu traveled to Taiwan from Amoy via the Pescadores, taking four days to cross the treacherous Taiwan Strait and arriving in a southern port near Taiwan prefectural city (now Tainan). Yu spent ten months on the island, trekking north over land to the sulfur mines in the area of Danshui and Keelung, and he recorded his experiences in this diary.[1]

As one of the earliest firsthand accounts of frontier Taiwan, the work was highly regarded by both Qing officials and the Japanese colonial officials who took over the island in 1895. Qing readers valued Yu's account not only for the information he recorded but also for his vivid descriptions and his prose style, which is unusually lively for a travel diary. Small Sea Travelogue is thus one of the most important texts for the study of Qing Taiwan. I translate here some of the highlights of Yu's travelogue, which is divided into three volumes.

Small Sea Travelogue, Vol. 1

In the first section, Yu described the circumstances surrounding his journey and the details of his voyage outward from Fujian toward the Pescadores and Taiwan. He vividly depicts the perils and the wonders of being at sea. Once he reached Taiwan, he established himself in Taiwan prefectural city, the seat of the local Chinese frontier administration.

I entered Fujian in the spring of 1691, passing through Jianning and Yanjin to reach the City of Banyans, Fuzhou. In the beginning of autumn, I left Fuzhou and traveled through Xinghua and Quanzhou to Shima in Zhangzhou. Before long, I also went to Zhangpu, Haideng, Longyan, Ningyang, all subordinate towns, as well as various villages along the shore, and then returned to Shima. Also I crossed to Xiamen (Amoy) by skiff, returning after five days. In 1692, I returned again to Fuzhou and stayed at the *yamen* of Wang Zhongqian. So I had traveled through six of the eight prefectures of Fujian. In the autumn of 1693, I went on duty to Taining. I moored my boat beneath the city walls of Shaowu, spent two nights there, and returned. The next year I went to Wuping in Dingzhou, going upstream from Yanjin. I climbed the heights of Tieyan and crossed the dangers of Jiulong. In the space of half a year, I went back and forth four times. Of all the mountains and streams and hidden depths, there was not a single one that I did not walk through and see with my own eyes. Thus, I completed my travels of the eight prefectures of Fujian.

The prestige of our dynasty is spread far and wide. The rebel Zheng [Koxinga] has rendered his allegiance. Taiwan lies far beyond the Eastern Ocean; since antiquity until the present day, there has never been a tribute mission sent to China. Now we have divided the land into districts and counties, established governmental offices, levied taxes and tribute, opened sea routes for continuous traffic back and forth, and added a ninth to the eight prefectures of Fujian; it is truly a feat. By nature I am addicted to travel and do not avoid obstacles or danger. I had often said that since Taiwan has already been put on the map, if I could not survey the place, I would not be satisfied. In the winter of 1696, there was a fire at the gunpowder storehouse at Fuzhou, more than 500,000 [*jin*]² of nitre gunpowder were destroyed with not a shred left. The person in charge was reprimanded and ordered to compensate for the loss. Jilong and Danshui in Taiwan produce sulfur rocks, and we were to go in search of it. I laughed joyfully and said, "It's my dream come true!" In the first month of 1697, I packed my luggage and observed the abstinences in preparation for travel. My colleagues, Master Yan Shengping (Youtao), Master Qiu Shaoyi, Master Hu Shenfu, Master He Xiangchen, Master Chen Ziwei, my cousin Zhao Lüzun, and my nephew Zhou Zailu, all bid me fond farewell. The servants Xu Wen, Yu Xing, and Long Dexi were asked to accompany me. Master Cao Lüyang sent me off, and Master Wang Yunsen traveled with me.

[First month] 24th—Noon, I went out of South Gate. I arrived at the Great Bridge [of Nantai] and met with rain. I stayed at Lu Yang's lodging place.

25th—The weather cleared slightly; I traveled thirty *li* and crossed the Wulong River. After the night, the fog began to clear and the river glistened like silk. Looking out at the reflection of the Net of Stars Pagoda in the harbor, it was like a needle hanging upside-down in the water. Therefore, I composed a quatrain:

> The billowing waves of the river flow day and night,
> From a distance I look at the summit of Mount Five Tigers.
> From Haimen gazing 3,000 *li*,
> All you can see is the floating Net of Stars Pagoda.

By night I arrived at Fangkou and saw a certain Master Shi and Master Dong Zanhou. Master Dong was the eldest son of the magistrate of Zhuluo, and Shi was his uncle. So I agreed to travel together with them.

26th—We passed Longing Peak, and I recalled that I had passed this peak six times since I had come to Fujian. In recent years my teeth have become soft and my hair gray. I was suddenly inspired and wrote this poem:

> For seven years I've been a servant in Min [Fujian],
> Six times I've been dyed by the dust of Longing Peak.
> All I have is the gray color of my temples,
> Going past once and returning anew again.

That night I stayed on Fisherman's Creek.

27th—We set out at dawn. We traveled by sedan chair in the morning light of a lightly cloudy sky. The villagers carried plows and led oxen, going back and forth over the mounds. The time when I would withdraw from service was drawing near, and I could not contain my excitement. I composed this poem:

> The color of the mountains is clearer in the dawn,
> The sound of the creek is quiet as it flows naturally.
> People speaking on the other side of the bank,

The barking of dogs emerges from a secluded corner
   of the village.
A light rain dampens my clothes,
A slight chill makes the traveler melancholy.
White clouds are really to be envied,
Rolling over the mountain peaks.

By noon we got to Puwei, the sedan-chair bearers placed the sedan
chair in the boat. Although I was taking a boat, I was actually sitting
in the sedan chair. The boatman held a bamboo pole and pulled the
boat while walking on the shore, the boat moved very quickly. Poling
a boat from shore and sitting in a sedan chair on a boat, two strange
things at once. This could only be seen at this place. Along the bank
were many old banyan trees, the roots and trunks were all twisted in
knots, in all sorts of strange configurations. There were more than ten
trees lined in a row for half a *li* that actually belonged to a single
trunk. I once moored the boat beneath these trees, and remember it to
this day. I still cherish its dense flourishing as I did in the past. . . .[3]

[Second month] 23rd— . . . After a while, black clouds spread in all directions, and the stars were totally obscured. I remembered that my
friend Master Yan Youtao had said, "At sea, in the pitch of night, you
cannot see a thing, but when you strike the water, you are able to
see." I struck it, and water splashed up sending rays of light flying like
dozens of bushels of bright pearls, spreading out over the surface of
the water, like crystals shimmering. After a long time it began to fade.
What a wondrous sight! In the middle of the night a slight breeze began to stir. The captain set the rudder in order preparing to set out.
Then I went to bed.

24th—Rising in the morning, I saw that the color of the sea had turned
from dark emerald to light black. Looking back, the islands of the
Pescadores could still be seen faintly. After a while, they slowly faded
beyond the clouds. In front of us, we could hazily see the various
mountains of Taiwan. Going on, the water turned pale blue, then became white, and then we saw the mountain peaks of Taiwan's prefectural city laid out in front of us. On the shore it was all shallow sand.
On the beach there were numerous fishermen's huts. Small skiffs were
continually going back and forth. Looking at Lu'er Gateway, we
could see it was the place where the sand spits of both shores came to-

gether. The "gateway" was over a *li* wide. When I looked at it, there did not seem to be anything terribly strange or dangerous. . . .

25th— . . . After two days, I began to pay calls. I saw Prefect Master Jin, Vice Prefect Master Qi, Registrar Master Yin, Prefect of Zhuluo Master Dong, and Prefect of Fengshan Master Zhu. Also through Vice Prefect Master Qi, I met my friend Master Lü Hongtu. We grasped each other's hands eagerly. He had not expected me to suddenly make an overseas journey and thought that I had fallen from the sky. I was really excited to meet an old friend in a strange land. We spent many a full day together and were even closer than we had been when we served together in Fuzhou. We wrote, shot arrows, composed songs, played pitchpots; there was nothing we did not do. In our leisure we discussed the ancient and the modern. We appreciated the strange and resolved doubts. Also we obtained a copy of the gazetteer of Taiwan prefecture and investigated Taiwan's conditions, poring over it together.

Taiwan is to the southeast of Fujian, separated by over 1,000 *li* of sea.[4] In past dynasties there were no links to China; the Chinese did not know that this piece of land existed. Even geographic maps, comprehensive gazetteers, and other such books, which contain very detailed records of all the barbarians, do not even include the name Taiwan. Only "Admiral Zheng He's Ocean Travels"[5] in the Ming compilation of state documents mentions "drawing well water at Chikan," but it does not specify where this "Chikan" is. Only the Pescadores, in the Ming, belonged to Tong'an county of Quan district in Fujian. Fishermen from Zhangzhou and Quanzhou all gathered there to pay the annual fishing taxes. During the Jialong period [1522–73], Liuqiu [the Ryukyus][6] occupied it. In the Ming, people held this territory in contempt and simply abandoned it. We have no means of verifying whether or not Liuqiu ever had sovereignty over Taiwan.

As for the people of Taiwan, the natives are savages. Their language cannot be understood in China. Moreover, they have no written language and no way to record events of earlier times. During the Wanli reign [1573–1620], the island was occupied by the Dutch (the Dutch are what we now call the "Red Hairs"). They built the two cities of Taiwan and Chikan (Taiwan is today called Anping, and Chikan is now the Tower of the Red Hairs).[7] From research we know the year was 1621. The two cities appear much like those in the pictures of buildings drawn by the Europeans. They are not more than ten sixth-acres in

area. Their purpose is primarily for stationing canons and defending
the port. There are no parapets or watchtowers as there are on the
city walls of China to secure the inhabitants. When our dynasty was
established, those in the four directions submitted [to the dynasty].
Only Koxinga held out at Jinmen [Quemoy] and Xiamen, making
numerous raids. . . .

. . . Fengshan county is located to the south [of the Taiwan prefectural capital]. Southward from the border of Taiwan county, it extends to the ocean by Shama jetty, a total of 495 *li*. From the shore
eastward to Dagou'a harbor at the base of the mountains, it is fifty *li*
wide. There are eleven villages of pacified savages, called Upper Danshui, Lower Danshui, Lili, Qieteng, Fangsuo, Dazeji, Yahou, and Da-
lou. The preceding are eight plains villages, which remit taxes and
perform corvée. There are those called Qieluotang, Langqiao, and Bei-
manan. These three are in the mountains. They only remit taxes and
do not perform corvée. In addition, there are the Kuilei savages and
the wild savages in the mountains, whose villages have no names.
Zhuluo district is located to the north. The pacified savage villages are
Xin'gang, Jialiuwan (pronounced Gelawan), Ouwang (pronounced
Xiaolang), Madou, etc., 208 villages, aside from which there are Ge'a-
nan (pronounced Geyalan), etc., 36 villages. Although these are not
wild savages, they do not remit taxes. It is hard to record everything
[about them]. North from the border with Taiwan county, to the
northwest corner, then turning to the great ocean by Big Jilong village
at the northeast corner, it extends 2,315 *li*. The [territory] under the
administration of the three counties encompasses only the plains between the mountain range and the shore. The wild savages in the deep
mountains do not communicate with the outside world. Outsiders
cannot enter; it is impossible to know the conditions there.

Small Sea Travelogue, Vol. 2

*After having settled in the prefectural city, Yu began to make preparations
for the sulfur expedition. In order to obtain this precious product, Yu was
compelled to travel north to Danshui and Jilong, where the sulfur mines
were located. To get to these remote regions, Yu must travel through indigenous territory and dense mountain jungle. What he encounters there is
so strange to him that he calls it "No-Man's Land." He is led on this trek
by local Chinese and indigene guides.*

Because of my sulfur mission, I spent over two months living in Taiwan prefectural city, buying cloth, oil, and sugar, smelting large kettles, getting knives, axes, hoes, and ladles made, ordering large and small wooden pails, making scales, rulers, peck and bushel measures, and making all sorts of other preparations. The cloth is to trade with the savages for sulfur ore. The oil and large kettles are for refining sulfur. The sugar is necessary because the workers must frequently drink and bathe with sugarwater in order to counter the poisonous sulfur fumes. The hoes are to level the earth and build platforms. The knives and axes are to chop firewood and clear weeds. The ladles are for removing the sulfur from the pots. The small buckets are for solidifying the sulfur. The large buckets are for storing water. The scale, ruler, peck, and bushel measures are for weighing and measuring various items. I also bought millet, salt, baskets, cauldrons, bowls and chopsticks, etc., for one hundred people. I estimate that I spent about 980 gold. I bought a large boat to transport it all. Having put about 70 percent of the supplies on board, I felt that the boat was overloaded and privately began to worry. So I halted the loading and bought another boat in order to transport the remainder; the cost was half that of the first boat. Someone said, "there are large and small boats, which can transport various amounts. Now you have not filled this one nearly to capacity; why have you spent more for no reason?" I said, "I suddenly became worried. I'm about to divide the cargo in two and have each boat transport half. It's not just for transporting the remainder." The speaker laughed to himself and left. Master Wang felt that the plans were already set and did not want to rearrange things. I thus dropped my plan to split the cargo in two.

My affairs having been settled, I planned to board the boat at dawn. Prefect Master Jin (name Zhiyang, sobriquet Dounan) and Vice Prefect Master Ji (name Tiwu, sobriquet Cheng'an) said to me, "Have you not heard how horrible the environment at Danshui is? Whenever people go there, they fall ill. Whenever they fall ill, they always die. Whenever the workers hear that they are being sent to Jilong or Danshui, they all sigh in despair as though being sent to the 'end of the world.' The custom is for navy men to change duty in the spring and fall, and they consider it great luck to return alive. If these tough workers are like this, how will you be able to bear it? Why don't you order a servant to go along while you yourself stay at the prefectural city to oversee operations from afar?"

I said, "For this journey we have hundreds of savages and crafts-men. Moreover, we will be going close to the wild savages. If we have no means by which to quell them, I'm afraid that there will be diffi-culties, causing trouble in the territories [which we control]. More-over, I have accepted this mission, how can I refuse to go?"

The next day, Lieutenant-Colonel Master Yin (name Fu) and Cap-tain Qi of Fengshan (name Jiacan), both from my native place, came to stop my journey. They said, "Last fall Zhu Youlong tried to plot sedition. Brigade-General Master Wang ordered a captain to lead a hundred men to guard Danshui. After only two months, not a single person returned. If it is like this going to Danshui, it will be even worse going to Jilong, which is beyond Danshui." Again they said, "A certain county functionary went with four companions but returned alone. These are all recent events; why don't you look out for your-self, Master?"

I laughed, "My life is governed by fate. Heaven controls it. What is the environment to me? I have thought it over carefully; I must go." Master Yin and prefectural military officer Master Shen (name Chang-lu) made herbal medicines and various other remedies such as pre-scriptions to ward off pestilence for me and bid me over and over to take care of myself.

Then there was my fellow-provincial, Master Gu (name Fugong) from Huangyan, who had followed his father, Mr. [Gu] Nanjin, to take up a post as regional commissioner in Jiangnan and live in Jing-kou. In 1659, he was abducted and taken to Taiwan. He lived in Tai-wan for a long time, becoming very familiar with the terrain. He and I had been like old friends since the first time we met. He, too, came to me and said, "The environment harms people, and the demon crea-tures cause trouble beyond what the expert can prepare for. If you wish to avoid difficult terrain and seek level ground, stay safe and avoid danger, you must consider everything. Do you know the sea routes? Sea-faring boats do not fear the open ocean; rather, they fear close mountains. They are not troubled by deep waters; rather, they are troubled by shallow waters. Boats are floating objects by nature, with masts to ride the wind and rudders to navigate the waters. Even though it is not easy for strong winds and waves to sink them, if they run into reefs, they will sink, and if they get stuck on sand bars, they will break up. Disaster will be immediate. Now, going from the pre-fectural city to Jilong, the boat must pass through sand and rapids, and if you meet with winds there are no ports in which to harbor. It is twice as dangerous as the open seas. How can it be better than going by land? Now you want to take me along, but if we must go by boat, then I wish to decline."

I said, "I'll follow your instructions."

Master Wang's plans were set, and in the end he boarded the boat. We could not convince him otherwise. I went with Master Gu and led a group of slaves; we took to the road in heavy carts. Fifty-five workers followed. It was the seventh day of the fourth month. We passed a savage village and changed carts. The carts were pulled by brown calves. We ordered local savages to drive. That day we passed the Dazhou Creek, Xin'gang village, Jialiuwan (pronounced Gelawan) village and Madou village. Although these were all the dwellings of savages, there were fine trees and shady woods. The houses were tidy and clean, not inferior to our own villages in China.

I said, "Who says that the savages are vile? How can you trust what others say?"

Master Gu said, "Xin'gang, Gelawan, Ouwang, and Madou were all major villages during the time of the rebel Zheng. He issued an order exempting all youths who could go to the town and study from forced labor, in order to gradually civilize them. The savages of the four villages thus know the value of agriculture and of saving and storing goods; every household is industrious and prosperous. Moreover, they are close to the prefectural city and are used to seeing the manners of the market town. Therefore, among all the savage villages their customs are superior. Ouwang is close to the ocean. It's not on the thoroughfare, but is especially prosperous and thriving; it's a pity you cannot see it. After this, I'm afraid that the farther we go, the more vile it will become."

Indeed I could see that the men and women of the four villages had uncoiffed hair and went without pants, still following their old customs. It was really base. At Madou we changed carts and headed for Daoluoguo. The savages could not understand the language of the servants. I saw that the officers had set out a meal for me while we were on the road, and thought that I should go over to them. We drove to Jialixing, and by the time that we arrived it was already the second watch. I asked where the sleeping quarters were to be, and they were in the camp. . . . I heard the water clock drip for half an hour, and then I went to bed.

[Fourth month] 8th—We still rode the same cart and returned to Madou village. We changed carts and crossed Maogangwei Creek and Tiexianqiao Creek and arrived at Daoluoguo village. It was almost dusk. I thought of Master Wang sailing on the large junk, riding the southern wind and covering a thousand *li* in a flash. I estimated that I would arrive behind him. So I traveled by night, crossing creeks such as Jishui and Bachang. It was already dawn when we reached Mount Zhuluo. I was so tired I fell asleep sitting up. Just when the day was getting hot, we crossed Niutiao Creek. We passed Damao village and crossed Shandie Creek. Then we passed Taliwu village and arrived at Chaili village, where we spent the night. I estimate that we traveled two days and nights by cart. On the cart, I was tired and wanted to sleep, but every time we got to a sheer cliff or a deep ravine, I would be startled awake again. The savage cart drivers I saw were all covered with blue-black tattoos. On their backs were outstretched wings of birds. From their shoulders to their navels they had net patterns cut in slanting strokes. On each shoulder there was the likeness of a human head, revolting and terrifying. From their wrists to their elbows, they piled tens of iron bracelets. Also there were some who used them to make their ears large.

10th—We crossed Huwei Creek and Xiluo Creek. The creeks were two or three *li* wide. One could walk on the sand flats, and when the carriages passed they left no tracks; it was like a kind of "sheet iron" sand. The sand and water were all black, due to the fact that the Taiwanese mountains are all colored by black earth. Another thirty *li* and we came to Dongluo Creek. It was exactly as wide as Xiluo Creek, but the water was deeper and more rapid. The buffaloes hitched to the shafts were afraid of drowning. They simply lay down and floated. Ten or so savage boys supported the wheels in order to get them across. Thus most of them did not sink below the surface. Once across, we met with rain. We galloped for thirty *li* and arrived at Dawu township, where we stayed the night. As for the savages that we saw that day, many more had tattooed their bodies. Their earrings became as large as plates. But they tied back their hair. Some had braids, some had little buns. Also they used three feathers from the chicken's tail as tassels which they stuck in their buns. The feathers swayed in the breeze. They thought it looked beautiful. There were also three young girls working with mortar and pestle. One of them was rather attractive. They appeared in front of outsiders naked, but their composure was dignified.

11th—We went thirty *li* and arrived at Banxian village. The host of the inn greeted the guests respectfully, setting out food and drink. He said, "Past this point it is mostly stone roads. Traveling by cart is not easy. Rest for a while to get rid of your fatigue." So we stayed overnight there. From Mount Zhuluo to this place, many of the savage women that we saw were white and pleasing.

12th—We passed Yasu village and reached Dadu village. All along the route were large and small clusters of rocks. The carts drove on top [of them]. Crouching all day we were extremely fatigued. On top of that there was the overgrown jungle. The grass buried you up to the shoulders. . . . The appearance of the savages turned increasingly vile.

13th—We crossed the Da Creek, passed Shalu village, and arrived at Niuma village. The village huts were very cramped. When it rained, they got totally wet. I borrowed a sleeping platform that the savages had set up outside the windows of the huts. I climbed a ladder and went up. Even though there was no door or railing, I was pleased that it was high and clean.

14th—It was cloudy and foggy and rained hard. We could not travel. After noon the rain stopped. I heard the sound of the ocean roaring; it was like the sound of the raging tidal bore at Hangzhou. It did not stop all day. A villager said: "The roar of the ocean is the evidence of rain."

The fifteenth and sixteenth it rained all day. The creek in front was agitated with new water. We did not dare proceed.

17th—A slight clearing of the skies. My bed faced the mountains, but they were blocked by fog for five days. I was disappointed at not being able to see the foothills. Suddenly I saw it clearing and was ecstatic. I thought of wild savages jumping from ridge to ridge. This mountain really is like a hedgerow; you cannot tell what the mountains that lie beyond are like. I was going to climb the foothills to see the view. A villager said, "Wild savages often hide in the jungle hunting deer. When they see people, they shoot arrows immediately. Be prudent and don't go!" I nodded to him but took my walking stick and, pushing aside weeds and thorns, made my way up. When I as-

cended the peak, the weeds were thick and tangled, and there was nowhere to place my feet. The trees in the forest were like hedgehog
bristles—branches connected and leaves overlapped. The shade was so
dense it was like night during the day. When I looked up to the heavens, it was like peering at the sky from the bottom of a well; from
time to time you could just get a glimpse. Although there was a
mountain directly in front of my eyes, the dense foliage blocked it, so
that I could not get a view. There were only wild apes jumping and
squatting above and below, making noises at the people, like old people coughing. Also there was an old ape, like a five-foot tall child,
squatting and glaring angrily. When the wind swept across the tops of
the trees, it made a soughing sound that chilled one to the bone. The
water from the waterfall flowed by. I looked for [the waterfall] but
could not find it. A long snake slithered out beneath my ankles, giving
me a fright. So I went back.

18th—It rained heavily again. It was the weather of a strong typhoon.
My clothes were soaked through. In front of the steps it was all mud.
One could not step through it. I paced up and down depressed, then
composed a poem:

> The savage huts are like ant hills,
> The thorny underbrush hangs down on the road.
> The typhoon wind invades the low window,
> The sea mist attacks the stairs.
> Avoiding the rain, I wear clogs everywhere,
> To the bed supported on tortoise shells is added a ladder.
> The stream in front has newly risen,
> I hesitate and wish to find a roosting place.

After a while, a savage woman arrived. Hair tangled and bone-thin,
her appearance was inhuman. She raised her hands and made hand
signals, as if she wanted something. I looked for some food and gave it
to her. When the villagers saw, they quickly waved her away, saying,
"This women knows magic. She is skilled at putting curses on people.
Do not let her get close."

25th—I took a cart together with Master Wang. We proceeded in double stages.[8] We crossed three high peaks and arrived at Zhonggang village, where we ate lunch. We saw a very fat ox outside the gate, which
was locked in a wooden cage. Its head was lowered and feet were
cramped; it was unable to stand up. The villagers said, "This ox is just

beginning to be put to the harness. We train it by this means." They also said, "At Zhuqian and Nankan on the route ahead, there are many wild oxen in the mountains . . . ."

[Beginning of the fifth month] After several days, all the heads of various villages arrived, namely from twenty-three villages: Balifen, Mashaoweng, Inner Beitou, Outer Beitou, Mt. Jizhou, Mt. Dadong, Little Jilong, Big Jilong, Jinbaoli, Nan'gang, Walie, Baizhe, Limo, Wu-liuwan, Leili, Laoli, Xiulang, Balangpan, Qiwuzu, Dadayou, Lizu, Fang'ayu, Mailizhekou. They were all led by the head village of Danshui. The local leaders were divided into head and vice chief. We gave them cheap wine, fed them sugar cubes, and gave them one *zhang*⁹ or so of cloth, and they all left happily. Moreover, we traded cloth with the savages for ore; for each seven feet of cloth we obtained one basket of ore.¹⁰ Weighing it, altogether we got about 270 or 280 catties.¹¹ The next day, savages, both men and women, arrived in a continuous stream carrying ore in *man'ge* [canoes].

The ore was variously brown and black. The color rich and the quality heavy, and there were sparks. When you rubbed it between the fingers, there was a wonderful soughing noise. If it is not like this, then it is inferior. The refining method: pound it into a powder, and let it dry in the sun. First put ten or so catties of oil into the kettle, slowly add the dry ore. Make a frame in the shape of a cross with large bamboo, and have two people hold each end and stir. The sulfur in the ore comes out upon contact with oil. As the oil and ore melt together, frequently add ore and oil until the kettle is full. You use approximately 800 or 900 catties of ore, and as for oil, the amount depends on the quality of ore. The workers from time to time scoop out some of the liquid with a metal spade and let it run down the side in order to examine it. If there is too much, they add ore; not enough, they add oil. If there is either too little or too much oil, then you will ruin the sulfur. If the ore is good and you use the appropriate amount of oil, then from one kettle you can get 400 or 500 catties of pure sulfur. If not, you can get anything from about 200 or so to a few dozen catties. Even though the key to the process lies in the oil, the workers attend to the strength of the fire; it seems as though this makes a slight difference. I asked the savages where the sulfur ore was produced and they pointed to the foothills behind the thatched hut. The next day I dragged Master Gu to go there.

We took a *man'ge* and ordered two savage boys to row. We entered by the stream; at the end of the stream was Inner Bai village. We called for some locals to guide us. We turned east and went half a *li*, then entered jungle. The stalks of the weeds were over one *zhang* high. We parted them with both hands and entered sideways. The hot sun touched the tips of the weeds and the hot summer air was steaming; it was oppressively humid. The path under the grass twisted and turned and was only wide enough for a snake to crawl on. Gu was well equipped for hiking and walked with the guide. They suddenly advanced; I followed behind with the attendants. I was only five paces behind him, yet we could no longer see one another. I was afraid we would lose each other. We would call to one another to gauge the distance of our separation.

We walked about two or three *li*, crossed two small streams (which we waded across), then again entered the deep jungle. The trees were dense and shady. Large or small we could not distinguish their names. Old vines wound around them like coiling dragons or serpents. When the wind passed leaves would drop, some as big as one's palm. Also there were giant trees that grew up splitting the earth. With two leaves sprouting, they were already ten spans big. The guide called these "cedar." When cedars begin to grow, they already have an entire trunk. Over many years they grow solid, but never increase in size. So they are the same in principle as bamboo. From the tops of the trees, there came the sounds of myriad types of birds. Though we could hear them, we could not see them. A cool wind hit the flesh, almost making me forget the sweltering heat. Again we crossed five or six hills and reached a large stream. The stream was four or five *zhang* wide. The water flowed over bare rocks, giving it an indigo color. The guide said that this water originally came from the sulfur caves, where there was a bubbling spring. I tested it with one finger and it was still quite hot. I leaned on my walking stick and crossed over by stepping on bare rocks. We went two or three more *li* and the forest suddenly ended; for the first time the mountains in front could be seen. Then we crossed a small peak, and I felt that the ground beneath my shoes was gradually getting hot. I saw that the color of the vegetation was a withered lifeless brown. As I gazed at the lower foothills of the mountain in front, I saw strands of white vapor rising, like mountain clouds being suddenly spit out, shaking and waving amid the blue peaks. The guide pointed and said, "That is the sulfur cave." When the wind passed, the sulfurous odor was horrible. We went another half *li*. No plants grew here and the ground was broiling hot. The mountains on both sides had giant rocks, which had been eroded by sulfur fumes, eaten away into powder. There were fifty or so streams of white vapor, all rushing out from under the ground. Pearl-like bubbles were spit up, flying up over a foot in the air. I hitched up my clothes and went over to the side of the cave and looked in. I heard an angry thunderous noise rocking the earth, and the sound of crashing waves and boiling cauldrons. The ground was precarious as though it were about to shake. It struck fear in my heart. Within an area of a hundred *mou*,[12] it was really like a giant boiling cauldron, and I was walking on the lid. The only thing that was keeping me from falling in was the fact that the hot air was causing it to swell up. Among the giant rocks on the right was one particularly large cave. Thinking that giant rocks would not fall, I climbed atop a rock and looked down. Poisonous flames assaulted me from the cave, making it impossible to look at it directly. When they hit my head, it felt as if my brain would split. I quickly retreated a hundred paces. On the left was a stream that made a sound like a toppling mountain. It was the source from which the bubbling spring came. I went back to the deep forest for a short rest. Then I followed the old path and returned. My clothes were infused with sulfur fumes, which would not disperse for days. For the first time, I realized that the ceaseless mountain-toppling, cliff-crumbling, ear-splitting noise was the sound of the bubbling in the sulfur caves. I wrote two poems to commemorate my visit:

> The Creator gathered these strange structures,
> A surging, bubbling spring in the high peaks.
> Angry thunder will flip the earth over on its axis,
> A poisonous fog shakes the cliff tops.
> In the emerald torrent the pine grows withered,
> In cinnabar mountains plants are about to go
>   up in flames.
> Fairy mountains Peng and Ying are far off in
>   my gaze,
> The boiling rocks welcome the gods.
>
> In May there are few travelers,
> On the western slope there is a volcano.
> Who knows where the bubbling spring lies?
> So I set out on a difficult journey.

Falling powder melts the precarious rocks,
The sulfur stains in script-like blotches.
A rumbling noise spreads for ten *li*,
It's not the echoing of the current.

People had said that the environment of this place was harmful, with contagious diseases and numerous perils. That was the judgment of the various gentlemen of Taiwan prefectural city. At first I did not believe them, but having been here only a short while, the slaves became sick, and nine out of ten of the workers fell sick! Even the cook got sick. There was no one to take charge of the cooking. Master Wang had barely escaped from drowning, and now had come down with dysentery and could not keep any fluids down. Day and night there were about seventy or eighty rows [of sick men], until gradually they overflowed the beds. By the side of my bed, there were sick men all around. All I could hear was their moaning and trembling, as though singing an endless chorus. I resented not having superhuman strength. How could I nurse all of them? So I sent them all back on a boat. Moreover, Master Gu had to return to the provincial capital on other business. I alone could not leave . . . .

Looking out over the plain, there is nothing but luxuriant grasses. The vigorous vegetation covers your head; the feeble vegetation comes up to your shoulders. When the carriage passes through this growth, it is like being in the underworld. The tips of the grasses graze your face and cut your neck. The mosquitoes and flies suck your flesh like starving vultures and hungry tigers; you cannot beat them off. The blazing sun beats down on you, and your neck and back are about to split open. You have already exhausted the suffering and toil of the human world. Then, when you get to camp, instead of four walls and a tiled roof, there is only thatch; from all sides the wind enters like arrows. In bed you constantly see the sky. The green weeds grow up into the bed, as soon as you pull them up they sprout again. When it rains, it is like a flood in the hut. After the rains have passed, you still have to wear clogs to bed for ten days. The strumming of the cicadas and the piping of the worms rise up from beneath the bed, and the tide reaches the steps from time to time. Going out of the hut, the weeds bury your shoulders, and the old trees are gnarled; it is indescribable. Horrid clumps of bamboo grow up in their midst. Within a foot of you not a thing can be seen. At night, cobras with their swollen necks make noises next to the pillows in every room. From time to time they snort like cows. They have the strength to swallow deer. Small snakes chase people and are as fast as flying arrows. At night, I do not dare go beyond the threshold of the hut. The sea wind howls angrily; everything resounds. The forests and valleys shake and rock. The hut and bed are on the verge of collapsing. In the middle of the night the apes howl, sounding like ghosts crying. A single lamp flickers, and I sleep next to those who are on the verge of dying from malaria. What are Ziqing's remote frontier and Xinguo's marshes next to this?[13]

Liu Zihou[14] said: "Bozhou is not a place fit for humans to live." Let Zihou know of this place, and he would regard Bozhou as a paradise. The night that I arrived, there was a fisherman who had built his hut south of the harbor, separated from my dwelling by the water. He had folded some cloth as a mat and pillow and had gone to sleep. In the middle of the night, arrows came in from the outside, piercing the top layer of the pillow twenty-eight times. Luckily, his brain was not injured. He remained in dreamland when another arrow entered, penetrating his arm. His companions pursued the bandits, but failed to capture them. When they examined the arrow, it turned out to be the type that the savages use to shoot deer. Also there was a villager killed on the road. This all happened within the space of a few days. My thatched hut is in No-Man's Land. From time to time I see savages coming and going in the jungle; no one can make out where they come from. When there are arrows being shot in the depths of night, how can I not be on guard? In this place, there are threats all around, and every minute I am on the verge of death! My body is not made of metal or stone; my strength is no greater than that of a mouse or rat. Moreover, I am in my hoary years and have an aged mother at home. How can I then forget the warning I received when I was getting ready to set forth, about remaining too long in a land of danger and death? It is just because I am resolute and brave by nature. I always advance and never retreat; in planning for others and planning for myself, I earnestly hope to accomplish something. Moreover, all my life I have been through dangers and encountered difficulties; why should I stop with just this one undertaking? Now I am old! If I were willing to stop in the middle of this endeavor, because of one thought of shame, would I not lose my former self? Now, those who have fallen ill have left, and those who have not fallen ill have also left out of fear of disease and danger. Who was left to complete this task? Would it not have been better not to have come then, rather than to leave early now? Who could force me? Now, since I have come, is it not useless to regret anything else? My will is habitually resolute. My spirit is so true that the mountain ghosts yield and the demon of disease also keeps far away from my sojourner's dwelling. Moreover, it was indeed due to my passion for travel that I came. I once said, "In searching for the exotic and visiting scenic spots, one must not fear risky inclinations: if the voyage is not dangerous, it will not be exotic; if the inclination is not risky, it will not be exhilarating." Taibo [Li Bo] climbed Mount Hua[15] and regretted not taking along one of Xie Tiao's[16] startling couplets; he scratched his head and complained to Heaven. Changli [Han Yu][17] climbed to the summit of Mount Hua and, crying bitterly, composed a letter taking leave of his family. The Magistrate of Huayin used a hundred stratagems to get him down, and only then was he able to descend.[18] They were all obsessed with a passion for travel. Although I would not dare to compare myself with the worthies of the past, what I have passed through on this journey would make Changli and Taibo envious. Moreover, Penglai island is in sight, and the waters of the Ruoshui can be cupped in the hand.[19] If Qin Shihuang and Han Wudi were to hear of this, would they not then roll over in their graves?[20]

Small Sea Travelogue, Vol. 3

In the last section, Yu described the completion of his expedition and his return to China. This section is filled with his observations about the relation between China and Taiwan, an island that had long been considered "beyond the seas" and remote from "China proper." Finally he made a plea both for the humanity of the native "savages" and for the benefits of colonizing Taiwan. Yu based his arguments on the need to civilize the "savages" and the need to strengthen China's position in the international arena. Upon arriving back in China, Yu gave his final judgment on the exotica he encountered and expressed his pleasure at returning to his home and old friends.

Since I have journeyed overseas and moreover have traveled to the farthest and most remote areas, personally traveling through No-Man's Land, walking over hill and dale, through the mountains and rivers, seeing the conditions, savage customs, and popular sentiment of all of Taiwan (not just being there myself but actually exploring), how can I not write something in order to leave a record by which to let people know of this world and these people? At the time, I would often go out at dawn with my walking stick, then take a boat at dusk, in order to survey the surroundings and explore the terrain.

. . . People argue that Taiwan is simply "a ball of mud beyond the sea that is unworthy of development by China. It is full of naked and tattooed savages who are not worth defending. It is a daily waste of imperial money for no benefit. It would be better to evacuate the people and vacate the land." Do they not know that if we abandon it, someone else will take it? If we vacate it, they will not have difficulty bringing in immigrants to populate it. Ai!

. . . The wild savages rely on their ferociousness and from time to time emerge and plunder, burning houses and killing people. Then they return to their lairs, and no one can approach them. Every time they kill someone, they remove the head and go back and cook it. They scrape the flesh from the skull and apply red and white paint to it. They place it in the doorway, and their fellows regard those with the most skulls as heroes. They live as if in a dream, as if drunk. They do not know to civilize [themselves]. They are really mere beasts! But they are just like tigers and leopards; if you come across them, they will bite. Like snakes and vipers, if you run up against them, they will bite. If you do not approach their caves, they have no intent of poisoning you.

. . . If we could civilize them with rites and righteousness; refine them with the *Book of Songs* and the *Book of Documents*; cultivate them in the way of storing what they have and preparing for shortages; regulate them with clothing, food and drink, marriage and funeral customs; make all of them understand love for relatives, respect for elders, obedience to their lords, and affection for superiors; enlighten their minds to the enjoyment of life, and repress their obstinate and hostile natures; then, at the longest, it would take one hundred years, and at the fastest, thirty years, to see their customs change and see them comply with the rites and teachings. How would they be any different from the Chinese?

. . . Because they are of a different kind, people discriminate against them. They see them without clothing and say, "They do not know cold." They see them walking in the rain and sleeping under the dew and say, "They do not get sick." They see them running for long distances with heavy loads and say, "They really have endurance." Ai! Are they not also human?! Look at their limbs, their bodies, their skin and bones; in what way are they not human, so that you say these things? You cannot gallop a horse all night; you cannot harness an ox crookedly, or else they will get sick. If oxen and horses are this way, how much the more so for people? . . . Enjoying fullness and warmth, suffering from hunger and cold, hating labor and delighting in idleness and pleasure, this is human nature. You may consider these people different, but what need is there to consider their nature different? The humanitarian gentleman will know not to reject my words. . . .

[Tenth month] 12th—Riding the slight breeze, I helped the boat along with a paddle. I could see the great Nantai Bridge. Young Zhou Xuanyu led several servants in a small skiff to welcome me. When I saw them, I was overjoyed. Xuanyu and I took the small skiff together and went to the great bridge, where we went ashore. Entering the city, we went to meet those good friends who had seen me off so long ago. Only Qiu Shaoyi, He Xiangchen, and my nephew Zhou Zailu were in. The others had either returned home or gone to other places, and we could not see them. Only Lü Hongtu crossed the ocean and returned before me. I was quite happy. Seeing once again the sights of the city, I remembered that for half a year I had been living in No-Man's Land. It was a world apart. I wonder how it compares with changing into a crane and going back [to Heaven as an immortal]. In the past I desired to travel overseas. I said that the waters of the Ruo-shui could be held in the hand, and that the three mountains of the immortals could be reached.[21] Now that my eyes have seen all of the vast wilderness, and my feet have exhausted the solitary precipices, I know that these so-called immortals are no more than a naked, tattooed race! Even if [Taiwan] is the elysium of the immortal islands Peng and Ying, it cannot compare to my hometown with its misty hazes over boundless waters and the fifes and drums of painted pleasure boats. These are extraordinary and wonderful rain or shine—quite enough to keep my thoughts attached [to them no matter where I go].

Excerpts from Ding Shaoyi's
Brief Record of the Eastern Ocean

The translated passage is a selection from Brief Record of the Eastern Ocean (Dongying zhilüe), *a lengthy travel account (8 juan) of Taiwan written by Ding Shaoyi in the nineteenth century, nearly two hundred years after Yu Yonghe. Ding Shaoyi was a native of Wuxi in Jiangsu. He traveled to Taiwan in the fall of 1847 as an aide to the circuit intendant of Taiwan, in which capacity he served about eight months. It was during this stay that he compiled his account. The account is divided into sixteen topics, such as taxes, schools, coastal defense, local products, "savage" villages, "savage" customs, and marvels. Ding traveled again to Taiwan in 1871. One noteworthy feature of the text is the fact that Ding returned to his record of 1847 and commented upon the historical changes that had taken place in the intervening decades. The text was first published by a Fujian publishing house around 1873. The translated passage is Ding's 1871 supplement to his entry on "Savage Customs."*

Supervising Censor Huang Yupu (Shujing), Senior Graduate Yu Canglang (Yonghe), and the various prefectural and county gazetteers lumped the raw and cooked savages together when they recorded savage customs. But all these texts recorded things that happened before the Yongzheng era. Today, most of the cooked savages marry virilocally and few marry uxorilocally, and they pass down a single surname. There is little difference from the Chinese settler population in terms of clothing, food, and conduct. Now that the various savages have become assimilated, they perform betrothals when they marry, and they bury the dead separately.[1] They distinguish between good and bad foods, and the women wear leggings and blouses, following many of the Chinese customs. It is only that they rarely have collars or sleeves on their clothing and seldom wear shoes. Nor have they established proper clan names, nor learned to read and write. To begin with, the conditions in the various savage villages already differed; now there is also a difference between the past and the present. So I chose to record the general conditions. Moreover, I am afraid that in a few more decades, once again a description of today's customs will no longer be fitting.

Prefect Deng Chuan'an (sobriquet Shuyuan), a native of Fuliang in Jiangxi, wrote in his *Measuring the Sea with a Calabash*: "During the Jiaqing reign [1796–1821], the female native chieftain Baozhu bedecked herself like a Chinese noble lady. In governance she used the law. Someone sent the officials an official communication stating that her tribe followed the law obediently and respectfully, not killing people and not rebelling. Even though this place is beyond the pale, how is this any different from China proper?" Popular legend has it that during the Zhu Yigui rebellion, a native chieftain of the Beinami, Wenji, guided troops to capture the bandits. The general rewarded him with the hat, robe, and shoes of the sixth rank, and also made his son a native chieftain.[2] He became dominant over the various native villages. He was presented with coral and pearls. Then he called himself the king of the Beinami. He hoped to obtain a beauty for his consort. In Taiwan city there was a courtesan who heard of this and happily volunteered to go. The savages value women (*zhongnü*) to begin with, and since he had gotten a courtesan, he doted on her to the extreme, doing whatever she commanded. Then they got rid of their old customs and were civilized with the rites and laws of China. Therefore, the seventy-odd villages of the Beinami are the most orderly, and their customs have long been different from those of other savages. "Baozhu" is not like the name of a savage woman; perhaps this so-called female chieftain is after all a courtesan?

In He Qiaoyuan's *History of Fujian* it is written:[3] "During the Yongle period [1403–24], Zheng He took to the seas and issued a proclamation to the various barbarian rulers. Only the Eastern Savages northeast of the Pescadores refused to submit to the treaty. Zheng He gave these people a bell to hang around the neck, thus making dogs of them."[4] Since I have traveled to the various savage villages both south and north, I have yet to see anyone wearing a bell. What is written cannot always be trusted.

The *Gazetteer of Zhuluo County* says: "Among all the various savages, the husband and wife are mutually devoted. Even when they are wealthy, [the savages] do not have maids and concubines or boy servants. For their entire lives they never go out the village gate. They hold hands when walking, and they ride together in the same carriage. They do not know the bitterness of being separated in life. They do not steal. They know not of gambling or gaming. Their world is like an unchiseled block of primeval Chaos."

The *Illustrations of the Flora and Fauna of Taiwan* says:[5] "When the harvest is in, the savages invite one another for a celebration. Men and women sit together unsegregated. Drinking and making toasts, they enjoy themselves. If a Han Chinese barges in, they pull him in to drink with them. They do not stop until they are drunk. When younger people meet their elders, they stand by the side of the road and wait for them to pass before they continue walking. When they come across one of their peers, they greet one another." These customs have still not changed. One can imagine that this is the world of Lord No-Cares and Getian.

Also, according to the Westerner Giulio Aleni's *Unofficial Records of a Geographer*:[6] "In North America, the farther north one goes, the wilder the people become. There are no city walls, no chiefs, and no writing system. Several families combined make up one village. By custom they are fond of drink. Attacking and killing are their daily business. Whenever they go out to battle, the entire family fasts and prays for victory. When they are victorious, they return. They cut off the enemy's head and use it to build a wall. If they go into battle again, the elders in the family immediately point to the skulls on the top of the wall to urge them on. Such is the extent of their bravura and belligerence. Recently, there have been European missionaries who have gone among them and urged them to worship God and cease their killing. Then they all changed entirely. Moreover, they had firm resolve; so once they reformed, they never transgressed. According to their custom, those who are wealthy are charitable. Whenever a family cooks a meal, they leave some food outside the gate. Passersby can partake as they please." These things that he recorded pertain to the native barbarians of the newly opened northern frontier of North

America, but their savagery is no different from the savages of Taiwan. Their ferocity was extreme, yet the Westerners have guided them with their senseless, confused religion and have finally changed their customs. So to say that the raw savages [of Taiwan] have absolutely no human morals despite their human appearance, and that they cannot be civilized with the Kingly Governance (*wangzheng*), is that not an injustice?![7]

Reference Matter

Notes

Introduction

1. There is some ambiguity in the English word "Chinese," since it refers to two different Chinese concepts, *Hua* and *Han*. The latter is a more restrictive term that refers to the majority Han Chinese ethnic group.

2. Yu Yonghe, *Pihai jiyou*, p. 1.

3. "Zheng Chenggong" in Mandarin Chinese.

4. See Yu Yonghe, *Pihai jiyou*, p. 31.

5. Shi Lang, *Jinghai jishi*, p. 60.

6. Millward, *Beyond the Pass*, p. 37; Waldron, *The Great Wall of China*, pp. 42–43.

7. In this work I use the word "comparable" in the sense of "suitable for comparison." See Perdue, "Comparing Empires," pp. 255–61; Adas, "Imperialism and Colonialism in Comparative Perspective"; Harrell, "Introduction"; and Millward, "New Perspectives on the Qing Frontier."

8. See Perdue, "Boundaries, Maps, and Movement."

9. The term "renegade province" is used in U.S. media to represent the PRC's position on Taiwan, but it is not a Chinese phrase. My thanks to Tom Christensen for pointing this out.

10. Foreign Desk, "China's Statement," p. 10.

11. See Christensen, "Posing Problems Without Catching Up." See also Cohen and Teng, *Let Taiwan Be Taiwan*.

12. This is not to deny that ethnic Chinese families on Taiwan, including my own, have ancestral ties to China, just as many Americans have ancestral ties to England.

13. For a critique of this "China as victim" approach, see Millward, *Beyond the Pass*, p. 16. On the problematic of applying "postcolonial discourse" to China, see Lee, *Shanghai Modern*, pp. 308–9.

14. For example, a recent publication of the National Museum of Chinese History includes this statement under the heading of "National Unification": "During the Qing Dynasty, the political, economic and cultural relations among various nationalities became increasingly harmonious, reinforcing the foundation of national unity" (Yu Weichao, *A Journey into China's Antiquity*, p. 164).

15. Doyle, *Empires*, p. 45.

16. Parry, "Problems in Current Theories of Colonial Discourse," p. 34; Thomas, *Colonialism's Culture*, p. 9.

17. See the Epilogue.

18. Said, *Culture and Imperialism*, p. 9.

19. Spurr, *The Rhetoric of Empire*, p. 5.

20. Williams, *Keywords*, p. 160.

21. Said, *Culture and Imperialism*, p. 9.

22. Thomas, *Colonialism's Culture*, p. 2.

23. As Peter Perdue ("Comparing Empires," p. 255) has provocatively argued: "The Qing Empire of China was a colonial empire that ruled over a diverse collection of peoples with separate identities and deserves comparison with other empires."

24. See ibid.; Perdue, "Boundaries, Maps, and Movement"; Shepherd, *Statecraft and Political Economy on the Taiwan Frontier*; and Hostetler, *Qing Colonial Enterprise*.

25. Ding, *Dongying zhilüe*, p. 79.

26. Hostetler, *Qing Colonial Enterprise*, pp. 37–41.

27. For example, the Qing required Han Chinese men to adopt the Manchu hairstyle of the queue.

28. On the multiethnic composition of the Qing military, see Crossley, "The Qianlong Retrospect of the Chinese-Martial (*hanjun*) Banners."

29. In Taiwan, the Qing recruited indigenous troops for deployment against rebellious Han settlers. In response, Han Chinese settlers sometimes forged alliances with rival indigenous groups against these troops; see Shepherd, *Statecraft and Political Economy on the Taiwan Frontier*. For more recent work on "ethnic politics" on the Taiwan frontiers, see Ka, *Fan toujia*.

30. Thomas, *Colonialism's Culture*; Stoler, "Rethinking Colonial Categories"; JanMohammed, "The Economy of Manichean Allegory"; Bhabha, *The Location of Culture*.

31. See, e.g., Millward, *Beyond the Pass*; Perdue, *China Marches West*; Gaubatz, *Beyond the Great Wall*; Shepherd, *Statecraft and Political Economy on the Taiwan Frontier*; Herman, "Empire in the Southwest"; Giersch, "'A Motley Throng.'"

32. Said, *Orientalism*; Said, *Culture and Imperialism*; Lowe, *Critical Terrains*; Greenblatt, *New World Encounters*; Spurr, *The Rhetoric of Empire*.

33. All this is not to argue, of course, that Qing colonial discourse is identical to European Orientalism (which itself had many variations, British, French, etc.). It is simply to say that Orientalism was not a uniquely European phenomenon and that the Chinese had a roughly equivalent discourse by which they produced their others (a category that included Europeans). Indeed, the very idea of comparison undermines the Orientalist notion that China is "utterly different" from the West and therefore beyond comparison. At the same time, this is not to say that Western colonial discourse theory is universally applicable without regard to cultural specificity. This study attempts to walk the fine line between these two extreme positions.

34. Gladney, "Representing Nationality in China," p. 94; Schein, "Gender and Internal Orientalism in China," p. 70.

35. See Crossley, "Thinking About Ethnicity in Early Modern China."

36. Despite the fact that the recent mapping of the human genome has demonstrated that there is no genetic basis for race, the current obsession with Tiger Woods shows that the idea of race is alive and well in twenty-first-century America.

37. For the development of nineteenth-century racial theory, especially the debate over monogenesis and polygenesis, see Young, *Colonial Desire*. See also Stocking, *Race, Culture, and Evolution*.

38. My research into issues of race and ethnicity builds on the work of scholars such as Pamela Kyle Crossley, Frank Dikötter, Stevan Harrell, Dru Gladney, and others. See Crossley, "Thinking About Ethnicity in Early Modern China"; Dikötter, *The Discourse of Race in Modern China*; Harrell, "Introduction"; and Gladney, *Muslim Chinese*.

39. Although I use the terms "race" and "ethnicity" in this work to describe Qing ideas about human difference, in referring to historical aspects of Qing frontier management I follow James Millward in using the term "ethnic." As Millward (*Beyond the Pass*, p. 14n) notes: "In describing these categories in general terms, it is extremely convenient to have a single word for this sort of distinction." Thus I speak of "ethnic policy," "ethnic groups," and "interethnic conflict." Whenever possible, I have avoided the awkward construction "race/ethnicity."

40. Crossley, "Thinking About Ethnicity in Early Modern China," p. 8.

41. Ching, *Becoming "Japanese."*

42. Said, *Culture and Imperialism*, p. 7.

43. Said, *Orientalism*, p. 54.

44. Schwartz, "The Geography Lesson," p. 36; Godlewska, "Map, Text, and Image"; Gregory, *Geographical Imaginations*.

45. Anderson, *Imagined Communities*, p. 15.

46. Thongchai, *Siam Mapped*, p. 17.

47. I propose that one key difference between the territoriality of nations and empires is that the boundaries of the nation are generally imagined as fixed, whereas the boundaries of the empire are often imagined as expandable.

48. Said, *Orientalism*, p. 54.

49. Liu-shi-qi, *Fanshe caifeng tukao*, p. 99.

50. Such information was either culled from the local gazetteers or based on officials' own observations during tours of inspection.

51. Travelers also composed poetry, which they often included in their narrative accounts.

52. The notion of the "travelogue" (*youji*) as a distinct Chinese genre is essentially a modern invention.

53. These include the genres of *shanshui hua* (landscape painting), *renwu hua* (figure painting), *huaniao hua* (bird-and-flower painting), and *jiehua* (ruled-line or architectural drawing). The format of such works included the painted handscroll, the hanging scroll, the painted album, the painted fan, the woodblock print, and the line drawing. The *tu* produced by such professionals are finely rendered *gongbi* works, painted in color on paper or silk. Less privileged travelers, and gazetteer compilers who did not enjoy the services of a professional painter, had to settle for producing their own drawings. These drawings served as the basis for the woodblock prints reproduced in the gazetteers. The quality of *tu* thus range from the painterly to the sketchy.

54. Elman, "Geographical Research in the Ming-Ch'ing Period."

55. See, e.g., Zeitlin, *Historian of the Strange*, p. 11.

56. Strassberg, *Inscribed Landscapes*.

57. Schafer, *The Vermilion Bird*, p. 128.

58. Yu Yonghe, *Pihai jiyou*, p. 27.

59. Dong, *Taihai jianwen lu*, p. 1.

60. Other similar, but less ambitious, anthologies include the *Geographic Collectanea of Imperial Dynastic Barbarian Colonies* (*Huangchao fanshu yudi congshu*) and the *Five Collected Works on the Frontiers* (*Bianjiang wuzhong*).

61. Wang Xiqi's mammoth travel anthology, for example, contains no pictures.

62. Liu-shi-qi, *Fanshe caifeng tukao*, p. 20.

63. Pratt, *Imperial Eyes*, p. 5.

64. It was the desire to see for himself that motivated Yu Yonghe, for example.

65. Quoted in Cahill, *Chinese Painting of the Late Ming Dynasty*, p. 39. Zhang Hong's comment further suggests that he viewed mimetic representation as an important function of painting. Zhang implied that what is pictured on silk directly correlates to, or imitates, that which is seen with the eyes. In representing "what he has seen" on silk, Zhang attempted to translate visual experience directly into visual artifact. In contrast, travel writing translates visual experience into words. Through the production of such an image, Zhang hoped to enable the viewer to "rely on the eyes," thereby deriving more authoritative knowledge, perhaps, than could be found through reading a travelogue.

66. The importance of visuality in late imperial Chinese travel writing is underscored by the fact that vivid description is commonly praised as *ruhua*, "like a painting," or *rutu*, "like a picture."

67. Travelers, including the famous Xu Xiake, frequently mention being inspired to travel by a desire to ascertain whether what they have heard about a particular place is either right or wrong. Moreover, travel writers often emphasize that they record only what they personally witnessed and exclude any material that could be considered hearsay. Thus, despite the fact that one subgenre of travel writing is called *wenjian lu* (records of things heard and seen), I would argue that seeing is still the privileged term: that is, *wen* is no good without *jian*.

68. Similarly, Anthony Pagden ("*Ius et Factum*") and Clifford Geertz (*Works and Lives*) have argued that it is through the sense of sight that the travel writer constructs the authority of his account.

69. See Pagden, "*Ius et Factum*."

70. Wu Xiqi, "Preface," in Zhai, *Taiyang biji*, p. 1.

71. The notion that only firsthand experience could guarantee the reliability of geographic information became a particular problem on the frontier. In Taiwan, for example, the dense jungle of the mountainous areas was often impenetrable to Chinese travelers. Such terrain was, therefore, impossible to map and difficult to document. When firsthand information was unattainable, hearsay had to substitute for empirical observations. For the frontiers, then, the expansion of geographic knowledge often went hand in hand with the extension of Chinese control.

72. Unlike landscape paintings, or other kinds of *hua*, which could stand on their own as objects of appreciation, these *tu* were generally produced and consumed in conjunction with written texts.

73. Cahill, *Chinese Painting of the Late Ming Dynasty*, pp. 206–7.

74. Cordell Yee is one notable exception.

75. Clunas, *Pictures and Visuality in Early Modern China*.

76. Maps and other *tu* were a central component of local gazetteers, as well as the more comprehensive *Yitong zhi*. Cosmological diagrams and

charts were produced with the hopes of making visible the "patterns of Heaven" (*tianwen*). Emperors as far back as the Liang dynasty (502–77) commissioned the painting of tribute illustrations (*zhigong tu*) to record the appearance of foreign peoples. Illustrated versions of the *Shanhaijing* (Classic of mountains and seas) were in circulation at least by Tao Qian's (365–427) time. Many of these *tu* have been analyzed by scholars of geography, cartography, and the history of science in China.

77. The role of the visual in anthropology has also become a subject of renewed interest in recent years; see Banks and Morphy, *Rethinking Visual Anthropology*.

78. Xia Xianlun, *Taiwan yutu*, p. 1.

79. Yee, "Chinese Maps in Political Culture," p. 91.

80. Strategic maps, of course, greatly aided the Qing in the conquest of frontier lands.

81. I include both Han Chinese and Manchus who wrote in classical Chinese. Because of my own linguistic limitations, I do not use Manchu sources.

82. For the Chinese settlement of Taiwan, see Knapp, "Chinese Frontier Settlement in Taiwan"; idem, *China's Island Frontier*; Shepherd, *Statecraft and Political Economy on the Taiwan Frontier*; Davidson, *The Island of Formosa*; Rubinstein, *Taiwan*; and Meskill, *A Chinese Pioneer Family*.

83. See Said, *Orientalism*, p. 3.

84. Doubtless I am guilty of a certain degree of essentialism in my attempts to outline "Qing colonial discourse" in this study. I would plead the reader's forbearance on the grounds that it is necessary first to delineate a general picture of this colonial discourse before we can begin to locate the heterogeneities, ruptures, and contradictions that are certain to be found within it. I have attempted to highlight these elements wherever possible.

85. Perdue, "Comparing Empires"; Perdue, "Boundaries, Maps, and Movement"; Perdue, *China Marches West*; Adas, "Imperialism and Colonialism in Comparative Perspective"; Shepherd, *Statecraft and Political Economy on the Taiwan Frontier*; Hostetler, *Qing Colonial Enterprise*.

86. Chang Lung-chih, "From Island Frontier to Imperial Colony." For recent theoretical work on the Japanese colonization of Taiwan, see Ching, *Becoming "Japanese."*

87. These terms are used by John Shepherd in his analysis of Qing Taiwan policy in *Statecraft and Political Economy on the Taiwan Frontier*.

88. "Green Gold" is a Chinese term for tea; see Etherington and Forster, *Green Gold*.

89. Thongchai, *Siam Mapped*, p. 17.

Interlude 1

1. Shepherd, *Statecraft and Political Economy on the Taiwan Frontier*, p. 1.
2. The "Zheng" regime is named after Koxinga (Zheng Chenggong) and his heirs. For Taiwan policy under this regime, see Shepherd, *Statecraft and Political Economy on the Taiwan Frontier*.
3. Ibid., p. 14.

Chapter 1

EPIGRAPH: My thanks to Allan Barr for bringing this passage to my attention.

1. TYJYS, *Qing Shengzu shilu xuanji*, p. 129.
2. Shi Lang, *Jinghai jishi*, p. 63.
3. Shi Lang was particularly aware of Dutch and Japanese interest in the island. Indeed, Shi secretly investigated the option of selling Taiwan back to the Dutch if the court rejected annexation.
4. Shi Lang, *Jinghai jishi*, p. 60.
5. This work identified the domain thus: "On the east reaching to the sea; on the west extending to the moving sands; to the utmost limits of the north and south" (trans. from Millward, *Beyond the Pass*, p. 37).
6. This theory was illustrated in a Song dynasty map; see Yee, "Reinterpreting Traditional Chinese Geographical Maps," p. 59.
7. Millward, *Beyond the Pass*, pp. 36–38; Waldron, *The Great Wall of China*, pp. 42–43.
8. Other maps emphasize the role of the Great Wall as a boundary defining the Chinese domain. A Ming edition of the "Gujin huayi quyu zongyao tu" from the *Lidai dili zhizhang tu*, for example, represents the Chinese domain bordered by ocean to the east and the south, the Great Wall to the north, and deserts and mountains to the west. Some maps depict a Chinese empire bordered by the Great Wall to the north, the sea to the east and the south, and mountain ranges to the west (Hu, *Visible Traces*, pp. 180, 187). Others used the Great Wall, the Gobi Desert, and the Yellow River to demarcate the boundaries of the Chinese domain on the north and northwest and the seas to demarcate the boundaries on the east and south (Millward, "'Coming onto the Map,'" p. 67; Yee, "Chinese Cartography Among the Arts," p. 154; idem, "Reinterpreting Traditional Chinese Geographical Maps," pp. 50, 59, 60).
9. Hu, *Visible Traces*, pp. 179–80.
10. Luo's map is reproduced in Yee, "Reinterpreting Traditional Chinese Geographical Maps," p. 50. Several important Song maps, which

continued to be reworked into the Qing, did not show anything on the seas and represented the waters as a blank.

11. Gao, *Taiwan fuzhi*, p. 11.

12. Zhongguo diyi lishi dang'an'guan, *Kangxi qiju zhu*, p. 1077. This claim is not strictly true since Hainan Island had been made a Chinese protectorate as early as the Song dynasty. Penghu, Jinmen and Mazu had also come under Chinese influence. These counterexamples only make this claim all the more interesting.

13. Chen Xueyi, "Ti 'Dongfan ji' hou," p. 27.

14. See Zeitlin, *Historian of the Strange*.

15. The "Gujin huayi quyu zongyao tu" from the *Lidai dili zhizhang tu*, for example, also shows the Country of Hairy People.

16. This map is reproduced in Hu, *Visible Traces*, p. 187.

17. According to legend, the ancient emperor Qin Shihuang had sent a mission overseas in search of these islands and the magical herbs of immortality.

18. The conception in the "Yugong" of the cosmographic ordering of the world was highly influential throughout Chinese history. As Needham (*The Shorter Science and Civilization in China*, p. 241) has argued, "All Chinese geographers worked under its aegis, drew the titles of their books from it, and tried unceasingly to reconstruct the topography which it contained."

19. Ibid., p. 239.

20. Such a scheme placed less emphasis on strict territorial borders than on the concept of radiating zones of influence.

21. This chart is reproduced in Henderson, "Chinese Cosmographical Thought," p. 207.

22. Ibid., p. 207.

23. Many Qing writers pointed out this etymological relation.

24. In various combinations, the term also refers to vassal states or outlying dependencies.

25. This spatialized political geography assumed that different locations had different customs, the more distant the more inferior.

26. Zhou Yuanwen, *Chongxiu Taiwan fuzhi*, p. 3.

27. See Millward, "'Coming onto the Map.'"

28. Yu Yonghe, *Pihai jiyou*, p. 9.

29. Edney, *Mapping an Empire*, p. 1.

30. Yee, "Traditional Chinese Cartography and the Myth of Westernization," p. 180.

31. Ibid.

32. As early as the Tang dynasty, Fan Chuo claimed to base his account of China's southern barbarians (*Manshu*) on direct observation.

Noted Yuan traveler Wang Dayuan wrote in the preface to his *Record of the Island Barbarians* (*Daoyi zhilüe*, 1349): "All these [details I recorded] were things which I personally observed on my travels, things which I heard and saw with my own ears and eyes. I did not record hearsay" (Thompson, "The Earliest Chinese Eyewitness Accounts of the Formosan Aborigines," p. 167). See chap. 4 of my dissertation for a discussion of direct observation in the pre-Qing era.

33. Zhou Zhongxuan, *Zhuluo xianzhi*, p. 36.

34. Hostetler, *Qing Colonial Enterprise*, p. 5.

35. Secondarily, classification served as an important authority structure of this and other geographic texts, a topic explored further in Chapter 5. Huang organized his ethnographic data into six categories: housing, diet, clothing and ornaments, marriage, funerals, and utensils/tools. Both classification and enumeration (numerical lists of villages, fruits, etc.) were important features of Qing geographic representation of Taiwan and served to create an effect of precision. In contrast, although distances between locations are given to the nearest *li*, quantitative measurement does not play large role in Qing geographic writing on Taiwan. For more on the specifics of Huang's ethnographic methodology and its relation to the rise of geography as a discipline in the Qing, see chap. 4 of my dissertation. On the question of quantitative measurement in other regions of the Qing empire, see Yee, *Taking the World's Measure*; Perdue, "Boundaries, Maps, and Movement"; Hostetler, *Qing Colonial Enterprise*; Smith, "Mapping China's World."

36. Lan, *Dongzheng ji*, p. 88.

37. See chap. 7 of my dissertation.

38. The "summer insect who knows not of ice" alludes to the Daoist parable from the *Zhuangzi*, which discusses the difficulty of understanding something beyond one's own experience.

39. See chap. 7 of my dissertation for the links between Qing ethnography/geography and the *zhiguai* genre of anomaly accounts.

40. The use of the terms *wei* (pretender) and *zei* (bandit) and the reference to Zheng Jing allow us to identify this map as a Qing map, dated between 1664 and 1681.

41. This edition essentially replicates the earlier map, with the addition of Taiwan peeking up from the bottom edge. In other words, the composition of the map had not been altered sufficiently to accommodate the depiction of the entire island. Nonetheless, "Taiwan" does appear where it had previously been absent.

42. The Jesuits dispatched a team to survey Taiwan in 1714.

43. Yee, "Traditional Chinese Cartography and the Myth of Westernization," p. 188.

44. Gao, *Taiwan fuzhi*, p. 5.
45. Hu, *Visible Traces*, pp. 193–95.
46. Chen Lunjiong, *Haiguo wenjian lu*, p. 34.
47. Smith, *Chinese Maps*, fig. 7.
48. Gao, *Taiwan fuzhi*, p. 26.
49. Ibid., p. 1.
50. This image became so deeply ingrained that one official expressed his surprise at finding that the Kangxi-Jesuit atlas oriented the mountains of the Central Mountain Range facing south rather than west as he had presumed—a result of the vertical orientation of Taiwan on this map. See Huang Shujing, *Taihai shicha lu*, p. 7.
51. Liu Liangbi, *Chongxiu Fujian Taiwan fuzhi*, p. 100.
52. Shi Lang, *Jinghai jishi*, p. 63.
53. Huang Shujing, *Taihai shicha lu*, p. 3.
54. Gao, *Taiwan fuzhi*, p. 25.
55. Qing writers commonly described the island as "facing the sea and backed by mountains," "rimmed by mountains," or "pillowing on mountains."

Chapter 2

An earlier version of this chapter appeared as "Taiwan as a Living Museum: Tropes of Anachronism in Late-Imperial Chinese Travel Writing," *Harvard Journal of Asiatic Studies* 59, no. 2 (Dec. 1999): 445–84, and is reprinted here with permission of the editors.

1. For a comparison of Miao marriage customs to those of Zhou times, see Chen Ding, *Dian Qian tusi hunli ji*. For a description of Nanhai instruments as survivals from the Han dynasty, see Zhou Zhongxuan, *Zhuluo xianzhi*, p. 160. See also Harrell, "Introduction," pp. 15–16.

2. There are many examples of barbarians representing the antithesis of Chinese decline. In "The Basic Annals of Qin" from the *Shiji*, for example, Duke Mu said to You Yu: "'China employs the Odes and Documents, its rites and music, its laws and regulations to govern the land, but even so there are times of chaos. Now the Rong and Yi people have none of these, so how can they bring about order? It must be very difficult, is it not?' You Yu laughed and replied, 'It is precisely because of these that China is in chaos! In ancient times when the sage rulers such as the Yellow Emperor created rites and music, laws and regulations, they took the lead in observing and carrying them out, and a small measure of order was achieved. But the rulers of later ages grow daily more arrogant and licentious, scrutinizing and berating their subjects in the name of the law, while their subjects, utterly exhausted, angrily reproach their superiors in

the name of benevolence and righteousness. So superior and inferior wrangle and revile one another, usurping and murdering until whole clans are wiped out. And all because of such things as rites and music, laws and regulations! The Rong and the Yi people are not like this. Superiors treat their inferiors with simplicity and thoughtfulness, while inferiors serve their superiors with loyalty and good faith, and the governing of the whole state is like the ordering of a single individual. No one knows why order comes about—such is the ordering of a true sage' " (Sima Qian, *Records of the Grand Historian, Han and Qin*, pp. 15–16).

3. Fabian, *Time and the Other*, pp. 1, 31.

4. Harrell ("Introduction") identifies three different "civilizing projects" on the Chinese frontiers, which he labels the "Confucian," the "Christian," and the "Communist."

5. Ibid., pp. 15–16.

6. Ibid., p. 16.

7. Both these rhetorical modes have longstanding precedents within the Chinese historiographic tradition. The idea of the "barbarian" as a repository of ancient virtues, for example, dates back to Zhou texts. In a study of early Chinese historiography, David Schaberg ("Foundations of Chinese Historiography," p. 100) writes of the rhetorical uses of the "wise barbarian" in Zhou texts: "Zhou's non-Chinese neighbors, like Herodotus's Egyptians and Ethiopians, rebuke the Chinese with an image of what they should be or used to be. The wise barbarian is as common a figure as the wise commoner in Eastern Zhou historiography, and serves some of the same purposes." The image of the "wise barbarian," of course, is played off against the more common image of the barbarian as the antithesis of civilized man.

8. Although representing two different visions of history, the rhetorics of privation and primitivism are not necessarily mutually exclusive. Individual writers might employ both modes at different rhetorical moments, or they might even combine tropes—an indication that privation and primitivism are, in many ways, two sides of the same coin.

9. Chen Di, "Dongfan ji," p. 27.

10. I am using modern place-names here.

11. Chen Di, "Dongfan ji," p. 27.

12. According to Harrell ("Introduction," p. 15), the association between knotting strings and "primitives" remained common in Chinese ethnographic descriptions through the 1950s.

13. Lewis, *Writing and Authority in Early China*, pp. 1–11.

14. Trans. from Ebrey, *Chinese Civilization: A Sourcebook*, p. 29.

15. This passage from the *Laozi* is repeated in nearly identical form in the *Zhuangzi*.

16. Chen Di, "Dongfan ji," p. 26.

17. Ibid., p. 27.

18. Trans. from Ebrey, *Chinese Civilization*, p. 28.

19. See Kawakatsu, *Gi Shin Nambokuchō*, pp. 33–43.

20. The images of primitivism in *Record* had particular appeal to the Qing audience: Qing travel writers and gazetteer compilers frequently quoted Chen Di's passage on the indigenes as the people of Lord No-Cares and Getian. They also incorporated Chen's tropes into their own compositions and elaborated on them.

21. Jia Ning, "Chen Di yu *Dongfan ji*," pp. 45–51.

22. See Wiens, *China's March Toward the Tropics*.

23. Legge, *The Sacred Books of China, The Li Ki*, p. 229.

24. Lin, *Taiwan jilüe*, p. 61.

25. Ibid., p. 62.

26. Legge, *The Sacred Books of China, The Li Ki*, pp. 369–70.

27. Luo Mi, *Lushi*, pp. 5.2a, 5.4b. It was said that people of antiquity would smear the blood of a sacrificial animal on their mouths when taking an oath.

28. Writers also drew on descriptions of barbarians from antiquity in texts such as the *Hou Hanshu* in constructing images of savagery.

29. Authors typically used references to "the people of Lord No-Cares and Getian," "the people of Fu Xi and Huangdi," or "Peach Blossom Spring" to idealize the natives.

30. Wu Chenchen, "Minyou ouji," p. 22.

31. Yu Yonghe, *Pihai jiyou*, p. 32.

32. See Lin, *Taiwan jilüe*, p. 64.

33. Yu Yonghe, *Pihai jiyou*, p. 33.

34. The phrasing also recalls Chen Di's use of this allusion.

35. For example, in the two earlier gazetteers, the section on "savage customs" contains only a single example of a trope of anachronism—"they burrow out caves to live in just like the folk of high antiquity"—but in Zhou's gazetteer the same section features twelve tropes of anachronism.

36. Zhou Zhongxuan, *Zhuluo xianzhi*, p. 164.

37. Wang Xianqian, *Zhuangzi jijie*, p. 550.

38. Zhou Zhongxuan, *Zhuluo xianzhi*, p. 158.

39. Yu Yonghe, *Pihai jiyou*, p. 37.

40. Ibid.

41. Thus China was known as "the land of moral principles and righteousness" (*liyi zhi bang*). By the same token, Confucian culture was not the exclusive preserve of the Han Chinese.

42. Shepherd, *Statecraft and Political Economy on the Taiwan Frontier*, pp. 362–94.

43. Fairbank, *The Chinese World Order*.

44. In Huang Shujing, *Taihai shicha lu*, p. 165.

45. Fabian, *Time and the Other*, p. 25.

Chapter 3

1. Moreover, with the defeat of the Zhengs, the Qing consolidation of power over Ming territory was now complete, and there seemed to be no compelling reason to extend the empire at this point.

2. See Shepherd, *Statecraft and Political Economy on the Taiwan Frontier*, p. 137.

3. Ibid., p. 145.

4. The Qing controlled intercourse between the island and the mainland by restricting shipping to the ports of Tainan in Taiwan and Amoy in Fujian. Between 1684 and 1732, the migration of Chinese families to Taiwan was forbidden, and the numbers of migrant farmworkers kept to a minimum. All these policies served to isolate Taiwan from the rest of the empire. See Shepherd, *Statecraft and Political Economy on the Taiwan Frontier*.

5. Yet the boundary between Qing territory and indigenous territory was unstable, and much of Qing policy toward Taiwan was concerned with drawing and redrawing this boundary line.

6. I borrow the term "imperial eyes" from Mary Louise Pratt (*Imperial Eyes*, p. 7). Pratt's "imperial eyes" belong to the "seeing-man" who looks out and possesses with his eyes.

7. Jiang Yuying, *Taiwan fuzhi*, p. 59.

8. Coming from the steppe, Manchu writers would not necessarily have shared Chinese attitudes toward grasslands. These representations of Taiwan's grasslands thus betray a Han Chinese chauvinist perspective.

9. The Chinese word for landscape is literally "mountains and waters" (*shanshui*), the two essential constituents of landscape.

10. Huang Shujing, *Taihai shicha lu*, p. 4.

11. Yu Yonghe, *Pihai jiyou*, p. 26.

12. Some declared that Taiwan had few natural products that could not be found on the mainland; see, e.g., Xu, "Taiwan suibi," p. 6.

13. Millward, *Beyond the Pass*, p. 37.

14. For more on theories of *qi* and their relation to the Chinese art of "siting," see Henderson, "Chinese Cosmographical Thought," pp. 216–22.

15. Yu Yonghe, *Pihai jiyou*, p. 22.

16. Ziqing is the sobriquet of Su Wu, a famous statesman of the second century B.C. sent by Han Emperor Wudi on a mission to the Xiongnu khan. He was imprisoned by the khan and later sent into the desert, where he lived for nineteen years as a shepherd. Xinguo refers to Wen Tianxiang (1236–82), who was famous for his loyalty to the Song dynasty and his resistance to the invading Mongols who overthrew the Song. In 1276 he was sent on a mission to a Mongol camp, where he was imprisoned. Later he escaped and fought with the imperial forces in Zhangzhou, Fujian. He was known for leading troops into the barbarian wilderness. He was honored with the title Lord of Xinguo.

17. Liu Zihou is the style name of Liu Zongyuan (773–819), a famous Tang dynasty (618–906) literatus who is often credited with establishing the travelogue genre. Bozhou is in present-day Guizhou. Yu Yonghe, *Pihai jiyou*, p. 27.

18. Yu's representation of the Taiwan frontier owes much to Tang dynasty literary treatments of the southern borderlands, works of exiles such as Han Yu and Liu Zongyuan, who portrayed the south as a barbarous and miasmic land. Many Qing literati came to see Taiwan as analogous to these earlier southern frontiers. For Tang dynasty exotica, see Schafer, *The Golden Peaches of Samarkand*.

19. McClintock, *Imperial Leather*, p. 30.

20. Although wilderness embodied desolation for most Qing literati, it also held out the promise of hidden treasure. The rumor of gold lying about for the taking in the mountains was a favorite of travel writers. Delicious tropical fruits and fragrant wild tea were said to grow deep in the mountains. Some pondered whether the unexplored island might after all prove to be the magical isle of Penglai, with its herbs of immortality. Others speculated whether it might be the fabled Land of Dogs. Ji Qiguang ("Taiwan zaji") reported a number of the island's marvels, including Gold Mountain, which produced giant boulders of gold; Jade Mountain, which was so tall that humans could not reach the summit, and which glowed like pure jade in the moonlight; Fire Mountain, a volcano that puffed fire and smoke; and a phoenix with feathers the colors of the rainbow.

21. He also wrote that the people of Taiwan were either descendants of pirates or rebels. See Ji Qiguang, "Taiwan zaji," p. 2.

22. The term "inner mountains" was sometimes also used to refer to the eastern side of the island, which was more generally known as "behind the mountains" (*shanhou, houshan*). Both terms reflected the Qing perspective on Taiwan as viewed from the Chinese mainland.

23. Lin, *Taiwan jilüe*, p. 64.

24. Yu Yonghe, *Pihai jiyou*, p. 32.

25. Zhou Zhongxuan, *Zhuluo xianzhi*, p. 295.

26. Gao, *Taiwan fuzhi*, pp. 2–5.

27. Zhou Zhongxuan, *Zhuluo xianzhi*, pp. 1–23.

28. Similarly, a Yongzheng-era scroll map of Taiwan represents few landmarks pictorially but renders Taiwan's landscape in exquisite detail. With its tall, craggy mountains, dense forests, sprawling bamboo groves, and empty, expansive plains, the map resembles a landscape painting. The enormously exaggerated trees, which tower to the same heights as the mountains, create the impression of a primeval wilderness. Images of nature on this map visually overwhelm the human traces on the landscape, which are few and far between. Both maps produce an image of Taiwan as pristine nature, untouched by the human hand.

29. Indeed, in 1725 Lan was enlisted to work on revisions of the imperial *Comprehensive Gazetteer*. In 1728, Lan was introduced to the Yongzheng emperor for discussions of geography and Taiwan policy, and he won praise from the emperor for his "Memorial on the Administration of Taiwan" ("Jingli Taiwan shu"). During his time in Taiwan, he wrote many important policy recommendations, often in Lan Tingzhen's name.

30. See Zhuang Jinde, "Lan Dingyuan di zhi Tai danglun," pp. 1–27; Shepherd, *Statecraft and Political Economy on the Taiwan Frontier*.

31. Lan, *Pingtai jilüe*, p. 32.

32. Ibid.

33. Ibid.

34. Yu Yonghe, *Pihai jiyou*, p. 22.

35. Lan, *Dongzheng ji*, p. 87.

36. The modern name for Shuishalian is Sun Moon Lake.

37. Lan Dingyuan (*Dongzheng ji*, p. 85) left this description of "floating fields": "The savages take bamboo and tie it to make rafts, and float them on the surface of the water. They make a mat of grass and fill it with dirt to farm and plant it with rice; these are called floating fields."

38. Ibid., p. 86.

39. Ibid., p. 89.

40. Shepherd, *Statecraft and Political Economy on the Taiwan Frontier*, p. 145.

41. Ibid., p. 182.

42. Ibid., p. 186.

43. Lan, *Dongzheng ji*, p. 87.

44. Spurr, *The Rhetoric of Empire*, p. 28.

45. Lan, *Pingtai jilüe*, p. 31.

46. Ibid, p. 30.

47. Zhou Zhongxuan, *Zhuluo xianzhi*, p. 113.

48. Ibid., p. 114.

49. In Shepherd, *Statecraft and Political Economy on the Taiwan Frontier*, p. 186.

50. Lan, *Dongzheng ji*, p. 3.

Chapter 4

1. Huang Shujing, *Taihai shicha lu*, p. 94.

2. Ibid.

3. Shi Lang, *Jinghai jishi*, p. 60.

4. See Stainton, "The Politics of Taiwan Aboriginal Origins."

5. *Taiwan Yearbook 2003*, pp. 3–8. See esp. pp. 5 and 7 for new government designations of indigenous groups.

6. See Shepherd, *Statecraft and Political Economy on the Taiwan Frontier*; Stainton, "The Politics of Taiwan Aboriginal Origins."

7. *Taiwan Yearbook 2003*, p. 4.

8. TYJYS, *Qing Shengzu shilu xuanji*, p. 133.

9. Gao, *Taiwan fuzhi*, p. 185.

10. The term *lei* was also used to refer to "subethnic" conflict in Taiwan: that is, conflict between Han Chinese groups of different regional origins.

11. See Dikötter, *Discourse of Race in Modern China*.

12. Huang Shujing, *Taihai shicha lu*, p. 1.

13. TYJYS, *Liuqiu yu Jilongshan*, pp. 1–2.

14. Yu Yonghe, *Pihai jiyou*, p. 20.

15. Ibid., p. 18.

16. Zhou Zhongxuan, *Zhuluo xianzhi*, p. 155.

17. Gao, *Taiwan fuzhi*, p. 187.

18. Fung, *A History of Chinese Philosophy*, p. 123; see *Mengzi* VIA 7.5 and 8.

19. Knoblock, *Xunzi*, p. 142.

20. Legge, *The Li Chi*, p. 229.

21. Legge, *The Chinese Classics*, pp. 354–55.

22. Chen Di, "Dongfan ji," p. 24. Chen Di also refuted Mencius's argument on universal human tastes with this observation:

According to custom they are fond of deer meat. They cut open the intestines and scrape out the newly swallowed grass, both excrement and the stuff that has not yet turned to excrement, and call it "hundred-grasses ointment." They eat this alone insatiably. When Chinese see this, they generally vomit. They eat pigs but do not eat chickens. They raise chickens and let them grow as they will, only taking the tail feather as a decoration. When they shoot pheasants, they also only pluck the tail feather. When they see Chinese eating chickens or pheasants, they generally vomit. So how can you judge which is the correct [sense of] taste? How can all tastes be the same? (Ibid., p. 26)

The idea that the Taiwan indigenes had particular tastes surfaced frequently in ethnographic descriptions: "they have a taste for liquor," "they have a taste for killing," "they have a taste for promiscuity," and so on. These were generally denigrating observations.

23. Lin Qianguang, *Taiwan jilüe*, p. 61.

24. Zhou Zhongxuan, *Zhuluo xianzhi*, p. 154.

25. Ibid.

26. Legge, *The Li Chi*, p. 228.

27. Dikötter, *Discourse of Race in Modern China*, p. 8.

28. In ibid., p. 27.

29. Millward, *Beyond the Pass*, pp. 37–38.

30. Yu Yonghe, *Pihai jiyou*, p. 38.

31. Ibid., p. 33.

32. Huang Shujing (*Taihai shicha lu*, p. 129) even wrote a poem on the subject: "Who says that they are of a different kind (*yilei*) or another flock (*qun*)? / Their genial warmth is like the spring; they could not bear for me to part. / I have heard that they changed the village name to Place Where the Horse Turned Back. / In later years I will remember the clouds of the eastern ocean."

33. Ibid., p. 166.

34. Huang included this detail as an implicit contrast to earlier travel writers who had described the savages as able to run barefoot over thorny ground, as if they had the hooves of horses.

35. Huang Shujing, *Taihai shicha lu*, p. 94.

36. Yu Yonghe, *Pihai jiyou*, pp. 36–37.

37. The first Qing schools were established in 1686, only two years after annexation, in four indigenous villages of Zhuluo county. Yet education was not a priority of the state during the early years of Qing rule on Taiwan, and expenditures in this area were limited. Yu urged a more serious commitment to the project of education and assimilation. Yu thus supported not only annexation but also the active transformation of Taiwan into a domain of Chinese civilization.

38. Huang Shujing, *Taihai shicha lu*, p. 94.

39. Crossley, *A Translucent Mirror*, p. 246.

40. Ibid., p. 225.

41. There were those who followed the Xunzian argument that human nature is inherently evil and in need of reforming and argued that the bellicose inborn nature of the savages could be transformed through active effort. Thus, there was some accommodation between racialist discourse and Qing imperial ideology.

42. See Dikötter, *Discourse of Race in Modern China*, p. 25.

43. Zhou Zhongxuan, *Zhuluo xianzhi*, p. 153.

44. Chen Wenda, *Fengshan xianzhi*, p. 80.

45. See Shepherd, *Statecraft and Political Economy on the Taiwan Frontier*.

46. Lan, *Pingtai jilüe*, p. 56.

47. Huang Shujing, *Taihai shicha lu*, p. 175.

48. Lan, *Pingtai jilüe*, p. 56.

49. At Shuishalian, Lan (*Dongzheng ji*, p. 86) complained that his enjoyment of the landscape was constricted by the fear of savages. He urged local officials to "cultivate virtue and transformation in order to thoroughly saturate their flesh. That will enable everyone to enjoy excursions here."

50. Ibid., p. 60.

51. This is one of the few cases in which we see the legal implications of race or ethnicity on the Taiwan frontier. My research has found no legal codification of "race" as a concept on the Taiwan frontier in the sense that we understand it in the United States. Although Qing statutes on Taiwan frequently made a distinction between Han and *fan* or, more specifically, between *shufan* and *shengfan* (for example, in establishing tax rates), these were not legal definitions of "race" per se. There were no laws equivalent to, for example, the blood-quantum rules in the United States, established by various legal statutes, which attempted to carefully define who was White and who was Colored (or [Native American] Indian, Chinese, etc.). Hence, as Shepherd (*Statecraft and Political Economy on the Taiwan Frontier*, p. 379) points out, the 1737 decree prohibiting intermarriage between Han Chinese men and indigenous women was promulgated for reasons of political expediency and not out of philosophical or moral opposition to "race mixing" as was the case with U.S. anti-miscegenation laws (see Chapter 8). The pertinent distinction in Qing law was between *min* (subjects) and non-*min*, and not necessarily between racial groups.

52. Ibid., p. 190.

53. Also known as the *Map of Taiwan's Savage Boundary* (*Taiwan fanjie tu*).

Chapter 5

1. Lan, *Dongzheng ji*, p. 260.

2. These various shades of meaning are present in the concepts of raw and cooked peoples. All these concepts imply a process of transformation, from the raw to the cooked, from the unripe to the ripe, from the strange to the familiar. The agent of transformation might be fire or it might be culture. I have chosen "raw" and "cooked" to translate the terms *sheng*

and *shu*, since they are the most flexible in meaning and best able to convey the opposition between nature and culture. I use these terms in their metaphorical, and not literal, senses.

3. Lévi-Strauss, *The Raw and the Cooked*, esp. pp. 334–42.

4. Dikötter, *Discourse of Race in Modern China*, p. 9. On "raw persons" and "cooked persons" see Lévi-Strauss, *The Raw and the Cooked*, p. 335.

5. West ("The Overflowing Well," p. 1) writes: "It is clear from the contexts in which the words appear that the terminology draws upon the trope of 'eating' as the governing master metaphor of cultural consumption in China. And when applied to foreigners, it describes a range of bipedal activities from the inedible and horrific (*sheng*) to the culturally palatable and nearly commensurate (*shu*), and indexes the appropriateness of their ingestion into Han culture."

6. In general, Chinese writers held the cooked in higher regard; yet, in some cases they considered the cooked sly and untrustworthy, and the raw, brutish but harmless (see ibid., p. 1). It is, therefore, impossible to arrive at a general definition for the raw and the cooked in premodern Chinese ethnography.

7. Liu Liangbi, *Chongxiu Fujian Taiwan fuzhi*, p. 101.

8. Pratt, *Imperial Eyes*, p. 6.

9. The earliest extant eyewitness account of the Taiwan indigenes, Chen Di's *Record of the Eastern Savages*, referred to them as the "Eastern Savages." Since Chen traveled only in the southwestern corner of Taiwan, he had limited contact with the indigenous people, and was not fully cognizant of their cultural diversity. Thus, he used the blanket term "Eastern Savages" to refer to the people of the island. After annexation, Qing writers largely dropped the appellation "Eastern Savages" in favor of the terms "native savages" (*tufan*), "tribal savages" (*shefan*), or just plain "savage" (*fan*). Despite their greater familiarity with the indigenous people, the earliest Qing writers still tended to speak of Taiwan's "savages" in generic terms.

10. Ji Qiguang (1684) mentioned the presence of "wild savages" on the island, and the *Gazetteer of Taiwan Prefecture* of 1696 noted in passing the existence of "raw savages" on Taiwan's eastern coast, who lived beyond Qing rule. When Yu Yonghe traveled on the island in 1697, old hands explained to him the difference between native savages and wild savages. Often, the terms "wild" and "raw" were used interchangeably.

11. Chang Yao-ch'i, "Pingpuzu sheming duizhaobiao," p. 1.

12. Zhou Zhongxuan, *Zhuluo xianzhi*, p. 154.

13. Both the inhabitants and the land of taxpaying villages were registered with the state and were therefore directly subject to state control.

14. Yu Yonghe, *Pihai jiyou*, p. 11.

15. Deng, *Lice huichao*, pp. 2–3.

16. Lu, "Taiwan shimo ouji," p. 9.

17. The nineteenth-century writer Shi Mi ("Chouban fandi yi," p. 256) also defined the raw and cooked in terms of submission to state authority but read this submission in cultural not fiscal terms: "One may distinguish those who are sincere in submitting from those who are not sincere by whether they wear the queue. Those who do not wear the queue harbor a mind to rebel. Those who wear the queue have already reformed into cooked savages."

18. Fan Xian, *Chongxiu Taiwan fuzhi*, p. 15.

19. Kangxi-era writer Lu Zhiyu ("Taiwan shimo ouji," p. 9), for example, wrote that both the raw and the cooked "in general hunt animals and drink blood. They are fond of killing and fighting."

20. Lan, *Dongzheng ji*, p. 59.

21. Huang Shujing, *Taihai shicha lu*, p. 155.

22. In ibid., p. 162.

23. As Huang Shujing (ibid., p. 167) wrote: "Their wild natures are hard to tame, they burn and plunder and kill people."

24. Lan, *Dongzheng ji*, p. 60.

25. "The Song of the Cooked Savage," which was recorded in the *Gazetteer of Gemalan* (Ke, *Gemalan zhilüe*), employed these opposing images of the raw and the cooked: "People fear the raw savages who are as fierce as tigers. People cheat the cooked savages as if they were as lowly as dirt. Fearing the strong and cheating the weak, people's hearts are really un-ancient."

26. One reason for such positive representations was that the "cooked savages" had provided auxiliary troops to the Qing as early as 1684, when Qing commanders called on villagers of the southwestern core to fight against Ming loyalist rebels. Such auxiliary troops proved vital again in 1721, during the Zhu Yigui rebellion, when they fought alongside Qing troops against the rebels.

27. In the *Qing Imperial Tribute Illustrations*, the raw savages are described as follows: "The men and women have their hair loose and are naked. Some cover their bodies with deerskins," and "they dwell in nests and caves, eat fur and drink blood. Naked, they do not know cold or heat" (TYJYS, *Qing zhigongtu xuan*, pp. 44, 56).

28. Lan, *Pingtai jilüe*, p. 63.

29. See Huang Shujing, *Taihai shicha lu*.

30. "Caps and belts" is a metonym for literati.

31. Liu Liangbi's *Taiwan Gazetteer* combined administrative, cultural, and territorial criteria: "The raw savages live far away in the inner mountains. Recently, they are also gradually submitting to civilization. The

cooked savages pay taxes and perform corvée. They are equivalent to subjects" (p. 101).

32. Lin, *Taiwan jilüe*, p. 62.

33. Gao, *Taiwan fuzhi*, p. 9.

34. The *Gazetteer of Fengshan County* of 1720 also reported ape-like people and belligerent headhunters living in the mountains: by the publication of the next *Gazetteer of Fengshan County* in 1764, these people were "raw savages" (see Chen Wenda, *Fengshan xianzhi*, p. 82; and Wang Yingzeng, *Chongxiu Fengshan xianzhi*, p. 60).

35. Zhou Zhongxuan, *Zhuluo xianzhi*, p. 295. The traveler's sense of dread was frequently compounded by the inability to survey the terrain. In conventional Chinese travel writing, the climax is presented as the moment when the traveler ascends to a high place, a mountain peak or a tower, and looks down upon the landscape spread beneath him. From this vantage, the traveler contemplated man's relation to nature, his own relation to history, or perhaps the governance of the locale. Indeed, an entire genre of classical poetry was devoted to "climbing a high place." In Taiwan, the traveler could gain no such privileged view. Travel writers frequently complained of climbing mountains only to have their vistas blocked by dense foliage; others did not dare enter the mountains at all. Travelers in Taiwan were therefore constantly plagued by what they could not see: headhunters and bandits lurking in the jungle, snakes hidden in the underbrush, ghosts and mountain spirits, and the invisible but deadly miasmas.

36. The government could more easily build roads on the flat and open terrain, again facilitating military control, as well as commerce and communication.

37. Lan, *Dongzheng ji*, p. 60.

38. In Huang Shujing, *Taihai shicha lu*, p. 170.

39. As the Kangxi-era writer Wu Chenchen ("Minyou ouji," p. 22) wrote around 1713–15: "The Han Chinese and the cooked savages live mixed together. Across the mountain ranges is the domain of the raw savages. Anyone who chases a wild animal and mistakenly crosses over into their territory and meets with raw savages will certainly be killed."

40. Yu Yonghe, *Pihai jiyou*, p. 32. Liu Liangbi's *Gazetteer of Taiwan Prefecture*, for example, described the raw savages as "dwelling in the deep mountains and tall ranges, screened by the forest, which is cut only by winding, twisted paths. They never see the sky or sun" (p. 106).

41. The boundary consisted of an island-wide set of trenches, known as earth-oxen, built from south to north ten *li* to the west of the foothills of the Central Mountain Range. The term "redline" is derived from the col-

ored line used to represent this boundary on maps. See Shi Tianfu, "Taiwan lishi dili yanjiu daji."

42. As John Shepherd (*Statecraft and Political Economy on the Taiwan Frontier,* p. 272) notes, a memorial of 1745, which refers to the "raw-savage boundary," clearly puts the Han and the cooked on one side and the raw on the other.

43. Fan Xian, *Chongxiu Taiwan fuzhi,* p. 15.

44. Such definitions not only territorialized the raw and the cooked but also captured the earlier meanings of "unfamiliar" and "familiar," with the raw located far away and the cooked nearer to the Han Chinese.

45. As geographic location assumed greater importance in the classification of the indigenes, gazetteer editors developed multiple subcategories to reflect this trend. The *Gazetteer of Taiwan Prefecture* of 1742 offered numerous subclassifications of the raw and the cooked, which were based on both territorial and administrative criteria: "submitted raw savages" (*guihua shengfan*), "newly submitted raw savages" (*xin'guihua shengfan*), "raw savages of the Transmontane Territory" (*shanhou shengfan*), "cooked savages who live near the mountains" (*yishan shufan*), "cooked savages of the flatlands" (*pingdi shufan*), "cooked savages of the plains" (*pingpu shufan*), "cooked savages of the foothills of the inner mountains" (*banju neishan shufan*), and "cooked savages of the shore" (*bianhai shufan*). This proliferation of labels represented an attempt to gain greater precision in representing the Taiwan indigenes, particularly the type of terrain they inhabited (see Liu Liangbi, *Chongxiu Fujian Taiwan fuzhi,* pp. 80–83).

46. Wu Ziguang, *Taiwan jishi,* pp. 88–89.

47. Yu Yonghe, *Pihai jiyou,* p. 33.

48. Lan, *Pingtai jilüe,* p. 56.

49. Several of the local gazetteers also explicated the connection between environment and human customs. As the *Gazetteer of Zhuluo County* of 1717 noted, quoting the *Hanzhi,* "The differences of hard and soft are connected to the wind and *qi* of the environment. This is called *feng.* The choice of good and evil follows inclinations of the ruler. This is called *su*" (Zhou Zhongxuan, *Zhuluo xianzhi,* p. 135). Thus customs (*fengsu*) were formed in the confluence of environmental and human influences.

50. Liu Liangbi, *Chongxiu Fujian Taiwan fuzhi,* p. 100.

51. Zhou Zhongxuan, *Zhuluo xianzhi,* p. 180.

52. Liu Liangbi, *Chongxiu Fujian Taiwan fuzhi,* p. 100.

53. Shen Qiyuan, "Tiaochen Taiwan shiyi zhuang," p. 5. The notion of transforming "fan" into "Han" is intriguing, but beyond the scope of this chapter.

54. As John Shepherd (*Statecraft and Political Economy on the Taiwan Frontier,* pp. 371–72) has shown, after annexation the Qing court pursued a conservative policy toward cultural transformation in Taiwan: "The civilizing mission of local magistrates (toward Han and non-Han alike) was to propagate Confucian civic culture and attitudes of submission to constituted authority rather than wholesale sinicization, although it was not always a simple matter for Chinese officials to distinguish Confucian attitudes from Han customs. To the extent the plains aborigine hunter-warrior culture led to the training of braves that could be enlisted by the state and a separate plains aborigine ethnic identity facilitated [Qing] policies of divide and rule . . . it was in the state's interest to oppose wholesale sinicization (which might erase ethnic divisions) while fostering the loyalty that came with 'civilization' and 'Confucianization.'"

55. The Qing also attempted to abolish footbinding among Han Chinese women, but failed.

56. In 1745, a memorial to the emperor reported cooked savages burning and looting in the guise of raw savages (Shepherd, *Statecraft and Political Economy on the Taiwan Frontier,* pp. 262–63).

57. In 1787, when the Qing was fighting the Lin Shuangwen rebellion, the emperor once more turned to Lan's writings as a source of key policy ideas, lessons that should have been learned. The Qianlong emperor was particularly interested in Lan's essays and made *Record of the Eastern Campaign* recommended reading for the governor-general and the field commander. Lan's influence, then, was more long-term than immediate. According to Zhuang Jinde ("Lan Dingyuan di zhi Tai danglun"), Lan was highly influential in turning Qing policy from one of passive containment to aggressive colonization.

58. In Shi Tianfu, "Taiwan lishi dili yanjiu daji," p. 95.

59. Luo Zhufeng, *Hanyu dacidian,* p. 242.

60. As the *Gazetteer of Taiwan Prefecture* noted: "As for the eastern side of the island, the azure mountains beyond the mountains, from north to south, none has submitted to civilization" (Gao, *Taiwan fuzhi,* p. 6).

61. Beginning with the map from the *Gazetteer of Fujian Province* of 1684.

62. I am indebted to Pat Giersch for his elegant translations of *shanhou* and *shanqian.*

63. The first gazetteer to include a map of Transmontane Territory was the *Gazetteer of Zhuluo County* of 1717, followed soon thereafter by the *Gazetteer of Fengshan County* of 1720. Chen Lunjiong's *Record of Things Seen and Heard at Sea (Haiguo wenjianlu)* of 1730 also contained a map of the eastern side of Taiwan. Yet these maps were the exception to

the general convention, and later gazetteers and cartographers did not necessarily follow their example. Early maps of Taiwan's eastern coast are thus rare.

64. Zhou Zhongxuan, *Zhuluo xianzhi*, pp. 20–23.

65. See *Taiwan fanjie tu*.

66. See Millward, "'Coming onto the Map.'"

67. Perdue, "Boundaries, Maps, and Movement," p. 274.

68. Yee, "Traditional Chinese Cartography and the Myth of Westernization," p. 181.

69. Perdue, "Boundaries, Maps, and Movement," p. 279.

70. A version of the Jesuit Atlas produced by Jean-Baptiste d'Anville was published in Jean-Baptiste du Halde's *Description de la Chine* (1735) and spread widely over Europe; see Perdue, "Boundaries, Maps, and Movement."

71. Yee, "Traditional Chinese Cartography and the Myth of Westernization," p. 191.

72. See Xia Liming, *Qingdai Taiwan ditu yanbianshi*.

73. Ibid., p. 63.

Chapter 6

Material for this chapter first appeared in the essay "Texts on the Right and Pictures on the Left: Reading the Qing Record of Frontier Taiwan," in *Writing and Materiality in China*, ed. Judith T. Zeitlin and Lydia H. Liu (Harvard University Asia Center, 2003, pp. 451–87) and is reprinted here with permission of the publisher.

1. TYJYS, *Qing zhigong tu xuan*, p. 3.

2. Crossley, "The Qianlong Retrospect of the Chinese-Martial (*hanjun*) Banners," p. 64.

3. As Laura Hostetler (*Qing Colonial Enterprise*, p. 56) argues, the Qianlong emperor placed great emphasis on the need for these illustrations to conform to a standardized format in order to ensure they be "uniform and complete." The *Tribute Illustrations* thus provided a medium for the orderly display of difference within the multiethnic Qing empire.

4. TYJYS, *Qing Gaozong shilu xuanji*, p. 93.

5. The pictorial depiction of foreigners has a long history in China; see Hostetler, *Qing Colonial Enterprise*, pp. 87–96. Thus, the Qing illustrations of the Taiwan indigenes had numerous precedents. The only images of Taiwan that might have been entirely new and unfamiliar to Qing viewers were the European-style copperplate engravings celebrating mili-

tary victories on the Taiwan frontier commissioned by the Qianlong emperor, a detailed discussion of which is beyond the scope of this book.

6. According to Tu Cheng-sheng ("Pingpu zuqun fengsu tuxiang ziliao kao"), there are nine "kinds" of ethnographic illustrations of the Taiwan indigenes extant, including one ethnographic map and several painted albums.

7. Xie, *Xuxiu Taiwan xianzhi*, p. 365.

8. The analysis in this chapter is not intended to condemn the "racism" of the Qing artists who produced the ethnographic pictures.

9. See Young, *Colonial Desire*.

10. As I demonstrate in Chapter 4, although Chinese intellectuals of this time did not theorize "race" as a distinct concept and certainly did not propose "scientific" theories of race, they were interested in questions of human difference.

11. Zhou Zhongxuan, *Zhuluo xianzhi*, p. 36.

12. Han Chinese customs, which are also recorded in the gazetteer, are not illustrated.

13. Hu, *Visible Traces*, pp. 72–75.

14. The illustrations include no pictures of weaving, a theme of later illustrations.

15. Furthermore, whereas the *Illustrations of Tilling and Weaving* show women engaged in indoor activities such as spinning and weaving, the *Zhuluo Gazetteer* contains no indoor scenes. Always represented in exterior landscapes, the indigenes are tied more closely to nature than the civilized Chinese.

16. See Hu, *Visible Traces*, p. 72; and Zhou Zhongxuan, *Zhuluo xianzhi*, p. 27. The scene of "Picking Betel Nuts" from the *Gazetteer of Zhuluo County* again reveals compositional similarities to the scene "Picking Mulberry Leaves" from the Kangxi *Illustrations of Tilling and Weaving*, as well as telling differences that reveal much about the artist's strategy for representing primitiveness. The Han Chinese depicted in "Picking Mulberry Leaves" use ladders to climb the mulberry trees; the savages depicted in "Picking Betel Nuts" scale the palms with bare hands and feet. The basket carrier in "Mulberry Leaves" stands waiting in the foreground with his baskets set behind him; the basket carrier in "Betel Nuts" lolls lazily on the ground. In place of the mulberry trees, extolled in classical literature as the food of the all-important silkworm, are exotic palms. There is also a subtext implicit in the gazetteer's inclusion of "Picking Betel Nuts" in place of "Picking Mulberry Leaves": the civilized Chinese pick mulberry leaves, an activity fundamental to sericulture; the savages pick betel, a non-nutritive nut enjoyed for its euphoric effects. The pic-

ture thus impresses on literati viewers the inferiority of savage culture, which values short-term enjoyment over "proper" economic activities.

17. Zhou Zhongxuan, *Zhuluo xianzhi*, p. 31.

18. The basic composition of this picture is patterned after conventional scenes such as the "fishermen's drinking party," a model of which appears in the *Mustard Seed Garden Manual of Painting (1679)*, the most widely used handbook of painting in late imperial China; see Sze, *The Mustard Seed Garden Manual of Painting*, p. 245. Both scenes contrast sharply with the *Manual's* model of "four people seated drinking," which depicts four gentlemen clothed in long robes, seated at a table in dignified postures with small cups placed in front of them: a picture of the civilized manner of drinking (ibid., p. 244).

19. See Hostetler, *Qing Colonial Enterprise*, pp. 159–80.

20. Huang Shujing, for example, commissioned illustrations of savage customs and flora and fauna, as well as a map of the island illustrated with ethnographic vignettes.

21. During his term of office in Taiwan, Liu-shi-qi supervised the production of a revised edition of the *Gazetteer of Taiwan Prefecture* along with his Han Chinese counterpart Fan Xian; see Liu-shi-qi, *Fanshe caifeng tukao*.

22. Ibid., p. 99.

23. Tu, "Pingpu zuqun fengsu tuxiang ziliao kao," pp. 2–3.

24. This album is known as *Illustrations of Savage Customs by Mr. Chen of Dongning (Dongning Chenshi fansu tu)*. Yu Weichao, *A Journey into China's Antiquity*, p. 203.

25. The illustrated albums of Taiwan do not fit the criteria Hostetler (*Qing Colonial Enterprise*, p. 159) establishes for the definition of "Miao albums": "The genre is defined both by its subject matter and by its form—illustrations and texts that delineate and categorize the different groups that lived within a given province, or occasionally a smaller administrative unit. Each named group receives one entry, consisting of an illustration paired with textual description." The illustrations of Taiwan depict particular customs, rather than particular groups, as will be seen below. Although there are a large number of "Miao albums" housed in various museums and libraries around the world, illustrations of the Taiwan indigenes are relatively rare. Since so many late imperial Chinese painted ethnographic albums were purchased by private collectors at the turn of the twentieth century and many others have undoubtedly been lost, it is impossible to speculate on the number of such works actually produced during the Qing.

26. Ibid., p. 159.

27. Ibid., pp. 159–60.

28. Ibid., pp. 166–67.

29. Ibid., p. 182.

30. Liu-shi-qi, *Fanshe caifeng tukao*, pp. 99–100.

31. Held in the National Taiwan Museum.

32. Liu-shi-qi, *Fanshe caifeng tukao*, p. 57.

33. A further visual association between the natives and monkeys is made in "Weaving Cloth." In this picture, two boys are shown climbing a large tree, while a group of women weaves in the shade. The boys are chasing after a monkey that has climbed far out on a limb. The older boy wears only a tunic, exposing his lower body; the younger boy is naked. Their brown skin is painted the same color as the monkey's fur. The older boy is posed in the same posture as the monkey, with one arm clinging to a branch and the other outstretched. The cartoon-like features of the boys, which are only briefly sketched, quite closely resemble those of the monkey's face.

34. Liu-shi-qi, *Fanshe caifeng tukao*, p. 62.

35. Tu, "Pingpu zuqun fengsu tuxiang ziliao kao," p. 17.

36. Yu Weichao, *A Journey into China's Antiquity*, p. 203.

37. "Dancing natives" also became a topos of travel poetry; see Liu-shi-qi, *Fanshe caifeng tukao*, pp. 14–16.

38. Ibid., p. 100.

39. Like Liu-shi-qi's illustrations, Chen Bishen's album, which similarly focuses on the cooked savages, is dominated by visual primitivism.

40. Liu-shi-qi's album contains no illustrations of Han Chinese women. Therefore, the comparison is only implicit.

41. See *Yiyu tuzhi*, Cambridge University Library.

42. The genre of tribute illustrations (*zhigong tu*) dates back at least to the Liang dynasty (502–57). The purpose of these works was to record the foreign envoys who submitted tribute to China. The official department in charge of receiving these tribute bearers recorded details of each country's customs, products, and geography. At the same time, pictures were made of representative figures from each country. The tribute system thereby served as an important means of collecting geographic information about the world beyond China. Like most geographic works of the Qing, the *Tribute Illustrations* go far beyond the earlier examples of this genre, which contained several dozens of figures at most. The Qing work also differs from its precedents, which pictured only male subjects, by including a pair of figures, one male and one female, to represent each group. In addition, whereas early *Tribute Illustrations* were based on interviews of foreign envoys received at the capital, the Qing version was (theoretically) based on illustrations made at the frontiers and submitted by officials to the Grand Council.

43. The woodblock print version contains only Chinese text, but Xie Sui's scrolls contain text in both Chinese and Manchu.

44. In the various figures of the *Tribute Illustrations*, we see racial difference visualized. Each pair of figures represents a distinct and idealized type, linked to a particular geographic location. The collection begins with the "Korean official" and "his lady," proceeds through various Southeast Asian and Western countries, and then illustrates a long parade of non-Han Qing subjects. Although the differences between each particular type are highlighted, certain general typologies also emerge through the groupings in this collection: the southern barbarian, the northern barbarian, the Muslim, the European barbarian, and the relatively civilized barbarians of the Qing protectorates of Korea, Liuqiu, and Vietnam. Within these general types, we sometimes find faces or postures repeated or other shared elements, such as the distinctive hats of the Muslims. As such, the collection serves as an aid both for the visual identification of particular peoples and for developing a more generalized racial taxonomy.

45. Zhuang Jifa, *Xie Sui "Zhigong tu" Manwen tushuo jiaozhu*, pp. 1–22.

46. In Xie Sui's scrolls, the costumes are rendered in precise detail, down to the patterning of the fabrics, and are elaborately painted in brilliant colors.

47. The notion that spectacle or display is central to the *Tribute Illustrations* is supported by the fact that information of strategic or administrative value is given short shrift in the annotations, despite the fact that there was no lack of such information in the local gazetteers and other texts.

48. Clunas, *Pictures and Visuality in Early Modern China*, p. 88.

49. Zhuang Jifa, *Gugong Taiwan shiliao gaishu*, pp. 252, 262.

50. Representations of the savage female in the *Tribute Illustrations* are comparatively less grotesque and less threatening. The women tend to be more fully clothed and less muscular than their male counterparts. Only one female figure in the set is depicted bare-breasted and bare-legged. The key signifier of the savage woman's ethnic difference is her bare feet, which form a sharp contrast with the small, bound feet of the ideal Chinese woman. Aside from this, the illustrators appear to have employed conventional notions of femininity in representing the savage women: they have demure facial expressions and are often fair-skinned, and a number of them are depicted with children. This gendered difference in the representation of the savage male and female is interesting in light of the fact that Qing travel writers and gazetteer compilers made much of the supposedly dominant role of women among the indigenous Taiwan-

ese. Qing writers frequently described what they saw as gender role rever-sal among the indigenous people. See Chapter 7.

51. See *Yiyu tuzhi*, Cambridge University Library, n.p.

52. TYJYS, *Qing zhigong tu xuan*, p. 16.

53. Ibid., p. 56.

54. See Zhuang Jifa, *Xie Sui "Zhigong tu" Manwen tushuo jiaozhu*, p. 41.

55. TYJYS, *Qing zhigong tu xuan*, pp. 58–60.

56. Nineteenth-century European artists employed similar techniques to express character through physiognomy, particularly in representing racial others, the urban poor, as well as "criminal types"; see Cowling, *The Artist as Anthropologist*.

57. Song, *Huanan bianjiang minzu tulu*, p. 86.

58. Ibid., p. 70.

59. Ibid., p. 87.

60. In Hostetler, *Qing Colonial Enterprise*, p. 169.

Chapter 7

An earlier version of this chapter appeared as "An Island of Women: The Discourse of Gender in Qing Travel Accounts of Taiwan," *International History Review* 20, no. 2 (June 1998): 353–70, and is reprinted here with permission of the editors.

1. Hu, *Visible Traces*, p. 187.

2. Gladney, "Representing Nationality in China"; Harrell, "Introduction"; Schein, "Gender and Internal Orientalism in China."

3. Stoler, "Rethinking Colonial Categories"; McClintock, *Imperial Leather*; Morgan, *Place Matters*.

4. Wong, "Ethnicizing Gender," p. 113.

5. Shepherd, *Statecraft and Political Economy on the Taiwan Frontier*, p. 44.

6. This generalization may have resulted from the greater Chinese fa-miliarity with the Siraya.

7. Trans. from Thompson, "The Earliest Chinese Eyewitness Ac-counts of the Formosan Aborigines," pp. 173–74.

8. Yu Yonghe, *Pihai jiyou*, p. 35.

9. Deng Chuan'an (*Lice huichao*, p. 10), for example, wrote: "According to savage custom, the men who marry uxorilocally are just like women who marry virilocally [in China]. Obedient and dutiful, they do not dare to take their own initiative; they are debased to such a degree."

10. Thompson, "The Earliest Chinese Eyewitness Accounts of the Formosan Aborigines," p. 181.

11. Shepherd, *Statecraft and Political Economy on the Taiwan Frontier*, p. 366.

12. McKann, "The Naxi and the Nationalities Question," p. 45.

13. *Taiping guangji*, p. 3629.

14. Diamond, "Defining the Miao," p. 103.

15. Ma, *Yingya shenglan*, p. 104.

16. Adas, "Imperialism and Colonialism in Comparative Perspective," p. 380.

17. The idea that there were parallels between the customs of the Taiwan savages and other Southeast Asian peoples was also noted by a number of Qing writers.

18. Yu Yonghe, *Pihai jiyou*, p. 19.

19. Ibid., pp. 18–19.

20. Liu-shi-qi, *Fanshe caifeng tukao*, p. 7.

21. Trans. based on Thompson, "The Earliest Chinese Eyewitness Accounts of the Formosan Aborigines," p. 196.

22. Ibid., pp. 192–93.

23. Melissa Brown ("On Becoming Chinese," p. 52) notes that specific rates of intermarriage cannot be estimated.

24. See *Qing huidian Taiwan shili*.

25. Ibid., p. 171.

26. "Miscegenation" is a specific, nineteenth-century racialist construct, first introduced into Anglo-American discourse in 1864 to replace the older term "racial amalgamation"; see Young, *Colonial Desire*, p. 144. The concept does not apply to the Qing case. Hence I use the term "intermarriage." For the shifting politics of intermarriage in Dutch colonies, see Stoler, "Rethinking Colonial Categories."

27. Shepherd, *Statecraft and Political Economy on the Taiwan Frontier*, p. 379.

28. Shepherd (ibid., p. 462n85) notes that the Dutch regarded intermarriage as a vehicle for Christianizing the Taiwan indigenes.

29. Jiang Shiche, *Taiyou riji*, p. 46.

30. The term "transculturation" was coined by Fernando Oritz in the 1940s. Mary Louise Pratt (*Imperial Eyes: Travel Writing and Transculturation*, p. 6) notes: "Ethnographers have used this term to describe how subordinated or marginal groups select and invent from materials transmitted to them by a dominant or metropolitan culture."

31. Brown, "On Becoming Chinese," p. 45.

32. See Antonio Tavares's forthcoming dissertation. The memoirs of American consul Charles LeGendre intriguingly mention the existence of "half-caste" communities in various regions of Taiwan; see e.g., Eskildsen, *Foreign Adventurers and the Aborigines of Southern Taiwan*, p. 51. If accu-

rate, LeGendre's observations indicate that intermarriage was not simply a mechanism for the "sinicization" and eventual racial assimilation of the Taiwan indigenes but a complex phenomenon that deserves further research.

33. See Brown, "On Becoming Chinese," p. 52.

34. Ding, *Dongying zhilüe*, p. 78.

35. Pratt, *Imperial Eyes*, p. 6.

36. Zhuoyuanting zhuren, "Zou Annan yuma huan xingrong," pp. 61–62.

37. Zhang Chang was a native of Pingyang during the Han dynasty who became governor of Chang'an under Han Emperor Xuan. He was famous for painting his wife's eyebrows.

38. Wu Ziguang, *Taiwan jishi*, p. 31.

39. See Ko, *Teachers of the Inner Chambers*.

40. Yang, "Jinru wenming lingyu de bensheng shandi funü," pp. 163–69.

Chapter 8

Portions of this chapter appeared in "Taiwan as a Living Museum: Tropes of Anachronism in Late-Imperial Chinese Travel Writing," *Harvard Journal of Asiatic Studies* 59, no. 2 (Dec. 1999): 445–84, and are reprinted here with permission of the editors.

1. Chen Di, "Dongfan ji," p. 24.

2. Yu Yonghe, *Pihai jiyou*, p. 33.

3. Xu, "Taiwan suibi," p. 6.

4. Deng, *Lice huichao*, pp. 9–12.

5. See Behdad, *Belated Travelers*.

6. See Schwartz, "The Geography Lesson," on textual baggage and imaginary geography.

7. For a discussion of the emergence of evidential scholarship, see Elman, *From Philosophy to Philology*.

8. Campany, "Chinese Accounts of the Strange," p. 449.

9. Campany, *Strange Writing*, p. 362.

10. The references to trading and the origins of the merchant tariffs are to a passage of the *Mencius*: "Of old time, the market-dealers exchanged the articles which they had for others which they had not, and simply had certain officers to keep order among them. It happened that there was a mean fellow, who made it a point to look out for a conspicuous mound and get up upon it. Thence he looked right and left, to catch in his net the whole gain of the market. The people all thought his conduct mean, and therefore they proceeded to lay a tax upon his wares. The tax-

ing of traders took its rise from this mean fellow" (trans. Legge, *The Works of Mencius*, pp. 227–28).

11. Sima Qian's account of the origin of money mentions spade-shaped and knife-shaped money: "When the farmers, the artisans, and the merchants first began to exchange articles among themselves, that was when currency came into being—tortoise shells and seashells, gold and copper coins, knife-shaped money and spade-shaped money. Thus its origin is very old" (Sima, *Records of the Grand Historian, Han and Qin*, p. 83).

12. The village trade monopolies in Taiwan were originally established by the Dutch. The Qing government also collected taxes from the indigenous people through Chinese tax farmers or monopoly traders. Under this system, the Chinese tax farmer paid the tribal tax on behalf of the village in return for the privilege of collecting it. He also was granted a trade monopoly over that village.

13. Puli (or Pu'ali) village was located in Danshui subprefecture.

14. The reference is to a passage in the *Chronicle of Zuo*, Xiang 4: "To be on good terms with the Jung [Rong] has five advantages. The Jung and Teih [Di] are continually changing their residence, and are fond of exchanging land for goods. Their lands can be purchased;—this is the first advantage" (Legge, *The Chinese Classics*, 5: 422–24). Wei Jiang was sent by Duke Dao of Jin to make peace with the Rong.

15. See note 14.

16. Deng made no reference to the fact that uxorilocal marriage was practiced in his own time.

17. Several passages in this classic work concern the divorcing of wives or divorced women.

18. A reference to Xi Zhi of Jin from the Spring and Autumn period, who wore crimson leather gaiters.

19. The reference is to a passage in the *Chronicle of Zuo* that describes the battle against the Wu at Ailing.

20. Anli village was located in Danshui subprefecture.

21. Chen Xueyi, "Ti 'Dongfan ji' hou," pp. 27–28.

22. The reference is to Ode 211, "Futian." The couplet reads, "He [the husbandman] will seek for thousands of granaries / He will seek for myriads of carts" (trans. Legge, *The Chinese Classics*, 4: 379). The poem concerns husbandry and agricultural sacrifices, as well as the relationship between the ruling class and commoners.

23. Shuili village was located northwest of Shuishalian.

24. Chushi Shengzi was a man of Wei from the Spring and Autumn period.

25. This notion of barbarians as ancestors of the Chinese in fact dates back to early texts such as the *Mencius* and the *Chronicle of Zuo*. The *Men-*

cius claims that Emperor Shun was an Eastern Barbarian, and that King Wen was a Western Barbarian. The *Chronicle of Zuo* depicts the Dongyi (Eastern Barbarians from an area near Shandong) as ancestors of the Chinese.

26. Cf. *Lunyu* 6.16: "The master said: When substance is ascendant over form, then you have primitiveness; when form is ascendant over substance, then you have ornateness. When form and substance are equally combined, then you have the superior man." Legge's (*Confucius*, p. 190) translation is: "Where the solid qualities are in excess of accomplishments, we have rusticity; where the accomplishments are in excess of the solid qualities, we have the manners of a clerk. When the accomplishments and solid qualities are equally blended, we then have the man of virtue."

27. Deng, *Lice huichao*, pp. 9–11.

28. This phrase was attributed to Zhu Fu, a military commander from the Latter Han; see "The Biography of Zhu Fu," in Fan Ye, *Hou Hanshu jijie*, pp. 401–8.

29. Wu Ziguang, *Taiwan jishi*, p. 27.

30. Ibid., p. 28.

31. Ibid., p. 30. This passage is a reference to the *Book of Rites* description of the practice of calling the soul.

Interlude 2

1. Shepherd, *Statecraft and Political Economy on the Taiwan Frontier*, pp. 161, 394.

2. See Gardella, "From Treaty Ports to Provincial Status."

3. Weiss and Weiss, *The Authentic Story of Taiwan*, p. 136.

Chapter 9

1. Eskildsen, *Foreign Adventurers and the Aborigines of Southern Taiwan*, p. 256.

2. See Eskildsen, "Of Civilization and Savages."

3. Eskildsen, *Foreign Adventurers and the Aborigines of Southern Taiwan*, p. 258.

4. Davidson, *The Island of Formosa*, p. 158.

5. On self-strengthening, see Speidel, "The Administrative and Fiscal Reforms of Liu Ming-ch'uan in Taiwan."

6. By the nineteenth century, the western side of the island was already dominated by the Han Chinese population and was fairly heavily settled.

7. To reverse the Kangxi emperor's words: China "gained much by possessing Taiwan and would lose much in not possessing it."

8. Zhou Zhongxuan, *Zhuluo xianzhi*, p. 295.

9. Luo Dachun, *Taiwan haifang bing kaishan riji*, p. 66.

10. Gardella, "From Treaty Ports to Provincial Status," p. 177.

11. See Eskildsen, "Of Civilization and Savages."

12. Luo Dachun, *Taiwan haifang bing kaishan riji*.

13. Ibid., p. 28.

14. Ibid., p. 34.

15. Ibid., p. 45.

16. Ibid., p. 46.

17. In ibid., pp. 120–21.

18. Luo Dachun, *Taiwan haifang bing kaishan riji*, p. 36.

19. Ibid., p. 70.

20. Kuang, "Taiwan fanshe kao," p. 35.

21. As in eighteenth-century descriptions of the raw and cooked savages, the plains-dwellers are given a more favorable representation than the mountain-dwellers. Kuang, however, placed more emphasis on physical differences between the two types than did eighteenth-century writers.

22. Huang Fengchang, *Taiwan shengshufan jishi*, p. 29.

23. Davidson, *The Island of Formosa*, pp. 110–22.

24. Thus, although he attributed negative qualities to the inborn natures of the savages, he constructed each tribe as possessing its own distinct nature.

25. Luo Dachun, *Taiwan haifang bing kaishan riji*, pp. 53–54.

26. Tu, "Pingpu zuqun fengsu tuxiang ziliao kao," pp. 13–14.

27. In his diary, Luo Dachun (*Taiwan haifang bing kaishan riji*, pp. iv–v) quoted a memorial by Shen that explained the link between opening the mountains and naval defense. Shen wrote: "People only know that today's opening the mountains is for the sake of pacifying the savages; they do not understand that today's pacifying the savages is really for the sake of naval defense. . . . Foreigners are drooling over Taiwan's territory, a situation that is not limited to one day or to one country."

28. Ibid., p. 60.

29. Ibid., p. 3.

30. Ibid., p. 59.

31. Huang Fengchang, *Taiwan shengshufan jishi*, p. 40.

32. See Eskildsen, "Of Civilization and Savages."

33. See Huang Fengchang, *Taiwan shengshufan jishi*.

34. Ibid., p. 52.

35. Chinese literati had long considered the failure to plan for the future as a basic characteristic of barbarians.

36. See Huang Fengchang, *Taiwan shengshufan jishi*; Luo Dachun, *Taiwan haifang bing kaishan riji*.

37. Wu Guangliang in Huang Fengchang, *Taiwan shengshufan jishi*, p. 45.

38. In Huang Fengchang, *Taiwan shengshufan jishi*, p. 51.

39. Shi Mi, "Chouban fandi yi," p. 256.

40. Huang Fengchang, *Taiwan shengshufan jishi*, pp. 37–49.

41. Ibid., p. 53.

42. Weiss and Weiss, *The Authentic Story of Taiwan*, pp. 120–21.

43. Xia Liming, *Qingdai Taiwan ditu yanbianshi*, p. 50.

44. Xia Liming (ibid., p. 63) notes that this was the first map of Taiwan to include, in rough outline, the eastern coastline.

45. Ibid., p. 106.

46. This image of Taiwan as half-Chinese and half-aboriginal was also supported in numerous Western maps of Taiwan, particularly those based on the Jesuit map of 1715; see Weiss and Weiss, *The Authentic Story of Taiwan*.

47. Xia Xianlun, *Taiwan yutu*, p. 1.

48. Ibid.

49. Ibid., p. 75.

50. Ibid., p. 2.

51. See Xia Liming, *Qingdai Taiwan ditu yanbianshi*, p. 52.

52. Xia Xianlun, *Taiwan yutu*, p. 69.

53. Gardella, "From Treaty Ports to Provincial Status," pp. 187–94.

54. Gardella, "From Treaty Ports to Provincial Status"; Myers, "Taiwan Under Ch'ing Imperial Rule"; Speidel, "Liu Ming-ch'uan in Taiwan"; Speidel, "The Administrative and Fiscal Reforms of Liu Ming-ch'uan in Taiwan."

55. Millward, *Beyond the Pass*, pp. 232–52.

Conclusion

1. Chi, *Quan Tai youji*, preface.

2. Ibid., pp. 1–2.

3. See Millward, *Beyond the Pass*, pp. 197–203. I take the term "culture blocs" from Millward.

4. Ibid., p. 197–201.

5. Hevia, *Cherishing Men from Afar*, p. 30.

6. See ibid., pp. 29–56.

7. Ibid., p. 32.

8. Crossley, *A Translucent Mirror*, p. 270.

9. Millward, *Beyond the Pass*, p. 202.

10. Millward, *Beyond the Pass*; Crossley, *A Translucent Mirror*; Crossley, "The Qianlong Retrospect of the Chinese-Martial (*hanjun*) Banners."

11. I am inclined to accept Crossley's use of the term "race," in its early modern sense, as an apt translation of the Chinese term *zu*; see Crossley, "The Qianlong Retrospect of the Chinese-Martial *(hanjun)* Banners."

12. Crossley, "*Manzhou yuanliu kao* and the Formalization of the Manchu Heritage," p. 780.

13. See Millward, *Beyond the Pass*, pp. 194–96.

14. Crossley, "*Manzhou yuanliu kao* and the Formalization of the Manchu Heritage," p. 780.

15. Dorothea Heuschert ("Legal Pluralism in the Qing Empire") has demonstrated that in the Mongol areas of the empire the Qing employed a pluralistic system of law, which mixed Mongol, Manchu, and Han Chinese legal codes and practices. In contrast to the practice in European colonies, Han Chinese living in these areas were tried according to local law and not according to the laws of "China proper." No such pluralistic system existed in Taiwan, which again speaks to the exclusion of the Taiwan indigenes from the Five Nations paradigm and the lower status of their culture in the eyes of the Qing.

16. Crossley, "The Qianlong Retrospect of the Chinese-Martial *(hanjun)* Banners," p. 85.

17. Shepherd, *Statecraft and Political Economy on the Taiwan Frontier*.

18. See ibid., pp. 395–410.

19. Ibid., p. 288.

20. Ka, *Fan toujia*, pp. 35–62.

21. Shepherd, *Statecraft and Political Economy on the Taiwan Frontier*, p. 280.

22. Liu Liangbi, *Chongxiu Fujian Taiwan fuzhi*; Fan Xian, *Chongxiu Taiwan fuzhi*; Wang Yingzeng, *Chongxiu Fengshan xianzhi*; Wang Bichang, *Chongxiu Taiwan xianzhi*.

23. Millward, *Beyond the Pass*, p. 201.

24. Liu Liangbi, *Chongxiu Fujian Taiwan fuzhi*, p. 33.

25. Millward, *Beyond the Pass*, pp. 232–45.

26. Millward (ibid., p. 251) calls this the "Hanization" of the empire.

27. Crossley, *A Translucent Mirror*, p. 347.

28. See Millward, *Beyond the Pass*, p. 251.

29. On nationalist discourse, see Duara, *Rescuing History from the Nation*.

30. Among the most famous group memorials protesting the Treaty of Shimonoseki submitted to the emperor in the spring of 1895 were a memorial signed by seventy scholars from the Hanlin Academy, a memorial signed by 155 officials from the Grand Secretariat, and one signed by 603 candidates for the *jinshi* examination; see Dawley, "Changes from the Periphery," p. 19.

31. See "The One-China Principal and the Taiwan Issue," a report by China's Taiwan Affairs Office and the Information Office of the State Council; excerpted in Foreign Desk, "China's Statement," p. 10. I am using the word "imaginary" here in the sense of "existing only in imagination: lacking factual reality."

Epilogue

1. Thomas, *Colonialism's Culture*, p. 1.
2. Ibid., p. 8.
3. Ching, *Becoming "Japanese."*
4. See Liao, "Postcolonial Studies and Multiculturalism in Taiwan." I do not address the re-colonization issue, which is covered eloquently by Liao.
5. I do not address the question of Taiwan Independence here, for I believe that this question should be settled not on the basis of historical or cultural criteria but by the democratic process. Although there is an implicit link between "decolonization" and "independence," the two concepts are not absolutely intertwined. That is, Taiwanese independence does not require decolonization, nor does decolonization preclude *unification* (not *re*unification) between Taiwan and China.
6. Millward, "New Perspectives on the Qing Frontier," p. 119.
7. Although most Hakka are native to Taiwan, historically they have been marginalized from the construct of "Taiwanese" identity, which is modeled on an idealized Hokkien-speaking (or "Hoklo") subject.
8. Ching, *Becoming "Japanese,"* pp. 19–24.
9. Hind, "The Internal Colonial Concept," p. 559.
10. Ching, *Becoming "Japanese,"* p. 30.
11. See Schein, *Minority Rules.*
12. Hind, "The Internal Colonial Concept." See also Hechter, *Internal Colonialism.*
13 See Adas, "Imperialism and Colonialism in Comparative Perspective," pp. 384–87.
14. Thomas, *Colonialism's Culture*, p. ix.
15. Eskildsen, *Foreign Adventurers and the Aborigines of Southern Taiwan*, p. 260.

Appendix A

1. Sections of this translation were first published as "Exploring China's Last Frontier" and are forthcoming in the *Hawaii Reader of Traditional Chinese Culture*, edited by Victor Mair.

2. Approximately 300,000 kilograms or 660,000 pounds.

3. One *li* is equal to approximately one-half kilometer. In the omitted portion, the author explained that he transferred to an ocean-going sampan.

4. The distances given by Yu in this diary are not necessarily accurate.

5. Admiral Zheng He, the great eunuch commander of the Ming fleet, led seven major naval expeditions between 1405 and 1433, exploring the seas as far as Africa.

6. Now Okinawa, a part of Japan.

7. Tower of the Red Hairs is located in Tainan, Taiwan.

8. This means that they skipped every other rest stop that would normally have been scheduled.

9. One *zhang* is equivalent to approximately 141 inches.

10. A Chinese foot is equivalent to approximately 14.1 English inches.

11. A catty is equivalent to approximately 1.33 pounds.

12. One *mou* is equivalent to approximately 733 square yards.

13. See note 16, p. 300, in Chapter 3.

14. See note 17, p. 300 in Chapter 3.

15. Li Bo (699–762) was a famous Tang dynasty poet and inebriate. Mount Hua is one of the five sacred mountains of China. It is located in modern Shaansi province, in the south of Huayin county. It was traditionally renowned as a Daoist holy place and as a scenic spot.

16. Xie Tiao (464–499) was famous for the originality of the couplets in his landscape poems.

17. Han Yu (768–824) was an eminent poet and essayist of the Tang dynasty.

18. In 803, Han Yu climbed Mount Hua with some companions. It is said in Li Zhao's *Supplement to the State History of the Tang* that when Han reached the summit, he became afraid that he would be unable to descend. He then wept and made out a last will to his family. The magistrate of Huayin eventually reached him and helped him to descend.

19. Penglai is one of three mythical islands of immortals located in the middle of the Eastern Sea. The Ruoshui is the name of a river said to run near the dwelling place of the goddess, the Queen Mother of the West.

20. According to legend, the ancient Emperor Qin Shihuang, founder of the Qin dynasty, sent a mission overseas in search of the three islands of the immortals and the magical herbs of immortality. Another legend has it that Emperor Wudi of the Han once met with the Queen Mother of the West and attempted to obtain the secrets of immortality from her.

21. The three mountains of the immortals are the mythical mountains Fangzhang, Penglai, and Yingzhou, said to be located in the middle of the Eastern Sea.

Appendix B

An earlier version of this translation first appeared as "*A Brief Record of the Eastern Ocean* by Ding Shaoyi," in *Under Confucian Eyes: Texts on Gender in Chinese History*, ed. Susan Mann and Yu-Yin Cheng (University of California Press, 2001), pp. 350–62, 457–61.

1. Earlier Chinese accounts noted that the dead were placed in the house uncoffined or buried under the house. Chen Di, for example, wrote in *Record of the Eastern Savages* (*Dongfan ji*, 1603): "They place the corpse on the ground in the midst of a blazing fire in order to dry it; when it is dried, they place it exposed in the house, uncoffined. When the house is dilapidated and they rebuild it, they dig a pit underneath and bury [the corpse] in a standing position, but with no mound to cover it, and the house is then again raised above it" (trans. from Thompson, "The Earliest Chinese Eyewitness Accounts of the Formosan Aborigines," 174). Here the idea is that the dead are buried apart from the living, a sign of "progress."

2. Ding does not specify the name of the "general" here. This seems fitting as he is relating an item of local lore, not historical fact.

3. The *History of Fujian* (*Minshu*), compiled by He Qiaoyuan (1558–1632), was published around 1628.

4. Zheng He was the famous palace eunuch-admiral who made a series of seven nautical expeditions during the period 1405–33. His voyages took him from Java to Mecca and to the coast of East Africa. One aspect of his diplomatic missions was to issue imperial proclamations declaring the emperor's majesty and virtue and then to obtain tribute from the rulers of various domains. It is still a matter of debate whether Zheng He ever reached the island of Taiwan. As Ding pointed out, this particular story is most likely apocryphal. One of the earliest references to this story can be found in Chen Di's *Record of the Eastern Savages*.

5. *Illustrations of the Flora and Fauna of Taiwan* (*Taihai caifeng tu*) was compiled by Censor Liu-shi-qi ca. 1746.

6. Giulio Aleni (1582–1649) was an Italian Jesuit who lived in China during the Ming. He is the author of a number of works in Chinese, including the *Unofficial Records of a Geographer* (*Zhifang waiji*).

7. This is a reference to a statement made by Lan Dingyuan in his *Record of an Eastern Campaign* (*Dongzheng ji*, 1722) to the effect that the savages had the outer appearance of human beings but lacked the morals of humans.

Works Cited

Adas, Michael. "Imperialism and Colonialism in Comparative Perspective." *International History Review* 20, no. 2 (1998): 371–88.

Anderson, Benedict. *Imagined Communities: Reflections on the Origin and Spread of Nationalism.* Rev. ed. London: Verso, 1991.

Banks, Marcus, and Howard Morphy, eds. *Rethinking Visual Anthropology.* New Haven: Yale University Press, 1997.

Behdad, Ali. *Belated Travelers: Orientalism in the Age of Colonial Dissolution.* Durham, N.C.: Duke University Press, 1994.

Bhabha, Homi K. *The Location of Culture.* London: Routledge, 1994.

Brown, Melissa J. "On Becoming Chinese." In *Negotiating Ethnicities in China and Taiwan,* ed. idem, 37–74. Berkeley: Institute of East Asian Studies and University of California Berkeley, Center for Chinese Studies, 1996.

Cahill, James. *Chinese Painting of the Late Ming Dynasty, 1570–1644.* New York: Weatherhill, 1982.

Campany, Robert. "Chinese Accounts of the Strange: A Study in the History of Religions." Ph.D. diss., University of Chicago, 1988.

———. *Strange Writing: Anomaly Accounts in Early Medieval China.* Albany: SUNY Press, 1996.

Chang, Lung-chih. "From Island Frontier to Imperial Colony: Qing and Japanese Sovereignty Debates and Territorial Projects in Taiwan, 1874–1906." Ph.D. diss., Harvard University, 2003.

Chang Yao-ch'i 張耀錡. "Pingpuzu sheming duizhaobiao" 平埔族社名封照表 (A comparative name list of plains aborigine villages). *Wenxian zhuankan* 文獻專刊 2, no. 1–2 (1951): 1–84.

Chen Di 陳第. *Dongfan ji* 東番記 (Record of the Eastern Savages). In *Minhai zengyan* 閩海贈言 (Words of praise from the Taiwan Sea), ed. Shen Yourong 沈有容, 24–27. TWWX, vol. 56. Taipei: Taiwan yinhang, 1959.

Chen Ding 陳鼎. *Dian Qian tusi hunli ji* 滇黔土司婚禮記 (Marriage rites of the tribal chieftains of Yunnan and Guizhou). 1651.

Chen Lunjiong 陳倫炯. *Haiguo wenjian lu* 海國聞見錄 (Record of things seen and heard at sea). TWWX, vol. 26. Taipei: Taiwan yinhang, 1958.

Chen Wenda 陳文達. *Fengshan xianzhi* 鳳山縣志 (Fengshan county gazetteer). TWWX, vol. 124. Taipei: Taiwan yinhang, 1961.

Chen Xueyi 陳學伊. "Ti *Dongfan ji* hou" 題東番記後 (On Reading Chen Di's *Record of the Eastern Savages*). In *Minhai zengyan* 閩海贈言 (Words of praise from the Taiwan Sea), ed. Shen Yourong 沈有容, 27–28. TWWX, vol. 56. Taipei: Taiwan yinhang, 1959.

Chi Zhizheng 池志徵. *Quan Tai youji* 全臺遊記 (Travelogue of all Taiwan). In *Taiwan youji* 臺灣遊記 (Taiwan travelogues), ed. TYJYS, 1–17. TWWX, vol. 89. Taipei: Taiwan yinhang, 1960.

Chinese Materials and Research Aids Service Center. *Catalog of the Chung-kuo Fang-chih Tsung-shu: Series 1, South China, Central China, North China, Northeast China, Northern Frontiers, Western China.* [Taipei:] CMRASC, 1971.

Ching, Leo T. S. *Becoming "Japanese": Colonial Taiwan and the Politics of Identity Formation.* Berkeley: University of California Press, 2001.

Christensen, Thomas J. "Posing Problems Without Catching Up: China's Rise and Challenge for U.S. Security Policy." *International Security* 25, no. 4 (2001): 5–41.

Clunas, Craig. *Pictures and Visuality in Early Modern China.* Princeton: Princeton University Press, 1997.

Cohen, Marc J., and Emma Teng, eds. *Let Taiwan Be Taiwan: Documents on the International Status of Taiwan.* Washington, D.C.: CTIR Publications, 1990.

Cowling, Mary C. *The Artist as Anthropologist: The Representation of Type and Character in Victorian Art.* New York: Cambridge University Press, 1989.

Crossley, Pamela Kyle. "*Manzhou yuanliu kao* and the Formalization of the Manchu Heritage." *Journal of Asian Studies* 46, no. 4 (Nov. 1987): 761–90.

———. "The Qianlong Retrospect of the Chinese-Martial (*hanjun*) Banners." *Late Imperial China* 10, no. 1 (June 1989): 63–107.

———. "Thinking About Ethnicity in Early Modern China." *Late Imperial China* 11, no. 1 (June 1990): 1–34.

———. *A Translucent Mirror: History and Identity in Qing Imperial Ideology.* Berkeley: University of California Press, 1999.

Davidson, James. *The Island of Formosa: Historical View from 1430 to 1900.* New York: Macmillan, 1903.

Dawley, Evan. "Changes from the Periphery: The Loss of Taiwan and Transformations in Late 19th Century China." Paper presented at the annual meeting of the New England Regional Association for Asian Studies, Oct. 2001.

Deng Chuan'an 鄧傳安. *Lice huichao* 蠡測彙鈔 (Measuring the sea with a calabash). TWWX, vol. 9. Taipei: Taiwan yinhang, 1958.

Diamond, Norma. "Defining the Miao: Ming, Qing, and Contemporary Views." In *Colonial Encounters on China's Ethnic Frontiers*, ed. Stevan Harrell, 92–116. Seattle: University of Washington Press, 1995.

Dikötter, Frank. *The Discourse of Race in Modern China*. Stanford: Stanford University Press, 1992.

Ding Shaoyi 丁紹儀. *Dongying zhilüe* 東瀛識略 (Brief record of the Eastern Ocean). TWWX, vol. 2. Taipei: Taiwan yinhang, 1957.

Dong Tiangong 董天工. *Taihai jianwen lu* 臺海見聞錄 (Record of things seen and heard in the Taiwan Strait). TWWX, vol. 129. Taipei: Taiwan yinhang, 1961.

Doyle, Michael. *Empires*. Ithaca: Cornell University Press, 1986.

Duara, Prasenjit. *Rescuing History from the Nation: Questioning Narratives of Modern China*. Chicago: University of Chicago Press, 1995.

Ebrey, Patricia Buckley, ed. *Chinese Civilization: A Sourcebook*. 2nd ed. New York: Free Press, 1993.

Edney, Matthew. *Mapping an Empire: The Geographical Construction of British India*. Chicago: Chicago University Press, 1997.

Elman, Benjamin A. *From Philosophy to Philology: Intellectual and Social Aspects of Change in Late Imperial China*. Harvard East Asian Monographs 110. Cambridge, Mass.: Council on East Asian Studies, Harvard University, 1984.

———. "Geographical Research in the Ming-Ch'ing Period." *Monumenta Serica* 35 (1981–83): 1–18.

Eskildsen, Robert. "Of Civilization and Savages: The Mimetic Imperialism of Japan's 1874 Expedition to Taiwan." *American Historical Review* 107, no. 2 (Apr. 2002): 388–418.

Eskildsen, Robert, ed. *Foreign Adventurers and the Aborigines of Southern Taiwan, 1867–1874: Western Sources Related to Japan's 1874 Expedition to Taiwan*. Taipei: Institute of Taiwan History, Academia Sinica, forthcoming.

Etherington, Dan M., and Keith Forster. *Green Gold: The Political Economy of China's Post-1949 Tea Industry*. Hong Kong: Oxford University Press, 1993.

Fabian, Johannes. *Time and the Other: How Anthropology Makes Its Object*. New York: Columbia University Press, 1983.

Fairbank, John King, ed. *The Chinese World Order: Traditional China's Foreign Relations*. Cambridge, Mass.: Harvard University Press, 1968.

Fan Xian 范咸, ed. *Chongxiu Taiwan fuzhi* 重修臺灣府志 (Newly revised gazetteer of Taiwan prefecture). 1747. TWWX, vol. 105. Taipei: Taiwan yinhang, 1961.

Fan Ye 范曄. *Hou Hanshu jijie* 後漢書集解, vol. 1. Beijing: Zhonghua shuju, 1984.

Foreign Desk. "China's Statement: 'The Right to Resort to Any Necessary Means.'" *New York Times*, Feb. 22, 2000, Sect. A, p. 10.

Fung, Yu lan. *A History of Chinese Philosophy*, vol. 1. Trans. Derk Bodde. Princeton: Princeton University Press, 1952.

Gao Gongqian 高拱乾, ed. *Taiwan fuzhi* 臺灣府志 (Gazetteer of Taiwan prefecture). 1696. TWWX, vol. 65. Taipei: Taiwan yinhang, 1960.

Gardella, Robert. "From Treaty Ports to Provincial Status, 1860–1894." In *Taiwan: A New History*, ed. Murray A. Rubinstein, 163–200. Armonk, N.Y.: M. E. Sharpe, 1999.

Gaubatz, Piper Rae. *Beyond the Great Wall: Urban Form and Transformation on the Chinese Frontiers*. Stanford: Stanford University Press, 1996.

Geertz, Clifford. *Works and Lives: The Anthropologist as Author*. Stanford: Stanford University Press, 1988.

Giersch, C. Pat. "'A Motley Throng': Social Change on Southwest China's Early Modern Frontier, 1700–1880." *Journal of Asian Studies* 60, no. 1 (Feb. 2001): 67–94.

Gladney, Dru. *Muslim Chinese: Ethnic Nationalism in the People's Republic*. Cambridge, Mass.: Council on East Asian Studies, Harvard University, 1991.

———. "Representing Nationality in China: Refiguring Majority/Minority Identities." *Journal of Asian Studies* 53, no. 1 (1994): 92–123.

Godlewska, Anne. "Map, Text, and Image: The Mentality of Enlightened Conquerors. A New Look at the *Description de l'Egypt*." *Transactions of the Institute of British Geographers*, n.s. 20 (1995): 5–28.

Greenblatt, Stephen, ed. *New World Encounters*. Berkeley: University of California Press, 1993.

Gregory, Derek. *Geographical Imaginations*. Cambridge, Mass.: Blackwell, 1994.

Hao Yulin 郝玉麟. *Fujian tongzhi* 福建通志 (Gazetteer of Fujian province). 1737. In *Yingyin Wenyuange siku quanshu* 影印文淵閣四庫全書, vols. 527–30. Taipei: Taiwan shangwu, 1983.

Harrell, Stevan. "Introduction: Civilizing Projects and the Reaction to Them." In *Cultural Encounters on China's Ethnic Frontiers*, ed. idem, 3–36. Seattle: University of Washington Press, 1995.

Harrell, Stevan, ed. *Cultural Encounters on China's Ethnic Frontiers*. Seattle: University of Washington Press, 1995.

Hartman, Charles. *Han Yu and the T'ang Search for Unity*. Princeton: Princeton University Press, 1986.

Hechter, Michael. *Internal Colonialism: The Celtic Fringe in British National Development*. New Brunswick, N.J.: Transaction, 1999.

Henderson, John B. "Chinese Cosmographical Thought: The High Intellectual Tradition." In *The History of Cartography*, vol. 2, book 2, *Cartography in the Traditional East and Southeast Asian Societies*, ed. J. B. Harley and David Woodward, 203–21. Chicago: University of Chicago Press, 1994.

Herman, John E. "Empire in the Southwest: Early Qing Reforms to the Native Chieftain System." *Journal of Asian Studies* 56, no. 1 (Feb. 1997): 47–74.

Heuschert, Dorothea. "Legal Pluralism in the Qing Empire: Manchu Legislation for the Mongols." *International History Review* 20, no. 2 (June 1998): 310–24.

Hevia, James L. *Cherishing Men from Afar: Qing Guest Ritual and the Macartney Embassy of 1793*. Durham, N.C.: Duke University Press, 1995.

Hind, Robert. "The Internal Colonial Concept." *Comparative Studies in Society and History* 26, no. 3 (July 1984): 543–68.

Hostetler, Laura. *Qing Colonial Enterprise: Ethnography and Cartography in Early Modern China*. Chicago: University of Chicago Press, 2001.

Hu, Philip K., ed. *Visible Traces: Rare Books and Special Collections from the National Library of China*. Queens, N.Y.: Queens Borough Public Library, 2000.

Huang Fengchang 黃逢昶. *Taiwan shengshufan jishi* 臺灣生熟番紀事 (Notes on Taiwan's cooked and raw savages). TWWX, vol. 51. Taipei: Taiwan yinhang, 1960.

Huang Qing zhigong tu 皇清職貢圖. In *Yingyin Wenyuange siku quanshu* 影印文淵閣四庫全書, vol. 594. Taipei: Taiwan shangwu, 1984.

Huang Shujing 黃叔璥. *Taihai shicha lu* 臺海使槎錄 (Record of a tour of duty in the Taiwan Strait). TWWX, vol. 4. Taipei: Taiwan yinhang, 1957.

Huang Shujing 黃叔璥, attr. *Taiwan fanshe tu* 臺灣番社圖 (A map of Taiwan's savage villages). Kangxi era. Held at National Taiwan Museum, Taipei.

JanMohammed, Abdul R. "The Economy of Manichean Allegory: The Function of Racial Difference in Colonialist Literature." In *Critical Inquiry* 12, no. 1 (1985): 59–87.

Ji Qiguang 季麒光. *Taiwan zaji* 臺灣雜記 (Miscellaneous records of Taiwan). In *Taiwan yudi huichao* 臺灣輿地彙鈔 (Collected works on Taiwan's geography), ed. TYJYS, 1–2. TWWX, vol. 216. Taipei: Taiwan yinhang, 1965.

Jia Ning 賈寧. "Chen Di yu *Dongfan ji*" 陳第與東番記 (Chen Di and the *Record of the Eastern Savages*). *Zhongyang minzu xueyuan xuebao* 中央民族學院學報 3 (Mar. 1983): 45–51.

Jiang Shiche 蔣師轍. *Taiyou riji* 臺遊日記 (Travelogue of Taiwan). TWWX, vol. 6. Taipei: Taiwan yinhang, 1957.

Jiang Yuying 蔣毓英, ed. *Taiwan fuzhi* 臺灣府誌 (Gazetteer of Taiwan prefecture). 1685. Beijing: Zhonghua shuju, 1985.

Jin Hong 金鋐, ed. *Fujian tongzhi* 福建通志 (Gazetteer of Fujian province). 1684. Beijing tushuguan guji zhenben congkan, vol. 35. Beijing: Shumu wenxian chubanshe, 1988.

Ka Chih-ming 柯志明. *Fan toujia* 番頭家 (The aborigine landlord: ethnic politics and aborigine land rights in Qing Taiwan). Taipei: Institute of Sociology, Academia Sinica, 2001.

Kawakatsu Yoshio 川勝義雄. *Gi Shin Nambokuchō* 魏晉南北朝 (The Wei, Jin, and Northern and Southern Dynasties). Chūgoku no rekishi 中国の歴史 (Chinese history), vol. 3. Tokyo: Kosaido, 1974.

Ke Peiyuan 柯培元. *Gemalan zhilüe* 葛瑪蘭志略 (Gazetteer of Gemalan). 1835. TWWX, vol. 92. Taipei: Taiwan yinhang, 1961.

Knapp, Ronald G. *China's Island Frontier: Studies in the Historical Geography of Taiwan*. Honolulu: University of Hawaii Press, 1980.

———. "Chinese Frontier Settlement in Taiwan." *Annals of the Association of American Geographers* 66 (1976): 43–59.

Knoblock, John. *Xunzi: A Translation and Study of the Complete Works*. 3 vols. Stanford: Stanford University Press, 1988, 1990, 1994.

Ko, Dorothy. *Teachers of the Inner Chambers: Women and Culture in Seventeenth-Century China*. Stanford: Stanford University Press, 1994.

Kuang Qizhao 鄺其照. *Taiwan fanshe kao* 臺灣番社考 (Investigation of Taiwan's savage villages). In *Taiwan yudi huichao* 臺灣輿地彙鈔 (Collected works on Taiwan's geography), ed. TYJYS, 35–40. TWWX, vol. 216. Taipei: Taiwan yinhang, 1965.

Lan Dingyuan 藍鼎元. *Dongzheng ji* 東征集 (Record of the eastern campaign). TWWX, vol. 12. Taipei: Taiwan yinhang, 1958.

———. *Pingtai jilüe* 平臺記略 (Record of the pacification of Taiwan). TWWX, vol. 14. Taipei: Taiwan yinhang, 1958.

Lee, Leo Ou-fan. *Shanghai Modern: The Flowering of a New Urban Culture in China, 1930–1945*. Cambridge, Mass.: Harvard University Press, 1999.

Legge, James, trans. *The Chinese Classics*. 5 vols. 1895. Reprinted—Hong Kong: Hong Kong University Press, 1960.

———. *Confucius: Confucian Analects, the Great Learning, and the Doctrine of Mean*. New York: Dover, 1971.

———. *The Li Chi*. Hong Kong: Hong Kong University Press, 1967.

———. *The Sacred Books of China: The Texts of Confucianism*, vols. 3–4, *The Li Ki*. Oxford: Clarendon Press, 1885.

———. *The Works of Mencius*. New York: Dover, 1970.

Lévi-Strauss, Claude. *The Raw and the Cooked*. Trans. John Weightman and Doreen Weightman. Chicago: University of Chicago Press, 1964, 1983.

Lewis, Mark Edward. *Writing and Authority in Early China*. Albany: SUNY Press, 1999.

Liao, Ping-hui. "Postcolonial Studies and Multiculturalism in Taiwan: Issues in Critical Debates." Working Papers Series, Washington State University, Department of Comparative American Cultures, 2000: 1–16.

Lidai dili zhizhang tu 歷代地理指掌圖 (Easy-to-use maps of geography through the dynasties). Ming. Held at Taiwan National Palace Museum, Taipei.

Lin Qianguang 林謙光. *Taiwan jilüe* 臺灣紀略 (Brief notes on Taiwan). TWWX, vol. 104. Taipei: Taiwan yinhang, 1966.

Liu Liangbi 劉良璧, ed. *Chongxiu Fujian Taiwan fuzhi* 重修福建臺灣府志 (Newly revised gazetteer of Taiwan prefecture, Fujian). 1742. TWWX, vol. 74. Taipei: Taiwan yinhang, 1961.

Liu-shi-qi 六十七. *Fanshe caifeng tukao* 番社采風圖考 (Illustrations of the savage villages). TWWX, vol. 90. Taipei: Taiwan yinhang, 1961.

Lowe, Lisa. *Critical Terrains: French and British Orientalism*. Ithaca, N.Y.: Cornell University Press, 1991.

Lu Zhiyu 魯之裕. *Taiwan shimo ouji* 臺灣始末偶紀 (Random notes on Taiwan from beginning to end). In *Taiwan yudi huichao* 臺灣輿地彙鈔 (Collected works on Taiwan's geography), ed. TYJYS, 9–10. TWWX, vol. 216. Taipei: Taiwan yinhang, 1965.

Luo Bi 羅泌. *Lushi* 路史 (A grand history). Shanghai: Hanfenlou, 1920.

Luo Dachun 羅大春. *Taiwan haifang bing kaishan riji* 臺灣海防並開山日記 (Diary of Taiwan's naval defense and opening the mountains). TWWX, vol. 308. Taipei: Taiwan yinhang, 1972.

Luo Zhufeng 羅竹風, ed. *Hanyu dacidian* 漢語大詞典. Hong Kong: Joint Publishing, 1988.

Ma Huan 馬歡. *Yingya shenglan* 瀛涯勝覽 (The overall survey of the ocean's shores). Trans. J. V. G. Mills as *Yingya shenglan*: "The Overall Survey of the Ocean's Shores." Cambridge, Eng.: Cambridge University Press for the Hakluyt Society, 1970.

McClintock, Anne. *Imperial Leather: Race, Gender and Sexuality in the Colonial Contest.* New York: Routledge, 1995.

McKann, Charles. "The Naxi and the Nationalities Question." In *Colonial Encounters on China's Ethnic Frontiers,* ed. Stevan Harrell. Seattle: University of Washington Press, 1995.

Meskill, Johanna Menzel. *A Chinese Pioneer Family: The Lins of Wu-feng, Taiwan, 1729–1895.* Princeton: Princeton University Press, 1979.

Millward, James A. *Beyond the Pass: Economy, Ethnicity, and Empire in Qing Central Asia, 1759–1864.* Stanford: Stanford University Press, 1998.

———. "'Coming Onto the Map': 'Western Regions' Geography and Cartographic Nomenclature in the Making of Chinese Empire in Xinjiang." *Late Imperial China* 20, no. 2 (Dec. 1999): 61–98.

———. "New Perspectives on the Qing Frontier." In *Remapping China: Fissures in Historical Terrain,* ed. Gail Hershatter, Emily Honig, Jonathan N. Lipman, and Randall Stross, 113–29. Stanford: Stanford University Press, 1996.

Morgan, Susan. *Place Matters: Gendered Geography in Victorian Women's Travel Books About Southeast Asia.* New Brunswick, N.J.: Rutgers University Press, 1996.

Myers, Ramon. "Taiwan Under Ch'ing Imperial Rule, 1684–1895: The Traditional Economy." *Journal of the Institute of Chinese Studies of the Chinese University of Hong Kong* 5, no. 2 (1972): 373–409.

Needham, Joseph. *The Shorter Science and Civilization in China,* vol. 2. New York: Cambridge University Press, 1981.

Pagden, Anthony. "*Ius et Factum*: Text and Experience in the Writings of Bartolome de Las Casas." In *New World Encounters,* ed. Stephen Greenblatt, 85–100. Berkeley: University of California Press, 1993.

Parry, Benita. "Problems in Current Theories of Colonial Discourse." *Oxford Literary Review* 9, no. 1–2 (1987): 27–58.

Perdue, Peter C. "Boundaries, Maps, and Movement: Chinese, Russian, and Mongolian Empires in Early Modern Central Eurasia." *International History Review* 20, no. 2 (1998): 263–86.

———. *China Marches West: The Qing Conquest of Central Eurasia, 1600–1800.* Cambridge, Mass.: Harvard University Press, forthcoming.

———. "Comparing Empires: Manchu Colonialism." *International History Review* 20, no. 2 (June 1998): 255–62.

Pingpu wenhua zixunwang 平埔文化資訊網 (Website of Plains Aborigine culture). Institute of Ethnology, Academia Sinica, Taiwan, 2000 (accessed Jan. 23, 2001). Available at www.sinica.edu.tw/~pingpu/index.html.

Pratt, Mary Louise. *Imperial Eyes: Travel Writing and Transculturation.* New York: Routledge, 1992.

Qing huidian Taiwan shili (Taiwan precedents from the Qing Institutes). TWWX, vol. 226. Taipei: Taiwan yinhang, 1966.

The Republic of China at a Glance (website; closed). Government Information Office, Taiwan, 2001 (accessed Jan. 23, 2001).

Rubinstein, Murray A., ed. *Taiwan: A New History.* Armonk, N.Y.: M. E. Sharpe, 1999.

Said, Edward. *Culture and Imperialism.* New York: Vintage Books, 1993.

——. *Orientalism.* 1st ed. New York: Pantheon Books, 1978.

Schaberg, David. "Foundations of Chinese Historiography: Literary Representation in *Zuozhuan* and *Guoyu.*" Ph.D. diss., Harvard University, 1995.

Schafer, Edward H. *The Golden Peaches of Samarkand: A Study of T'ang Exotics.* Berkeley: University of California Press, 1963.

——. *The Vermilion Bird: Tang Images of the South.* Berkeley: University of California Press, 1967.

Schein, Louisa. "Gender and Internal Orientalism in China." *Modern China* 23, no. 1 (1997): 69–98.

——. *Minority Rules: The Miao and the Feminine in China's Cultural Politics.* Durham, N.C.: Duke University Press, 2000.

Schwartz, Joan M. "The Geography Lesson: Photographs and the Construction of Imaginative Geographies." *Journal of Historical Geography* 22 (1996): 16–45.

Shen Qiyuan 沈起元. "Tiaochen Taiwan shiyi zhuang" 條陳臺灣事宜狀 (A detailed statement on Taiwan matters). In *Qing jingshi wenbian xuanlu* 清經世文編選錄 (Selected writings on Taiwan statecraft), 2–5. TWWX, vol. 229. Taipei: Taiwan yinhang, 1966.

Shen Yourong 沈有容, ed. *Minhai zengyan* 閩海贈言 (Words of praise from the Taiwan Sea). TWWX, vol. 56. Taipei: Taiwan yinhang, 1959.

Shepherd, John. *Statecraft and Political Economy on the Taiwan Frontier, 1600–1800.* Stanford: Stanford University Press, 1993.

Shi Lang 施琅. *Jinghai jishi* 靖海紀事 (Record of pacifying the seas). TWWX, vol. 13. Taipei: Taiwan yinhang, 1958.

Shi Mi 史密. "Chouban fandi yi" 籌辦番地議 (Proposal for the dispensation of savage lands). In *Zhi Tai bigao lu* 治臺必告錄 (Records on Taiwan governance), ed. Ding Yuejian 丁曰健, 252–58. TWWX, vol. 17. Taipei: Taiwan yinhang, 1959.

Shi Tianfu 施添福. "Taiwan lishi dili yanjiu daji" 臺灣歷史地理研究搭記 (Research notes on Taiwan's historical geography). *Taiwan fengwu* 臺灣風物 39, no. 2 (1989): 95–98.

Sima Qian. *Records of the Grand Historian, Han and Qin.* Trans. Burton Watson. 3 vols. New York: Columbia University Press, 1993.

Smith, Richard J. *Chinese Maps: Images of "All Under Heaven."* New York: Oxford University Press, 1996.

———. "Mapping China's World: Cultural Cartography in Late Imperial Times." In *Landscape, Culture and Power in Chinese Society*, ed. Wenhsin Yeh, 52–109. Berkeley: University of California, Center for East Asian Studies, 1988.

Song Guangyu 宋光宇, ed. *Huanan bianjiang minzu tulu* 華南邊疆民族圖錄 (Illustrations of frontier minorities of southern China). Taipei: National Central Library, 1991.

Speidel, William M. "The Administrative and Fiscal Reforms of Liu Ming-ch'uan in Taiwan, 1884–1891: Foundation for Self-strengthening." *Journal of Asian Studies* 35, no. 3 (May 1976): 441–59.

———. "Liu Ming-ch'uan in Taiwan, 1884–1891." Ph.D. diss., Yale University, 1967.

Spurr, David. *The Rhetoric of Empire: Colonial Discourse in Journalism, Travel Writing, and Imperial Administration.* Durham, N.C.: Duke University Press, 1993.

Stainton, Michael. "The Politics of Taiwan Aboriginal Origins." In *Taiwan: A New History*, ed. Murray A. Rubinstein, 27–44. Armonk, N.Y.: M. E. Sharpe, 1999.

Stocking, George W., Jr. *Race, Culture, and Evolution: Essays in the History of Anthropology.* Rev. ed. Chicago: University of Chicago Press, 1982.

Stoler, Ann Laura. "Rethinking Colonial Categories: European Communities and the Boundaries of Rule." *Comparative Studies in Society and History* 31 (1989): 134–61.

Strassberg, Richard E. *Inscribed Landscapes: Travel Writing from Imperial China.* Trans. idem. Berkeley: University of California, 1994.

Sze, Mai-mai, ed. *The Mustard Seed Garden Manual of Painting.* Bollingen. Princeton: Princeton University Press, 1992.

Taiping guangji 太平廣記 (Accounts widely gathered in the Taiping era). Taipei: Wenshizhi chubanshe, 1987.

Taiwan fanjie tu 臺灣番界圖 (Map of Taiwan's savage boundary). Qianlong era, ca. 1760. Held at Fu Ssu-nien Library, Academia Sinica, Taiwan.

Taiwan Yearbook 2003 (website). Government Information Office, Republic of China (Taiwan), 2003 (accessed Sept. 9, 2003). Available from www.gio.tw/taiwan-website/5-gp/yearbook/chpt02.html.

Taiwan yinhang jingji yanjiushi (TYJYS) 臺灣銀行經濟研究室, ed. *Liuqiu yu Jilongshan* 流求與雞籠山 (The Ryukyus and Mount Jilong). TWWX, vol. 96. Taipei: Taiwan yinhang, 1964.

————. *Qing Gaozong shilu xuanji* 清高宗實錄選輯 (Selections from the Veritable Records of the Qianlong reign). TWWX, vol. 186. Taipei: Taiwan yinhang, 1964.

————. *Qing Shengzu shilu xuanji* 清聖宗實錄選輯 (Selections from the Veritable Records of the Kangxi reign). TWWX, vol. 165. Taipei: Taiwan yinhang, 1963.

————. *Qing zhigong tu xuan* 清職貢圖選 (Selected drawings of Qing tribute bearers). TWWX, vol. 180. Taipei: Taiwan yinhang, 1963.

————. *Taiwan wenxian congkan* 臺灣文獻叢刊 (Taiwan literary collectanea; TWWX). 309 vols. Taipei: Taiwan yinhang, 1957–72.

————. *Taiwan yudi huichao* 臺灣輿地彙鈔 (Collected works on Taiwan's geography). TWWX, vol. 216. Taipei: Taiwan yinhang, 1965.

Teng, Emma Jinhua. "A Brief Record of the Eastern Ocean by Ding Shaoyi." In *Under Confucian Eyes: Texts on Gender in Chinese History*, ed. Susan Mann and Yu-yin Cheng, 350–62, 457–61. Berkeley: University of California Press, 2001.

————. "Exploring China's Last Frontier: Excerpts from Yu Yonghe's *Small Sea Travelogue*." *Asian Pacific American Journal* 4, no. 1 (1995): 89–107.

————. "An Island of Women: The Discourse of Gender in Qing Travel Accounts of Taiwan." *International History Review* 20, no. 2 (June 1998): 353–70.

————. "*Pihai jiyou*: An Early Exploration Account of Taiwan." In *Hawaii Reader of Traditional Chinese Culture*, ed. Victor Mair. Honolulu: University of Hawaii Press, forthcoming.

————. "Taiwan as a Living Museum: Tropes of Anachronism in Late-Imperial Chinese Travel Writing." *Harvard Journal of Asiatic Studies* 59, no. 2 (Dec. 1999): 445–84.

————. "Texts on the Right and Pictures on the Left: Reading the Qing Record of Frontier Taiwan." In *Writing and Materiality in China*, ed. Judith T. Zeitlin and Lydia H. Liu, 451–87. Cambridge, Mass.: Harvard University Asia Center, 2003.

————. "Travel Writing and Colonial Collecting: Chinese Travel Accounts of Taiwan from the Seventeenth Through Nineteenth Centuries." Ph.D. diss., Harvard University, 1997.

Thomas, Nicholas. *Colonialism's Culture: Anthropology, Travel, and Government*. Princeton: Princeton University Press, 1994.

Thompson, Laurence. "The Earliest Chinese Eyewitness Accounts of the Formosan Aborigines." *Monumenta Serica* 23 (1964): 163–204.

Thongchai Winichakul. *Siam Mapped: A History of the Geo-Body of a Nation*. Honolulu: University of Hawaii Press, 1994.

Tu Cheng-sheng 杜正勝. "Pingpu zuqun fengsu tuxiang ziliao kao" 平埔族群風俗圖像資料考 (Study of research materials on ethnographic illustrations of the Plains Aborigines). Paper presented at the Pingpu zuqun yu Taiwan lishi wenhua conference 平埔族群與臺灣歷史文化會, Academia Sinica, Taiwan, 1998.

TYJYS, see Taiwan yinhang jingji yanjiushi 臺灣銀行經濟研究室

Waldron, Arthur. *The Great Wall of China: From History to Myth*. Cambridge, Eng.: Cambridge University Press, 1990.

Wang Bichang 王必昌. *Chongxiu Taiwan xianzhi* 重修臺灣縣志 (Gazetteer of Taiwan county, revised). 1752. TWWX, vol. 113. Taipei: Taiwan yinhang, 1961.

Wang Xianqian 王先謙, ed. *Zhuangzi jijie* 莊子集解 (Collected explanations of the *Zhuangzi*). Beijing: Zhonghua shuju, 1954.

Wang Yingzeng 王瑛曾, ed. *Chongxiu Fengshan xianzhi* 重修鳳山縣志 (Gazetteer of Fengshan county, revised). 1762. TWWX, vol. 146. Taipei: Taiwan yinhang, 1962.

Weiss, H., and B. J. Weiss, eds. *The Authentic Story of Taiwan*. Knokke, Belgium: Mappamundi, 1991.

West, Stephen H. "The Overflowing Well: Esthetic and Gendered Borders in the Song-Jin Imagination." Unpublished paper, n.d.

Wiens, Herold J. *China's March Toward the Tropics*. Hamden, Conn.: Shoe String Press, 1954.

Williams, Raymond. *Keywords: A Vocabulary of Culture and Society*. Rev. ed. New York: Oxford University Press, 1983.

Wong, Sau-ling. "Ethnicizing Gender: An Exploration of Sexuality as a Sign in Chinese Immigrant Literature." In *Reading the Literatures of Asian America*, ed. Shirley Geok-lin Lim and Amy Ling, 111–30. Philadelphia: Temple University Press, 1992.

Wu Chenchen 吳桭臣. *Minyou ouji* 閩遊偶記 (Random notes on Fujian travels). In *Taiwan yudi huichao* 臺灣輿地彙鈔 (Collected works on Taiwan's geography), ed. TYJYS, 11–28. TWWX, vol. 216. Taipei: Taiwan yinhang, 1965.

Wu Ziguang 吳子光. *Taiwan jishi* 臺灣紀事 (Taiwan memoranda). TWWX, vol. 36. Taipei: Taiwan yinhang, 1959.

Xia Liming 夏黎明. *Qingdai Taiwan ditu yanbianshi* 清代臺灣地圖演變史 (History of the development of maps of Taiwan during the Qing dynasty). Taipei: Zhishufan chubanshe, 1996.

Xia Xianlun 夏獻綸. *Taiwan yutu* 臺灣輿圖 (Geographic maps of Taiwan). TWWX, vol. 45. Taipei: Taiwan yinhang, 1959.

Xie Jinluan 謝金鑾, ed. *Xuxiu Taiwan xianzhi* 續修臺灣縣志 (Gazetteer of Taiwan county, revised). 1807. TWWX, vol. 140. Taipei: Taiwan yinhang, 1962.

Xu Huaizu 許懷祖. *Taiwan suibi* 臺灣隨筆 (Random jottings on Taiwan). In *Taiwan yudi huichao* 臺灣輿地彙鈔 (Collected works on Taiwan's geography), ed. TYJYS, 3–8. TWWX, vol. 216. Taipei: Taiwan yinhang, 1965.

Yang Baiyuan 楊百元. "Jinru wenming lingyu de bensheng shandi funü" 進入文明領域的本省山地婦女. *Taiwan wenxian* 19, no. 4 (1968) 163–69.

Yee, Cordell D. K. "Chinese Cartography Among the Arts: Objectivity, Subjectivity, Representation." In *The History of Cartography*, vol. 2, book 2, *Cartography in the Traditional East and Southeast Asian Societies*, ed. J. B. Hartley and David Woodward, 128–69. Chicago: University of Chicago Press, 1994.

———. "Chinese Maps in Political Culture." In *The History of Cartography*, vol. 2, book 2, *Cartography in the Traditional East and Southeast Asian Societies*, ed. J. B. Hartley and David Woodward, 71–95. Chicago: University of Chicago Press, 1994.

———. "Reinterpreting Traditional Chinese Geographical Maps." In *The History of Cartography*, vol. 2, book 2, *Cartography in the Traditional East and Southeast Asian Societies*, ed. J. B. Hartley and David Woodward, 35–70. Chicago: University of Chicago Press, 1994.

———. "Taking the World's Measure: Chinese Maps Between Observation and Text." In *The History of Cartography*, vol. 2, book 2, *Cartography in the Traditional East and Southeast Asian Societies*, ed. J. B. Hartley and David Woodward, 96–127. Chicago: University of Chicago Press, 1994.

———. "Traditional Chinese Cartography and the Myth of Westernization." In *The History of Cartography*, vol. 2, book 2, *Cartography in the Traditional East and Southeast Asian Societies*, ed. J. B. Harley and David Woodward, 170–202. Chicago: University of Chicago Press, 1994.

Young, Robert. *Colonial Desire: Hybridity in Theory, Culture and Race*. New York: Routledge, 1995.

Yu Weichao, ed. *A Journey into China's Antiquity*, vol. 4. National Museum of Chinese History. Beijing: Morning Glory Publishers, 1997.

Yu Yonghe 郁永河. *Pihai jiyou* 裨海記遊 (Small sea travelogue). TWWX, vol. 44. Taipei: Taiwan yinhang, 1959.

Zeitlin, Judith. *Historian of the Strange: Pu Songling and the Chinese Classical Tale*. Stanford: Stanford University Press, 1993.

Zhai Hao 翟灝. *Taiyang biji* 臺陽筆記 (Notation book on Taiwan). TWWX, vol. 20. Taipei: Taiwan yinhang, 1958.

Zhongguo diyi lishi dang'an'guan 中國第一歷史檔案館, ed. *Kangxi qiju zhu* 康熙起居注 (Record of the Kangxi emperor's daily actions, from rising to retiring), vol. 2. Beijing: Zhonghua shuju, 1984.

Zhou Yuanwen 周元文, ed. *Chongxiu Taiwan fuzhi* 重修臺灣府志 (Gazetteer of Taiwan prefecture, newly revised). 1712. TWWX, vol. 66. Taipei: Taiwan yinhang, 1960.

Zhou Zhongxuan 周鍾瑄, ed. *Zhuluo xianzhi* 諸羅縣志 (Gazetteer of Zhuluo county). 1717. TWWX, vol. 141. Taipei: Taiwan yinhang, 1962.

Zhuang Jifa 莊吉發, ed. *Gugong Taiwan shiliao gaishu* 故宮臺灣史料概述 (Summary of historical materials on Taiwan in the Palace Museum). Taipei: National Palace Museum, 1995.

———. *Xie Sui "Zhigong tu" Manwen tushuo jiaozhu* 謝遂《職貢圖》滿文圖説校註 (Xie Sui's Manchu version of the *Qing Imperial Tribute Illustrations*). Taipei: National Palace Museum, 1989.

Zhuang Jinde 莊金德. "Lan Dingyuan di zhi Tai danglun" 藍鼎元的治臺讜論 (The remonstrances of Lan Dingyuan on the governance of Taiwan). *Taiwan wenxian* 臺灣文獻 17, no. 2 (1966): 1–27.

Zhuoyuanting zhuren 酌元亭主人. "Zou Annan yuma huan xingrong" 走安南玉馬換猩絨 (On a journey to Vietnam a jade horse miniature is exchanged for crimson velvet). In *Zhaoshi bei* 照世杯 (The cup that reflects the world), 53–63. Shanghai: Shanghai gudian wenxue chubanshe, 1956.

Character List

The entries are ordered letter by letter, ignoring word and syllable breaks, with the exception of personal names, which are ordered by surname and then by given name.

baimiao 白描
Bai Miao tu 百苗圖
banju neishan shufan 半居內山
　熟番
bantu 版圖
Baodao 寶島
Baozhu 寶珠
bi 蔽
bian 變
biange 變革
bianhai shufan 邊海熟番
Bianjiang wuzhong 邊疆五種
bie 別
biezhong 別種
Binfengtu 豳風圖

Cai Fangbing 蔡方炳
cailian qu 採蓮曲
cang 藏
Canglang 滄浪
Cao Junyi 曹君義
caodi 草地
Chen Bishen 陳必琛
Chen Di 陳第
Chen Liang 陳亮

Chen Lunjiong 陳倫炯
Chen Wenda 陳文達
Chen Xueyi 陳學伊
chenglan 呈覽
Chi Zhizheng 池志徵
chizi 赤子
chong 重
Chouban fandi yi 籌辦番地議
Chuci 楚詞
chulei 畜類
Chunqiu 春秋
cun 村

Da Ming yitong zhi 大明一統志
Da Qing 大清
Da Qing yitong yutu 大清一統
　輿圖
Da Qing yitong zhi 大清一統志
Daode jing 道德經
Daoyi zhilüe 島夷志略
datong 大同
Deng Chuan'an 鄧傳安
Dianyi tushuo 滇夷圖說
dili 地理
dili zhi 地理志

Ding Shaoyi 丁紹儀
diqi 地氣
ditu 地圖
dongfan 東番
Dongfan ji 東番記
dongfan zhi yi 東番之夷
Dongning Chenshi fansu tu 東寧
    陳氏番俗圖
dongyi 東夷
Dongying zhilüe 東瀛識略
Dongzheng ji 東征集

e 惡
Erya 爾雅

fan 番
Fan 蕃
Fan Chuo 范綽
Fan Xian 范咸
fanben xiugu 反本修古
Fang Junyi 方濬頤
Fangzhang 方丈
fanjie 番界
fanjing 番境
fanli 藩籬
fanmin 番民
fanshe fengsu tong 番社風俗通
"Fansu jingu shuo" 番俗近古說
Fansu liukao 番俗六考
fei renlei 非人類
fei wo zulei, qi xin bi yi 非我族類
    其心必異
fenbie 分別
feng 風
Fengshan xianzhi 鳳山縣志
fengshui 風水
fengsu 風俗
Fengsu tongyi 風俗通義
fengsu tu 風俗圖
fengtu zhi 風土志
fengwu tu 風物圖
fenye 分野

fu jiaohua 服教化
Fu Xi 伏羲
fugu 復古
Fujian haifangzhi 福建海防志
Fujian sheng ditu 福建省地圖
Fujian tongzhi 福建通志
fumu guan 父母官

Gao Gongqian 高拱乾
Gao Ru 高儒
Gaoshan zu 高山族
ge 割
gengzhi tu 耕織圖
Getian 葛天
gongbi 工筆
gonghui 公繪
Gu Yanwu 顧炎武
guandai zhi qu 冠帶之區
guangfu 光復
Guangyu tu 廣輿圖
guanlan 觀覽
guanwai 關外
guihua 歸化
guihua she 歸化社
guihua shengfan 歸化生番
Gujin Huayi quyu zongyao tu 古今
    華夷區域總要圖
Gujin tushu jicheng 古今圖書集成
Gujin xingsheng zhi tu 古今行勝
    之圖

Haiguo wenjian lu 海國聞見錄
hainei 海內
haiwai 海外
Han 漢
Han Wudi 漢武帝
hanfan (cruel savage) 悍番
Hanfan 漢番 (Chinese and savage)
Hanhua 漢化
Hanjian 漢奸
Hanshu 漢書
Hanzhi 漢志

heiren 黑人
hoan'a 番仔
Hou Hanshu 後漢書
houshan 後山
"Houshan zongtu" 後山總圖
hua (painting) 畫
Hua (Chinese) 華
hua (transform) 化
huafan 化番
huang 荒
Huang Di 黃帝
Huang Fengchang 黃逢昶
Huang Shujing 黃叔璥
Huangchao fanshu yudi congshu
　皇朝蕃屬輿地叢書
Huangchao Zhongwai yitong yutu
　皇朝中外一統輿圖
huangfu 荒服
Huang Ming dayitong ditu 皇明
　大一統地圖
Huangyu quanlan tu 皇輿全覽圖
huaniao hua 花鳥畫
huawai 化外
Huayi yitong tu 華夷一統圖
Huayi zhi fen 華夷之分
Huayi zhi jiao 華夷之交

Ji Qiguang 季麒光
jian 見
Jiang Shiche 蔣師轍
Jiang Yuying 蔣毓英
jiaohua 教化
Jiaqing 嘉慶
jiehua 界畫
jiewai 界外
Jiexie 羯羯
"Ji fanshe fengsu" 記番社風俗
ji huoshan 紀火山
Jin (dynasty) 晉
Jin (Jurchens) 金
Jinghai jishi 靖海紀事
jinghua 精華

Jinghua yuan 鏡花緣
"Jingli Taiwan shu" 經理臺灣書
Jingman 荊蠻
jinshi 進士
jiufu 九服
juan 卷

kaishan fufan 開山撫番
Kangxi 康熙
kaogu 考古
kaozheng 考證
Kuang Qizhao 鄺其照
Kuilei 傀儡

laihua 來化
Lan Dingyuan 藍鼎元
Lan Tingzhen 藍廷珍
Lao 獠
Laozi 老子
lei 類
li (miles) 里
li (reason) 理
li (ritual or propriety) 禮
Li Ruzhen 李汝珍
liangfan 良番
liangmin 良民
Lice huichao 蠡測彙鈔
Lidai dili zhizhang tu 歷代地理
　指掌圖
lifan tongzhi 理番同知
Liji 禮記
Lin Qianguang 林謙光
Lin Shuangwen 林爽文
Liu Liangbi 劉良璧
Liu Mingchuan 劉銘傳
Liu Zongyuan 柳宗元
Liuqiu (Ryukyu) 流求/琉球
Liu-shi-qi 六十七
liyi zhi bang 禮儀之邦
"Liyun" 禮運
louhei 陋黑
Lu Zhiyu 魯之裕

Lunyu 論語
Luo Dachun 羅大春
Luo Hongxian 羅洪先
Luo Mi 羅泌
Lushi 路史

Mai 蓮
Man 蠻
Manbao 滿保
Manshu 蠻書
Man, Yi, Zhen, Fan 蠻夷鎮藩
Manzhou yuanliu kao 滿州源流考
Manzu 滿族
meidi 美地
meng 蒙
Mengzi 孟子
Miao 苗
Miao Man tu 苗蠻圖
min 民
minfan jietu 民番界圖
Ming 明
Minyou ouji 閩遊偶記
Mudanshe 牡丹社

neidi 内地

Pan 潘
Panhu 盤瓠
Penglai 蓬萊
pi 癖
pifa 披髮
Pihai jiyou 裨海記遊
pingdi shufan 平地熟番
pingpu shengfan 平埔生番
pingpu shufan 平埔熟番
pingpuzu 平埔族
Pingtai jilüe 平臺記略
Pisheye 比舍耶

qi (abandon) 棄
qi (spatial energy) 氣
"Qian li" 愆禮

qiangfan 強番
"Qianhoushan zongtu" 前後山總圖
Qianlong 乾隆
qidi 棄地
Qin 秦
Qin Shihuang 秦始皇
qing 情
qishi 歧視
Qu 娶
quan Tai 全臺
Quan Tai youji 全臺遊記
qun 群

ren 人
Ren Fang 任昉
renji budao 人跡不到
renmin 人民
renwu hua 人物畫
ru bantu 入版圖
ru tuji 入圖籍
ruhua 如畫
rumao yinxue 茹毛飲血
Ruoshui 弱水
rutu 如圖

Sancai tuhui 三才圖會
shanchuan tu 山川圖
shandi funü 山地婦女
shandi tongbao 山地同胞
shanggu 上古
Shanhai jing 山海經
shanhou 山後
shanhou shengfan 山後生番
shanqian 山前
shanshui hua 山水畫
"Shanxing" 善性
she (tribe / village) 社
She (ethnic group) 畬
Shefan 社番
Shen Baozhen 沈葆楨
Shen Nong 神農

Shen Qiyuan 沈起元
Shen Yourong 沈有容
sheng 生
shengdi 生地
shengfan 生番
shengfan jie 生番界
shengjing 生境
shenqu 神區
shi 史
Shi Lang 施琅
Shi Mi 史密
Shiji 史記
Shijing 詩經
shu 熟
shudi 熟地
shufan 熟番
shujing (cooked territory) 熟境
Shujing (Classic of History) 書經
Shuowen jiezi 説文解字
shuyi 熟夷
Shuyi ji 述異記
Sihai zongtu 四海總圖
Siku quanshu 四庫全書
siyi 四夷
Su Bai 蘇拜
suan 算
Suishu 隋書

Taigong 太公
taigu zhi min 太古之民
Taihai caifeng tu 臺海采風圖
Taihai shicha lu 臺海使槎錄
Taiping guangji 太平廣記
Taiwan fanshe kao 臺灣番社考
Taiwan fanshe tu 臺灣番社圖
Taiwan haifang bing kaishan riji
　臺灣海防並開山日記
Taiwanhua 臺灣話
Taiwan jilüe 臺灣記略
Taiwan jishi 臺灣紀實
Taiwan lüetu 臺灣略圖
Taiwanren 臺灣人

Taiwan shengshufan jishi 臺灣
　生熟番紀事
Taiwan shimo ouji 臺灣始末偶記
Taiwan suibi 臺灣隨筆
Taiwan yudi huichao 臺灣輿地
　彙鈔
Taiwan yutu 臺灣輿圖
Taiwan zaji 臺灣雜記
Taiyang biji 臺陽筆記
Taiyou riji 臺遊日記
tan 坦
Tao Qian (Yuanming) 陶潛(淵明)
"Taohuayuan ji" 桃花源記
Tiaochen Taiwan shiyi zhuang
　條陳臺灣事宜狀
tianbian 天變
tianwen 天文
*Tianxia jiubian fenye renji lucheng
　quantu* 天下九邊分野人跡路程
　全圖
tongyi 統一
tu 圖
tuanjie 團結
tufan 土番
"Tufan fengsu" 土番風俗
tuguan 土官
tunfan 屯番
turen 土人
tushuo 圖説

Wa 佤
wan 頑
Wang Bichang 王必昌
Wang Dayuan 汪大淵
Wang Fuzhi 王夫之
Wang Kaitai 王凱泰
Wang Qi 王圻
Wang Xiqi 王錫祺
Wang Yingzeng 王瑛曾
wanghui 王會
wangzheng 王政
wangzi xiongfan 王字兇番

wei 偽
Wei Jiang 魏絳
Wei Yuan 魏源
weiguihua 未歸化
weiru bantu 未入版圖
wen (culture) 文
wen (hear) 聞
wenhua 文化
Wenji 紋吉
wenjian lu 聞見錄
Wenxian tongkao 文獻通考
Wokou 倭寇
Wu 吳
Wu Chenchen 吳枨臣
Wu Guangliang 吳光亮
wufen fan yu Han 無分番與漢
Wuhuai shi 無懷氏
wuren zhi jing 無人之境
Wuti Qingwen jian 五體清文鑑
Wu Ziguang 吳子光

Xi Shi 西施
Xia Xianlun 夏獻綸
xian 險
xiang 鄉
xianghua 向化
xian jiangshan 獻江山
Xiao He 蕭何
Xiaofanghuzhai yudi congchao
　小方壺齋輿地叢鈔
xiaoyaoyou 消搖遊
Xie Sui 謝遂
xin 心
xing 性
xingsi 形似
xinguihua shengfan 新歸化生番
Xinjiang 新疆
xiongfan 兇番
Xiyu tongwen zhi 西域同文志
Xu Huaizu 徐懷祖
Xu Shu 徐澍
Xu Xiake 徐霞客

xuechu 穴處
xueju yechu 穴居野處
Xunzi 荀子

"Yangzhou shiri ji" 揚州十日記
yanxue shengfan 巖穴生番
Yao 瑤
yefan 野番
yeju 野居
Yelang 夜郎
yeren 野人
yeshi shi 野史氏
yi (barbarian) 夷
yi (change) 易
yi (righteousness) 義
yi (strange) 異
Yijing 易經
yilei 異類
Yingzhou 瀛州
yipi 衣皮
yipi duanfa 衣皮斷髮
yishan shufan 倚山熟番
yisu 異俗
yixing 異性
Yixing 一行
yiyu 異域
Yiyu tuzhi 異域圖志
yizhong 異種
Yong 庸
Yongzheng 雍正
youji 遊記
Yu Yonghe 郁永河
Yu ditu 輿地圖
yuanyou 遠遊
Yugong 禹貢
Yuzhi Gengzhi tu 御製耕織圖

zei 賊
Zengding Guangyu ji quantu 增訂
　廣輿記全圖
Zhai Hao 翟灝
Zhang Chang 張敞

Zhang Hong 張宏
Zhao 招
Zhao Rugua 趙汝适
zhen 眞
Zheng 鄭
Zheng Chenggong (Koxinga)
　鄭成功
Zheng He 鄭和
Zheng Jing 鄭經
Zheng Xuan 鄭玄
zhengming 正名
zhi (record) 志
zhi (substance) 質
zhifang waiji 職方外記
zhigong tu 識貢圖
zhiguai 志怪
zhong 種
Zhong Kui 鍾馗
Zhongguo 中國
zhonglei 種類
zhongnan qingnü 重男輕女
zhongnü qingnan 重女輕男

Zhongwai yijia 中外一家
zhongzu 種族
Zhou Chen 周臣
Zhou Yuanwen 周元文
Zhou Zhongxuan 周鐘瑄
Zhouli 周禮
Zhu Yigui 朱一貴
zhuan 篆
zhuang 莊
zhuangmao 狀貌
Zhuangzi 莊子
Zhufan zhi 諸番志
Zhunjun pingding Taiwan fanshe
　jilüe 準軍平定臺灣番社紀略
Zhuoyuanting zhuren 酌元亭主人
ziyou 自遊
"Zou Annan yuma huan xing-
　rong" 走安南玉馬換猩絨
zu (blocked) 阻
zu (tribe) 族
zulei 族類
Zuozhuan 左傳

Index

European imperialism, 253; classical, 255; differences among powers, 8; domination relationships, 174; similarities to Qing imperialism, 10. *See also* Imperialism

Evidential scholarship (*kaozheng*): empirical research, 195–96, 201; influence, 196; methods, 204; popularity, 196; return to antiquity goal, 196; study of geography, 19; study of indigenous Taiwanese customs, 194–95, 196; textual research, 49, 50, 200–202, 205

Fabian, Johannes, 61, 79
Fairbank, John King, 20, 77, 239
Fan (domain), 41–43
Fan (savage), 43
Fan Xian, 160
Fang Junyi, *Brief Account of the Soldiers' Pacification of Taiwan's Savage Villages (Zhunjun pingding Taiwan fanshe jilüe)*, 219
Fanjie, see Savage boundary
"Fansu jingu shuo," *see* "Discourse on the Resemblance of Savage Customs to Those of Antiquity"
Fansu liukao, see Investigation of Savage Customs in Six Categories
Farming, *see* Agriculture
Feminism, 193
Fengshan county: establishment, 47; illustrations of indigenes, 164, 165, 167; maps, 88; rebellions, 92
Fengshui, 57
Fengsu tongyi, see Comprehensive Account of Folkways
Fengsutu, see Ethnographic illustrations
Field-allocation system (*fenye*), 56–57

Flowers in the Mirror (Jinghua yuan, Li Ruzhen), 174, 191–92
Forests, *see* Jungles and forests of Taiwan
Formosans, *see* Indigenes, Taiwanese
France, naval blockade of Taiwan, 234–36
Frontier officials: analogy to parents, 227; as audience for travel writing and topographic illustrations, 21; collection of ethnographic information, 101–2, 150; collection of geographic information, 17–18, 45–46; criticism of settler treatment of indigenes, 77–78; illustrated ethnographic albums commissioned by, 156–57; illustrations produced by, 150; need for maps, 45–46, 150; paintings of, 9; relations with Han Chinese settlers, 11–12; relations with indigenes, 9, 11; tours of inspection, 117
Frontier studies (*bianjiangxue*), 251–52, 254
Fujian province: maps of, 52; settlement, 98; Taiwan as prefecture of, 47, 51, 57
Fujian sheng ditu, see Map of Fujian Province
Fujian tongzhi, see Gazetteer of Fujian Province
Fu Xi, 64, 69, 70

Gao Gongqian, 47
Gazetteer of Fengshan County (1720), 116
Gazetteer of Fujian Province (Fujian tongzhi), 51, 52, 88, 145
Gazetteer of Taiwan County (1720), 54

Harvard East Asian Monographs
(* out-of-print)

Harvard East Asian Monographs

Harvard East Asian Monographs

Harvard East Asian Monographs

89. Sung Hwan Ban, Pal Yong Moon, and Dwight H. Perkins, *Rural Development*

*90. Noel F. McGinn, Donald R. Snodgrass, Yung Bong Kim, Shin-Bok Kim, and Quee-Young Kim, *Education and Development in Korea*

91. Leroy P. Jones and Il SaKong, *Government, Business, and Entrepreneurship in Economic Development: The Korean Case*

92. Edward S. Mason, Dwight H. Perkins, Kwang Suk Kim, David C. Cole, Mahn Je Kim et al., *The Economic and Social Modernization of the Republic of Korea*

93. Robert Repetto, Tai Hwan Kwon, Son-Ung Kim, Dae Young Kim, John E. Sloboda, and Peter J. Donaldson, *Economic Development, Population Policy, and Demographic Transition in the Republic of Korea*

94. Parks M. Coble, Jr., *The Shanghai Capitalists and the Nationalist Government, 1927–1937*

95. Noriko Kamachi, *Reform in China: Huang Tsun-hsien and the Japanese Model*

96. Richard Wich, *Sino-Soviet Crisis Politics: A Study of Political Change and Communication*

97. Lillian M. Li, *China's Silk Trade: Traditional Industry in the Modern World, 1842–1937*

98. R. David Arkush, *Fei Xiaotong and Sociology in Revolutionary China*

*99. Kenneth Alan Grossberg, *Japan's Renaissance: The Politics of the Muromachi Bakufu*

100. James Reeve Pusey, *China and Charles Darwin*

101. Hoyt Cleveland Tillman, *Utilitarian Confucianism: Chen Liang's Challenge to Chu Hsi*

102. Thomas A. Stanley, *Ōsugi Sakae, Anarchist in Taishō Japan: The Creativity of the Ego*

103. Jonathan K. Ocko, *Bureaucratic Reform in Provincial China: Ting Jih-ch'ang in Restoration Kiangsu, 1867–1870*

104. James Reed, *The Missionary Mind and American East Asia Policy, 1911–1915*

105. Neil L. Waters, *Japan's Local Pragmatists: The Transition from Bakumatsu to Meiji in the Kawasaki Region*

106. David C. Cole and Yung Chul Park, *Financial Development in Korea, 1945–1978*

107. Roy Bahl, Chuk Kyo Kim, and Chong Kee Park, *Public Finances During the Korean Modernization Process*

108. William D. Wray, *Mitsubishi and the N.Y.K, 1870–1914: Business Strategy in the Japanese Shipping Industry*

Harvard East Asian Monographs

Harvard East Asian Monographs